THE LAW AND POLICY OF THE WORLD TRADE ORGANIZATION

THE LAW AND POLICY OF THE WORLD TRADE ORGANIZATION

Marko Nikolić

SOCIETY Publishing

www.societypublishing.com

The Law and Policy of the World Trade Organization

Marko Nikolić

Society Publishing
4164 Lakeshore Road
Burlington, ON L7L 1A4
Canada
www.societypublishing.com
Email: orders@arclereducation.com

ISBN: 978-1-83441-120-0 (Hardcover)

ABOUT THE AUTHOR

Marko obtained his Master's degree from the University of Belgrade Faculty of Law in 2014. He specialized in Criminal Law, Family Law, and Environmental Law. He spent his Master's year studying international child abduction in the modern world. He was employed in the Ministry of Defense's Legal Department and was also working as a legal secretary in numerous educational institutions. His freelance engagements are including more than 40 longterm clients and he also established a consulting agency in 2021. He is the head of the sector in a company specializing in intellectual property and his focus is in trademarking. In addition to professional literature editing, he published a novel on the subject of history and mythology in 2020. Out of office his main focus are environmental and ecological issues.

TABLE OF CONTENTS

LIST OF FIGURES

PREFACE

Border trade is one of the signature features of globalization. Goods, services, and capital are exchanged across the world with a previously unmatched pace and volume. While commerce makes development and growth possible, it also produces tensions because countries want to balance local priorities and international obligations. Struggles over tariffs, subsidies, intellectual property, and services are no longer an isolated issue but a part of a web of interlinked interactions within an integrated international system where regulations must be transparent, predictable, and enforceable. Without a secure legal and institutional framework, international trade would become protectionism, discrimination, and ongoing conflict between nations.

The establishment of an integrated global trading system has reshaped the way states engage each other in trade. This institution defines the game rules for market access, oversees commitments, and provides for a dispute to be resolved. It is not just a regulator, but a negotiation forum as well, balancing developed and developing economies' interests. Its structure addresses virtually every sector—agriculture, manufacturing, technology, intellectual property, and services—and therefore is at the center of economic life today. Acquaintance with its law and policy is therefore essential in comprehending how the world negotiates, competes, and cooperates in the 21st century.

The book *The Law and Policy of the World Trade Organization* is designed to provide a comprehensive and systematic analysis of the WTO's legal and institutional framework. It combines introductory explanations with penetrating analysis, offering students and professionals alike an accessible yet challenging introduction to the subject. Each chapter delineates basic principles, underscores general agreement, and explains how policy and law function in practice. Clarity of doctrine is balanced with real-world examples so that readers know how rules play out in practice on contemporary trade issues. From basic concepts to advanced debate, the book equips readers with the ability to understand, criticize, and participate in the WTO regime.

Chapter 1 introduces the World Trade Organization, emphasizing its history, objectives, structure, and membership. It follows the evolution from the General Agreement on Tariffs and Trade (GATT) to the formation of the WTO in 1995. The chapter indicates why there was a need for a multilateral institution, how it is distinct from earlier trading agreements, and what function is served by its principal organs like the Ministerial Conference, the General Council, and expert committees. This background enables readers to better understand the institutional machinery underpinning world trade governance.

Chapter 2 explains the fundamental rules of WTO law. They are non-discrimination, most-favored-nation (MFN) treatment, national treatment, reciprocity, and transparency. It describes how these principles lie at the foundation of the trading system, ensuring equality as well as liberalization. It continues to explain the exceptions and flexibilities embedded in these principles, which are the political bargains making different states members of the same system.

Chapter 3 explains extensively the WTO agreements and legal regime. It informs us about how the Marrakesh Agreement established the WTO, how annexes contain agreements regarding goods, services, and intellectual property, and how plurilateral agreements are placed within the framework. The chapter provides an overview of major agreements such as GATT, GATS, and TRIPS within the broader legal framework. The overview establishes how WTO law works as a bundle of obligations for members.

Chapter 4 deals with goods market access. Chapter 4 explains tariff bindings, tariff reduction commitment, and prohibition of quantitative restrictions. The chapter explores special treatment for industrial and agricultural products and illustrates how market access negotiations have overshadowed trade rounds. Special attention is given to tackling issues in tariff escalation, non-tariff trade barriers, and preferential trade arrangements. This section brings out tension between multilateral liberalization and regional trading agreements.

Chapter 5 examines trade in services within the General Agreement on Trade in Services (GATS). It explains how GATS differs from GATT, both in its positive-listing character and modes of supply. The chapter summarizes state commitments, regulating services concerns, and the rise of digital trade. It refers to fields such as finance, telecommunications, and professional services, showing how services liberalization is altering economies everywhere.

Chapter 6 addresses intellectual property rights under the TRIPS Agreement. It explains minimum copyright, patent, and trademark requirements, as well as those related to enforcement. The chapter also addresses the controversies of TRIPS, particularly on access to medicines, technology transfer, and public health. It highlights balancing the protection of innovation and ensuring fair access to fundamental goods. It illustrates how intellectual property became one of the most contentious aspects of trade law.

Chapter 7 deals with trade remedies and safeguards. Chapter 7 outlines the legal structure of anti-dumping measures, countervailing duties, and safeguard actions. The chapter explains why these instruments are being permitted in the context of the normal rule of liberalization, and how they are used by states to retaliate for unjustified actions or unexpected rises in imports. Case studies provide illustrations of how trade remedies tend to be at the center of conflict, reflecting divergent interests of domestic industries and international commitments.

Chapter 8 examines the mechanism of dispute settlement, widely considered the WTO system's crown jewel. It details the sequence from consultations to panel decisions, Appellate Body appeal, and enforcement. The chapter considers the virtues of the mechanism—binding decisions and high rates of compliance—as well as its existing challenges, including paralysis of the Appellate Body. They are introduced to key conflicts that have influenced international trade law and to arguments regarding reforming the system.

Chapter 9 explores the WTO and developing countries. It touches on special and differential treatment provisions, activities for building capacity, as well as disputes over equity and fairness in the trading system. The chapter highlights how developing countries used the WTO as a bulwark against prejudice and as a platform through which to advance their interests. It also explores the traditional complaints that the system is biased towards richer members and pays no heed to development priorities.

Chapter 10 explores challenges and opportunities for the WTO in the present and future. It addresses current challenges such as rising protectionism, trade wars, e-commerce, environmental sustainability, and rising regional trade agreements. The chapter also considers proposed reforms, from modernizing dispute settlement to new bargaining arenas. This forward-looking analysis asks readers to contemplate whether the WTO is still useful in a changing global economy.

The book is a generalist text. Law students and academics will enjoy it as a general introduction to WTO law. Economists and policy analysts will appreciate the convergence of legal thinking with policy discourse. Practicing lawyers, trade negotiators, and officials can look at it as a handbook for the rules, procedures, and dispute resolution. Business leaders and civil society groups will discover the influence of trade law on development, intellectual property, services, and international markets. Finally, this book is for everyone who is interested in learning how rules of international business are formed, enforced, and tested, and how those rules regulate our world.

Chapter 1

Introduction to the World Trade Organization

Contents

INTRODUCTION TO THE WORLD TRADE ORGANIZATION

The World Trade Organization (WTO) is an important global trade organization established to regulate and encourage international trade among nations. Founded in 1995, the WTO evolved from the General Agreement on Tariffs and Trade (GATT), which had controlled international trade since 1948. The founding of the WTO was a significant step in the direction of a more formalized and legally binding approach, broadening its ambit to include trade in services as well as intellectual property. The primary aims of the WTO include promoting free trade, settling disputes, and forming a negotiating forum. Importantly, the organization seeks to provide a fair platform for developing as well as developed nations, ensuring that each member is able to make their voice heard when it comes to trade rules that govern their economies. Such inclusivity is important in maintaining economic stability in the world and fostering growth through enhanced cooperation in trade. Perhaps the most crucial role of the WTO is to serve as an intermediary in trade disputes. In a world economy where there will inevitably be conflicting interests, the WTO provides an official process for resolving trade disputes between member countries.

Figure 1.1. Introduction to the World Trade Organization (WTO).

Source: https://media.geeksforgeeks.org/wp-content/uploads/20240122111508/World-Trade-Organization.webp.

The procedure would be one of consultations and, in extreme cases, official adjudication by panels and an appellate body composed of international trade law specialists. Not only does this system of dispute resolution aim to find fair outcomes but also to preserve the integrity of the multilateral trading system. By offering a neutral platform for the settlement of disputes, the WTO spares the world trade wars and hostilities that have catastrophic economic implications. Such an arrangement is required because countries commonly face informal and formal barriers resulting in a higher degree of tensions and protectionist measures undermining global trade efforts. Furthermore, the World Trade Organization has an essential role to promote liberalization of trade as well as economic growth across its member nations. Through its agreements, the WTO promotes countries to reduce tariffs and non-tariff barriers, making a pro-free-trade situation. According to research, liberalization of trade can yield enormous economic benefits, such as increased competitiveness, innovation, and enhanced consumer access to goods and services. While not controversy-free, the work of the WTO will create a rules-based trading system that can withstand market and geopolitical ups and downs. It is required to adapt constantly to the changing world environment, and this includes addressing new issues such as digital trade and environmental sustainability. As nations navigate this complex dance of development and trade, the role of the WTO in enabling equitable growth remains the most critical (Figure 1.1).

Definition and Purpose of the World Trade Organization (WTO)

Essentially, the WTO is an international forum established to oversee and facilitate world trade relations among states. Established in 1995, the WTO was the product of a series of trade talks, specifically the Uruguay Round, and is the direct successor of the GATT. The fundamental purpose of the WTO is to provide an environment for its members to negotiate trade agreements to reduce tariffs as well as other trade obstacles. By enabling an open and foreseeable trading regime, the organization seeks to expand international trade flows, generate economic growth, and improve living standards worldwide. This institutional framework emphasizes member states' responsibility to adhere to mutually agreed rules and settle disputes in an orderly manner, rendering the WTO a key figure in the world economic order. Other than encouraging trade liberalization, the WTO plays a significant role in ensuring that international trade affects economic and environmental sustainability. Integration of trade and climate policies has gained prominence as nations grapple with the impact of their economic activities on the planet. Other writings, such as those of the Working Group on Trade, Investment, and Climate Policy of The Frederick S. Pardee Center for the Study of the Longer-Range Future, articulate the need to formulate trade rules in accordance with climate goals. In this case, the crossroads of investment agreements with climate change mitigation efforts is a demonstration of the WTOs ability to reshape global economic standards. By encouraging environmentally sustainable trade practices, the WTO can significantly influence its member nations to go after environmentally conscious development objectives alongside conventional economic goals (Ackerman et al., 2016). Furthermore, the mandate of the WTO extends beyond providing a bridge for trade to encompass the regulation of capital flows, particularly in the wake of global financial crises. As the Pardee Center Task Force on Regulating Capital Flows pointed out in its reports, the complexities of capital account regulation reveal trade agreement-trade policy tensions and effective macroeconomic policy. The reports stress the concerns of developing nations for their limited ability to use devices of regulation due to existing trade and investment agreements, most notably the large economic players like the United States. Thus, the WTO stands at a crossroads, where its role as a facilitator of trade must change to accommodate the socio-economic concerns of the day, and offer a framework that is beneficial both for economic development and sovereign capacity in governance (Anderson et al., 2013).

Historical Context and Formation

The history of the WTO goes as far back as the post-World War period when there was a desperate demand for economic stability and cooperation internationally. The war had created behind it an incredible devastation that called for the establishment of a regulatory system that would cut down disputes on trade and ease economic cooperation between states. This led to the creation of the GATT in 1947, which would facilitate international trade by reducing tariffs and other forms of trade barriers. GATT was a precursor of the WTO, to which it introduced an appreciation of multilateral trade agreements as a way of enhancing economic interdependence and averting the protectionist measures that devastated the interwar period. Thus, GATT provided a lead to the eventual establishment of a more robust institutional structure that could address the complexity of the present-day global trade. As the global economy evolved, so did the need for a stronger framework comprising not only goods but also services and intellectual property. This change witnessed the inception of the WTO in 1995, which added more depth to trade negotiations and new trade dispute-settling mechanisms between member countries. The WTO was the outcome of the Uruguay Round of talks, when it was evident that economic opening-up required a more integrated system considering various elements of trade, including labor rights and environmental policies. The new organization was designed to be a more holistic institution for coping with the multi-dimensional nature of international trade and therefore facilitating greater cooperation among member states. The move toward more holistic trade management is precipitated by the dynamic nature of international relations and growing awareness among various stakeholders in shaping trade policy. The creation of WTO was also motivated by international politics and economic reforms taking place in the world, particularly by rising emerging economies and changing power dynamics. China and India began becoming deep influences in the global marketplace, thereby necessitating a more flexible and adaptive organizational structure. The creation of WTO also trailed massive sociopolitical transformations in other regions of the world, showing intricate interrelations between society and economics. In such a context, the understanding of the origin of the WTO over history requires an examination of the interaction of institutionals, such as governments and multinational corporations, and how they shape trade policy. The complexities of experience of nations summarize the complexities entailed in this adjustment, describing how identity networks, shaped by local and global forces, play a vital role in negotiating the deals at the WTO (Ergur et al., 2014; Kerremans et al., 2013).

Importance in Global Trade

The relevance of international trade cannot be forgotten, particularly in establishing economic interdependence among nations. The WTO plays a pivotal role in fostering such interdependence by developing a systematic method of negotiating and settling trade disputes. The international trade agreement provides a level playing field, allowing countries to compete on an equal basis and hence fuels economic growth. For instance, enforcing agreements such as the Trans-Pacific Partnership (TPP) seeks to open up trade with lower tariffs and other trade barriers between member countries. Such institutions not only enhance trade potential but also stimulate investments that can trigger growth among member nations. Such interdependence renders the principles upheld by the WTO central to sustaining global economic relationships and triggering prosperity across borders (Fergusson et al., 2015). Furthermore, international trade transcends economic figures; it is important for political stability and societal cohesion. Trade agreements foster state cooperation, which has the effect of lessening tension by intertwining their interests economically. By enhancing economic relations, states are less likely to go to war, appreciating the mutual benefits of economic collaboration. As seen in cooperative organizations, countries that engage in bilateral trade are likely to collaborate on more abstract political and societal issues, such as global security or climate change. The experience of the exporters in countries such as Uganda demonstrates that establishing relationships with international customers can lead to competitiveness and robustness in the global markets. The emphasis on soft competitiveness factors (SCFs), such as business ethics and relations among people, reflects the degree to which trade can benefit not only economies, but also the quality of diplomatic relations between nations (Wiegratz et al., 2008). In addition to its economic and political effects, international trade has a pronounced effect on socio-economic development, particularly in emerging markets. A well-efficient system of international trade provides these countries with access to larger markets, by which they can diversify their export base and induce domestic economic growth. Trade can enhance technology transfer, education, and innovation, advancing poverty alleviation and development goals. Gains in trade are not shared equally because there exists a disparity between developed and developing nations. These gaps must be filled to achieve the objective of inclusive growth as international trade has the tendency to expand disparities at times. Policymakers and institutions like the WTO must pursue policies that ensure balanced patterns of trade so that all nations, particularly those in the developing nations, are able to convert the possibilities of international trade into sustainable growth. The balance of interests in global trade is thus crucial to the creation of a fair economic setting capable of fostering the growth of all participating countries (Figure 1.2).

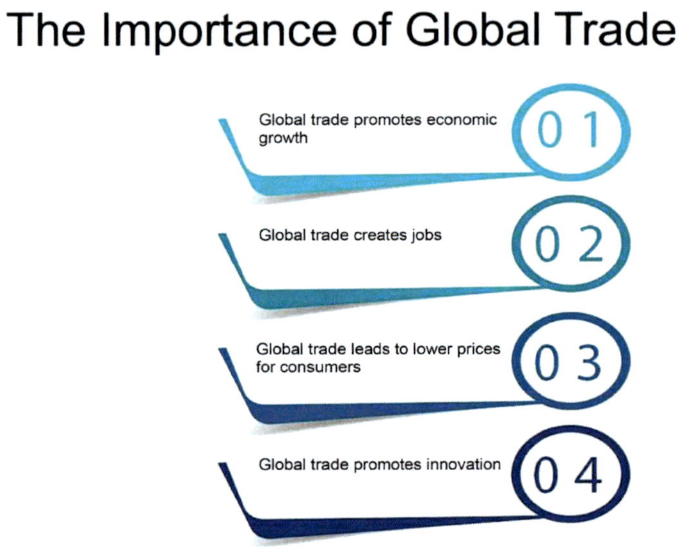

Figure 1.2. The importance of global trade.

Source: https://fastercapital.co/i/Global-Trade--Trade-Talks-at-the-Jackson-Hole-Symposium--A-New-Era--The-Importance-of-Global-Trade.webp.

1.1. STRUCTURE OF THE WORLD TRADE ORGANIZATION (WTO)

WTO boasts an organizational framework grounded on an arrangement for the facilitation of multilateral trade agreements and settlement of disputes among member states. It was created in 1995, and the WTO has both an adjudicative and legislative function in that it helps make trade rules while also acting as a mechanism by which disagreements over rules arise between countries can be settled. The organization at its basis is based upon a collection of agreements governing different aspects of trade, such as goods, services, and intellectual property. In establishing a system of rules governing world trade, the WTO aims at encouraging predictability and openness in trade relations and thereby bring nations to exercise open communication and trade. This organizational structure reflects the body's commitment to equity and principles of non-discrimination, thereby creating an environment that fosters economic cooperation and economic development. In the center of WTO operations are its various governing bodies, specifically the Ministerial Conference and the General Council. The supreme decision-making body is the Ministerial Conference, meeting every two years to consider and settle issues related to international trade policy. Between these occasions, the General Council, consisting of representatives from each member country, enables ongoing consultations and the implementation of previously reached agreements.

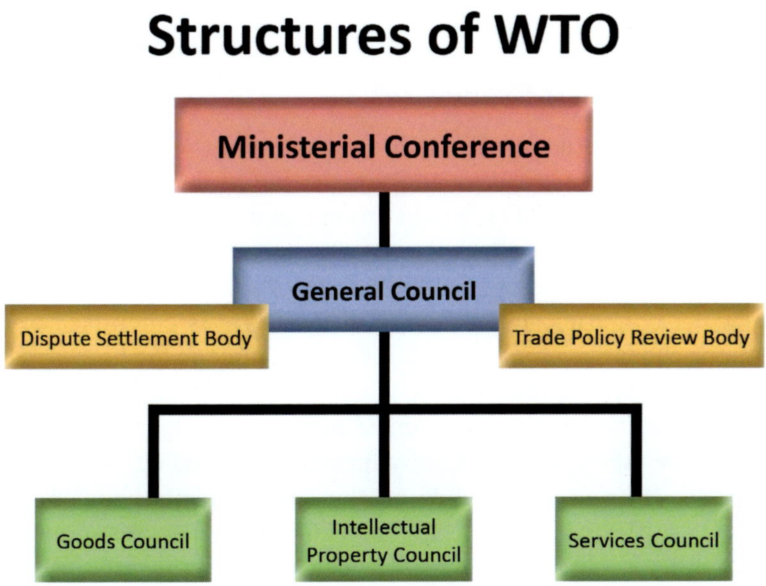

Figure 1.3. Structure of the World Trade Organization (WTO).

Source: https://www.drishtiias.com/images/uploads/1613553941_image3.jpg.

This dual structure allows for a balance of general policy direction and particular operational management, providing members with a number of ways in which to participate and make decisions. In addition, the WTO also contains expert committees which address specific fields, such as agriculture and services, providing a more specialist reaction to the complexities of international trade. This tiered organizational framework ensures the WTO's efforts towards balancing various member interests, as well as trade governance coherence on the international stage. Global economic trends as well as trade dispute dynamics have guided development in the structure of the WTO. The WTO has been facing increasing challenges in adapting its frameworks to member states' unilateral actions, underscoring the need for adaptive institutional frameworks. The challenges that face us today, such as the invoking of national security exceptions, point out to the weakness of the WTOs conflict resolution mechanisms and call for drastic rethinking of the existing architecture. As evident from arguments over national security and trade, the need to develop flexible architectures that can address new challenges like climate change and cybersecurity while reinforcing multilateralism is crucial. These trends emphasize not only the necessity to sustain the existing institutional setup but also the rebirth of the organizations' role in safeguarding trade against the threats of contemporary economic uncertainties (Dethier et al., 2025; Trujillo et al., 2020) (Figure 1.3).

1.1.1. Organizational Framework

Institutional design of the World Trade Organization (WTO) is central to the explanation of the WTO structure and functioning in the world trade context. Established in 1995, the WTO revolves around an institution of norms centered on enhancing international trade and economic cooperation. The norms include non-discrimination, transparency, and the encouragement of fair competition among member countries. The structure of the WTO is comprised of several bodies, among them the Ministerial Conference, which is the highest decision-making body, and the General Council, which is charged with general operation. These entities function jointly to oversee negotiations, resolve disputes, and implement trade agreements, thereby providing a stable and predictable trading system. Its success depends on the commitments being fulfilled by member states, reflecting the delicate balancing act between national interest and international cooperation in trade. Secondly, the complexity of the WTOs organizational structure also reflects the intricacy of worldwide trade patterns. The dynamic interaction among actors, including member states, non-state actors, and private sectors, also reflects the requirement for adaptive governance structures. As trade problems continue to shift, the WTO must be proactive in adapting to challenges such as digital trade and sustainable development. The ability to adapt is crucial as it allows the organization to remain relevant and address the changing needs of its members. Surprisingly, research on corporate sustainability management shows that organizations respond with tensions when addressing multiple dimensions, including economic, social, and environmental. Through examining the governance of its members, the WTO can utilize similar approaches to resolve the paradoxical tensions encountered in international trade, in effect leading to an inclusive conversation working towards better practices and policies in trade (Ozanne et al., 2016). Having a robust organizational structure necessitates constant review and modification to ensure that the WTO is well-equipped to meet the advanced needs of an evolving environment of trade. In this regard, public policy plays a fundamental role in shaping the contextual drivers of trade interactions. Policymakers need to devise regulations that are aligned with the underlying principles of the WTO as well as address the matter-of-fact issues that member states encounter. Corporate sustainability management studies show that the public policy function is critical in forming and destroying organizational performance (Callin et al., 2016). The synthesis between the public policy and the WTO's goals can lead to improved outcomes, as it helps in keeping the tensions among member nations with a view to sustainable trade practice at bay. Lastly, the success of the WTOs organizational framework depends on its ability to foster cooperation and a conducive environment for world trade growth.

1.1.2. Key Institutions and Bodies

The World Trade Organization (WTO) is a central institution in the arena of global commerce, since the primary institution for managing international trade. Established on January 1, 1995, the WTO replaced the General Agreement on Tariffs and Trade (GATT) and introduced a stronger regime, making the world's trading systems more stable and transparent. One of its key functions is the settling of disputes, governed by the Understanding on Rules and Procedures Governing the Settlement of Disputes (DSU), which has played a central role in settling trade disputes among member states. During its initial decade, the DSU successfully settled 324 complaints, more than were resolved under GATTs nearly half-century rule, and demonstrates the WTOs capacity to facilitate effective dialogue among its members while keeping the rules in check. However, the ongoing DSU reform negotiations suggest the challenges the organization is facing in maintaining political consensus as well as operational efficiency in the midst of a shifting world environment (Zimmermann, 2025). The WTO governance structure is sophisticated, with a number of principal organizations which each address various aspects of trade regulation. The Ministerial Conference, comprising all 164 member states, is the supreme decision-making organ and convenes at least biennially. To complement it, routine administration is managed by the General Council, addressing issues of procedure as well as implementation of agreements. Specialized councils and committees address such fields as trade in services, intellectual property, and regional trade agreements, enabling concentrated debate conducive to effective trade policy. Besides, the WTO Secretariat plays a critical role in coordinating activities, providing technical assistance, and bringing research results to ensure member countries trade-related activities. This multi-level arrangement is the

WTOs commitment to providing a friendly environment for the accommodation of diverse member interests with regard to attaining overall economic growth (International Labour Office, 2003). In addition to its fixed institutions, the WTO is faced with a complex system of challenges which erode its operational legitimacy and psychological integrity. While the DSU has facilitated colossal progress in settlement, the ineffectiveness of political decision-making in the institution has created a sizeable imbalance. Recurrent discussions on the DSU review, initiated in 1997, have not yielded substantial reforms that would correct weaknesses in the system. In addition, disparities in member capabilities can heighten conflicts between developed and developing nations, necessitating an improvement in participation in decision-making. As such trends unfold, the viability of the WTOs core mandates is questioned, necessitating new governance approaches that address the changing requirements of global trade while upholding the institutions' original underpinnings (Zimmermann, 2025) (Figure 1.4).

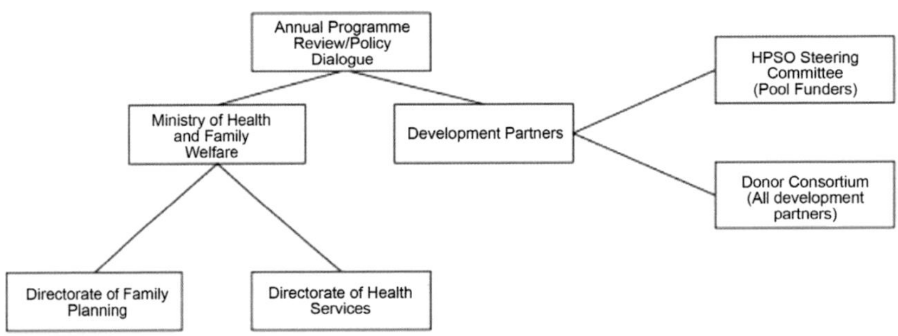

Figure 1.4. Key institutions and bodies.

*Source:*https://www.researchgate.net/profile/Birger-Forsberg/publication/7076366/figure/fig1/AS:216496560185344@1428628210021/Overview-of-main-institutions-and-coordinating-bodies-in-the-HPSP-in-Bangladesh.png.

1.1.3. Membership and Governance

The organizational setup of the World Trade Organization (WTO) has a critically significant role in determining how member states deal with each other and collaborate within the global trading system. As a member of 164 countries, the governance system of the WTO is built around norms of consensus-driven decision-making and openness. This approach allows all the member states, regardless of their size or economic power, to participate in the decision-making process, generating a sense of inclusiveness and collaboration. However, the complexity of the rules of consensus can extend negotiations, particularly where there are conflicting interests at stake. With the organization persevering to evolve in response to new global trade challenges, such as digital commerce and sustainable development, the functioning framework of governance is also bound to evolve accordingly to keep it effective and reflective of its multi-diverse membership (Schipani et al., 2025). Not only does WTO membership reflect economic engagement, but there is also an accompanying obligation to adhere to its rules and commitments. Member countries must harmonize their domestic policies and trade conduct with WTO agreements at times, generating pressures between national sovereignty and international commitments.

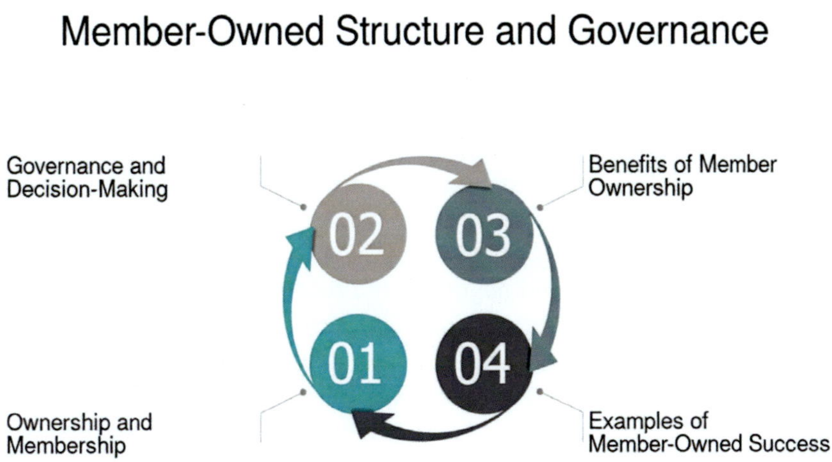

Figure 1.5. Membership and governance.

Source: https://fastercapital.co/i/Credit-union--How-to-join-a-credit-union-and-what-are-the-benefits--Member-Owned-Structure-and-Governance.webp.

For instance, countries are often requested to comply with laws adopted by the WTO, which in most cases is challenging for less resourceful developing nations. Besides, joining for new members could also be a painful experience because the prospective members must negotiate the terms of membership and, as a result, some significant reforms in their trade policy to comply with WTO norms (Junhai et al., 2001). Membership, nonetheless, is typically desirable because it widens access to wider markets and defends against discriminatory trade action. WTO governance not only involves its institutions' functioning but also the capacity of its institutions to adapt to changes in the international trade environment. With increasing dynamism and complexity of international trade, there has been inquiry into the effectiveness of the WTOs model of governance. For example, the proliferation of bilateral and regional trade agreements threatens the traditional multilateral trading system in which the WTO is enshrined. In order to remain in the public eye, the organization must re-tune its governance frameworks to support evolving patterns of trade and enhance cooperation between members. Dispute resolution mechanism reinvention and streamlining negotiations is an essential step to resolve member issues and uphold the principles of fair trade. While the world economy keeps evolving, the management of the WTO must be constantly evaluated and reformed to make it suitable for its diverse membership as well as to ensure an equitable trading climate (Schipani et al., 2025) (Figure 1.5).

1.2. FUNCTIONS OF THE WORLD TRADE ORGANIZATION (WTO)

WTO has a pivotal role in facilitating international trade by its multifaceted functions. One of its primary functions is to provide a platform for negotiation of trade among member countries with a view to reducing trade barriers and creating a more open and predictable trade world. This position is vital, as it enables nations to sit down and negotiate and resolve trade issues collectively, thus fostering economic collaboration. Furthermore, the WTOs negotiation system has both provisions for developed and developing countries, signifying the organization's focus on fair international trade mechanisms. Because trade agreements have a tendency to situate economic policies, the emphasis on cooperation is a preeminent vehicle through which the WTO ensures equitable trade agreements between its multicultural membership (Odermatt et al., 2014). In addition to being a negotiating forum, the WTO also serves as a umpire of trade disputes. Through its Dispute Settlement Mechanism (DSM), it is at the center of the resolution of disputes arising from the interpretation of trade agreements. By providing for an orderly means of resolving disagreements, the WTO upholds the integrity of international trade rules so that members do not contravene their commitments. Along with instilling an impression of fairness, this function facilitates adherence by member nations through the potential for punishment or retaliatory trade in the guise of sanctions. Because disagreements have the tendency to hinder trade flows to a great extent, the effectiveness of the DSM is essential in maintaining stability in the global trading system (Bonnal et al., 2005). The ability of the WTO to resolve disagreements also assists in confidence-building among members, thus enhancing the general effectiveness of world trade relations. The WTO also assists in the world trading system by overseeing the execution and administration of the trade agreements. This role involves tracking member states' trade policies to ensure consistency with WTO obligations to foster transparency and accountability. Through a mechanism of requiring members to report on their trade measures from time to time, the WTO sees to it that nations adhere to their commitments and the ideals of equitable trade. Moreover, the agency offers technical assistance and capacity building to developing nations to assist them in fully understanding the intricacies of international trade regulations. This pedagogic role plays a significant role in leveling the playing field, enabling poor nations to compete on an equal basis in international markets and thus supporting the general goal of equitable economic development (Odermatt et al., 2014). Therefore, the WTOs multiple roles underscore its vanguard role in establishing and overseeing the international trading system (Figure 1.6).

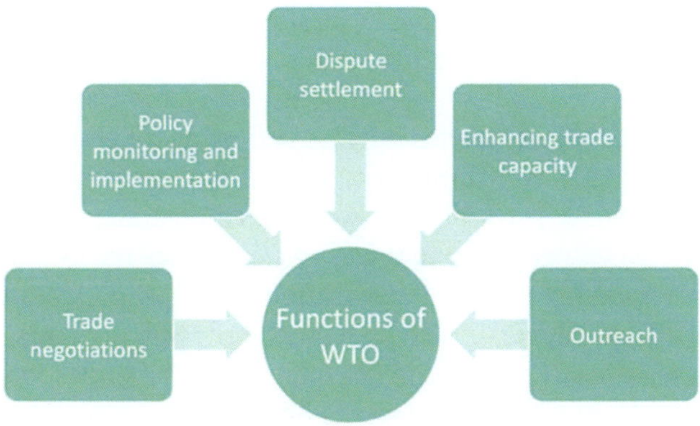

Figure 1.6. Functions of the World Trade Organization (WTO).

Source: https://wallstreetmojo-files.s3.ap-south-1.amazonaws.com/2023/06/functions-of-WTO.png.

1.2.1. Trade Negotiations

Negotiations for trade under the umbrella of the World Trade Organization (WTO) are at the core of international trade norm construction and emergence. The relevance of these negotiations is underscored by the complexity and historic nature of agreements such as the Trade-Related Aspects of Intellectual Property Rights (TRIPS). The agreements that emerged out of the Uruguay Round, 1986–1994, demonstrate the complexity of issues negotiators faced in reconciling changing national interests and economic circumstances. Particularly highlighted is the inclusion of provisions for geographical indications, reflecting long traditions and providing benefits to producers but also created intense arguing between member states on intellectual property norms and substitutes in agricultural trade (Geuze et al., 2025). Then, therefore, trade negotiations not only provide rules but also navigate a landscape of historical legacies and existing economic interests. WTO negotiations often feature the dynamic tensions between the developed and the developing nations, especially in specific sectors such as agriculture. As with the case of the Doha Development Agenda from the WTO Ministerial Meeting of 2001, developing countries have aired their grievances over agricultural subsidies and market access. The variations in the way these nations interact and compete in foreign markets demonstrate the challenge at the bargaining table. Evidence indicates that trends in agricultural trade vary geographically, and this has raised speculation regarding the necessity of using customized policies to balance these disparities effectively. In particular, the impacts of trade reforms by industrialized nations, notably OECD countries, on regions of high agricultural reliance have significant implications for regional economic growth prospects as well as risks to developing country rural poverty reduction (Wilson et al., 2025). Present controversies in trade negotiations not only reflect timely economic issues but also reflect wider geopolitical dynamics and development goals. The complexity of multilateral trade talks, as in those conducted under the WTO umbrella would demonstrate, calls for a precise balancing act between opposing interests. As countries try to protect domestic industries while pursuing bigger liberalization schemes, collaborative dialogue becomes increasingly critical. Recent talks also point towards the need for adaptive strategies in order to confront emerging challenges, such as market access barriers and sustainability concerns. By facilitating the collective culture, the WTO enables member states to collaborate in addressing the intricacies of international business, maintaining the organization's fundamental goal of promoting free and fair trade and catering to the different wishes of its members.

1.2.2. Dispute Resolution Mechanism (DRM)

The World Trade Organization's (WTO) DRM plays a significant role in maintaining the legitimacy and viability of international trade law. Implemented by the Dispute Settlement Understanding (DSU), this system marks a departure from the softer forms of the General Agreement on Tariffs and Trade (GATT) to one with more emphasis on legalism and compliance. The GATT had relied on diplomatic negotiations, which often led to less than optimal solutions, the parties resorting to non-compliance without much penalty. The DRM of WTO attempts to fix these lacunae by presenting a more formal means of conflict resolution, thus introducing more accountability between member states. Yet, even in light of all this, there is the question of making sure that the solution delivered through this system is fair and just for all the interested parties involved (Khansari et al., 1996). In practice, the success of the WTOs DRM relies on the communication and cooperation of its member states. At times, disputes arise from some trade concerns (STCs) which are initially solved through informal meetings during committee sessions. Such informal negotiations can serve to defuse tensions before disputes are brought to formal levels. The Sanitary and Phytosanitary Measures (SPS) and Technical Barriers to Trade (TBT) committees are a prime example of this dynamic working effectively; although thousands of notifications are traded every year, only a fraction of those escalate into disputes requiring adjudication. This forward-looking approach is testament to the role of dialogue and negotiation in the world of trade and highlights the ongoing process of improvement in rules governing these discussions (Wolfe et al., 2020). The necessity for reform of the WTO's dispute settlement procedures has become more apparent as international trade tensions escalate. Strengthening the DRM is crucial in order to increase members' confidence in the system and make it remain relevant in light of changing trade practices. Reform proposals focus on the requirement of increased communication and transparency among WTO members, capable of resolving disputes at an earlier stage in development and preventing them from escalating to formal dispute proceedings. By promoting a compliance and cooperative culture via more effective notification procedures and strengthened accountability mechanisms, the WTO can better meet its mandate of promoting equitable trade. Hence, resolving the inherent issues in the DRM not only resolves conflicts but also complements a more balanced and equitable international trading regime (Wolfe et al., 2020) (Figure 1.7).

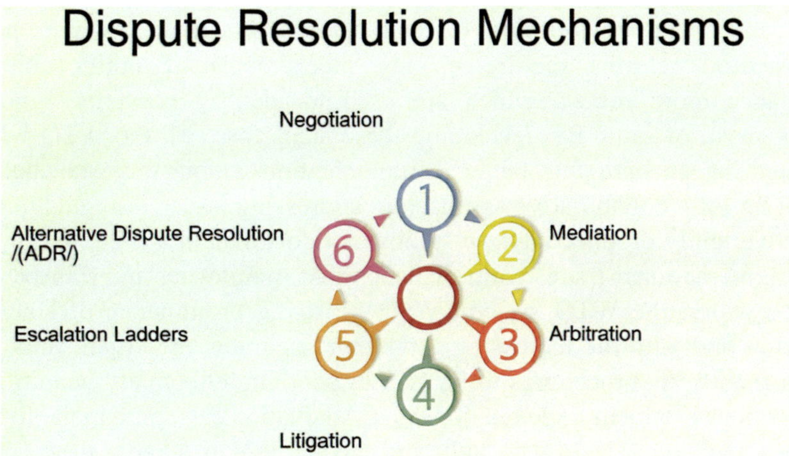

Figure 1.7. Dispute resolution mechanism (DRM).

Source: https://fastercapital.co/i/Legal-issues--How-to-avoid-legal-issues-and-comply-with-regulations-when-outsourcing-team-tasks--Dispute-Resolution-Mechanisms.webp.

1.2.3. Monitoring and Transparency

Monitoring and transparency are central components of the World Trade Organizations (WTO) system in international trade. These components ensure that trade rules are adhered to, providing an environment of equitable practice in trade among member states. By establishing explicit rules of checking compliance, the WTO aims to limit the likelihood of disputes due to misinterpretation or terms of agreement violations. This emphasis on supervision not only enhances trust among trading nations but also provides channels for dispute settlement through which nations can pursue redress in a structured manner, thereby guaranteeing stability in the global trading system. Such openness is crucial since it interprets trade policy complexity and aids in coordinating varied member countries' trade strategies with broader economic and development goals, that is, democracy and human development (Woods, 2025). The WTO has moved towards making internal as well as external transparency of its operations and decision-making efficient. The activities by the organizations involve different frameworks that seek to encourage clearer communication among the member states, thereby bringing more overall efficiency in trade negotiations.

But it should be mentioned that the existing structures still face challenges in handling complex, opaque behind-the-border regulatory externalities, which can impede the free flow of trade agreements. That is why proposals for structural reforms require making mechanisms of notification and surveillance more robust, which are used to identify possible regulatory barriers ahead of time. By developing these steps forward, the WTO will be facilitated in encouraging better communication among its stakeholders, advocating for a collaborative approach in addressing issues of regulation that can inadvertently produce adverse spillovers (Hoekman et al., 2025). Further, the new international trade world demands that monitoring and transparency continue within the WTO system. With the rising prominence of emerging economies and with the increasing complexity of trade, the organization will need to modify its procedures to be able to continue effectively handling the complications of global trade relationships. Adaptation can come in the form of using new technologies for data gathering and analysis to enhance the feedback mechanisms that are used to make policy decisions. Increased transparency will allow member nations to gain the vision that they need to address the intricacies of global markets and to promote the practice of trade that is not only fair but also conducive to long-term economic growth. In general, effective monitoring and transparency constitute the bedrock of WTO legitimacy and effectiveness to promote a peaceful trading environment that benefits all members (Hoekman et al., 2025; Woods, 2025).

1.3. PRINCIPLES OF THE WORLD TRADE ORGANIZATION (WTO)

The WTO is guided by a number of principles whose intent is to promote equitable trade and economic cooperation among nations. Central to these principles is the most-favored-nation (MFN) treatment, under which member states are bound to accord the same trade advantage to all WTO members. The principle is intended to ensure that none of the members is treated differently in any fashion, providing a level playing field for trade. Furthermore, the rule of national treatment requires imported and domestic goods to be treated equally after crossing the border, in order to eliminate discrimination according to the product. All these are basic cornerstones in building a stable and clear business environment that enables countries to engage in international trade while minimizing conflict and trade wars to bare essentials, thus contributing to the improvement in the stability of the global economy. Another core principle of the WTO is that of transparency, which requires members to openly publish their rules and policies in a transparent manner and to notify the WTO in the event of any modifications.

Transparency is required to build the trust between nations and promote compliance with global trade standards. Transparency enables business and governments to make more informed choices because now they are able to clearly understand the environment of trading and operate within it. Furthermore, the WTO encourages participation of members in a comprehensive system of rules that governs trade negotiations so that all countries, large or small, and powerful or powerless, can join in formulating international trade policy. This makes the process equitable and checks the dominance that is usually characteristic of trade negotiations, leveling the playing field of the global trade system. The intersection of trade and environmental policy has become increasingly significant in the WTO principles' discussion. As globalization develops further, the environmental implications of the trade policy cannot be overlooked. The WTO principles must evolve and incorporate sustainability into its framework to deal with these issues. For instance, there have been discussions regarding environmental goods and services focused on restructuring what these are in the WTO architecture in a bid to provide it with greater ability to fight climate change. As has been mooted in discussions among experts such as those in the Working Group on Trade, Investment, and Climate Policy, the potential for trade agreements to aid or hinder climate objectives is significant (Ackerman et al., 2016). This dynamic dialogue in the WTO mirrors the necessity of balancing trade and environmental interests in today's world, casting the organization's relevance in addressing global challenges (Buzan et al., 2014) (Figure 1.8).

Figure 1.8. Principles of the World Trade Organization (WTO).

Source: https://fastercapital.co/i/World-Trade-Organization--How-to-Understand-and-Comply-with-the-World-Trade-Organization-Rules-and-Dispute-Settlement-Mechanism--Key-Principles-of-the-World-Trade-Organization.webp.

1.3.1. Most-Favored-Nation (MFN) Treatment

The MFN is instrumental in playing a vital role in the WTO system by ensuring that any preferential terms of trade accorded by a member is accorded to all members. This non-discrimination promotes justice and equality in international trade because countries cannot extend preferential terms of trade selectively to specific partners. Rather, any good arrangement, whether in terms of tariffs, quotas, or trade rules, has to be extended to all WTO members so as to promote a competitive trading system. The application of the MFN principle is the foundation on which the common objective of the WTO to create a stable and predictable global trading system with the capacity to spur economic growth and development among members is founded, illustrating how highly interdependent global economies rely on equitable trade practices to thrive. The MFN treatment plays a pivotal role towards preventing discrimination in trade and defense of member states against unreasonable trade barriers. The norm is aimed at addressing terms-of-trade externality whereby nations would otherwise charge high tariffs in their quest for competitiveness. The General Agreement on Tariffs and Trade (GATT) that existed before the WTO was geared towards eliminating such obstacles by instituting a rules-based regime that ensured nations lowered trade barriers mutually and reciprocally. As recorded by existing literature, the basic principles of GATT, like MFN, are bargaining regulations that help governments handle the intricacy of protectionism in trade and avoid the inefficiency provoked by the externality of terms-of-trade, thereby establishing equilibrium in international trade relations as a whole (Bagwell et al., 2025). The MFN principle further demonstrates how entangled trade policy can lead nations towards cooperative rather than competitive strategies. Within the WTO framework, MFN treatment encourages predictability and transparency, which are the virtues required in promoting global supply chains and global trade. In the absence of this standard, countries unilaterally enjoying preferential terms can weaken the multilateral trading regime, paving the way for a fragmented global economy. Being dedicated to MFN, the member countries express their commitment to ensuring sound trade agreements that are mutually favorable to both countries involved. This framework not only ensures market efficiency but also economic growth among member countries, making them engage more constructively at the international level, thus illustrating the applicability of MFN treatment in the broader context of global relations and trade (Giacalone et al., 2007) (Figure 1.9).

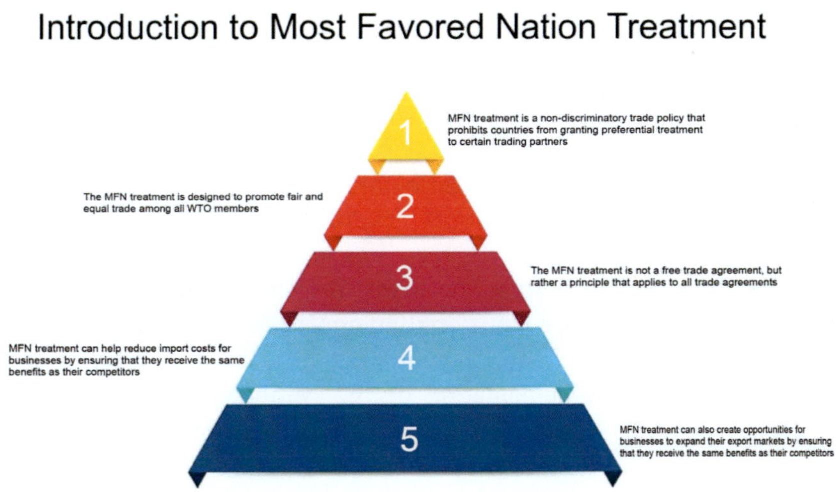

Figure 1.9. Most-favored-nation (MFN) treatment.

Source: https://fastercapital.co/i/Trimming-Import-Costs--Most-Favored-Nation-Treatment-Explained--Introduction-to-Most-Favored-Nation-Treatment.webp.

1.3.2. National Treatment Principle

The National Treatment Principle is a cornerstone of the World Trade Organization (WTO) framework, offering a fundamental rule for WTO member nations regarding treatment of foreign goods and services. Specifically, the principle mandates that imported products that enter into a domestic market receive treatment that is no less favorable than that of similar domestic products. This is a provision that assists in preventing discrimination against foreign competitors, thereby creating a more level playing field for international trade. The assurance of nondiscrimination treatment not only assists in fostering equitable competition but also inspires countries to remove protectionist obstacles that could hinder trade relations. The National Treatment Principle is robust in how it can contribute towards the overall aspirations of the WTO, which are to reduce barriers to trade as well as promote open and transparent trading regimes between member states. Applying the National Treatment Principle is not an easy task, particularly when account is taken of state trading enterprises (STEs). As has been noted by the Canada-Wheat WTO panel decision, the principle of non-discrimination must be applied with care in the face of unique domestic farm policies. The panels' rulings, in trying to resolve the United States' grievances regarding Canada's single-desk wheat marketing mechanism, underscored the complexity of juggling national interests and the requirement to guarantee compliance with the National Treatment Principle. This decision underscored the WTO's approach to governing STEs in accordance with GATT Article XVII, emphasizing the value of openness in the way these entities operate and comply with international trading regulations. Therefore, ongoing discourses on STEs reflect the delicate balance between achieving fair trade practices and giving in to the different economic frameworks unique to member states. Moreover, the National Treatment Principle was significantly influenced by situations such as the Singapore Ministerial Conference, which highlighted the dichotomy between liberalization and protectionism domestically. As much as the ministerial attempted to address several matters that concern international trade, it could not provide a clearly articulated proposal for effective implementation of the National Treatment Principle among members. Most significantly, ineffective handling of market access and anti-dumping policies brought to the forefront the continued challenge for members to adhere to principles of non-discrimination. As countries chart intraindigenous and extraterritorial trade policies, the implications of such advances remain symbolic of the continued challenge to make the WTOs goal of promoting fair trade a reality. Consequently, the relationship between international trade regulations and national interests remains a key aspect of the debate surrounding the National Treatment Principle and its application in practice, deciding the destiny of world trade.

1.3.3. Transparency and Fair Competition

Transparency and fair competition are key concepts within the framework of the World Trade Organization (WTO) because they instill the trust required for multilateral trading relationships. Transparency refers to the unobstructed passage of information, making member states and stakeholders cognizant of trade policy, rules, and processes. Transparency is important in creating a forum for all players in trade to carry out their activities on a level playing field. Without transparency, countries could establish hidden trade barriers or discriminatory trade practices, leading to extreme imbalances in competition. By having specific rules to mandate member states to offer trade-related information, the WTO aims to promote equity, reduce misunderstandings, and prevent disagreements, thereby making trading activities among states smoother, which is vital to ensuring stability in the international trading system (Hoekman et al., 2017).

Figure 1.10. Transparency and fair competition.

Source: https://fastercapital.co/i/Price-fixing--Price-Leadership-vs--Price-Fixing--Ethical-Considerations--Transparency-and-Fair-Competition.webp.

Moreover, emphasis on fair competition reflects the WTOs commitment towards guaranteeing an even playing ground for all members. Free competition is the concept that all trading partners, regardless of nationality, have an equal chance of accessing market opportunity without discriminatory action being taken against them. The WTO guidelines encourage level trade rules and the removal of unfair subsidies that will imbalance the forces of the market. The establishment of well-defined rules against anti-competitive behavior will allow nations to engage in confidence in international trade with the assurance of rights protection. This promotes not only economic growth but the higher potential for innovation, as companies are encouraged to compete based on the quality of their products and services and not on uneven terms based on protectionism or lack of regulatory oversight (Hoekman et al., 2017). Within broader debates regarding fair competition and openness, the evolution of procedural rights and the position of civil society are of particular note. Emergence of participation rights represents an important shift in how stakeholders handle trade policy and regulation on the international scene. Initially, procedural rights were limited, but as the demand for increased transparency picked up pace, progressively more and more recognized the virtue in open conversation. Democratic states such as those in Europe have led in demanding openness and civil society engagement in trade discourse. Though, there is consent on representation because various political traditions shape the views that are held on civil involvement in governance. A middle ground, that includes various views, can enhance the efficacy of the WTO to ensure transparency supports fair competition, and the organization's goal to ensure cooperative trade relations among its members (Figure 1.10).

1.4. IMPACT OF THE WORLD TRADE ORGANIZATION (WTO) ON GLOBAL TRADE

The WTO plays an important role in the trend in international trade by establishing a rules-based framework of international trade. In offering a negotiating forum and mechanism for settling disputes, the WTO stimulates member countries to exchange more freely and with more confidence. One of its main aspects of influence is the expansion of the Trade Facilitation Agreement (TFA) to streamline customs procedures and assist member country transparency. Recent studies indicate that Latin American and Caribbean countries, disproportionately affected by the COVID-19 crisis, have progressed significantly in TFA implementation, with an average regional coverage of 71% as of 2023 (Herreros et al., 2023). This achievement proves the WTO's ability to impart nations with harmonious trade behavior, thereby increasing international trade flow and production linkages. Further, the WTO modus operandi transcends traditional trade facilitation, addressing the complicated interconnection of trade and global matters, such as climate change. The organization's ongoing debates reflect the imperative of harmonizing trade policy with ecological care, a matter increasingly at the forefront of the international agenda. It has identified the WTOs capability to facilitate a transition to climate-friendly action by revisiting existing trade agreements and incorporating environmental concerns within them (Ackerman et al., 2016). For instance, examining foreign investment treaties as tools to direct investment in the direction of climate mitigation objectives emphasizes the WTOs unique role in reconciling these two objectives. Through promoting policies that harmonize trade and environmental stewardship, the WTO not only promotes economic growth but also a robust global system of trade. The impact of the WTO on global trade has extensive implications, reaching the socioeconomic fabric of member nations. Through promoting free trade, the organization promotes the generation of employment opportunities, innovation, and consumer choice. Meanwhile, the benefits of trade liberalization can be unevenly distributed, and social equity as well as environmental issues can arise. The WTO thus has the challenge of balancing its policies to both promote trade and correct the imbalances that are caused by globalization. The inclusion of provisions that promote fair trade practice and environmentally responsible management is hence important in developing an inclusive international trading system. As countries keep defining the future of post-pandemic recovery, the WTO's contribution towards promoting cooperative and sustainable trade policies will be vital in formulating well-balanced and robust global trade relations.

1.4.1. Trade Liberalization Effects

Trade liberalization directly affects global economic forces, particularly its impact across various sectors, including industries and services. By reducing tariffs and other trade barriers, countries can make foreign services and products more readily available, hence encouraging domestic industry competition and innovation. Services, too, often relegated to the secondary background of trade negotiations, are increasingly recognized as major economic drivers. Countries liberalizing their service sectors experience increased growth rates and better standards of living, suggesting that the benefits of trade liberalization do not hold in traditional sectors such as manufacturing and agriculture alone. The potential benefits from trade liberalization in services, for instance, are likely to outshine those derived from goods trade, thereby pointing towards the need for comprehensive trade agreements covering services as much as other sectors (James, 2009). The intricacy of trade liberalization also encompasses how it affects the environment, particularly in the case of environmental goods (EGs). Research indicates that reductions in tariff and non-tariff barriers can significantly enhance the exportation of EGs from one country to another. Interestingly, it is found that tariff reductions in the exporting country have a bigger impact on its EG exports compared to identical reductions in the importing country. This asymmetric effect serves to put forward the necessity of proactive tariff negotiations in trade liberalization experiences. The environmental theme reinforces the proposition that trade liberalization needs to consider not only economic growth but also environmentally sound practices because trade policy reforms can foster greener economies as well as enhance total trade balances for nations (Fang et al., 2015). Besides this, the ongoing process of trade liberalization under the auspices of the World Trade Organization (WTO) is evidence of strengthening consensus about its benefits and drawbacks. The complexities of navigating trade agreements, especially amid fluctuating economic conditions and disparate regulatory frameworks, call for utmost priority and coordination among member countries. One of the needed challenges comes from the resistance to negotiations, particularly for more emphasis on services and environmental goods. Countries, including the United States, are prompted to take unilateral measures to open up their markets, not only placing them in a favorable position in international trade but also compelling other nations, including developing countries, to conform to these high standards. Therefore, encouraging a free trade environment is more than mere economic benefit, creating an interdependent global marketplace in preparation for innovative development and sustainability (James, 2009) (Figure 1.11).

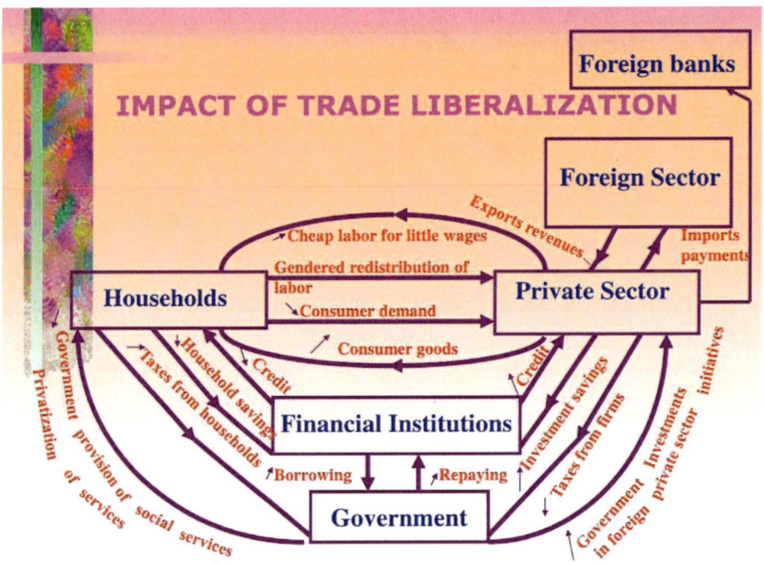

Figure 1.11. Trade liberalization effects.

Source: https://external-content.duckduckgo.com/iu/?u=https%3A%2F%2 Fimage1.slideserve.com%2F3496796%2Fimpact-of-trade-liberalization-l.jpg&f=1&nofb=1&ipt=806b0429bc3d17890a2acfcf95ef08842f27bbcc5ebfd3e7d3d6932115d670c0.

1.4.2. Economic Growth and Development

The nexus between economic growth and development is commonly ascribed to the paradigms of international trade, particularly as described by the World Trade Organization (WTO). Economic growth, a stat measured most times through growth in Gross Domestic Product (GDP), reflects the quantitative aspect of an economy's performance. Growth can be due to any variety of causes like accumulation of capital, technical progress, and increasing labor productivity. Real development, however, goes beyond quantitative growth; it entails qualitative improvement in living standards, equitable distribution of riches, and sustainability. WTO has a significant function in facilitating trade liberalization, enabling countries to get access to larger markets, attract more foreign investment, and achieve a stronger competitive edge in the world. Such an arrangement of trade agreements enables countries to make use of their unique endowments and hence improves their economic growth as well as external shock resistance (Rush et al., 2007). As countries exchange across the globe under the patronage of the WTO, intricate mechanisms of demand and supply modification impact domestic economies considerably. For instance, developing nations are likely to gain an export boost since tariffs are reduced and market access has opened up, allowing them to avail themselves of their comparative advantages to the fullest. This integration of trade is required for countries like Indonesia, whose participation in initiatives like the ASEAN Free Trade Area (AFTA) has significantly influenced the evolution of specific export industries like crude palm oil. The regional cooperation exemplified by AFTA is a demonstration of how economic blocks can enhance intra-regional trade, with the ultimate aim of economic development of member nations. But whereas trade fuels growth, it is likewise demanding in the context of sustainability and even-balanced development, with the need for a carefully calculated move by policymakers in remedying such complex issues (Febrianti et al., 2015). The dynamic shift in global trade through forums like the WTO necessitates an improved understanding of the link between economic growth and development. Sustainable economic growth calls for convergence between expanded trade liberalization and offsetting the imbalances that might arise from it. The fast-growing United States-China trade deficit is worrisome in terms of long-term financial stability and its potential impact on international economic arrangements. Economic integration can be volatile, especially if national interests are undermined by geopolitical tensions, as has occurred in the U.S.-China relationship. Thus, although the WTO aims at facilitating international trade, it also has to facilitate negotiations on equitable economic opportunities so that all nations, particularly developing nations, can benefit from globalization without compromising their long-term development goals (Rush et al., 2007).

1.4.3. Influence on Trade Policies of Member Countries

The effect of the World Trade Organization (WTO) on the trade policies of the member countries is far-reaching and varied. When nations accede to the WTO, they pledge to respect a set of rules and regulations relating to international trade agreed upon by members. This agreement creates a framework where trade policy has to conform with wider international standards, effectively making them more credible and stable. For example, developing nations such as Turkey have deliberately phased into the international trading order through their accession to the WTO. By entering into undertakings to end trade barriers and subsidization, these nations not only gain greater access to markets but also enhance their competitiveness on the global platform. The WTO system hence plays a pivotal role in shaping national policies by promoting openness, responsibility, and compliance with fair trade norms as required for boosting economic growth and prosperity within member nations (Bektaş et al., 2018). Besides, the WTOs negotiations and decisions have a central role to play in refashioning agricultural policy, an important part of most nations' trade. The member states have to maneuver complex rules for market access, subsidies, and domestic support, which the WTO regulates to ensure fair trading practices. This applies particularly in nations like Turkey, whose agriculture trade remains a major sector of the economy.

Figure 1.12. Influence on trade policies of member countries.

Source: https://external-content.duckduckgo.com/iu/?u=http%3A%2F%2Fblog.volkovlaw.com%2Fwp-content%2Fuploads%2F2025%2F03%2Ft.jpeg&f=1&nofb=1&ipt=2f8d5e510de263568eab1357ac56e5841048778315af2fe10fc8e96d3bd0c6bf.

Through the imposition of rules all member states must comply with, the WTO directs domestic agriculture policy, compelling countries to reimagine policies promoting international competitiveness along with global standards. In addition, agricultural subsidy policy progressively confronts countries with balancing domestic interests against international commitments, echoing the dynamic tension between national sovereignty and international trading standards embodied by the WTO (Bektaş et al., 2018). More broadly, the WTO is a vital forum for economic collaboration with implications not only on trade deals but even on member countries' overall economic strategies. The organization provides a venue for discourse and negotiation, where members can coordinate their economic policies. Coordination of this kind is highly pertinent under the G-20 framework, where trade policies and economic regulation are highly debated across large economies. The implications of these talks have spill-over impacts on member nations' trade policies, supporting global trade regimes and norms. The effectiveness of such groupings in allowing consistent trade policies accentuates the WTO's umbrella role in creating a common global trading environment, despite ongoing debate about its efficacy and responsiveness to emerging economic issues (Figure 1.12).

1.5. CRITICISMS OF THE WORLD TRADE ORGANIZATION (WTO)

The WTO has been criticized extensively since its establishment, primarily regarding its role in poor nations. Critics have claimed that the WTO perpetuates unequal outcomes from international trade by favoring affluent nations at the disadvantage of others, making them dependent on others. This is based on the argument that decision-making in the WTOs reflects mainly the interests of powerful member states to the detriment of ostracizing other less developed nations. As they struggle to compete on an unlevel platform, the policies of the WTOs can be a source of, rather than a solution to, poverty, the critics maintain. Besides, it is argued by critics whether the organization actually responds to issues of labor rights and environmental policies, which raise concerns of a more inclusive and fair trade negotiation strategy (Brassett et al., 2012). Adding to the enormous pile of criticism against the WTO is its perceived transparency and accountability, raising serious doubts among stakeholders. It is commonly asserted that the WTO negotiation processes are shut to the public, offering little space for public knowledge and involvement. Such lack of openness not only deters trust but also fosters doubts regarding the legitimacy of the organizations decision-making. Critics say the secrecy could serve corporate interests at the expense of common citizens, thus diminishing the credibility and efficiency of the WTO as an authority. Beyond this, there are calls for more profound reforms that would enable greater stakeholder involvement in the process of conducting trade and enhance mechanisms of accountability in a bid to ensure stakeholders' interests are suitably represented and considered (Brassett et al., 2012). Lastly, the WTO has been blamed for being unable to stay ahead of the ever-changing global environment of trade, particularly taking into consideration new economic trends and challenges emerging. The breakdown of the Doha Round in 2016 highlighted elemental weaknesses in the organization's institutional design and governance, calling into question its relevance in contemporary issues in trade. Stakeholders are convinced that unless there is substantive reform, the WTO risks being rendered obsolete, unable to address critical challenges such as electronic trade, global warming, and supply chain sabotage at the international level. As louder demands for the institutional reforms are made, the supporters underscore the necessity to evolve the WTO so that it remains at the core of facilitating fair and balanced global trade systems that are sensitive to the needs of all nations (Basedow et al., 2018) (Figure 1.13).

Figure 1.13. Criticisms of the World Trade Organization (WTO).

Source: https://pwonlyias.com/wp-content/uploads/2024/03/15-65e1dfa1830bd.webp.

1.5.1. Allegations of Favoring Developed Nations

The World Trade Organization (WTO) has been continually accused of having a bias towards favoring developed nations within the arena of international trade. Critics argue that the organization's policies and framework are disproportionately skewed to favor wealthier nations, building an inequality-driven system on an international scale. For instance, the WTO rules imposed are such that they target the interests of the economically advanced nations to be able to exert major influence over trade negotiations. This has led to accusations that developing countries are overlooked and lack the ability to dictate their trade fate. Therefore, the WTO's function and structure contribute to a process of developed nations maintaining their competitive edge at the cost of the poorer nations aspiring to ascend in an uneven international trade process. These imbalances are evident through several WTO agreements, which are perceived to have been drafted with the capabilities of developed nations, rather than developing ones. For example, free trade deals tend to focus more on intellectual property rights that favor multinational corporations based in richer nations, and this makes it challenging for poorer nations to have access to vital technologies. This has been of concern regarding the adverse impacts on poorer countries' agriculture and medical sectors, whose necessary commodities and innovations are inhibited. They have cited the necessity to adjust these accords to create a more balanced trading system, which takes cognizance of and caters to the unique problems of developing countries, in an effort to ensure that the principle of fair trade is upheld in the global economy. Furthermore, charges of biases against developed countries are also levied at the WTO enforcement mechanism. The dispute settlement system, intended to provide a just resolution of trade disputes, has been criticized as less accessible to developing nations. The latter are often denied the economic and legal capital necessary to pursue a sophisticated legal dispute before the panels of the WTO. Doe v. Unocal Corp case also involves broader issues of multinational corporate accountability and human rights when multinationals are apt to act in developing nations. This situation is a repeat of the WTOs approach, proving that unless radical change occurs, the institution may continue to permit channels that advance the interests of developed economies by undermining emerging economies, in effect maintaining an economic imbalance that defies the tenets of fairness in trade.

1.5.2. Environmental and Labor Concerns

In the context of global commerce, employment and environmental concerns have been critical issues reflecting the crossroads of economic progress and ecological wholeness. The World Trade Organization (WTO) seeks to encourage international trade, but its resulting increase places immense pressure on the environment and working conditions. With the push towards competitiveness, unregulated trading can lead to environmental degradation, unsustainable consumption of resources, and adverse impacts on workers' well-being. This calls for moral examination on the part of nations in ensuring that trade does not take place at the expense of environmental health or workers' welfare. Policymakers are then charged with crafting institutions that act to balance economic interests against environmental stewardship and equitable labor practices, cultivating an environment for trade conducive to growth while sustaining itself. The relationship between environmental impact and unionization has gained increased attention among scholars, where the potential for organized labor to engage in sustainability is highlighted. According to studies that have analyzed data from the OECD countries, increased levels of unionization correlate negatively with per capita carbon dioxide emissions, a factor that suggests that the representation of workers can promote environmentally sustainable practices. By advocating for workers' rights and proposing policies that curtail ecological damage, labor unions have the ability to synthesize workers' interests with those of environmentalists. The movement of this force is the complex interplay at work, calling for labor policy to be better comprehended for its impacts on the environment, particularly under the global trade regime of the WTO (Alvarez et al., 2019). As the process of globalization continues to redefine trade patterns, the freight transport industry is in the middle of environmental and labor disputes. The global supply chain growth has awakened high levels of concern with regard to how such activities affect the workforce and the environment. With the extensive implications on health and safety, freight transportation trends must consider the echoing effects on exporting and importing nations. Tackling these issues calls for creative organizing practices and policies that reduce harm and focus on the health of workers and ecosystems as much as possible. Furthermore, the dynamic character of international trade demands cooperation to set standards that defend labor rights while promoting sustainable approaches. Under such paradigms, the WTO can help build a trade environment that not only fosters economic development but also promotes labor and environmental integrity, resulting in a sustainable international economy (Hricko et al., 2011).

1.5.3. Calls for Reform and Improvement

The World Trade Organization (WTO) has come to be more and more under pressure to reform and improve, particularly of its operating structures and models of governance. The complexity of modern trade necessitates a review of decision-making procedures, negotiating techniques, and resolution of disputes. Critics argue that existing processes do not do enough to address challenges facing us today, including the explosion of regulatory externalities with the potential to undermine trade agreements. For example, proposals to have a critical mass approach taken in negotiations have emerged, the aim of which is to provide more inclusive and effective dialogue between member states. By accepting that the WTO is an incomplete contract which must self-enforce, the parties can learn its limitations and where it can be changed to enhance the organizations relevance and efficacy in the face of a changing global landscape (Hoekman et al., 2025). Moreover, thematic sessions at the WTO have also been onboarded as a strategy for facilitating debate and seeking major issues with regard to international trade. The organization has held more than 100 thematic sessions over the last few years, which are used as a platform for member states to examine the success stories and failures of existing agreements. These meetings have ensured the sharing of experience in implementation, which is vital in understanding challenges faced by member states, especially developing countries. However, the effectiveness of these meetings is still uncertain, and the majority of committees fail to optimize their utilization. In order to better utilize their potential, reform initiatives should aim at deeper participation by capital-based administrators and incorporate future-looking agendas that address pertinent global trade issues (Wolfe et al., 2020).

Figure 1.14. Calls for reform and improvement.

Source: https://external-content.duckduckgo.com/iu/?u=https%3A%2F%2Fres.cloudinary.com%2Fmomentum-media-group-pty-ltd%2Fimage%2Fupload%2Fv1655708843%2FMyBusiness%2Fnew_articleimage%2Freform-blocks-myb.jpg&f=1&nofb=1&ipt=c117d91fb45c26b32383a73af1e9378ff75e50b573466a863ddebb568820132c.

Lastly, WTO reform calls are a reflection of a general need for increased transparency and active interaction among member countries. In a more integrated global trade as well as regulatory methods, the organization must adapt by making its surveillance and monitoring abilities stronger. The proposed reforms should tackle material shortfalls in the discussions on subsidies, regional trade agreements (RTAs), and impacts of the dispute settlement outcome. By addressing these regions, the WTO will be in a position to create an even stronger environment conducive to cooperation and understanding among its members. An organized reform process, such as the application of best practices and investment in virtual meeting technologies, will be central to the maximization of the effectiveness and responsiveness of the WTO over the next several years (Wolfe et al., 2020) (Figure 1.14).

1.6. THE WORLD TRADE ORGANIZATION (WTO) IN THE 21ST CENTURY

The role of the WTO in the world today is replete with numerous challenges as well as opportunities for us moving into the 21st century. Perhaps the most significant challenge for the WTO is a diminution of popular support for open markets among major OECD countries. This is a direct consequence of economic imbalances that have occurred within these economies, leading to an anti-globalization backlash. The erosion of confidence in the multilateral trade order poses an existential issue regarding its eventual sustainability, particularly given the growing trend of protectionism in popular opinion. The legitimacy of the WTO is at stake and will have to steer these public perceptions successfully to restore the organizations relevance and effectiveness in global governance, Higgott et al. (2009) assert. As the world economy changes, the WTO struggles with institutional issues that go beyond simple trade negotiations. The impasse of the Doha Round is quintessential of the challenges of reaching agreement on a divisive and complex agenda. In addition, clarity must be provided in delineating the WTOs goals as member states look to focus on more urgent global concerns, including climate change and sustainable development. The case at the hand is symptomatic of a key turning point, questioning whether the WTO can remain a suitable forum for fostering international trade amid rising regional preferentialism. These questions need to be answered because, otherwise, they might undermine the organizations core role as the arbiter of global standards and rules of international trade, according to Higgott et al. (2009). One of the immediate issues for the WTO is how it can tackle new global issues, specifically those associated with agriculture and sustainable development. The existing structure is perceived to be archaic and incapable of adequately responding to new challenges such as climate change, global food security, and poverty in developing countries. The challenge of balancing trade in agriculture with redressing these pressing global needs becomes increasingly complicated. As noted in, the WTOs sustained interest in conventional agricultural issues undermines its capacity to adequately address modern crises that affect global health and economic stability. In the absence of an imagined governance system with a stress on sustainability and resiliency, the WTO could continue to remain inconsequential as an institution that promotes cooperation at the international level in order to address 21st-century challenges.

1.6.1. Challenges Facing the World Trade Organization (WTO)

The WTO today is confronted with a myriad of issues that denigrate its timeliness and efficacy in the face of rapid-change globalization. The most fundamental one is possibly the increased complexity of global governance, which stems primarily from the very rapid economic integration and interdependence between nations. As clearly demonstrated by recent international summits, global leaders' inability to reach binding agreement reflects a broader trend of disaffection from multilateral institutions like the WTO. This is further complicated by the rise of multinational corporations whose existence cuts across borders and tends to transcend the economic influence of medium-sized countries, rendering the trends of international trade and preference more complex. In order to break through this soil so thoroughly, the WTO will have to re-imagine its institutions and strategies to construct collaboration between a broadening galaxy of actors and interests, and therefore reestablish its role within the global trading system (Hillman et al., 2018). Moreover, the eroding confidence in multilateralism further complicates the WTOs work since countries get increasingly drawn towards protectionism and bilateral trade agreements. Such tendencies not only undermine the organization's foundations of free commerce and cooperation but also tend to establish splintered economic arrangements difficult to control effectively. As seen in recent economic bloc evolutions like ASEAN, nations are following regional integration models that steer clear of traditional multilateral frameworks (Olmedo-Peralta et al., 2016). The WTO must rethink its approach in order to continue being an effective forum for trading deal negotiations and the resolution of disputes. Absent meaningful reform, the institution could fall behind other models of economic cooperation that may not necessarily prefer collective decision-making or common trade benefit. An important aspect of revitalizing the WTO is to update its governance structure and mandate based on the emerging dynamics of global trade. Since the institution operates in a world characterized by complexities and interdependencies, it must embrace new-style approaches that enhance its efficiency and responsiveness. This can entail reshaping the mechanism of resolving conflicts, renewing trade law, and promoting inclusivity in the member states, especially the marginalized within traditional trading systems. Additionally, its currency needs to be sustained through a renewed commitment to issues such as climate change and income inequality, which demand collective action worldwide (Hillman et al., 2018). In so doing, the WTO will be in a position to serve as a central driver not only of trade but even more general international coordination to ensure that it maintains a leading position in shaping a rules-based economic order (Figure 1.15).

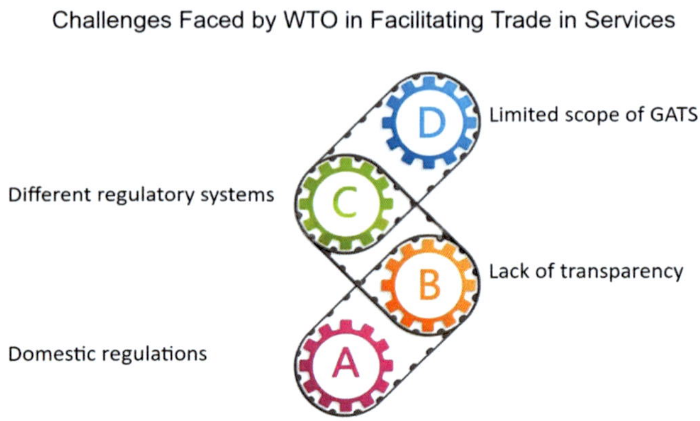

Figure 1.15. Challenges facing the World Trade Organization (WTO).

Source: https://fastercapital.co/i/Beyond-Goods--Exploring-WTO-s-Role-in-Facilitating-Trade-in-Services--Challenges-Faced-by-WTO-in-Facilitating-Trade-in-Services.webp.

1.6.2. Role in Addressing Global Issues

The World Trade Organization (WTO) is a global organization that plays a central role in the global economy, aimed at governing international trade relations and addressing some of the world's problems. With a rules-based trading system, WTO has facilitated outstanding growth of global GDP during the last few decades. Not only does the system foster economic development, but also addresses problems generated by globalization, such as trade imbalances and protectionism. Moreover, the WTO also plays an important role in global cooperation through the promotion of discussion between member countries. Despite the issues, such as the dilemma of national interest and policy reform disputes, the potential of the WTO to fairly regulate international trade relations remains the utmost priority since new issues keep emerging in our more complicated globalized world (Hoekman et al., 2017). However, while its pioneering work is recognized, the WTO is increasingly unable to keep pace in addressing global issues of the day, particularly in the areas of agriculture, climate change, and sustainability. Its existing framework struggles to address pressing challenges in regard to agricultures multifunctionality in the 21st century, with a stark disconnect between its established guidelines and the pressing demands from climate crises and food security. This lack strongly undermines whether the existing WTO regime can easily address issues of governance in modern times, considering that the issues target developing nations experiencing hunger and poverty. Considering such a disadvantage, the majority of scholars advocate for the reformulation of the WTOs model of governance in an attempt to adapt to the demands of modern global trade in light of environmental necessity and social inequality (Kim et al., 2025). To revitalize the WTOs position in attempting to address these cross-cutting challenges, there must be an honest and open discussion among member nations. While preferential trade arrangements have emerged as the necessary vehicle for a higher level of cooperation, these policies are normally not enough without the solid foundation that the WTO provides. The Agreement on Trade Facilitation is a good example of how member states can innovate and address issues surrounding development in a collective manner. By ensuring timely adaptation of its priorities and allowing for valuable debates regarding issues of emergent importance to trade policy, the WTO can become more relevant. Ultimately, this emphasizes the need for member states to share a commitment to common objectives and synergize their efforts in the face of the intricate challenges undermining international stability and prosperity during the 21st century (Hoekman et al., 2017).

1.6.3. Future Prospects and Adaptations

With the ongoing development of the international economy, the WTO must adapt to emerging challenges and opportunities due to technological advancements and shifting economic paradigms. Advances in digital trade and e-commerce offer opportunities and threats to traditional trade frameworks. The WTO faces the colossal task of framing guidelines that grant equitable access to online markets and combat concerns such as data privacy, cybersecurity, and intellectual property. The members, including nations and private enterprises, must unite to form guidelines that benefit not only growth but also equity in online trade. It is essential that the WTO remain up to date with such trends by establishing an environment that boosts innovations and protects the interests of all the stakeholders involved in international trade. Furthermore, future developments of the WTO can also be pushed by pressing environmental concerns and sustainable development demands. With growing environmental degradation and resource exhaustion, trade policies must integrate environmental considerations into their frameworks. This incorporation can take the shape of green free trade agreements or incentives towards adopting green practices. Economic policies are gradually recognizing the significance of maintaining growth in balance with nature, thus further accelerating the need for the WTO to bridge this process. By taking a lead on the environment, the

WTO can shape the way nations do business, and trade can drive a sustainable future rather than expanding existing issues. Not only does this align with long-term global stability but also the needs and aspirations of ever greener consumers and investors, as outlined in contemporary literature (Arriola et al., 2025). Additionally, the future of the WTO also hinges on its ability to address the complex geopolitics that shape global trade patterns. Increasingly, protectionism and trade wars threaten the liberal trading order promoted by the WTO since its inception. With governments grappling with rising nationalism and economic particularism, the organization must de-escalate tensions and facilitate cooperation among members. This may involve modifying existing systems or creating new mechanisms of conflict resolution that are more attuned to the nuances of the contemporary global setting. Through promoting communication and understanding, the WTO can actively seek to reduce the negative effects of such tensions while facilitating greater balanced trade for more players. Ultimately, geopolitical realities will have to be adjusted to by the organizations in order for their viability and relevance in the coming years (Alexander et al., 2014).

SUMMARY

An examination of the WTO, there is a need to recognize how central it stands in facilitating a rules-based system of international trade. The WTO has been instrumental in fostering international trade, and significantly contributed to increased global GDP growth in recent decades. But its relevance is contested, particularly during the midst of complexity of a global digital economy and with ongoing servicification of production. Dissensus among WTO members regarding priority in trade policy has prevented necessary reforms, which reflect underlying tensions over the effects of national policy on the world markets. These tensions therefore prevent meaningful debate and rule-making processes, particularly on such long-brewing topics such as agricultural policy and emerging issues of world trade concerns. The ability of the WTO to navigate through these challenges will be critical in maintaining the cooperative framework crucial to successful trade relations and general economic stability (Hoekman et al., 2017). Further, the widespread dissatisfaction with regard to the WTOs dispute resolution mechanisms and openness provisions introduces a further layer of complexity to its functional role. The reform of these aspects is also imperative not only to recover confidence among the member states but also to enhance the capability of the organization to solve contemporary trade grievances. As preferential trade arrangements grow in prominence, they underscore the need to have a robust rules-based platform provided by the

WTO. While such agreements can facilitate increased bilateral cooperation, they constitute half-measures to the new global trade issues that need solving at the multilateral level. The recent Trade Facilitation Agreement is an example of how, despite significant differences, member countries are able to arrive at incremental reform through collective problem-solving of development concerns. Having substantive discussions regarding the future and direction of international trade will be the driving force for revitalizing the role of the WTO and attaining multilateral engagement in the rule-making process (Higgott et al., 2009). To propel these intricate issues, the WTO stands at the juncture that necessitates reflection and action. Systemic problems will be stabilized by stabilizing its problems such as eroding popular backing for open markets in OECD nations and increasing rises of regionalism. Even more importantly, establishing clarity on the WTO agenda and priorities for the 21st century will be crucial to its legitimacy and effectiveness as a governing body. A lack of proper response to these pressing concerns can undermine not only the position of the WTO as a leading player in the world's trade setting but the reliability of global economic rule of law overall. Member nations must see that they employ an active policy, seeking dialogue which is geared towards fairness and equitability in trading arrangements. It is through an energetic drive towards reform that the WTO can maintain its pillar role in facilitating international trade in an increasingly complex world (Higgott et al., 2009).

As a world center institution, the WTO serves as a negotiating facilitator and maintains rules meant to support world economic stability. Among the greatest strengths of the WTO is that it stresses multilateralism, urging its member nations to unite in combat against trade challenges. The approach of multilateralism is integral in promoting equitable trade relations and reducing conflict among nations. The WTO's guidelines, including most-favored-nation treatment and national treatment, strive towards creating a level playing field such that liberalization through trade can be availed equally by all member nations. As a focal international organization, the WTO demonstrates how coordinated cooperation may declaw the complexity induced by dissimilar national interests and thereby help toward a unified international economy. The WTO also covers various trade issues through specialized agreements, such as those involving sanitary and phytosanitary (SPS) measures. Buth's work informs us as to how states move regulatory powers across these domains with the implication that principal-agent theory will need to be supplemented with consideration of domestic interest groups cost-benefit calculations. SPS measures are specially relevant because they directly impact public welfare, linking health standard and trade policy. This intersection captures the conflict between national and international regulation. Governments would like to institutionalize international cooperation in SPS measures beyond the WTO due to fear of the political cost associated with foregoing policymaking power. The process of decision-making hence captures an advanced bargain among maintaining national discretion and conforming to international norms (Buthe et al., 2008). The interplay between globalization and the roles of the WTO is also depicted through its function in settling disputes. The DSU helps guarantee a necessary means of resolving trade disputes, allowing nations to resolve complaints in an orderly fashion and avoiding the chances of trade wars. The WTO aids in making sure that trade disputes do not escalate into broader geopolitical concerns by offering a formal system for the resolution of disputes. This capability is particularly important with the greater connectivity of international trade and its sophistication. The DSU is the commitment to preserving a rules-based trading order and reconciling the various interests of member states. The dynamic nature of world trade, however, requires the institutions to be periodically reviewed to adapt to new challenges so as to maintain their relevance in facilitating cooperation among states (Blockmans et al., 2012).

REFERENCES

1. Ackerman, F., Bernasconi, N., Cabré, M. M., Corbett, J., et al. (2016). Trade in the balance: Reconciling trade and climate policy: Report of the Working Group on Trade, Investment, and Climate Policy. https://open.bu.edu/bitstream/2144/22909/1/Pardee_TradeClimate_110316final.pdf (accessed on 30th October 2025).
2. Alexander, D. J., Baigent, S., Banks, J., Belser, J. A., Blumenkrantz, D., Bosch, J., et al. (2014). One-way trip: Influenza virus' adaptation to gallinaceous poultry may limit its pandemic potential. https://core.ac.uk/download/36778404.pdf (accessed on 30th October 2025).
3. Alvarez, C. H., McGee, J. A., & York, R. (2019). Is labor green? https://core.ac.uk/download/287623724.pdf (accessed on 30th October 2025).
4. Anderson, S., Aruaz, A., de Paula, L. F., Francis, J., et al. (2013). Capital account regulations and the trading system: A compatibility review. https://open.bu.edu/bitstream/2144/22903/1/_Capital-Controls-Eng_201303.pdf (accessed on 30th October 2025).
5. Arriola, C., Somwaru, A., & Zahniser, S. (2025). The European Union's framework for climate change adaptation: Implications of agriculture's adaptation through sustained yield growth. https://core.ac.uk/download/pdf/6567631.pdf (accessed on 30th October 2025).
6. Bagwell, K., & Staiger, R. W. (2025). GATT-think. https://core.ac.uk/download/pdf/6606912.pdf (accessed on 30th October 2025).
7. Basedow, R. (2018). Strengthening the World Trade Organization–Critical demands for imperative success: Identifying politically viable options for incremental reform. https://core.ac.uk/download/322823605.pdf (accessed on 30th October 2025).
8. Bektaş, E. Ö. (2018). The impact of agricultural trade agreements and negotiations of World Trade Organization on the agricultural international trade–Turkey. https://core.ac.uk/download/649506081.pdf (accessed on 30th October 2025).
9. Bignami, F. E. (2003). Three generations of participation rights in European administrative proceedings. https://core.ac.uk/download/62561835.pdf (accessed on 30th October 2025).
10. Blockmans, S., Kostanyan, H., & Vorobiov, I. (2012). Towards a Eurasian Economic Union: The challenge of integration and unity. https://core.ac.uk/download/55791446.pdf (accessed on 30th October 2025).
11. Bonnal, P., Losch, B., & Van Vliet, G. (2005). Setting up and management of public policies multifunctional purpose: The case of developing countries–

Capitalization of research results on the multifunctionality of agriculture and rural areas. http://agritrop.cirad.fr/550307/1/document_550307.pdf (accessed on 30th October 2025).

12. Brassett, J., Richardson, B., & Smith, W. (2012). Private experiments in global governance: Primary commodity roundtables and the politics of deliberation. https://core.ac.uk/download/9562440.pdf (accessed on 30th October 2025).
13. Büthe, T. (2008). The globalization of health and safety standards: Delegation of regulatory authority in the SPS Agreement of the 1994 Agreement Establishing the World Trade Organization. https://core.ac.uk/download/62553315.pdf (accessed on 30th October 2025).
14. Buzan, B., & Lawson, G. (2014). Rethinking benchmark dates in international relations. https://core.ac.uk/download/8792633.pdf (accessed on 30th October 2025).
15. Callin, J., Carrington, M., Gupta, S., Luchs, M., et al. (2016). Managing the tensions at the intersection of the triple bottom line: A paradox theory approach to sustainability management. https://core.ac.uk/download/213067655.pdf (accessed on 30th October 2025).
16. Colyer, D. (2025). *Green Trade Agreements: Comparison of Canada, US and WTO*. https://core.ac.uk/download/pdf/7055450.pdf (accessed on 30th October 2025).
17. Dethier, J. J. (2025). *World Bank Policy Research: A Historical Overview*. https://core.ac.uk/download/pdf/6236014.pdf (accessed on 30th October 2025).
18. Ergur, A., Ünsal, A., Biggart, N. W., Bourdieu, P., Buğra, A., Özbilgin, M., Pamuk, Ş., et al. (2014). Between a rock and a hard place: Corporate elites in the context of religion and secularism in Turkey. https://core.ac.uk/download/29203963.pdf (accessed on 30th October 2025).
19. Fang, H., He, Q., Peng, B., Wang, Y., et al. (2015). Trade liberalization and trade performance of environmental goods: Evidence from Asia-Pacific Economic Cooperation members. https://core.ac.uk/download/213088391.pdf (accessed on 30th October 2025).
20. Febrianti, R. (R.), & Rani, F. (F.). (2015). Pengaruh Asan-Free Trade Area terhadap pertumbuhan ekspor crude palm oil Indonesia 2003–2012. https://media.neliti.com/media/publications/31994-ID-pengaruh-asan-free-trade-area-terhadap-pertumbuhan-ekpor-crude-palm-oil-indonesi.pdf (accessed on 30th October 2025).
21. Fergusson, I. F., McMinimy, M. A., & Williams, B. R. (2015). The Trans-Pacific Partnership (TPP): In brief. https://core.ac.uk/download/33615878.pdf (accessed on 30th October 2025).

22. Froese, M. D. (2025). Trade friction, dispute settlement and structural adjustment, or, why Canada-Wheat doesn't matter in North American trade relations. https://core.ac.uk/download/pdf/6689991.pdf (accessed on 30th October 2025).

23. Geuze, M. (2025). The provisions on geographical indications in the TRIPS Agreement. https://core.ac.uk/download/pdf/7035287.pdf (accessed on 30th October 2025).

24. Giacalone, R. (2007). Is European inter-regionalism a relevant approach for the world or just for Europe? *Jean Monnet/Robert Schuman Paper Series, 7*(14). https://core.ac.uk/download/5080855.pdf (accessed on 30th October 2025).

25. Herreros, S. (2023). Digital and sustainable trade facilitation in Latin America and the Caribbean: Regional report 2023. https://core.ac.uk/download/642876964.pdf (accessed on 30th October 2025).

26. Higgott, R. A. (2009). Not just a "second order" problem in a wider economic crisis: Systemic challenges for the global trading system. https://core.ac.uk/download/47382.pdf (accessed on 30th October 2025).

27. Hillman, J. A. (2018). Multilateral economic institutions and U.S. foreign policy: Hearing before the Subcomm. on Multilateral Int'l Dev., Multilateral Insts., & Int'l Econ., Energy, & Envtl. Pol'y of the S. Comm. on Foreign Relations, 115th Cong., Nov. 27, 2018 (Statement of Jennifer A. Hillman). https://core.ac.uk/download/213035760.pdf (accessed on 30th October 2025).

28. Hoekman, B. (2025). Proposals for WTO reform: A synthesis and assessment. https://core.ac.uk/download/pdf/6293366.pdf (accessed on 30th October 2025).

29. Hoekman, B., & Schuman, R. (2017). Bolstering global trade governance: A work program for the WTO presented by the High-Level Board of Experts on the Future of Global Trade Governance. https://core.ac.uk/download/322823606.pdf (accessed on 30th October 2025).

30. Hricko, A., De Lara, J., Matsuoka, M., & Gottlieb, R. (2011). Global trade impacts: Addressing the health, social and environmental consequences of moving international freight through our communities. https://core.ac.uk/download/71358287.pdf (accessed on 30th October 2025).

31. International Labour Office. (2003). *Training Policies for Vulnerable Groups in Central and Eastern European Countries*. https://core.ac.uk/download/5129384.pdf (accessed on 30th October 2025).

32. James, S. (2009). Service to the economy: Removing barriers to "invisible trade." https://core.ac.uk/download/71341724.pdf (accessed on 30th October 2025).

33. Junhai, L., & Schipani, C. A. (2001). Corporate governance in China: Then and now. http://www.wdi.umich.edu/files/Publications/WorkingPapers/wp407.pdf (accessed on 30th October 2025).

34. Kastenberg, J. E. (2003). Enforcing internationally recognized human rights violations under the Alien Tort Claims Act: An analysis of the Ninth Circuit's decision in *Doe v. Unocal Corp.* https://core.ac.uk/download/72053008.pdf (accessed on 30th October 2025).

35. Kerremans, B., & Orbie, J. (2013). Theorizing EU trade politics. https://core.ac.uk/download/55851683.pdf (accessed on 30th October 2025).

36. Khansari, A. M. (1996). Searching for the perfect solution: International dispute resolution and the new World Trade Organization. https://core.ac.uk/download/641030372.pdf (accessed on 30th October 2025).

37. Kim, C. G., Koo, W. W., & Moon, W. (2025). World Agriculture Organization (WAO): New global governance for agricultural trade. https://core.ac.uk/download/pdf/6672600.pdf (accessed on 30th October 2025).

38. La Porta, R., López-de-Silanes, F., & Shleifer, A. (2008). The economic consequences of legal origins. *Journal of Economic Literature, 46*, 285–332. https://doi.org/10.1257/jel.46.2.285 (accessed on 30th October 2025).

39. Liberati, A., Altman, D. G., Tetzlaff, J., Mulrow, C. D., Gøtzsche, P. C., Ioannidis, J. P. A., Clarke, M., et al. (2009). The PRISMA statement for reporting systematic reviews and meta-analyses of studies that evaluate health care interventions: Explanation and elaboration. *PLoS Medicine, 6*, e1000100–e1000100. https://doi.org/10.1371/journal.pmed.1000100 (accessed on 30th October 2025).

40. Nelson, R. M. (2009). The G-20 and international economic cooperation: Background and implications for Congress. https://core.ac.uk/download/33598162.pdf (accessed on 30th October 2025).

41. Odermatt, J., & Wouters, J. (2014). Comparing the 'Four Pillars' of global economic governance: A critical analysis of the institutional design of the FSB, IMF, World Bank, and WTO. https://core.ac.uk/download/163076631.pdf (accessed on 30th October 2025).

42. Olmedo-Peralta, E. (2016). The regulation of competition and innovation in the European Union and Spain: Opportunities for the Philippines and the ASEAN. https://core.ac.uk/download/132742999.pdf (accessed on 30th October 2025).

43. Ozanne, L. K., Phipps, M., Weaver, T., et al. (2016). Managing the tensions at the intersection of the triple bottom line: A paradox theory approach to

sustainability management. https://core.ac.uk/download/213067655.pdf (accessed on 30th October 2025).

44. Rush, S. (2007). Can increased trade prevent conflict with China? https://core.ac.uk/download/56727795.pdf (accessed on 30th October 2025).
45. Schipani, C. A., & Liu, J. (2025). Corporate governance in China: Then and now. https://core.ac.uk/download/pdf/7057192.pdf (accessed on 30th October 2025).
46. Spinanger, D. (2025). The WTO after the Singapore ministerial: Much to do about what? https://core.ac.uk/download/pdf/6796319.pdf (accessed on 30th October 2025).
47. Trujillo, E. (2020). An introduction to trade and national security: New concepts of national security in a time of economic uncertainty. https://core.ac.uk/download/322820161.pdf (accessed on 30th October 2025).
48. Wiegratz, J. (2008). Beyond harsh trade? The relevance of 'soft' competitiveness factors for Ugandan enterprises to endure in global value chains. https://core.ac.uk/download/51232.pdf (accessed on 30th October 2025).
49. Wilson, J. S. (2025). Liberalizing trade in agriculture: Developing countries in Asia and the post-Doha agenda. https://core.ac.uk/download/pdf/6372903.pdf (accessed on 30th October 2025).
50. Wolfe, R. (2020). Informal learning and WTO renewal: Using thematic sessions to create more opportunities for dialogue. *Bertelsmann Working Paper*, 24/02/2020. https://core.ac.uk/download/287647977.pdf (accessed on 30th October 2025).
51. Wolfe, R. (2020). Reforming WTO conflict management: Why and how to improve the use of "specific trade concerns." *Bertelsmann Working Paper*, 24/02/2020. https://core.ac.uk/download/287647976.pdf (accessed on 30th October 2025).
52. Woods, N. (2025). Accountability in global governance. https://core.ac.uk/download/pdf/6248858.pdf (accessed on 30th October 2025).
53. Zimmermann, T. A. (2025). WTO dispute settlement at ten: Evolution, experiences, and evaluation. https://core.ac.uk/download/pdf/9310951.pdf (accessed on 30th October 2025).

Chapter 2

Fundamental Principles of WTO Law

Contents

INTRODUCTION

The World Trade Organization (WTO) plays a key role in the global economy by offering a multilateral trading regime that ensures fair competition and reduces trade barriers among its member countries. As the principal international organization that governs the trade relations, the WTO aims to ensure trade movements as smooth, predictable, and free as possible. It is important to understand the fundamental principles that underpin WTO law so that one can better see how international trade agreements are created and applied.

These principles not only facilitate cross-border trade but also connect with other world challenges like economic development and the environment. By defining the trading system, the WTO seeks to promote balance between the interests of different nations, in a manner of cooperation within an increasingly interdependent world. At the center of the WTO's working lies ideas such as most-favored-nation (MFN) treatment, national treatment, and openness. The MFN principle demands that any one member's trade advantage extended to another has to be extended to all other members, a sense of equality among countries.

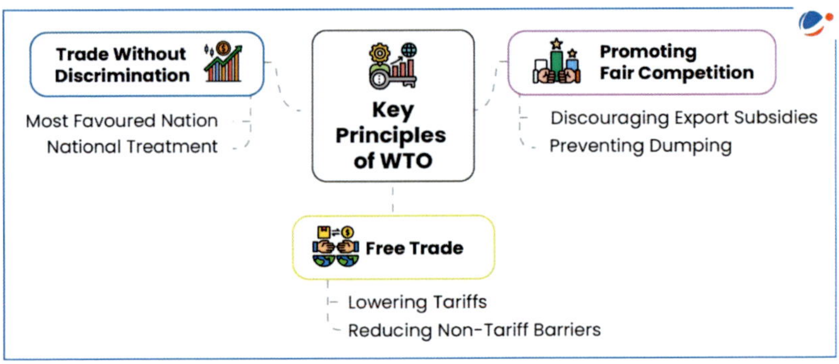

Figure 2.1. Fundamental principles of World Trade Organization (WTO) law.

Source: https://d2av8kbir6lh9m.cloudfront.net/uploads/kjBTnwUH1o01rmp-WqC270jLrA8UP1W3I8oVNABAp.jpg.

The national treatment principle ensures that after products have entered a market, they are given the same treatment as locally produced products, ending discrimination against imports from abroad. Transparency is emphasized by making it mandatory for member countries to publish their trade policies and regulations, which fosters confidence and accountability in the trading process. Collectively, these principles constitute the legal framework of WTO law and strive to bring about a stable and predictable trading world in the interest of all member countries. The convergence of WTO law with other international problems such as climate policy and human rights discloses the complex challenges facing modern trade governance. Recent discussions have highlighted the necessity for WTO rules to align with environmental imperatives as well as emerging problems that are linked with sustainable development. For example, taking into consideration the effect of international trade on climate change means re-evaluating existing agreements to make them beneficial not only for economic development but also for environmental protection. Law scholars, including authors of a recent report by the Working Group on

Trade, Investment, and Climate Policy, advocate a more nuanced approach to investment agreements that could redirect investment to climate-friendly ventures. This evolution of WTO law underscores the requirement to harmonize trade behaviors with the general principles of human development and human rights, thereby reflecting the interdependent nature of global challenges (Figure 2.1).

Definition of World Trade Organization (WTO) Law

WTO Law is the totality of legal rules and conventions governing trade among member states in the framework of the World Trade Organization (WTO). At the heart of this definition is the pivotal role played by the different legal documents in facilitating trade relations. These instruments cover the General Agreement on Tariffs and Trade (GATT), the General Agreement on Trade in Services (GATS), and the Agreement on Trade-Related Aspects of Intellectual Property Rights (TRIPS), among others. They collectively serve as a foundation for establishing norms to reduce trade obstacles, promote equitable competition, and provide transparency in international business. As such, WTO Law is not just a dispute-settlement process but an instrument of multilateral cooperation and economic growth compatible with the overarching missions of the mandates of the organization. WTO Law is characterized by some fundamental principles, including most-favored-nation (MFN) treatment, national treatment, and transparency. The MFN principle is that any preference in trade accorded to a single trading country must be extended automatically to all WTO member countries, thereby promoting equality in trade relations. National treatment is the requirement of equal treatment of foreign goods compared to domestic goods once goods are in a market to prevent protectionism. Transparency, on the other hand, is the stipulation that member states all make their rules and trade practices public so that everyone understands what the rules are and operates based on the same perception of the rules. The interaction of these tenets not only democratizes trade but also renders international trade more predictable and stable and is fundamental to the development of an environment conducive to economic growth and development. The validity of WTO Law is continuously challenged and debated in legal and academic circles. Scholars such as Deborah Z. Cass have examined the constitutionalization of WTO Law and its impact on legitimacy and democracy within the global trading system (Pauwelyn et al., 2006). The intricacies involved in making the balance between state sovereignty and the need for international governance of trade concerns can be understood through such examination. Also, many conferences, such as those held at the European University Institute, have considered transnational social norms and their legal patterns and the resulting implications for WTO

Law (Pauwelyn et al., 2004). These arguments showcase the evolving nature of trade law and the continuous adjustment to the new dynamics of international trade. Through its bargaining of legal norms that encompass a broad spectrum of interests, WTO Law aims not merely to regulate trade, but also serves as a crucible for the management of greater social and economic issues that transcend the boundaries of countries.

Importance of World Trade Organization (WTO) in Global Trade

The WTO plays an important role to ensure liberal and rule-based international trade. At its very center is the guarantee of a system of agreed rules to be followed by member countries, which enhances predictability and stability in cross-border economic transactions. By encouraging reductions in tariffs, the WTO encourages greater market access, which in turn means greater competition and choice for consumers. Besides, the organization acts as an international trade disputes mediator, providing a formal process for the resolution of any arising disputes. Through this process, not just international trade order is maintained but, also, confidence among traders is established, resulting in investment and foreign economic activity leading to growth and development globally. Another key area of the WTOs intervention in global trade is its commitment to openness and harmonization of trade practices among nations. Through the supply of standards for international trade and the requirement of nations to notify changes in trade practice, the WTO promotes accountability and reduces opportunities for conflicts.

The WTO proactively encourages member nations to adopt globally recognized standards, enhancing product quality and safety traded. As testifies the development of international standard-making, the WTO's stance testifies to a critical approach towards trade rules and their creation. Following recent rulings, such as the US—Tuna II case, the WTO emphasized the need for procedure reform when establishing international standards, evidencing the trend towards more openness and inclusiveness in international trade practice (Delimatsis et al., 2018). The WTO's influence on global trade also encompasses responding to and facing challenges present in the world today, such as economic disparity and environmental sustainability. As the world's economy expands, the institution has realized that it needs to engage with emerging challenges that affect the balance of trade. An effort to integrate sustainable development goals into trade policy signifies a shift towards equity in aligning economic expansion with the environment. Moreover, through encouraging open debate amongst its members, the WTO seeks to counteract inequalities that are likely to result from globalization. The principles guiding its governance, such as non-discrimination and reciprocity, are geared towards protecting the interests of both developed and developing nations so that trade will be an impetus to equitable prosperity across the world (Figure 2.2).

Figure 2.2. Role of WTO (World Trade Organization) in international trade.

Source: https://www.batheories.com/wp-content/uploads/international-trade.png.

Overview of Fundamental Principles

The WTO is founded on a body of basic principles which provide the foundation for its jurisprudence and trade relations among nations. The principles like MFN treatment and national treatment work towards creating a level playing field between the member nations. MFN treatment mandates that any preferential treatment provided by a member to another member be provided to all members of the WTO, creating a non-discriminatory platform of trade practices. Similarly, the principle of national treatment ensures that foreign products are dealt with equally as domestic ones to prevent local protectionism. All these principles together, in conjunction, not only bring about competition and efficiency in international markets but also assist the overall goals of economic advancement and a fair trading system, as hinted by scholars examining the WTO law constitutionalization, such as in Cass (Pauwelyn et al., 2006). In addition to encouraging equity in trade, the inherent values of WTO law reflect support for transparency and reciprocity among states. Translating to the requirement that trade policies and regulations be made accessible to the public, so they can make informed decisions on matters related to trade, this principle of transparency aids in building trust among members and minimizing uncertainties in trade relations. Reciprocity, nevertheless, means that concessions made by one country should be followed by similar behavior by others, which ensures the exchange to be balanced and to everyone's advantage. Such values do not only facilitate the flow of trade but also help in large measure to coordinate international trade activity with broader developmental goals like human development and human rights. Such harmonization of ethical issues is increasingly valued to be imperative towards ensuring sustainable and fair trade regimes (Normand, 2025). Further, one of the key aspects of WTO law is the ability to adapt and align with the evolving challenges of the era. The underlying core principles make a robust pillar upon which to respond to changing issues such as digital trade, environmental protection, and social accountability. For instance, when members are negotiating rules on e-commerce and technology transfer, non-discrimination and national treatment principles guide the negotiations so that new agreements do not undercut the prevailing trade rights. The WTO has also had dialogues where trade intersects with social policy, encouraging debate on human rights and labor standards in foreign trade. These developments confirm how the foundation of WTO law can ensure that trade works to serve wider social values, showing evidence of an understanding that economic life should support human welfare and promote inclusive growth (Normand, 2025; Pauwelyn et al., 2006).

2.1. MOST-FAVORED-NATION (MFN) PRINCIPLE

The MFN principle is one of the pillars of the World Trade Organization (WTO) system and reflects the principle of non-discrimination in trading relations among nations. Under this principle, any preferential terms of trade granted by a member nation to another shall extend automatically to the other WTO member nations. This is one of the central mechanisms that not only ensures equitable trading conditions but also ensures that risks of trade fragmentation arising from the implementation of preferential terms of trade are reduced. The historical background of the MFN principle underscores its importance in preserving a multilateral trading system in order to prevent discriminatory practices which would result in trade wars and destabilization of the economy. Thus, the MFN principle encourages international economic integration while it encourages nations to lower the barriers to trade collectively, embracing the spirit of cooperation that is behind the WTOs goals. In explaining the implications of the MFN principle, it is essential to identify how it relates to the principle of reciprocity that also aims to enhance the functional dynamics of trade agreements. Reciprocity posits that concessions offered by one state are expected to be reciprocated with similar concessions from other members, hence offering a balanced trading platform. In combination, these principles work to balance terms-of-trade externality found in scholarly research, where countries would otherwise exercise excessive protectionism to suit their own economic agendas at the expense of others. MFN principle and reciprocity work to neutralize each other the reduction of trade barriers as well as the promotion of a stable global platform for trade. The resulting synergy is critical for upholding the laws and negotiations governing trade relations, providing the parameters needed to decipher the complexities of international trade. Secondly, the MFN principle has strategic significance in the capacity to create long-term relations among states trading internationally. Because nations choose to be MFN, they are showing their loyalty to a rules-based trading order that respects fairness and equality. This commitment may act as a disincentive against unilateral taking of trade action, effectively safeguarding against the threat of protectionist posturing in the future. Critics have also raised concerns that by offering concessions all around, countries risk undermining their leverage in bilateral deals. But proponents respond that the long-term benefits through stability, certainty, and fairness well outweigh any concern. The success of MFN principle in facilitating cooperation and avoiding conflict bears witness to its prominence in the WTO law framework, thereby cementing its position as a pillar of global governance of trade (Figure 2.3).

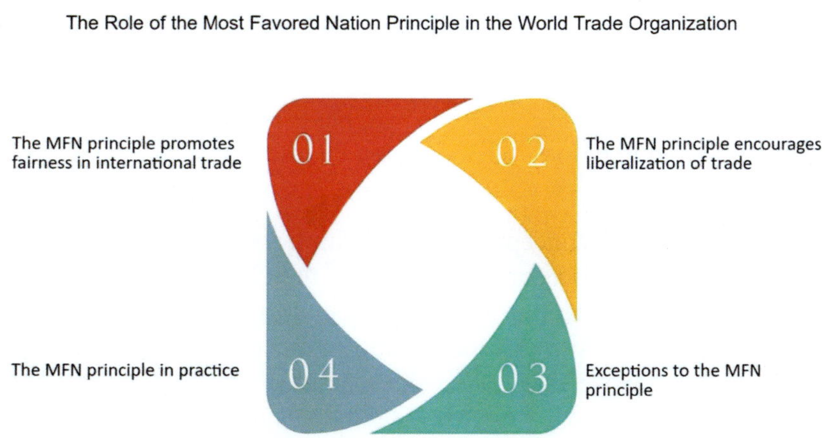

Figure 2.3. Most-favored-nation (MFN) principle.

Source: https://fastercapital.co/i/The-Most-Favored-Nation-Rule--A-Pillar-of-WTO-s-Success--The-Role-of-the-Most-Favored-Nation-Principle-in-the-World-Trade-Organization.webp.

2.1.1. Explanation of Most-Favored-Nation (MFN) Status

The MFN status is a central precept under World Trade Organization (WTO) law, serving as the anchor for international trade relations. Essentially, MFN dictates that preferential terms of trade agreed by one WTO member to another be passed on to all other members to ensure non-discrimination among trading partners. The principle allows for the historical context of protectionism in trade, which can result in excessive tariffs and trade barriers as it did during the Great Depression in the 1920s and 1930s. MFN mechanism not only establishes a more equitable trading environment but also minimizes the adverse effects of the "terms-of-trade externality," a situation whereby one-sided rules of trade can generate inefficiencies in global markets (Bagwell et al., 2025).

Figure 2.4. The most-favored-nation (MFN) status.

Source: https://fastercapital.co/i/Driving-Global-Prosperity--Most-Favored-Nation-and-Trade-Liberalization--What-is-Most-Favored-Nation---MFN---status.webp.

Moreover, the MFN concept functions within the broader framework of general reciprocity that also constitutes part of the GATT and the WTO as a whole. Reciprocity leads nations to accept trade terms that capture the highest possible mutual benefit, further accentuating interdependent world economic conditions. By stipulating that concessions granted to one nation are to be reciprocated exactly by all members, MFN attains balance of trade in concessions, ultimately leading to reduced tariffs and improved market access over borders. This reciprocal exchange reinforces GATTs original purpose of eliminating discriminatory treatment and creating a successful system of world trade where fair treatment prevails. Thus, MFN not only insulates against trade retaliation but also fortifies cooperative trade relationships between nations (Bagwell et al., 2025). While helpful, use of MFN status is not controversy-free. Criticizers believe that while MFN assists in bringing a level playing ground among member states, it does so by weakening national sovereignty unintentionally. For instance, multilateral treaties like the Multilateral Agreement on Investment (MAI) have been characterized as reconfiguring the balance of power between domestic legislating and international trade obligations. This tension challenges the level of national sovereignty in trade negotiations and how far states can proceed in adopting regulations according to public interest, especially when such regulations might be against international trade provisions under the MFN regime. Therefore, while MFN status is a significant principle of non-discrimination in trade, it is crucial to consider its implications for domestic governance and the need to balance carefully between global integration and national policy autonomy (Figure 2.4).

2.1.2. Implications for Member Countries

The effects of WTO law on member countries are multifaceted and extensive, impacting economic stability, trade, and domestic policy. Entry into the WTO binds countries to adhere to a code of principles that seeks to promote equitable and free trade. This alignment necessitates a comprehensive reorganization of national laws and enforcement mechanisms into harmony with WTO agreements. Countries must implement policies that adhere not only to liberalization of trade but also to basic labor and environmental standards, which sometimes may conflict with the local customs and economic methods. These commitments give a framework under which countries can enhance their exports and attract foreign investment, resulting in economic development. But such growth must be weighed against social development and welfare goals, especially for the developing countries that can potentially have an unequal burden of keeping up with these rigorous standards (Fields et al., 2003). In balancing the terms to member states, consideration must be given to the social dimension of WTO commitments. The meeting point of labor rights and trade law ensures countries adhere to international labor standards, thereby influencing domestic labor markets and social policy. As postulated in most arguments regarding labor standards, the compulsion to comply can have the impact of driving positive change, including improved labor conditions and reduced exploitation. Nevertheless, it is also critical to recognize that these changes can have the impact of triggering resistance, particularly from industries that rely on low-cost labor. The member nations must balance the moral demands of labor protections with the fiscal realities of competitiveness in trade. The reforms in labor standards under WTO agreements can prove difficult initially to emerging economies but have the potential to lay the foundation for long-run sustainable development and better living standards (Fields et al., 2003). Further, WTO law extends to the intellectual property domain, affecting member states' intellectual property protection and promotion of innovations. The framework the WTO provides demands respect for intellectual property rights by nations, which may encourage creativity and technological advancement. This emphasis is problematic, particularly for developing countries that may struggle to uphold stringent intellectual property requirements while simultaneously seeking to advance public health and access to knowledge. Initiatives such as those discussed at recent treaty negotiations reaffirm the significance of a paradigm of rights strong enough to harmonize intellectual property law and human rights. To this effect, member states must function under these nuances without derogating from their obligation to uphold human rights and the public interest while aiming for a balanced and just trading environment.

2.1.3. Case Studies Illustrating Most-Favored-Nation (MFN) Application

Most-favored-nation application is of especial significance in understanding the functioning of international trade agreements, particularly against the context of the World Trade Organization (WTO). A significant case study reflecting the impact of MFN is the entry negotiations of nations to the WTO. In these cases, applicant states negotiate in a bilateral fashion with existing members, illustrating the double effect of the MFN rule: the hardened bargainer effect and the free-rider effect. The first emboldens the applicant by creating bargaining leverage as member states must consider the implications of withholding preferential terms from one state and giving them to another. Conversely, the free-rider phenomenon can hurt the negotiations in which current members stand to gain from concessions without giving anything in return, making it more difficult for the applicants to achieve successful accession and WTO standards compliance (Lai, 2025). Looking at the history of the General Agreement on Tariffs and Trade (GATT), one is able to identify the secret purpose and structure that includes the MFN principle. GATT was established as a response to the adverse economic impacts of high tariffs during the 1920s and 1930s, a situation that was favorable to the terms-of-trade externality. The terms lead nations to practice excessive protection that becomes detrimental in the absence of a trade pact. The MFN provision of GATT was directed at making trading conditions equal by preventing discrimination among members. Through the assistance of recent theoretical discussions, the core precepts of GATT like reciprocity and non-discrimination are contended to serve as indispensable tools to reverse the inefficiencies caused by such externalities in trading relations (Bagwell et al., 2025). In a more practical context, case studies of MFN applications can help illuminate how these theoretical frameworks come to fruition in practice. For instance, countries that are negotiating accession to free trade agreements often wind up balancing the expectations set under MFN treatment against their own internal economic realities. Looking at specific cases where countries won or lost as a result of their MFN commitments, one can then think about the broader implications for international trade policy. These examples illustrate the sophistication of maintaining equal treatment in the midst of diverse national interests, ultimately highlighting the necessity of stable and predictable rules to form successful international trade relationships. This complex environment illustrates how the MFN principle is a bargaining lever and a source of conflict, with implications on trade negotiations globally (Bagwell et al., 2025; Lai, 2025).

2.2. NATIONAL TREATMENT PRINCIPLE

The Principle of National Treatment is a cornerstone of World Trade Organization law that mandates member states to treat foreign goods, services, and capital at least as favorably as domestically produced ones once these goods have penetrated the market. The principle draws its roots from a broader objective of fair competition and reduction of protectionism in international trading situations. In offering equal treatment, WTO members seek to do away with discrimination to allow firms from different countries to compete on an even plane. This provides foreigners more access to markets, ultimately facilitating international economic integration and more consumer choices across borders. Therefore, the National Treatment Principle is not only essential to protect importers but also to enhance confidence in the trading system, ensure investment, and enable international trade relations. An important component of the National Treatment Principle is its application in the context of product regulation and standard-setting. Disputes tend to be raised about measures that, although otherwise in furtherance of legitimate national interests like environmental conservation or public health, can unduly prejudice imported merchandise. An example of this is the treatment of "like products" under GATT Article III, which has been central to such disputes, with the focus of examining whether a measure is discriminatory or necessary in accordance with the principle. Previously established case law indicates that while consumer preference will be a significant factor in establishing market conditions, this is to be balanced against the National Treatment Principle to prevent unreasonable barriers to trade. The resolution of disputes regarding ethical public policy norms, as underscored in recent studies, underscores the importance of enhancing the application of consumer choice together with the underlying law principles of WTO, particularly with respect to sustainability and health regulation (Berg et al., 2011). Furthermore, the implications of the National Treatment Principle extend to the field of taxation and home regulation. In cases where nations adopt business taxes, the principle calls for a reconsideration of domestic consumption and taxation thereof. For instance, new tax systems, like destination-based cash flow taxes, can be designed that comply with WTO regulations while ensuring fair treatment for both foreign and domestic firms. Striving for alternatives to existing methods of taxation not only promotes compliance with the National Treatment Principle but also lowers the risk of trade discrimination disputes. Such methods, which juggle international obligation and domestic policy goals, have the potential to generate a national interest and international trade commitments-enabling environment (Grinberg et al., 2017). As such issues evolve, the function of the National Treatment Principle is in no doubt to establish a rules-based trading system that improves fairness and economic advancement globally (Figure 2.5).

Figure 2.5. The national treatment principle.

Source: https://external-content.duckduckgo.com/iu/?u=https%3A%2F%2Fwww.transnationalmatters.com%2Fwp-content%2Fuploads%2F2024%2F06%2Fusers_7dd1dc79-7cb9-40c2-b5f8-d0e040fa311b_generations_b9d1bc99-2666-402f-aced-b6ec8e21ac8d_Default_a_group_of_international_lawyers_sits_around_a_large_t_0.webp&f=1&nofb=1&ipt=bc9f0bdb4d74a30bead700c8abcec5021bf0e63d9d3ad83fb4c47779873390b4.

2.2.1. Definition and Significance of National Treatment

The principle of national treatment is the cornerstone of World Trade Organization (WTO) law that mandates that foreign persons, services, and products receive the same treatment as their domestic counterparts after entering the market. It is a non-discrimination policy that is crucial in providing equal competition and preventing protectionism since it mandates that governments prevent enacting legislation or policies that can prefer domestic entities to those foreign. By ensuring equality of treatment, national treatment not only justifies the pillars of free trade but also promotes effective functioning of the internal market. Such provisions enable the economies to integrate at an international level to ensure the free movement of services and goods and thus enhance economic efficiency and innovation in member states. The significance of national treatment transcends the mere assurance of market access parity; it is an expression of the commitment of nations to deal with each other reciprocally justly. In a world where national policies can directly affect international economic relations in real-time, maintaining national treatment is fundamental in avoiding tensions triggered by felt injustices. Critics of investment agreements such as the proposed Multilateral Agreement on Investment (MAI) argue that provisions intended to protect foreign investors have a tendency to restrict the sovereignty of states and freedom to regulate. This perspective highlights the fine line of upholding national interests against pursuing international legal norms on fair competition, raising pertinent questions of regulatory sovereignty and global trade agreements' externalities into domestic regulation (Stumberg et al., 1998). Besides, national treatment has significant implications for government subsidies and competitive advantage that can be generated through local measures. In the background of shifting economic realities, namely with geo-economic rivalries and trans-border rivalry, national treatment is still relevant with the necessity for countries to navigate complex regimes of subsidies in WTO agreements. With the breakdown of conventional categorization of subsidies, laying new norms and embracing a cooperative framework to regulate subsidies assumes priority (Hoekman et al., 2020). National treatment not only avoids distortions caused by subsidies that are provided in the home market but also makes it possible for countries to solve issues that arise from spillover of competition collectively. Such adaptability and responsiveness to international economic problems continues to reaffirm the central place that WTO law and international trade in general give to national treatment.

2.2.2. Comparison with Most-Favored-Nation (MFN) Principle

The MFN clause is a cornerstone in WTO law architecture structure that reflects the essence of non-discrimination in trade relations. The clause mandates that all favored trading terms extended to one member state be extended to all members to encourage equality in trading. The significance of the MFN principle does not only echo in its role as a force behind globalization but also in its power to reverse cases of trade discrimination. By the assurance that all member states equally enjoy favorable terms of trade, the MFN principle serves to fight excessive protectionism that could be widespread without such a principle, providing a stable and predictable trading atmosphere (Bagwell et al., 2025). This inherent characteristic of the WTO collectively enhances global collaboration and confirms the interrelatedness that characterizes modern economic relations. Comparison with other components of WTO law, however, reveals nuances, as in the instance of trade agreements like the draft Multilateral Agreement on Investment (MAI). While the MFN principle seeks to ensure non-discrimination among states, critics indicate that agreements such as the MAI can erode state sovereignty and national administration. Proponents of the MAI assert that it is built on a multilateral sovereignty framework with the purpose of ensuring economic integration; however, its opponents argue that it would disproportionately favor foreign investors over local legislation. This tension illustrates the manner in which the MFN principle might sometimes find itself in a multi-dimensional interaction with broader agreements that contradict traditional notions of sovereignty and mastery (Stumberg et al., 1998).

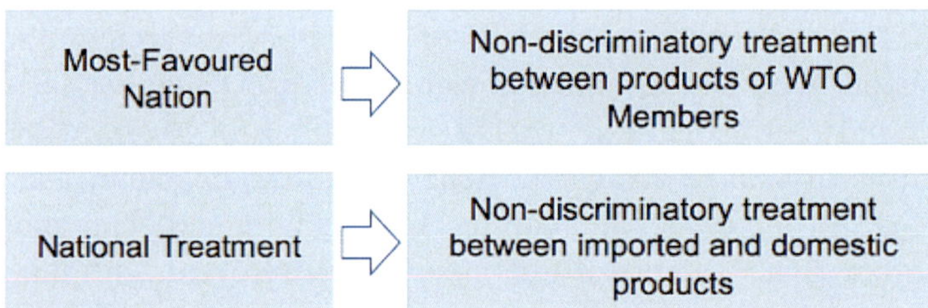

Figure 2.6. National treatment comparison with most-favored-nation (MFN) principle.

Source: https://cdn-images.prepp.in/public/image/39e5405b9d04f6a81a027029eb583dd2.png?tr=w-512,h-182,c-force.

Therefore, while the MFN principle aims for a fair playing field among nations, its interaction with investment agreements generates uncertainty regarding the balance of power between international economic cooperation and national regulatory self-determination. More discussion of the MFN principle is intended to emphasize its complementary nature with other core WTO principles such as transparency and reciprocity. Transparency is highly essential in bringing trade practices into view and making them accessible to all members in order to realize a more balanced trading world. Reciprocity, on the other hand, gives impetus to the idea that concessions by one member will be responded to by analogous concessions from others. In addition to the MFN principle, these determinants counteract the inefficiencies and uncertainties normally created by liberalized trade, specifically concerning protectionist tendencies encapsulated in previous trade policies. Positive aspects of such an interrelation speak of the multi-dimensional role played by institutions like the WTO in creating a cooperative framework that supports negotiation over conflict in international trade transactions. Thus, although the MFN principle assures equal treatment and prevents discrimination, it performs optimally in combination with principles that encourage dialogue and reciprocation between member states (Bagwell et al., 2025) (Figure 2.6).

2.2.3. Examples of National Treatment in Practice

National treatment, one of the founding doctrines of World Trade Organization (WTO) law, ensures foreign goods and services no less favorable treatment than domestic goods and services. One best example of the application of national treatment is in the frame of the General Agreement on Tariffs and Trade (GATT). Under GATT, member countries are required to abolish discriminatory tariffs and rules that would be inimical to imported goods. For instance, when the European Union put regulations on the safety of food imports, the provisions were drafted in a manner that addressed local producers and imports equally, thereby fulfilling the national treatment obligation. This approach not only enhances fairness in trade relationships but also attempts to pre-empt protectionist policy which can distort market forces, keeping in view the importance of transparency and fairness in the international trade system. Another operational expression of national treatment exists in investment agreements, namely the proposed Multilateral Agreement on Investment (MAl). This agreement framework invites equal treatment of foreign investors in contrast to domestic participants. Its proponents are convinced that MAl safeguards foreign investments through the imposition of stringent non-discrimination principles to guarantee that foreign investors enjoy rights akin to those of domestic investors. Its detractors are convinced that such designs could dissolve the regulatory powers of nation-states, as seen in controversy surrounding how the MAls ability could derail domestic governance and law-making capabilities. This critique illustrates the conflict between ensuring protection for foreign investment and protecting state sovereignty in the enforcement of local regulation, raising significant questions regarding the implications of national treatment for economic governance (Stumberg et al., 1998). National treatment is also coming into conflict with broader humanitarian interests, specifically concerns regarding human rights and development. When states adopt a priority on the non-discriminatory treatment of foreigners, they also foster a conducive environment for foreign investment, which can enhance human development indicators. For instance, when a country successfully implements national treatment regimes, it not only achieves growth in terms of foreign direct investment but can also enhance social indicators such as health and education. National treatment thus extends beyond economic interactions per se, having an impact on human rights and development internationally (Normand, 2025). It is thus a double-edged sword that can be utilized to advance economic interests as well as social good, and whose use requires thoughtful consideration in trade agreement-making as well as domestic policymaking.

2.3. TRANSPARENCY IN TRADE REGULATIONS

Transparency is at the core of the effectiveness of WTO trade regulations. As the global economy becomes increasingly integrated, free discourse between nations regarding their regulatory regimes is essential. Transparency promotes confidence among member states because it not only provides them with information about what rules are in effect but also about how the rules come into effect. The transparency offered by open rules reduces the likelihood of dispute, since countries know what to anticipate from each regarding a specific trade practice. As has been shown in the US—Tuna II case, the applicability of examining international standards based on transparency has attracted the spotlight, with arguments on how to make standard-setting processes more legitimate and equitable within the WTO framework (Delimatsis et al., 2018). Hence, not only is transparency a procedural necessity but also an underlying principle that drives mutual understanding and cooperation in international trade. Moreover, the procedural soundness of regulatory processes relies considerably on transparency. Regulations lacking open, transparent processes favor particular groups of stakeholders at the cost of others, hence hindering equitable trade practices. The WTO transparency obligation not only requires member states to furnish timely and full information regarding trade measures but also to incorporate participation and public involvement in the measures. The two-faceted requirement guarantees that several voices are being heard, making the regulatory system more inclusive. The evolving landscape of international standard-setting reflects growing realization of a need for greater transparency; as the WTO moves toward a more assertive position as a standards mediator, the governance system of global standards has also to adapt with these requirements. Such reforms, termed by some as "global standard-setting 2.0," are paramount to ensuring that rules are founded on common and not special interests (Delimatsis et al., 2018). Thus, increased transparency can make a significant impact on the efficiency of trade rules through more transparent rules and abolishment of uncertainty. The transparency not just prevents conflicts but also improves confidence in and foreign investment in the trade process. Trading partners and investors will be more inclined to take part in markets where they know the rules and procedures ruling trade transactions. This produces a more secure trading environment in which economic prosperity can flourish as a consequence. Transparency, however, has a downside in having to balance the need to protect confidential data against the public's right of information. These are issues to be overcome in making international trade laws legitimate. Shifting transparency mechanisms within institutions such as the WTO can result in a more equitable, participatory, and effective global trading system ultimately to the advantage of all stakeholders involved (Figure 2.7).

Figure 2.7. Transparency in trade regulations.

Source: https://external-content.duckduckgo.com/iu/?u=https%3A%2F%2Ftse2.mm.bing.net%2Fth%2Fid%2FOIP.uXcWAJXMApbky8VPAs-xqfgHaEM%3Fr%3D0%26pid%3DApi&f=1&ipt=3d9fa95e915fa3cee15136ccea17029090f0eb3d749e7667531e6fec2c231613.

2.3.1. Importance of Transparency in World Trade Organization (WTO) Law

The concept of transparency in WTO law serves to function as a basis for establishing trust and accountability among member countries. Transparency fosters an environment where trade rules and obligations are clearly articulated, allowing countries to make informed decisions. When transparency is lacking in other nations' policies and operations, chances are high that there will be misinterpretation and conflict. For instance, transparent standard-setting procedures are necessary as presented globally whereby standards are usually taken up under environments that are not transparent and inclusive. This underlines the necessity to restructure the process of establishing standards at the global level in such a way that all interested parties are adequately represented. In essence, an open system not only enhances collaboration between WTO members but also results in a stable trade world. Second, the connection between transparency and procedural fairness is extremely interlinked in WTO law. As already indicated in the case of international standard-setting, openness is key to ensuring that all countries, regardless of their economic status, have a voice in shaping trade standards. The recent emphasis by the Appellate Body on reviewing the processes through which international standards are developed is a milestone towards people-holding-accountability. This analysis implies that the design of standards must then comply with the principles of openness and deliberation and thereby minimize exclusion. To this end, the WTOs critical standpoint not only safeguarded the interests of developing or small nations but also ensured the legitimacy of the overall trading system, including equal access to international trade discourse. Besides, transparency is also an important mechanism in averting difficulties in dealing with political pressures from influential trading blocs. For example, such policies such as the EU Neighbourhood Policy that govern nations towards liberalization and privatization of public services can be subject to inconspicuous negotiations regarding a wide range of stakeholders. The transparency entailed under the WTO model aims at countering these inequalities of power and encouraging participatory policy-making. By making such policies publicly debatable and disclosed, the WTO establishes a platform under which member nations can hold one another accountable. Through doing so, this commitment to transparency not only enhances the credibility of WTO law but also establishes an open platform that is receptive to involvement by various groups of individuals, thus speeding up global economic development in a fair and equitable manner (Figure 2.8).

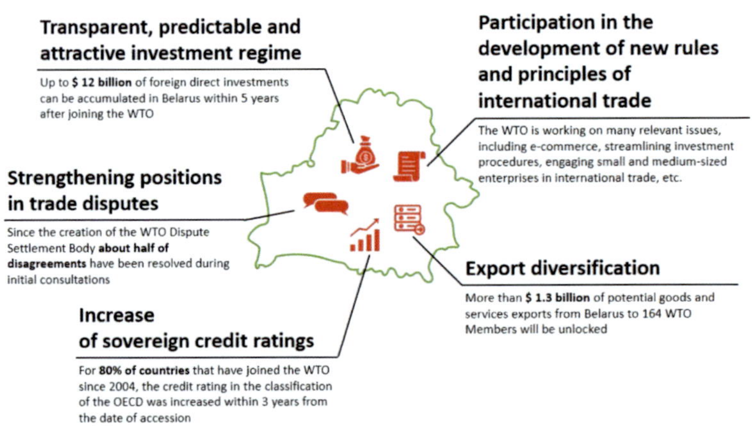

Figure 2.8. Importance of transparency in World Trade Organization (WTO) law.

Source: https://mfa.gov.by/kcfinder/upload/images/DVD/23.02.27_wto_info2_eng_2.jpg.

2.3.2. Mechanisms for Ensuring Transparency

Transparency is a fundamental principle built into the World Trade Organization (WTO) rules and operations, serving as a significant mechanism for fostering confidence among member nations. The WTO places strong reliance on members making their trade policies and regulations widely available so that all stakeholders can engage with full awareness. This communication reduces misinterpretations and divergences that may otherwise arise in trade negotiations and disputes. Moreover, effective communication procedures encourage accountability among nations in a way that the trading activities align with agreed undertakings. By compelling members to report on their trade measures from time to time, the WTO encourages a culture where openness becomes a key theme in the world of trade, which ultimately leads to greater economic cooperation and cohesion among nations. One of the most vital instruments for ensuring WTO institutions' transparency is the Trade Policy Review Mechanism (TPRM). It triggers routine examination of members' countries' trade practice, thereby enabling member states to scrutinize and criticize members' policies and measures.

Through the TPRM, the WTO aims to establish a comprehensive understanding of the members' trade and economic policies, hence their adherence to agreed principles. These reviews not only encourage compliance but also highlight areas which need improvement or reform. When nations implement these reports, they gain valuable lessons that can be applied to correct their own policy and build a culture of collective responsibility. The TPRM is thus an essential safeguard against opaque practices, as it maintains the commitment to transparency in high levels within the international trading regime. Outside institutions such as the TPRM, the WTOs emphasis on trade negotiations illustrates the critical need for transparency to support successful international trade relations. For instance, Trade Promotion Authority (TPA) in the US illustrates how legislative frameworks can encourage transparency through setting clear negotiating goals and congressional oversight processes. This authority ensures that trade agreements are negotiated with involvement from elected lawmakers, thereby increasing public awareness and sensitivity of trade issues. Embedding accountability in these negotiations is also in the larger interest of engaging stakeholders and ensuring that trade agreements benefit more people. In addition, initiatives like the G20 focus on enhancing accountability in economic institutions around the world further accentuate the interconnectivity of transparency with other fundamental principles of WTO law, ultimately seeking a more stable and predictable international trading system (Beth et al., 2014; Brown et al., 2025).

2.3.3. Consequences of Lack of Transparency

The principle of transparency constitutes the foundation of the functioning of the World Trade Organization (WTO) and its regulation. Lack of transparency has the potential to lead to an enormous extent of misunderstanding among the member states regarding trade commitments and obligations. Unless countries disclose information regarding their trade policies adequately, the resulting lack of clarity can be a trigger for disputes that could otherwise be negotiated amicably. Such lack of transparency not only undermines the ability of member countries to monitor one another but also reduces the overall credibility and faith in the WTO system.

This breakdown of trust can give rise to additional conflicts, where members do not trust one another's intentions and commitment to mutually agreed terms and standards. Therefore, the lack of transparency undermines the basic processes which promote cooperation and stability within the international trading system. Also, the consequences of bad transparency extend beyond the immediate trade relationship to affect broader governance arrangements associated with international law. The inability to define transparently the functions of the WTO can be a cause of legitimacy and authority problems, discerditing the role of the institutions as a mediator of disputes in trade. Without transparency, member states tend to act on their own, discrediting the multilateral trading system and fostering an environment of competitiveness rather than cooperation. This is even more so due to the intricate and interdependent nature of international trade, where the action of one nation can make a big difference for others. Without the kind of open communication and openness in negotiations and decision-making, the WTO stands the risk of becoming an institution where power struggles will be the watchword over brotherly partnership, rendering it less effective as a forum for ensuring fair trade practices (Helfer et al., 2003). Lastly, the political ramifications of a breakdown in transparency within WTO proceedings can have direct effects on human development and democratic engagement in member states.

Without sufficient disclosure, citizens become disempowered and out of touch with policymaking choices with a direct effect on their economic well-being. That failing public understanding and engagement can strangle democratic processes, leading to further disillusionment with global institutions and their perception of unaccountability. If the public do not understand or engage with the complexity of trade policy, then their ability to advance their rights and interests is crucially diminished. These instances serve to emphasize the need for more transparency in the WTO to promote not only fair trade practices but democratic participation and public trust in global governance institutions (Woods, 2025) (Figure 2.9).

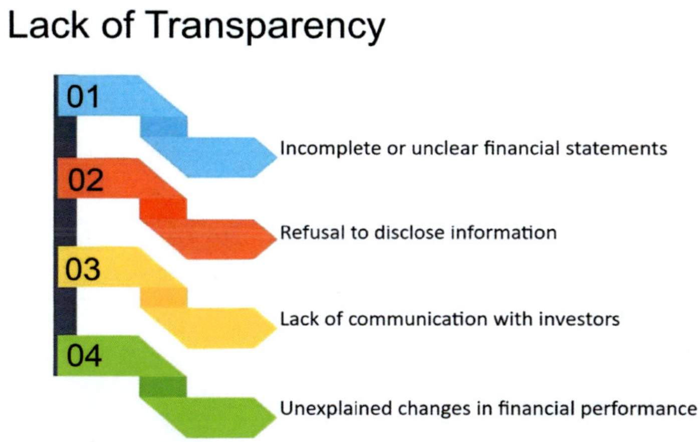

Figure 2.9. Consequences of lack of transparency in World Trade Organization (WTO) law.

Source: https://fastercapital.co/i/Insider-trading-tips--Recognizing-warning-signs-and-red-flags--Lack-of-Transparency.webp.

2.4. TRADE LIBERALIZATION

Free trade liberalization is one of the fundamental principles guiding World Trade Organization (WTO) law, guaranteeing free movement of goods and services between member nations. This ensures increased exchange of goods and services by having countries drop tariffs, quotas, and other barriers to international trade. Trade liberalization enables an open trading system, hence guaranteeing competition and growth, eventually enjoyed by consumers in the form of decreased prices and varied products. As nations proceed towards open economies, non-discrimination and reciprocity become increasingly significant, so that all member states are an active participant in the global economy on an equal footing. Trade liberalization also fosters interdependence among nations, creating networks of economic relations that create political stability and peace—a fundamental objective articulated in the overall objectives of the WTO. But liberalization of trade comes with its own baggage, particularly in policy convergence across jurisdictions. The e-commerce phenomenon introduced complexity into international trade, where governments must deal with stress resulting from differing regulatory systems. Laid out in the context of US and EU policymaking modalities, these disparate regulations can inhibit the maturation of the global marketplace that is by design global but regulated locally. In order to properly utilize the gains of trade liberalization in the age of the digital era, policymakers will need to converge their respective policy frameworks. The call for a uniform regulatory strategy mirrors the interconnected nature of today's markets, whereby the effects of one jurisdiction's policies will resonate across others, influencing aggregate trade dynamics and economic relations (Mann, 2025).

Figure 2.10. Trade liberalization.

Source: https://cdn.sketchbubble.com/pub/media/catalog/product/optimized1/d/6/d64ac74f848f87f4f5d8ebbc6acd790bb9159bf2147568163528f2e8c37b2aa8/trade-liberalization-slide1.png.

Furthermore, the consequences of trade liberalization are not only economic but also touch social and political institutions, particularly in the third world. Implementing policies of economic openness is likely to be accompanied by calls for privatization and deregulation, as the EU Neighbourhood Policy shows in which it addresses liberalization and privatization of public services in the neighboring countries (Hall et al., 2006). This dynamic illustrates the way liberalization of trade can spur transformational reforms in governance systems, compelling countries to react to global markets' competitive pressures. While such developments may stimulate growth and development, they may also represent serious challenges, including the danger of dismantling public welfare services and inequality. Thus, an approach to trade liberalization in an integrated manner is necessary, sharing the gains widely while safeguarding essential public interests (Figure 2.10).

2.4.1. Concept of Trade Liberalization Under World Trade Organization (WTO)

The WTO notion of trade liberalization is a central tenet of global trade that aims at reducing barriers to trade, which in turn results in a fair and more competitive market. By the promotion of tariff reduction and non-tariff barriers elimination, the WTO has established a system where member countries can engage in free trade, ensuring maximum efficiency in the allocation of resources. This alignment not only facilitates freer exchanges among nations but also maximizes the economic growth prospects of the parties involved. Additionally, trade liberalization promotes the nondiscrimination norm, codified in the Most-Favored-Nation and National Treatment provisions, that causes states to treat trading partners equally, hence contributing to a stable and clear trading atmosphere vital for sustainable economic development. Trade liberalization has more than just enriching effects; it also constitutes closely integrated domestic policy considerations and standards of governance. As trade increasingly intersects with national policy, there has been pressure on member states to guarantee openness and transparency in the making of their trade policy.

This has seen an increase in attempts to increase the profile and accountability of trade decisions in government. As noted, there have been suggested openness frameworks by which one can juxtapose these initiatives across various trading counterparts (Isaac et al., 2025). Not only do these frameworks highlight the growing importance of public involvement in trade policy, they also address the changing nature of international trade whereby local interests are not held back. Furthermore, trade liberalization via the WTO has the tendency to expose the thin line that governments must walk between international commitments and domestic concerns. The imperative of free trade policies must be pitted against the potential adverse effects of such policies on domestic industry and employment.

This built-in tension underpins the relevance of the WTO as a negotiating and dispute-settlement platform among member nations, allowing for negotiations to pursue innovative resolutions to new trade controversies. The platform set by the WTO allows for the establishment of consensus-driven strategies that are geared towards expanding market access while not sacrificing individual countries socio-economic interests (Caswell et al., 2025). Therefore, trade liberalization is not only established as a means of economic integration but also as a central part of global management that needs to be handled carefully to provide equitable benefits to all member nations.

2.4.2. Benefits of Reducing Trade Barriers

Reducing trade barriers has monumental economic benefits, primarily by leading to increased global trade and competition. When countries eliminate tariffs and quotas, they facilitate the entry of enterprises into foreign markets, hence promoting economic growth. This higher level of trade creates higher efficiency and innovation, since local manufacturers must continually adapt to survive in the face of the challenges of a more competitive global market. According to the definition by the World Trade Organization (WTO), removing trade barriers encourages countries to specialize in producing goods and services in which they enjoy a comparative advantage, hence optimizing resource allocation around the world. Such systems can develop higher consumer welfare, as lowered trade barriers translate to lower prices and greater varieties of products made available to consumers. In addition, the reduction of trade barriers contributes to the world's pursuit of sustainable development by promoting green behavior. With an increasingly integrated world trade, countries are compelled to sign up to and abide by higher environmental standards as mentioned in reports on the trade-climate policy nexus (Ackerman et al., 2016).

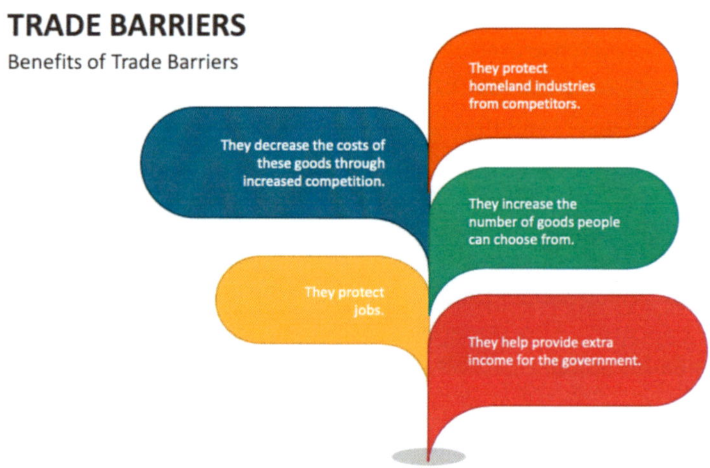

Figure 2.11. Benefits of reducing trade barriers.

Source: https://www.collidu.com/media/catalog/product/img/8/7/8730a755c712ac25602b956526660af99d70bed291d0153fba7d529885c5691c/trade-barriers-slide4.png.

When trade policies are designed with sustainability in mind, they stand to enable nations to exchange green technology and adopt best practices for environmental management between trading states. Such effective transfer of knowledge and technology not only allows states to tackle climate change but also demonstrates the worth of aligning environmental and trade policies, hence proving that dismantling trade barriers can benefit economic and ecological goals equally. Further, reducing trade barriers can foster nation-to-nation diplomacy and lead to international stability. Nations achieve interdependencies by exchanging goods and services with other nations, leading to cooperation and decreased war possibilities. This is enhanced by the general principles of the WTO that utilize rules-based trade arrangements to establish equitable competition and avenues of conflict resolution (Chang et al., 2004). Trade agreements increase discussion and cooperation on matters across the world, from economic partnership to shared environmental goals. The lowering of trade barriers, thus, can encourage nations to create confidence to cooperate more in solving problems confronting the world. Benefits of reducing trade barriers, thus, extend beyond economics to encompass overall impacts on global relations and global efforts towards sustainable development (Figure 2.11).

2.4.3. Challenges Faced in Achieving Trade Liberalization

Achieving trade liberalization is plagued with issues that can go a long way in hindering the progress in the international trading system. Various nations have varying economic interests, levels of development, and political incentives, thus it becomes difficult to negotiate. For instance, it is often that less developed countries would be at a disadvantage, facing restrictions in trade from more developed economies while attempting simultaneously to adopt policies of liberalization. This sort of imbalance is observed in the challenge faced by Caribbean countries as they negotiate access into multilateral trade negotiations like the Free Trade Area of the Americas (FTAA). As the in-depth analysis of their participation illustrates, the individual conditions and exposures of these nations render them unable to bargain on favorable terms in these agreements, painting a significant hurdle in achieving equitable liberalization in trade (Bishop et al., 2003). The second major factor of challenges faced in liberalization in trade is the cross-link between the strategies of trade and environmental concerns. The ever-present tension between seeking freer trade and fighting climate change has become increasingly critical, particularly amidst the process of globalization. Regulations to facilitate trade inevitably have the side effect of diluting environmental standards, thereby impacting the endeavor to fight climate change. Reports by the Working Group on Trade, Investment, and Climate Policy underscore the difficulty of bridging trade agreements like the Trans-Pacific Partnership (TPP) and the Transatlantic Trade and Investment Partnership (TTIP) with climate objectives. As much as these agreements aim to promote economic interdependence, they overlook critical environmental implications, thus making it more difficult to bridge trade liberalization with sustainable development (Ackerman et al., 2016). Furthermore, geopolitical factors add yet another layer of complexity to the problem of trade liberalization. Instability and shifting power dynamics may upset collaborative efforts at trade by creating conflicts that hinder negotiations. Common aims are overshadowed by national interests, giving rise to protectionism that defies the ideals of trade liberalization. The consequences of such positions are evident in the disruption caused by unilateral policies and trade wars that can be triggered by policy jingoism. With countries emphasizing sovereignty and economic interests, the predominate objective of liberalizing trade becomes even more difficult to attain. This brings into focus the importance of a concerted effort to navigate the geopolitical landscape effectively to establish an environment within which trade liberalization is possible, and thus remains focused on the substance of diplomatic negotiation and negotiation as being the fundamental principles of WTO law (Figure 2.12).

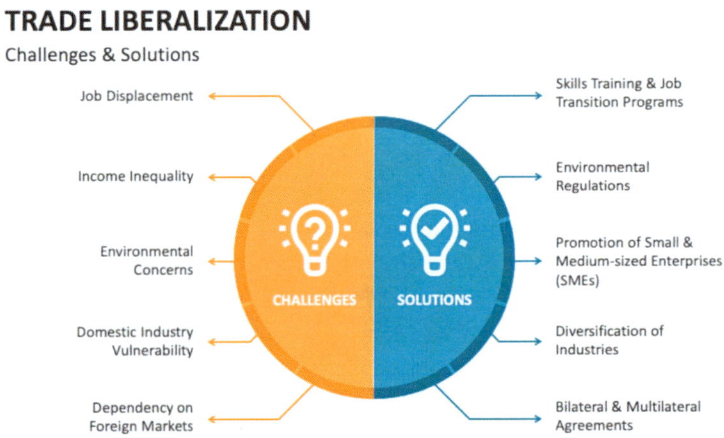

Figure 2.12. Challenges faced in achieving trade liberalization.

Source: https://www.collidu.com/media/catalog/product/img1/d/6/d6efb-97279cf3bc7d18221305f2046a2a32176f33f1e74bcd51d547621f29b18/trade-liberalization-slide4.png.

2.5. DISPUTE RESOLUTION MECHANISM (DRM)

The World Trade Organization (WTO) DRM represents a core framework for addressing disputes that would arise among member countries concerning trade agreements and laws. Central to the success of the DRM is its emphasis on objectivity and adherence to predetermined legal standards, which is crucial in building confidence between different states. The system is designed to provide a structured way of settling disagreements by panels and the Appellate Body, such that countries can settle disputes without resorting to unilateral action, which can increase tensions. As the importance of stable trading relations grows, particularly in an interdependent-leaning world economy, the function of the DRMs as enforcers of compliance with trade norms cannot be overstated. By offering a forum where grievances are heard in law, the WTO ensures a consistent and orderly world trading system.

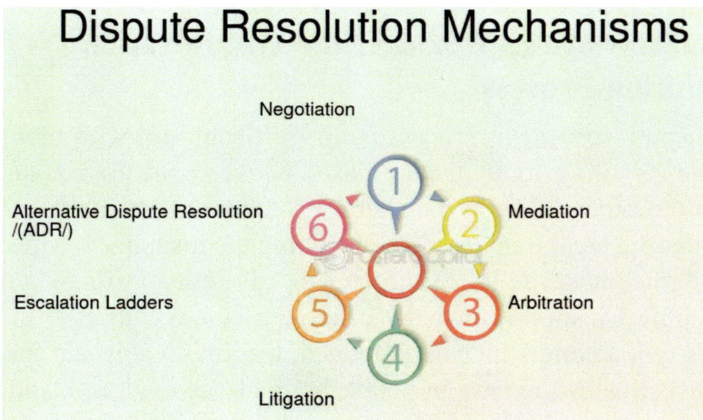

Figure 2.13. Dispute resolution mechanism (DRM).

Source: https://fastercapital.co/i/Legal-issues--How-to-avoid-legal-issues-and-comply-with-regulations-when-outsourcing-team-tasks--Dispute-Resolution-Mechanisms.webp.

The intricacy of the DRM is emphasized in its procedural commitments, requiring open and equitable practices. This includes reporting requirements and timelines that require members to be in good faith, which ensures the system's validity. The facility of appeal under the authority of the Appellate Body also supports the system; it is an appeal mechanism for panel decisions, making those decisions legally uniform. Critics have, however, argued about the matter of potential extra-national political ideologies influencing such judicial hearings, questioning the independence of international tribunals. The debate on judicial independence and state control has important implications for the efficacy of the DRM, requiring constant assessment of how structural variables within the WTO affect judicial decisions (Helfer et al., 2005). In addition, the DRM not only seeks to resolve disputes but also achieves the general objectives of the WTO, such as fostering economic growth and protecting human rights as emphasized in numerous scholarly examinations. The link between human development and dispute resolution is evident in the sense that equal economic development is attained through fair trade practices, and states can also uphold levels of human rights. Such harmony paints a picture of a deeper interdependency where efficient resolution of disputes not only means adherence to law of trade but also leads to sustainable human development. As nations address the complexities of international trade, the morality in the DRM provides a foundation to balance national interests and mutual moral responsibility, thus lending legitimacy to international trade standards (Normand, 2025) (Figure 2.13).

2.5.1. Overview of the World Trade Organization (WTO) Dispute Resolution Process

The WTO dispute settlement process is a significant tool with the purpose of resolving and handling trade-dispute cases between member countries. The backbone of the process lies in the Dispute Settlement Understanding (DSU), which provides the legal framework for handling the disputes. If a member state believes its rights under the WTO agreements have been infringed upon, it can initiate a dispute by approaching the offending country. In case the bilateral consultations fail, a complaint can be lodged, leading to a panels appointment. The panel investigates the case in detail, reviews the evidence, and listens to legal representations before submitting a report. This formal process not only tries to bring an end to disagreement but also enforces the general principles of multilateral trade agreements through the enforcement of established rules and norms. After the report of the panels is made public, it may be appealed to the Appellate Body, a higher court in the WTO dispute resolution system. The Appellate Body's task is to review the legal aspects of the panel's decision, ensuring consistency in interpretations of WTO agreements in different cases. The two-tiered system contributes to the integrity of the dispute settlement mechanism, promoting fairness and predictability in international trade. The parties may either implement the recommendations or negotiate among themselves, achieving the spirit of cooperation inherent in WTO law. If the implementation does not occur within a given time period, the successful party can request authorization to be able to impose trade sanctions, establishing a crucial enforcement tool that reinforces the authority of international trade agreements. Moreover, the WTO dispute settlement procedure embodies exceedingly crucial principles that are in line with broader international legal systems, namely those of human development and human rights. Underlying its function is the commitment to a rules-based system where disputes are resolved by established procedures instead of by individual choices, thus instilling a culture of stability and consistency in international trade (Normand, 2025).

Conversely, however, problems persist with decentralization, compliance, and legitimacy in the system, especially as the nature of world trade patterns evolves (Helfer et al., 2003). Accordingly, while efficacious in resolving disagreements, the WTOs process must be scrutinized continuously in order to stay current with these issues as well as to remain relevant and beneficial for all member nations. Through these complexities, the WTO continues to promote equitable trading relations reflecting the foundational tenets of its system of law.

2.5.2. Key Features of the Dispute Settlement Understanding (DSU)

The DSU acts as a core system within the World Trade Organization (WTO) that sets forth the rules and procedures through which member countries resolve their differences. Enacted in January 1995, DSU emphasizes the need for consultations between parties in conflict, establishing a formal mechanism through which disputes are resolved quickly. Automatic panel establishment is one of the typical features as such panels are mandated to examine cases within a reasonable framework, eschewing delays prevalent with previous arrangements under the General Agreement on Tariffs and Trade (GATT). Further, the DSU facilitates the effectiveness of the systems with the incorporation of specific deadlines for compliance and responses, placing further importance on prompt settlement and response to international trade agreements. All these factors collectively facilitate the effectiveness of the WTOs dispute settlement system, demonstrating its position in the middle as ensuring trade order between nations. One of the most important aspects of the DSU is the appeal mechanism, under which panel decisions can be appealed and remanded for review by an Appellate Body. This level of review is critical to ensuring that the disputes are resolved not simply fairly but also in a manner consistent with WTO norms, and hence the credibility of the system as a whole. In addition, the DSU guarantees the retaliatory powers in the event of a member state's failure to comply with the rulings acquired after controversies. It serves as a deterrent to infringement, contributing to the DSU as an instrument that can convince members to comply with international norms. The ability to sanction non-compliance equally enhances the functional integrity of the system, enabling the WTO to maintain its status as a forum for cooperative trade relations for its member states, as highlighted in debate over the sophistication of Preferential Trade Agreements (PTAs) (Hyams et al., 2017). With all these strengths, the DSU has had its own weaknesses, particularly on the procedural deficits that have been observed in recent years. Critics indicate that the compliance stage of disputes does not have adequate coordination, which may result in inefficiencies as well as protracted conflict. For example, the disconnection between the procedure of retaliations and determinations for compliance indicates a requirement for reform to improve clarity and usability of the system. In addition, the ongoing negotiations concerning the revision of the DSU reflect remaining uncertainties, particularly regarding the response to issues in PTAs and how they will affect compliance with WTO rules (Grimmett et al., 2004). As captured in Ambassador Ronald Saborío Sotos remarks, the conquest of such procedural uncertainties is crucial in order to ensure the legitimacy and functioning effectiveness of the WTOs dispute settlement mechanism so that it can continue to be resilient amid shifting global trade flows.

2.5.3. Notable Cases and Their Outcomes

The World Trade Organization (WTO) has ruled a number of landmark cases that recall its underlying principles, particularly in the area of dispute settlement as well as trade regulation. One of them is a prominent case in point: the United States — Gasoline case, which was a turning point in terms of national treatment commitments. In this instance, the Appellate Body found that the United States had violated Article 2 of the General Agreement on Tariffs and Trade (GATT) by imposing stricter rules on imported gasoline than on domestic products. The ruling highlighted the importance of equal treatment of imported items, a key factor in ensuring equal competition in foreign trade. The decision not only legalized the WTOs power to enforce compliance but also set a precedent that was applied to other trade barriers and domestic regulations cases, reflecting the delicate balance of national and international commitments. Another important case highlighting the working efficacy of WTO law is the China — Audiovisual Products case. Here, the Appellate Body found China's restrictions on foreign audiovisual products to be inconsistent with the commitments under GATT. The ruling emphasized the transparency rule and prohibition against arbitrary discrimination in trade measures. The adverse findings obliged China to examine its rules on imports of audiovisual products to align with WTO requirements. This case reconfirmed the importance of compliance and the dedication of the WTO to giving member states tools for standing up against unfair trade practices. It is a reminder of the importance of countries keeping their word, thus maintaining a safe environment for trade founded on the rule of law in international relations. Lastly, the EC — Hormones case demonstrates how the WTO balances health and safety standards with the values of trade liberalization. The European Communities were found to have violated GATT obligations by banning imports of beef products treated with hormones on the basis of unfounded health risks. The Appellate Body ruled that members may exercise discretion to implement health measures, but these must be based on evidence and not constitute arbitrary discrimination or disguised protection against trade. This case foregrounded the WTO's mandate of seeking evidence-based grounds for implementing trade-restrictive measures, in order to ensure that countries do not use public health to mask protectionist ends. The outcome reaffirmed the basic requirement of states to balance national health policy with the basic principles of the WTO such that trade measures are justified, reliable, and transparent (BALTA et al., 2017; Helfer et al., 2005).

2.6. SPECIAL AND DIFFERENTIAL TREATMENT (SDT)

The concept of SDT under the auspices of the World Trade Organization (WTO) has been crucial in facilitating developing countries' integration into the international trade regime. This legal mechanism grants these nations favorable treatment because of their personalized economic issues and stages of development. By the grant of less stringent obligations and extended periods of transition for trading arrangement compliance, SDT aims at the promotion of economic growth and diversification in the developing world. However, the effectiveness of these provisions has come under increasing attacks as some nations use their developing-country status to avoid commitments that would facilitate fair competition and sustainability in global trade. Such an abuse of privilege discredits the multilateral trading system and has resulted in pressure for reform to redefine the qualifications and ensure compliance among member states wishing to benefit from SDT. As observed in past trade negotiations, difficulties of SDT are exemplified by the case of member states like China, which presented itself as a developing member while simultaneously becoming one of the world's leading trading powers. Despite the economic emergence of China, it has been accused of using its developing status to access special treatment provisions reserved for less economically advanced nations. Others complain that the current system allows for enormous variation in obligations among members. For instance, whereas other nations follow guidelines established, Chinas inconsistent compliance with some obligations—such as transparency and notification obligations—cast doubts on the legitimacy of the system. The developing imbalance will impede negotiations on pressing global issues like fisheries subsidies and e-commerce norms and, therefore, underline the need for a renewed analysis of SDT against new global economic realities (Hu et al., 2019). Further, the nexus between environmental standards and SDT adds more complexities to the WTO regime. The Generalized System of Preferences (GSP) is a prominent system where developed nations offer non-reciprocal tariff preferences to developing countries as a means of encouraging economic development within these countries. Recent debates have examined how conditionality bestowed under such preferences may be inconsistent with values of non-discrimination fundamental to the WTOs system of law. The European Communities GSP, for example, has been altered to include special incentive arrangements subject to compliance with the environment. This raises questions regarding the legality and fairness of linking trade benefits to abiding by specific environmental standards, given that developing nations often have daunting barriers to compliance with such measures. Ultimately, although SDT is aimed at fostering equitable trade relationships, it also brings into question matters of exploitation and the consequences of conditionality in free trade agreements which would ultimately undermine central WTO precepts (Switzer et al., 2008) (Figure 2.14).

Figure 2.14. Special and differential treatment (SDT).

Source: https://www.ptun-surabaya.go.id/wp-content/uploads/2023/09/Gambar-Artikel-Rasa-Takut-5.png.

2.6.1. Purpose of Special and Differential Treatment (SDT) Provisions

The SDT provisions incorporated in the World Trade Organization (WTO) system serve to address inequalities experienced in the international trading system. The provisions are designed to provide developing countries with more favorable terms of trade, taking into consideration their unique economic challenges and the need for flexibility in their trade obligations. This approach is an articulation of one of the core principles of the WTOs objectives to promote equitable trade. By allowing developing nations to implement weaker commitments, SDT provisions aim to enhance their economic growth and integration into the global economy. This arrangement is also in question, particularly because there are industrialized countries that argue that certain nations misuse these concessions to evade the requirements that all WTO members are supposed to comply with, thus rendering multilateral trade agreements to be less holy, as evidenced by US and EU complaints about misuse of SDT provisions (Hu et al., 2019). The use of SDT provisions also evokes the concept of equity under international trade law towards a more equal world trading order. For instance, the provisions allow developing countries to postpone tariff reduction and grant them longer periods for taking on commitments, thereby allowing their economies to acquire competitiveness and stability. Such differential treatment is crucial in the context of history where developing nations entered the multilateral trading system with built-in vulnerabilities. Sheltering them to allow them to effectively absorb the impact of international trade is a situation that is conducive to economic growth. However, today's membership category debates expose the tensions inherent within the SDT architecture as more influential developing economies like China undermine the overall objective of equitable trade by using their development status to their advantage while involving themselves more and more in global markets (Hu et al., 2019). Furthermore, the special and differential treatment negotiations expose broader dynamics of sovereignty and control in international trade agreements. SDT provisions have been criticized by people such as defenders of the Multilateral Agreement on Investment (MAI) on grounds that such mechanisms undermine state sovereignty by subjecting domestic policy to international scrutiny and investor protections. Such arguments raise fundamental questions about the functions of states in the shaping of their trade regimes, making SDT provisions both a development assistance and a source of contention in the state sovereignty debate. As countries navigate the complexities associated with SDT, ongoing debate will establish the effectiveness and future practice of these provisions towards ensuring not only the interests of developing nations but also ensuring a robust, fair, and sustainable multilateral trading environment.

2.6.2. Categories of Developing Countries in World Trade Organization (WTO) Law

The division of developing countries in WTO law is of utmost significance in mapping the topography of international trade and ensuring equitable membership among member states. Developing countries are generally divided into various categories based on economic standing, institutional capacity, and some vulnerabilities. This differentiation enables the WTO to tailor its agreements and commitments to the unique challenges of these nations, such as limited resources and less developed negotiating strength. By acknowledging such differences, the WTO aims to establish a more balanced trading environment that will enable developing countries to effectively play their roles in the global economy and advance their economic growth and development. This cryptic categorization not only affects trade negotiation but also affects the compliance of trade obligations, upholding the potential of preferential treatment and flexibilities in obligations as may be the case. Moreover, the special and differential treatment (SDT) norms enshrined in WTO law further reinforce the obligations of developed countries towards supporting the development agenda of their developing counterparts. These are principles that underpin a range of concessions including extended periods for compliance with trade disciplines as well as technical assistance arrangements. Through the consolidation of these instruments, the WTO seeks to alleviate disparities in trade relations and facilitate the full enjoyment of the inherent right of developing countries to diversify their economic capacities. The constant disputes about such provisions, however, show the face-off between the need for fair trade practices and the complexities of global business. For instance, the effect of SDT is dampened by ineffective implementation, and it raises questions regarding the operational lifespan of such commitments and their actual application in real life (Normand, 2025). Furthermore, the categorization of developing countries also intersects with broader issues of global management and human advancement. Whilst the WTO seeks to associate trade and sustainable development, intellectual property and human rights legal models increasingly influence developing nations' trade policies. Since these have been established in many international conventions, the intersections necessitate a fuller context of developing countries' commitments under the WTO framework. Importantly, the impact of intellectual property rights on access to essential commodities, such as medicine and technology, illustrates the delicate balance that must be struck between encouraging innovation and ensuring access. Hence, with new agreements and proposals coming into being, a sustained debate about these intersecting regimes offers an opportunity to reconsider categorizing developing countries in WTO law, more importantly in human rights (Helfer et al., 2007).

2.6.3. Critiques and Effectiveness of These Provisions

The WTO operates in a sphere that focuses on its major principles, most notably encouraging free trade and non-discrimination among its members. But there are criticisms that its provisions are ineffective. One of them is the so-called democratic deficit of the WTO, where decision-making favored developed countries over developing countries. This imbalance has necessitated calls for reform to make its governance structure more inclusive. The opponents argue that the regulations that are established by the WTO are at times ineffective in addressing the specific issues that are faced by the less economically powerful nations and thus undermining the organization's overall legitimacy and effectiveness in reaching equitable trade resolutions, as scrutinized in relevant scholarly work, e.g., Pauwelyn et al. (2006). A key criticism focuses on the enforcement mechanisms established in the WTO framework. Although the mechanism of dispute settlement aims to compel compliance and provide remedies for violations, its effectiveness is questionable. The overwhelming majority of members bemoan undue delays in the decision-making process and the complexity of settling legal controversies. This implicates the voluntariness of the states to comply with judgments, particularly when measures taken do not align with their economic interests or political ambitions. The disparity in implementation similarly works to amplify system ills within the organization, such as the disparities in the compliance capabilities across the different member states that can undermine the level of trust necessary for a cooperative international trading system, as mentioned earlier in academic discussions regarding the interaction between international and constitutional law (Helfer et al., 2003). Moreover, the principles of openness and accountability in WTO provisions have also been very much criticized for being de facto circumscribed in their application. Even if the organization avows to hold such principles, some have attacked the actual negotiation and decision-making processes as not being open enough. This deficiency not only chases away more comprehensive stakeholder engagement but also feeds into the suspicion that the institution's legitimacy is questioned. Transparency is required to foster trust between member states and enhance the credibility of WTO economic governance. Without reforms focused on accountability, the institution can ever more become a stranger to the very norms it is meant to advance, ultimately undermining its utility as an integral actor in the global trading regime (Helfer et al., 2003; Pauwelyn et al., 2006).

SUMMARY

The fundamental WTO law principles form the basis of defining global trade dynamics. The WTO framework relies on pillar principles like most-favored-nation treatment, national treatment, and transparency in a bid to reduce trade barriers and promote fair trading practices among the member nations. The principles facilitate a global trading system that aims to enhance global economic cooperation, with a view to ending up in shared prosperity. Since trade itself is ever more being shaped in reaction to challenges such as technology and shifting power dynamics within economies, the principles of the WTO will have to be periodically examined to guarantee that they remain effective in addressing current challenges. Also, the complexity of the international trading world makes the imperative of an integrated approach to WTO law more pressing. As countries grapple with fragmentation of public international law, it is crucial to examine how different legal frameworks cope with one another. The threats facing the WTO, including tensions among members and the establishment of preferential trade agreements, demonstrate the kind of fragmentation in trade regulation. Managing these tensions requires an acute understanding of both conflict of norms and conflict of laws, as hinted at in discourse over public international laws complexities. Therefore, the WTO must evolve in response to these changing challenges while remaining true to its very foundations in order to preserve its usefulness. Finally, in order to realize the goals outlined in the WTO agreements, member states must be willing to engage in cooperative measures and ongoing dialogue. Strengthening the role of the WTO as a referee for trade disputes and the institution itself will be crucial to ensure effective global governance. Through this, the norms of WTO law cannot only be a foundation for trade but also a motivator for sustainable development and economic justice. As the worldwide dialogue concerning world trade broadens, the WTOs ability to adapt to new realities will decide if it will be successful in advocating for a steady and inclusive worldwide economic order, which will guarantee the organization effectively addresses the increasing issues of globalization as well as trade relationships and stays on course to its fundamental principles.

Deeply embedded at the core of the WTO law is a vibrant repository of fundamental principles governing international trade. These are principles, including non-discrimination, transparency, and equal competition, which are geared to ensure an equal trade environment among member states. Non-discrimination is unique in that it merges the MFN and National Treatment principles in the sense that the benefits of trade given to one member must be extended to all members to guarantee an equal feeling of trade relationships. Transparency, yet another basic principle, calls for members to publish their trade practices and regulations, allowing for well-informed decision-making. These basic principles are called for not only in formulating trade policies but also in meeting the mixed interaction between world trade patterns and national economic realities. Furthermore, the integration of labor standards into trade arrangements is a mere reflection of the evolving nature of international economic law. Over the last decades, trade negotiations have placed greater stresses on labor rights, whereby the complex interaction between economic policies and labor relations has found itself in the spotlight. The recognition of fundamental labor standards, as reaffirmed in many bilateral agreements, underlines the significance of countries maintaining a balance between economic growth and ethical labor standards. For instance, inclusion of labor standard provisions in trade agreements like NAFTA places a commitment to defend workers' rights above free trade pursuit. Greater acknowledgment of labor issues within trade negotiations indicates an evolving view of where economic and social dimensions intersect within WTO law (Baumert et al., 2008). Moreover, the ongoing debate on imposing international labor standards demonstrates the intricacy of balancing diverse economic interests. Although some Third World nations bemoan that rigid codes of labor might undermine their competitive edge, there are others who recognize the ethical imperative to impose an international minimum of labor rights across the globe. The central labor standards agreement is one key step towards bridging this disparity, aiming to end the race to the bottom situation where countries would compromise on labor standards in a bid to attract investment. Others do, however, oppose the applicability and use of such standards in different economic conditions. It is important to comprehend the roles of various stakeholders, particularly that of developing nations, so that one may be able to handle the intricacies of international labor standards and their integration in the overall framework of WTO law (Fields et al., 2003).

REFERENCES

1. Ackerman, F., Bernasconi, N., Cabré, M. M., et al. (2016). Trade in the balance: Reconciling trade and climate policy: Report of the Working Group on Trade, Investment, and Climate Policy. https://open.bu.edu/bitstream/2144/22909/1/Pardee_TradeClimate_110316final.pdf (accessed on 30th October 2025).
2. Bagwell, K., & Staiger, R. W. (2025). GATT-think. https://core.ac.uk/download/pdf/6606912.pdf (accessed on 30th October 2025).
3. Balta, F., Düzlü, Ö., İbiş, O., et al. (2017). The hidden though flourishing justification of intellectual property laws: Distributive justice, national versus international approaches. https://core.ac.uk/download/216959393.pdf (accessed on 30th October 2025).
4. Baumert, J., Heuschel, D., Johnson, K., et al. (2008). International cooperation on trade and labor issues. https://core.ac.uk/download/5118835.pdf (accessed on 30th October 2025).
5. Beth, R. S., Cooper, W. H., & Fergusson, I. F. (2014). Trade promotion authority (TPA): Frequently asked questions. https://core.ac.uk/download/20318565.pdf (accessed on 30th October 2025).
6. Bishop, M. D., & Chandler, S. J. (2003). Opportunities and challenges: The Caribbean involvement in the Free Trade Area of the Americas. https://core.ac.uk/download/144226511.pdf (accessed on 30th October 2025).
7. Bronckers, B., Charnovitz, S., Lydgate, E. B., Horn, H., Howse, R., Trebilcock, M., et al. (2011). Consumer preferences and the national treatment principle: Emerging environmental regulations prompt a new look at an old problem. https://core.ac.uk/download/16671807.pdf (accessed on 30th October 2025).
8. Brown, A. J., Strube, D., Oliveira, I., Joy, M., & Callaghan, M. (2025). G20 2014: Reform of the international organizations, financial regulation, trade, accountability and anti-corruption. https://core.ac.uk/download/pdf/30673851.pdf (accessed on 30th October 2025).
9. Caswell, J. A., Orden, D., Otsuki, T., et al. (2025). The role of product attributes in the agricultural negotiations. https://core.ac.uk/download/pdf/6545995.pdf (accessed on 30th October 2025).
10. Chang, S. W. (2004). Interaction between trade and competition: Why a multilateral approach for the United States? https://core.ac.uk/download/62547461.pdf (accessed on 30th October 2025).
11. Delimatsis, P. (2018). Global standard-setting 2.0: How the WTO spotlights

ISO and impacts the transnational standard-setting process. https://core.ac.uk/download/213020038.pdf (accessed on 30th October 2025).

12. Fields, G. S. (2003). International labor standards and decent work: Perspectives from the developing world. https://core.ac.uk/download/5131022.pdf (accessed on 30th October 2025).
13. Grimmett, J. J. (2004). Dispute settlement in the World Trade Organization (WTO): An overview. https://core.ac.uk/download/5121057.pdf (accessed on 30th October 2025).
14. Grinberg, I. (2017). A destination-based cash flow tax can be structured to comply with World Trade Organization rules. https://core.ac.uk/download/141869901.pdf (accessed on 30th October 2025).
15. Hall, D. (2006). EU neighborhood policy: Implications for public services and trade unions. https://core.ac.uk/download/67095.pdf (accessed on 30th October 2025).
16. Helfer, L. R. (2007). Toward a human rights framework for intellectual property. https://core.ac.uk/download/62563252.pdf (accessed on 30th October 2025).
17. Helfer, L. R., & Slaughter, A. M. (2005). Why states create international tribunals: A response to Professors Posner and Yoo. https://core.ac.uk/download/62563361.pdf (accessed on 30th October 2025).
18. Helfer, L. R., Hathaway, O. A., Goldstein, J., Lutz, E., Chayes, A., Raustiala, K., et al. (2003). Constitutional analogies in the international legal system. https://core.ac.uk/download/62563345.pdf (accessed on 30th October 2025).
19. Hoekman, B., & Nelson, D. (2020). Rethinking international subsidy rules. *Bertelsmann Working Paper*, 28/02/2020. https://core.ac.uk/download/287647974.pdf (accessed on 30th October 2025).
20. Hu, W. (2019). China as a WTO developing member, is it a problem? *CEPS Policy Insights*, No. 2019/16, November 2019. https://core.ac.uk/download/286731365.pdf (accessed on 30th October 2025).
21. Hyams, A., & Villalta Puig, G. (2017). Preferential trade agreements and the World Trade Organization: Developments to the dispute settlement understanding. https://core.ac.uk/download/151161965.pdf (accessed on 30th October 2025).
22. Isaac, G. E. (2025). Increasing the openness of the trade policy process: Challenges and implications. https://core.ac.uk/download/pdf/7035281.pdf (accessed on 30th October 2025).
23. Lai, E. L. C. (2025). The most-favored nation rule in club enlargement

negotiation. https://core.ac.uk/download/pdf/7359258.pdf (accessed on 30th October 2025).

24. Mann, C. L. (2025). Transatlantic issues in electronic commerce. https://core.ac.uk/download/pdf/6719983.pdf (accessed on 30th October 2025).
25. Michaels, R., & Pauwelyn, J. (2011). Conflict of norms or conflict of laws? Different techniques in the fragmentation of public international law. https://core.ac.uk/download/62547229.pdf (accessed on 30th October 2025).
26. Normand, R. (2025). Separate and unequal: Trade and human rights regimes. https://core.ac.uk/download/pdf/6248885.pdf (accessed on 30th October 2025).
27. Pauwelyn, J. H. B. (2004). Non-traditional patterns of global regulation: Is the WTO 'missing the boat'? https://core.ac.uk/download/62562456.pdf (accessed on 30th October 2025).
28. Pauwelyn, J. H. B. (2006). Book review. https://core.ac.uk/download/62562748.pdf (accessed on 30th October 2025).
29. Stumberg, R. (1998). Sovereignty by subtraction: The Multilateral Agreement on Investment. https://core.ac.uk/download/70374926.pdf (accessed on 30th October 2025).
30. Switzer, S. (2008). Environmental protection and the generalized system of preferences: A legal and appropriate linkage? https://core.ac.uk/download/9053220.pdf (accessed on 30th October 2025).
31. Woods, N. (2025). Accountability in global governance. https://core.ac.uk/download/pdf/6248858.pdf (accessed on 30th October 2025).

Chapter 3

The WTO Agreements and Legal Framework

Contents

INTRODUCTION

The World Trade Organization (WTO) is a keystone of the world trading system, established to facilitate trade everywhere on the globe by creating a vast network of laws that will span trade agreements between members. With the pace of globalization quickening, the function of the WTO has come under scrutiny, with critics posing that it is not evolving with shifting patterns in trade. WTO agreements address various aspects of trade like tariffs, subsidies, and intellectual property rights, in an attempt to harmonize trade practices and resolve disputes collectively. Beyond advancing economic cooperation among nations, the agreements also offer a legal framework that advances predictability and stability in international trade relations, necessary to foster investment and economic growth. But the WTO is beset with several problems that undermine its efficacy and pertinence in today's complicated trading atmosphere. Most member nations are turning more and more to bilateral and plurilateral agreements, which, although appear to be advantageous in the short run, weaken the multilateral trading systems power. Critics assert that this evolution to splintered trade relationships results in a "crisis of legitimacy" for the WTO, as it no longer remains capable of fulfilling its original role of governing global trade agreements. As maintained by recent analyses, patterns across and outside the organization emphasize the necessity of re-evaluating its capacity to address common issues of trade effectively; without fundamental reforms, the WTO is likely to lose its role as a key player in global trade (Bäumler et al., 2020). Knowing how the WTO agreements function requires a comprehensive consideration of the principles behind them and the structure that governs them. Key thematic areas, such as labor rights, environmental protection, and food security, illustrate the linkages between trade and significant global issues impacting society and the economy (N/A, 2006). Addressing these themes is an endeavor by the WTO to implement a fair policy on trade with respect to the socio-economic implications of the policies of its member nations. However, as the global landscape evolves, the efficiency of these agreements needs to be evaluated periodically to ensure that they remain in consonance with contemporary realities. This essay will analyze the complexity of the WTOs legal framework and how it can catch up with new challenges, providing insight into the organizations future in a more interconnected world.

Definition of the World Trade Organization (WTO)

The WTO is an important organization in the contemporary structure of global trade. Established in 1995, it took over from the General Agreement on Tariffs and Trade (GATT). The WTO provides an official framework for trade agreement negotiations and settlement of disagreements among member nations. It works with the general aim of promoting fair and free trade, thereby expanding world economic cooperation. Through the imposition of consistent international trade rules, the WTO serves as a platform where its 164 member states negotiate to reduce trade restrictions, tariffs, and other barriers to international exchange. The organization demonstrates the principles of non-discrimination, transparency, and predictability that are fundamental to the stability and dependability of the trading system. Besides, the role of the WTO is not just to facilitate trade since it also engages in environmental sustainability and development policy debate (Anderson et al., 2013). The WTO's legal basis is based on a succession of agreements that lay out rules for the regulation of multiple aspects of trade. Of these, the three most significant are the GATT, the General Agreement on Trade in Services (GATS), and the Trade-Related Aspects of Intellectual Property Rights Agreement (TRIPS). GATT, established originally to regulate the trade in goods, targets tariffs and non-tariff restrictions, with GATS targeting liberalization in the service sectors, as services are increasingly becoming vital to global economic activity. TRIPS refers to intellectual property rights, trying to balance the interests of innovation and access. The agreements coexist in an effort to evolve a harmonious body of law that oversees country-to-country trade relations, therefore enabling countries to attain maximum economic benefits while balancing complex issues such as regulatory differences and development imperatives (Ackerman et al., 2016). In addition to its fundamental deals, the WTO also plays an important role in responding to emerging challenges to global trade. The body is freely debating the matter of trade implications on climate policy, seeking consensus between economic growth and environmental conservation. For instance, recent Pardee Center analyses identify tensions between climate policy and trade rules as proof of the need for a more integrated model of governance, one attuned to the interdependence of environmental and trade policy. The capacity of global investment treaties to direct capital flows towards initiatives that are climate-friendly is a sign of the changing complexity of trade within the context of global sustainability goals. Thus, the WTO not only serves as a regulator but also as a forum for member nations to navigate the multifaceted world of contemporary issues related to trade, making it even more relevant in the debate regarding sustainable development and economic cooperation (Anderson et al., 2013).

Importance of World Trade Organization (WTO) Agreements in Global Trade

The WTO agreements play an important role in guiding and promoting international trade by creating a rules-based system that fosters stability and predictability. The agreements serve as important legal tools that guide all areas of global trade, allowing the member countries to approach complex trade relationships with confidence. By establishing rule-based, predictable rules of practice in trade, such as tariffs, import quotas, and trade remedies, WTO agreements minimize trade disputes and enhance cooperation among nations. This emphasis on predictability of the law is particularly crucial in a global economy with rapidly changing market forces and geopolitics. Without such arrangements, the threat of trade-related conflict grows, which causes economic uncertainties that can hurt international supply chains and cross-border commercial relationships. In addition to putting in place a legal basis, the WTO agreements also emphasize the importance of inclusive international trade. Plurilateral agreements, as highlighted in recent research, are now effective tools for resolving specific problems among a subset of countries, complementing the larger WTO framework. For example, sectoral agreements on information technology and telecommunications not only circumvent roadblocks in trade negotiations but also contribute to improving global governance of trade generally. The coming into existence of such issue-based plurilateral agreements reflects an innovative reaction to evolving trade complexities and the demand for flexible solutions.

Figure 3.1. The World Trade Organization (WTO) agreements.

Source: https://currentaffairs.adda247.com/wp-content/uploads/multisite/sites/5/2025/06/05111356/Nicaragua-Becomes-101st-WTO-Member-to-Accept-Fisheries-Subsidies-Agreement.jpg.

In initiating cooperation on specific trade matters, the agreements are capable of generating economic growth and enhancing increased integration among the member countries, with its acute role in the grand scheme of WTO agreements (Nakatomi et al., 2013). In addition, the effect of WTO agreements goes beyond legal frameworks to shape the competitive environment for developing countries. The Agreement on the Application of Sanitary and Phytosanitary Measures (SPS Agreement) is a prime example of how these frameworks can enable countries, especially those that have less developed agricultural industries, to participate in international markets. By keeping the international standards under the CODEX Alimentarius, the SPS Agreement is a platform in which developing countries can more effectively exploit their agricultural exports.

However, the effectiveness of such participation is generally undermined by the lack of institutional capacity, as these countries may not be capable of attending high-level negotiations required to affect standards. Without technical capacity and support, their interests might be maintained on the margins of the global trading space (Chowdhury et al., 2008). The WTO agreements are therefore not only legal but also vital tools that facilitate equitable access to global trade for all member states (Figure 3.1).

Overview of the Legal Framework Governing the World Trade Organization (WTO)

The WTO legal system is primarily founded on a series of agreements that govern international trade between member countries. The agreements are the foundation of a multilateral trading system established to make trade go as smoothly and predictably as possible. Each of the agreements addresses separate areas such as tariffs, trade in services, and technical barriers to trade, thereby forming a broad legal structure that simplifies international commerce. The General Agreement on Tariffs and Trade (GATT), as subsequently evolved into the WTO framework, is a critical pillar of this system, encouraging negotiations that are aimed at reducing trade barriers and facilitating greater cooperation between states. As the dynamics of trade evolve, the legal instruments of the WTO must evolve to cope with emerging challenges, demonstrating the importance of an adaptive legal system that reflects the imperatives of contemporary trade and members' interests. A fundamental component of the WTOs legal framework is the design of mechanisms for the settlement of disputes that enable member nations to resolve trade conflicts in an orderly environment. Desiring to provide timely and equitable solutions, these mechanisms help to ensure the integrity of international trade agreements. The Understanding on Dispute Settlement (DSU) is most critical, as it defines recourse procedure through law in the event of a dispute so that members abide by the undertakings under the various agreements. Having such mechanisms in place also contributes to the image of the WTO, as it can assure member states that their rights will be protected. Hence, the DSU not only favors compliance with WTO agreements but also facilitates general cooperation and concord among diverse trading partners, thereby making the entire legal framework of the organization more effective. The legal structure further comprises provisions that recognize the unique needs of developing countries in the global trading arena. These provisions, as part of arrangements such as the Agreement on Trade-Related Aspects of Intellectual Property Rights (TRIPS) and the Subsidies and Countervailing Measures Agreement, are intended to address imbalances that are present in the global marketplace. For instance, while the SPS Agreement makes international food standards legal, it simultaneously points to the challenges confronting developing countries in living up to the expectations, as explained in discussions of CODEX standards (Chowdhury et al., 2008). Moreover, the lack of effectiveness of the existing legal tools to address labor mobility in trade agreements also reflects the lack of effectiveness in addressing the intricacies of emerging economies (Ramjoue, 2025). Lastly, these elements reflect on the importance of the WTOs legal framework in ensuring equitable trade relations as well as addressing the social and economic aspects of its heterogeneous membership (Figure 3.2).

Figure 3.2. The legal framework governing.

Source: https://assets.entrepreneur.com/content/3x2/2000/1597249627-GettyImages-1085970542.jpg.

3.1. HISTORICAL BACKGROUND OF THE WORLD TRADE ORGANIZATION (WTO)

The history of the WTO is at the forefront of understanding its legal framework and governance. The WTO was established in 1995 based on the General Agreement on Tariffs and Trade (GATT), which itself was originally formulated in 1947 as a means of expanding international trade by reducing tariffs and trade barriers. The transition from GATT to WTO was not a mere name change but was a revolutionary change in the world trade machinery. WTO had a broader mandate covering services, intellectual property, and dispute settlement mechanisms, which offered a coverage of the complexity of modern commerce that could not be undertaken under GATT. Such a transformation was an increasing awareness of the mutual relationships between development, trade, and economic policies around the globe and the necessity for a more efficient legal framework to manage the diverse interests of member nations. The establishment of the WTO also indicated a response to increasing globalization of business and the attendant economic interdependencies. With rising world trade, the concerns relating to trade disputes, market access, and regulatory standards increased as well. The Uruguay Round talks, which were held between 1986 and 1994, played a key role in redefining the global trade regulations. The negotiations witnessed massive agreements like the Trade-Related Aspects of Intellectual Property Rights (TRIPS) and the General Agreement on Trade in Services (GATS). The inclusion of such agreements in the WTO law marks a shift towards the recognition of the importance of different spheres of the economy and the need for the supremacy of rules that facilitate trade while being sensitive to the interests of every member state (Chang et al., 2004). The WTO has, therefore, been central in the facilitation of economic cooperation between countries in the quest for the creation of a level playing field in international trade. In appreciating the history of the WTO, there is a need to highlight contributions of various international institutions and agreements which paved its way. The concept of trade preferences, particularly in the context of the Generalized System of Preferences (GSP), highlights how developing nations have for long been helped by industrialized states through non-reciprocal tariff preferences. These arrangements were designed to promote the economies of developing countries, stimulate industrialization, and further incorporate them into the world trading system (Switzer et al., 2008). Under the umbrella of the WTO, these preferential treatments constantly change, raising the issues involving the environment and sustainable development. Consequently, the WTO's historical evolution is a reflection of the tension it seeks to mediate: encouraging free trade and ensuring the fair distribution of the dividends of globalization among its diverse membership, thus remaining relevant in the economic discussions of our times.

3.1.1. Formation of the World Trade Organization (WTO) in 1995

The creation of the WTO in 1995 is a milestone in the history of regulation of international trade. Following the Uruguay Round negotiations between 1986 and 1994, the WTO aimed to establish a complete legal system that would administer international trade. The WTO adopted the General Agreement on Tariffs and Trade (GATT), which had been the prominent multilateral trade agreement since 1947. By the transition to a robust institutional framework, the WTO aimed to enhance trade liberalization and enforce global trade legislation better. This was a consequence of growing recognition of the necessity of an organization that would be able to provide a more formalized system for resolving conflicts, as well as assist in negotiating on behalf of member nations, and thereby compensate for the defects of its predecessor, GATT. At the center of establishing the WTO was the understanding that a rules-based process of resolving trade conflicts would be acceptable to all member states, particularly those who had poor bargaining power. Unlike negotiation-based systems that can favor strong nations, the WTO regulations provided a legal framework that granted weaker countries a bargaining chip to make stronger nations comply with agreements made.

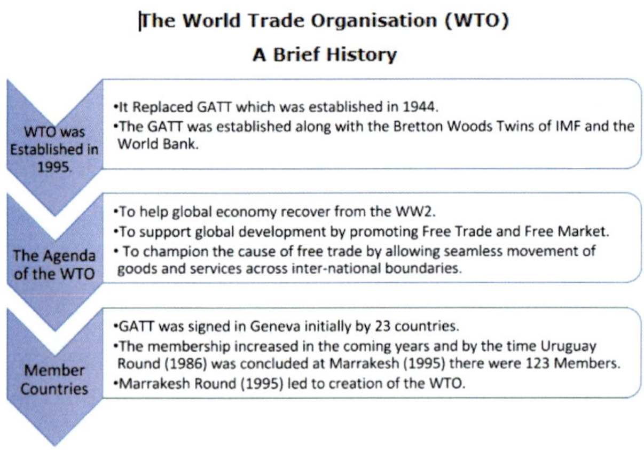

Figure 3.3. Formation of the World Trade Organization (WTO) in 1995.

Source: https://d18x2uyjeekruj.cloudfront.net/wp-content/uploads/2017/09/word-image52.jpeg.

Such an arrangement relies on an essential aspect of international politics where domestic interests are reconciled with world governance aspirations. As evident in recent research, the United States, upon acceding to the WTO, experienced the merits of a rules-based system in resolving trade disagreements. Such a leaning underscored the effects on international law and the new tendency towards a system that weighed competing interests in the different member nations and resulted in more equitable trade relationships (Brewster et al., 2006). In addition, the establishment of the WTO did not only strengthen the body of law surrounding trade but also underscored the intricacies involved in attaining further economic integration between nations. For instance, whereas the WTO wanted to help decrease trade barriers and promote international cooperation between nations, there were several structural issues that continued to exist worldwide. The inequalities in economic capability among members reflected the challenges confronting regional trade groups, like those within the Arab world, as they attempted to replicate the successful integration exhibited within the European Union. As this discourse was intimated in recent times, overcoming these challenges demands deep-seated reforms in economic agreements with a focus on highlighting reform that favors the interests of the collective good ahead of national state interests (Malkawi et al., 2007). Thus, the establishment of the WTO is both a sweeping step towards world trade regulation and a sign of the negotiations that have persisted in terms of international economic integration (Figure 3.3).

3.1.2. Evolution from the General Agreement on Tariffs and Trade (GATT)

The shift from the GATT to the World Trade Organization (WTO) is a radical change in global trade governance, encapsulating legal advancement and enhanced operational modalities. Initially introduced in 1947, GATT was significant in regulating global trade by emphasizing tariff reductions and trade liberalization. But when the weakness of GATT was unveiled through its shortcomings, particularly with respect to dispute settlement and the coverage of non-tariff barriers, the need for a stronger institutional system arose. With more complex trade since the inclusion of services and intellectual property, the weakness of GATT has spawned negotiations that ultimately led to the Uruguay Round. This transformation not only broaden the agenda of trade treaties but also paved the way for the WTO, fundamentally restructuring the way the member nations engage with each other within the global economic system. The establishment of the WTO in 1995 marked a pivotal transformation from a predominantly negotiation-based system to a comprehensive rule-based system. This development was important in that it gave an institutional framework to the settlement of trade disputes, thereby evening out the playing field between powerful as well as weak states. The legal systems of the WTO created a system of binding obligations and a formal process for dispute settlement, which dispensed with the erstwhile extensive use of bilateral negotiations, tending to favor stronger economies. As noted, "strong states are privileged by negotiation-based forms of dispute-settlement," whereas rule-based procedure of the WTO offers developing countries forums to enforce strong states to fulfill their promises (Brewster et al., 2006). In doing so, the WTO not only demonstrates a commitment towards equitable trade practice but also introduces a paradigm shift within global relations by shifting the focus towards legal remedy instead of negotiations. One central feature of this change is the incorporation of Special and Differential Treatment (SDT) provisions that aim to remedy the ideological development disparities between member states. During the Doha Round, such provisions were focal points in the negotiations, with the positions' divergences between developed and developing nations under the WTO platform. The SDT facilitates special trade rules that consider the particular issues of developing nations, thereby promoting inclusiveness in international trade (Manero-Salvador et al., 2025). Arguments regarding the development and effectiveness of such provisions are an expression of broader concerns to promote fair trade and assist sustainable development. With member states steering these complex negotiations, the WTOs model continues to evolve in response to the shifting outlines of international trade, balancing the interests of each party while reasserting its fundamental legal commitments (Figure 3.4).

Figure 3.4. General Agreement on Tariffs and Trade (GATT).

Source: https://external-content.duckduckgo.com/iu/?u=https%3A%2F%2Fthfvnext.bing.com%2Fth%2Fid%2FOIP.0ZM50NpdERTwS8ELZdwBVQHaFu%3Fcb%3Dthfvnext%26pid%3DApi&f=1&ipt=a2f2821ec038600383988aeb0898afea23f885897fda27f03b0783e0fe4e5ae5.

3.1.3. Key Milestones in World Trade Organization (WTO) History

The establishment of the WTO in 1995 was a significant milestone in regulating world trade, superseding the General Agreement on Tariffs and Trade (GATT) that had existed since 1948. WTO resulted from the Uruguay Round negotiations that started in 1986 and took an almost eight years trajectory. This set of negotiations resulted in the addition of various sectors of trade-related issues, including services, intellectual property rights, and trade-related investment measures to the legal framework of the WTO. Another feature, the establishment of the Dispute Settlement Understanding (DSU), further augmented WTOs effectiveness by allowing member nations to resolve trade disputes in an organized manner. This milestone not only embodied the evolving complexities of international trade but also established the foundation for an expanded and rule-based multilateral trading system, emphasizing the position of legal rules within trade pacts. The second milestone was achieved with the Doha Development Round, launched in 2001 with the goal of correcting trade imbalances unfairly placed on developing countries. This ambitious round sought to enhance facilitation of trade, agricultural liberalization, and capacity-building in developing countries. However, negotiations were plagued by a number of challenges that reflected divergences in priorities between developed and developing nations. The complexity of intellectual property and agricultural subsidy issues illustrated the requirement of solutions to be in line with the WTOs legal framework and equitable in nature. Though the Doha Round is far from any final conclusion, it reiterated the value of continuous dialogue and development of WTO agreements to balance emerging global challenges, looking at the organization's role in facilitating a fairer trading system for all its members. The evolving mandate of the WTO in global trade governance is also manifested through its activism on issues beyond traditional trade, such as environmental sustainability and public health. The recognition of the interdependence of trade with these essential sectors was seen in the COVID-19 pandemic, which accentuated the importance of cooperative structures in addressing cross-border emergencies. The roll-out of waivers against patent coverage for vaccines and drugs has spurred controversy regarding intellectual property rights and their impact on public health. Such controversies are comparable to past attempts to harmonize trade policy with sustainable development objectives. As witnessed with these ongoing debates, the WTO continues to develop its legal frameworks in an effort to promote resilience and inclusivity within international trade. The alignment of global issues with trade policy illustrates the importance of the WTOs adaptability as well as that of its agreements to be conversant with contemporary concerns, as witnessed with the sentiments expressed in Engel et al. (2025) and Gustafson et al. (2015).

3.2. STRUCTURE OF THE WORLD TRADE ORGANIZATION (WTO)

The organization of the WTO is a complex plan working towards facilitating international trade through a series of agreements that span all elements of international business. The WTO's core is the members who negotiate and implement the trade rules, with the main decision-making body being the General Council. This framework allows for the administration of a number of agreements, including those for goods, services, and intellectual property.

The legal system of the WTO is also established in its constituent agreements, which provide a platform for dispute settlement, monitoring compliance, and state openness. This institutional structure not only allows for rational domination of international trade but also prioritizes interdependence among trade agreements and world-order consequences on international economic cooperation. Furthermore, the legal norms governing how various WTO agreements intersect significantly impact multilateral negotiations. The WTO faces varying legal regimes — conditionality, separation, and open rules — each governing how countries can seek cross-issue cooperation. For instance, conditionality enhances multilateral cooperation where stakes in environmental policy are low compared to those of trade welfare.

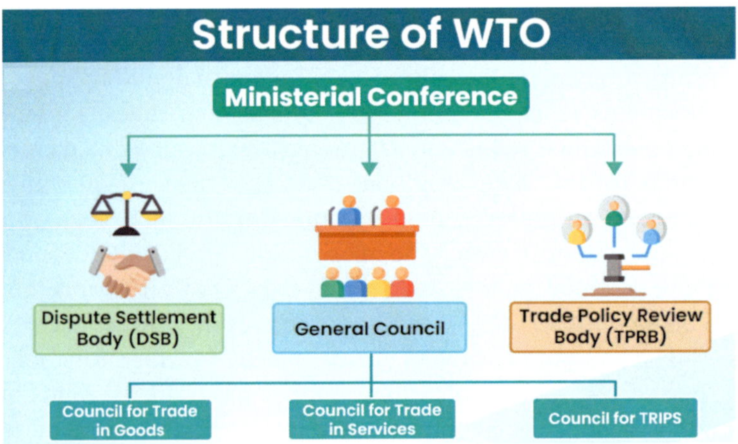

Figure 3.5. Structure of the World Trade Organization (WTO).

Source: https://external-content.duckduckgo.com/iu/?u=https%3A%2F%2Fcdn.educba.com%2Facademy%2Fwp-content%2Fuploads%2F2024%2F06%2FStructure-of-WTO.png&f=1&nofb=1&ipt=ff9fc22fc049843d700529f0d32479208b618e081481aeed6be9fc08b029359f.

Conversely, when compliance costs are high, these conditional measures deter cooperative initiatives. The dynamic nature of such legal systems justifies the importance of flexibility to allow the WTO to be responsive while solving complex global issues while having trade agreements being sound and effective to facilitate international cooperation (Conconi et al., 2001). In light of the geo-economic tensions of the day, it is clear that the WTO must evolve so that it can properly address collective action problems. Present rules on subsidies domestic and the spillover impacts thereof have proved to be insufficient. Present classifications of subsidies as being prohibited or actionable fail to capture the varied realities in trade terms of the day. To respond to this, more detailed guidance might be constructed, perhaps through a specialized work program at an future Ministerial Conference (Hoekman et al., 2020). The program would introduce subsidy regime expertise, developing a more robust evidence base to support subsequent negotiations, and finally enhancing the capacity of the WTOs institutional structure to address emerging international trade issues (Figure 3.5).

3.2.1. Overview of the Organizational Framework

The World Trade Organization (WTO) is a sophisticated web of agreement and legal frameworks, designed to regulate international trade among member nations. In essence, the WTO is framed to coordinate negotiations, oversee enforcement of trade agreements, and resolve disputes that arise between countries. This organizational structure is not only procedural in character but is closely linked to the success of the multilateral trading system. The critical analysis identifies a breakdown in the political consensus that leads to successful negotiation, as seen in the stalemated Doha Round, which has so far failed to deliver new frameworks for trade negotiations. This slowing down and associated lack of institutional learning signal a larger ill within the WTO that uncovering requires a new collective understanding of its roles and purposes, as witnessed in recent communiqués by member states that highlight the deficiency of political will and respect of obligations (Wolfe et al., 2018). The WTO's framework of law comprises several different agreements that regulate everything from various aspects of international trade. Of all these, the Agreement on Trade-Related Aspects of Intellectual Property Rights (TRIPS) is pivotal to setting intellectual property rights standards. The relationship between various international parties, including governments and multinational drug companies, makes it even harder to implement such rules. Insofar as the attempts of Brazil and South Africa to navigate TRIPS in an effort to gain increased access to HIV/AIDS medication illustrate, the implications of such legal frameworks extend beyond sheer compliance—they have a tendency to inform governmental policy-making. Hence, the dynamic relationship of different stakeholders in the structure of WTOs highlights how clashing interests create significant alterations in global health governance, showing an image of the role of the organizations in enabling and constraining national ability to act within crucial health crises (Christian von Soest et al., 2025). Furthermore, the efficacy of the WTOs organizational structure relies significantly on the transparency and accountability level of its member states. The compliance problems on notification issues bring into focus a critical point: the incomplete or tardy information provided by members can in fact seriously undermine the surveillance function of the WTO. Membership group reports have reported a growing sense of disappointment with the absence of shared vision and spirit of cooperation, which has extremely serious consequences for organizational coherence within the WTO. Enhancing transparency would also alleviate possible compliance issues in addition to creating a sense of renewed emphasis among members to achieve collective objectives. Addressing these failures is essential in revamping the WTOs effectiveness in ensuring its very basic function of promoting equitable and fair international trade practices in an increasingly complicated global setting (Wolfe et al., 2018).

3.2.2. Roles of the Ministerial Conference and General Council

The Ministerial Conference and the General Council are at the center of the World Trade Organization (WTO) as the most important deciding bodies guiding the organization's policies and activities. The Ministerial Conference, convened every two years or thereabouts, gathers trade ministers from member states to negotiate major aspects of international trade agreements and respond to emerging international problems in a responsive manner. It is at these conferences that major decisions on trade policy, directions for negotiations, and institutional change are made, embodying the collective will of the member states. This structure allows for extensive discussion and negotiation, which is absolutely essential in unraveling the complex tapestry of world trade—especially as nations try to reconcile their respective national interests with international obligations. As the political environment becomes increasingly divided, the role of the Ministerial Conferences to mediate between disparate interests becomes increasingly significant in avoiding a fragmented trade regime. The General Council, working in a more continuous capacity, is tasked with overseeing the day-to-day operations of the WTO as well as the enforcement of trade agreements negotiated at Ministerial Conferences. Such a dual role involves legislative in the sense of helping to create and formulate new trade rules, as well as executive in the sense of enabling it to administer dispute settlement processes. Its rulings, whether consensus or by vote, carry a significant weight in terms of compliance with and observance of WTO agreements. As the global economic environment continues to evolve, the General Council is confronted with complex legal structures that incline towards blurring the lines between trade and broader concerns such as national security and environmental problems. Overlaying these areas tends to enhance the weight of the choices made by the General Council, since it becomes a mediator that attempts to strike a balance between trade obligations and other pressing national interests and hence provide stability in international trade. Over the past few years, the Ministerial Conference and the General Council functions have been called into question in the light of the WTO's role in an increasingly dynamic world. The increasing fragmentation of trade and security issues, as pointed out in recent research, means that these organizations must adapt and revamp their proceedings to remain effective. For instance, proposals for reform of the decision-making process and increased transparency have emerged as central issues in the WTO debate. Furthermore, with an expansion of the agenda to include behind-the-border regulation, there needs to be continued communication and negotiation to establish common understanding among member nations. These reforms can promote organized political processes and enhance collective participation to ensure that the WTO will remain effective in the face of the intertwining problems of trade policy and regulatory interests since both the Ministerial Conference and General Council are able to adjust to these demands (Heath et al., 2020; Hoekman et al., 2025) (Figure 3.6).

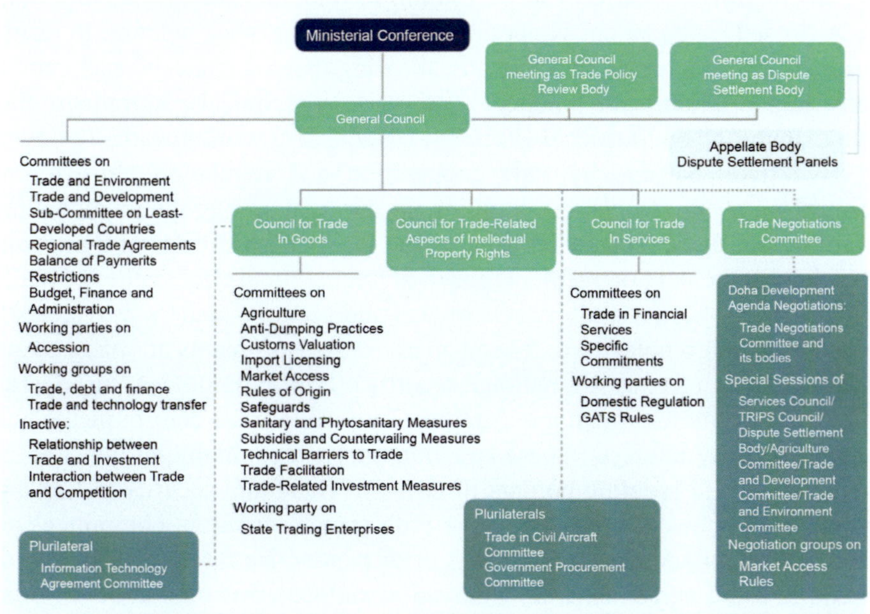

Figure 3.6. Roles of the ministerial conference and general council.

Source: https://www.wto.org/images/img_tif/wto_organigram800_e.png.

3.2.3. Functions of Various World Trade Organization (WTO) Bodies and Committees

WTO functions through numerous bodies and committees, all of which are specific to address other areas of international trade and agreements. These different entities are required to oversee the enforcement of WTO agreements as well as harmonize the negotiations between member countries. For instance, the Trade Negotiations Committee plays a central role in organizing and facilitating the negotiations for trade agreements, and the Committees on Trade and Environment and Trade and Development focus on mainstreaming environmental considerations and development needs into trade policy. Such committees serve not only as forums for discussion but also ensure cooperation among members to ensure that both developed and developing countries' opinions are considered. In addition, the cooperation between various bodies facilitates overall regulation of trade through facilitating a joint effort that supports the entire system under which international trade takes place. Significantly, specialized agencies in the WTO ensure trade rule adherence and fulfillment of commitments by member nations. As an example, the Dispute Settlement Body is the primary platform for resolution of trade disputes via an organized process to settle agreement violations. It also plays a vital function to ensure the rule of law in international trade by allowing member states to seek redress against unjustifiable trade practice. Also, various technical committees, such as the Committee on Technical Barriers to Trade, also work towards removing excessive trade barriers by state cooperation and regulation transparency. These roles are fundamental in building up the trust among the members and preventing conflicts, thereby reinforcing the legal and institutional framework that underpins the WTO agreements and their international effectiveness. Finally, the interactivity between the WTOs organs and security matters provides still another layer of complexity to its endeavors. As governments are increasingly translating trade interests into national security affairs, committees must operate within such dynamics which are changing, balancing trade commitments with changing security interests. These contemporary events highlight the strain as nations attempt to redefine borders in terms of trade and security policy. For example, where health crises converge with trade regulation, committees are assessing how to address best the impact of pandemics throughout the world on trade law and agreements. By innovation and experimentation on different strategies—such as organized political dialogue or legalism—the WTO is then able to effectively counter these complexities and develop its leadership in the new global relations paradigm (Heath et al., 2020). For this purpose, familiarity with each WTO agency and committee and its role is vital to comprehending their importance in developing the legal framework of global trade.

3.3. KEY WORLD TRADE ORGANIZATION (WTO) AGREEMENTS

In the WTO framework, large agreements comprise the foundation of global trade law, controlling the rights and obligations of member nations. The General Agreement on Tariffs and Trade (GATT), signed in 1947 and more recently under the WTO framework, is exemplary for its promotion of reducing barriers to trade and providing equal opportunities for competition. The GATT principles, including the Most Favored Nation (MFN) and National Treatment, are based on the commitment towards the non-discrimination of trade practices. Besides this, the Trade-Related Aspects of Intellectual Property Rights (TRIPS) Agreement plays a key role in maintaining the balance between the intellectual property protection and access to products required.

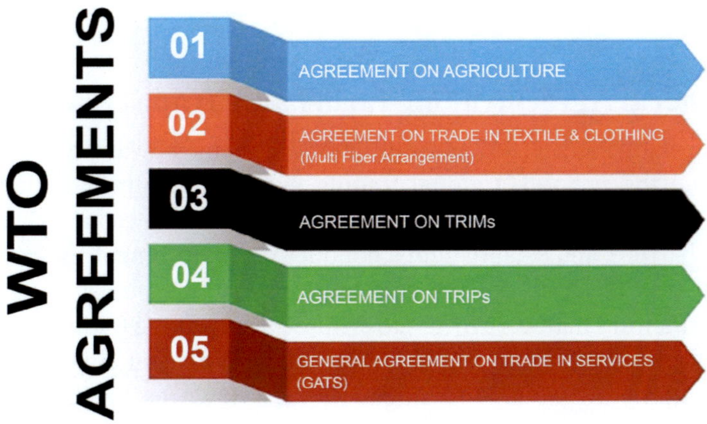

Figure 3.7. Key World Trade Organization (WTO) agreements.

Source: https://www.nextias.com/blog/wp-content/uploads/2024/08/wto-agreements.png.

The operation of these accords reveals complex legal arrangements that are aimed at promoting trade while considering the socio-economic conditions of different countries. The flexibility of the WTOs legal framework allows member countries to reconcile their trade undertakings with different economic objectives. For instance, even though they are bound by many agreements, members can still employ lawyering and litigation to construct the meaning of rules to suit their interests (Santos et al., 2012). Nations, particularly developing ones, can employ this interpretative capability as a strategy such that they can utilize legal tools to further their economic agenda and protect their regulatory sovereignty. By re-defining what is meant by "legal capacity," one realizes that states can pursue market access while also safeguarding their domestic policies, producing a more comprehensive analysis of how flexibility operates in terms of the WTO. Moreover, the inclinations which states, and particularly powerful ones like the United States, exhibit towards a rule-based system of dispute settlement reveal the intricacies of international trade politics. This kind of system prefers small states since it gives them the opportunity to hold powerful states to the terms of their agreements, a move that helps to level the stakes in international disputes (Brewster et al., 2006). International courts and settled legal systems present might change domestic bargaining power, which influences governments' ways of negotiating as well as enforcing trade agreements. Understanding this dynamic is also key to comprehending wider implications of WTO agreements on members states' trade practices, but also on their domestic regulatory institutions and the exercise of sovereignty in the international economy (Figure 3.7).

3.3.1. General Agreement on Tariffs and Trade (GATT)

The GATT, established in 1947 as a multilateral agreement, was the key institution to coordinate the pre-WTO global trading system until the establishment of the World Trade Organization in 1995. GATT aimed at reducing tariffs and other trade barriers and establishing a conductive environment for international business. It was the basis for the national treatment and most-favored-nation treatment principles that were meant to ensure parity among trading partners and minimize discriminatory conduct in foreign trade. With changing trade patterns, GATT had numerous rounds of negotiations, known as the GATT Rounds, which in an increasingly widening scope shifted away from tariffs to cover negotiations on services and intellectual property, ultimately establishing an organization that was able to deal with the complexities of international trade in the modern era. While GATTs accomplishments were immense, it was besieged with enormous issues that would ultimately lead to its restructuring into the WTO format. Member states were struggling to have sufficient enforcement channels to ensure member states adhered to the pacts, as GATT lacked substantive powers to punish violators. The limitation came to be more pronounced as globalization became more robust, promoting more interdependence among economies and sharply highlighting the necessity of an institution powerful enough to address a broader range of matters pertaining to trade. The WTO emerged out of this context, with an aim to remedy the deficiencies of GATT by establishing a more robust legal and institutional basis. The transition from GATT to WTO was not one of labels alone, but a radical shift towards an even more systematic and enforceable system of trade rules that tried to deal with the intricacy in international trade. An examination of the legacy of GATT within the WTO agreements confirms the intricate dance between past trade regulation and contemporary legal orders. As the development of the WTO continues apace, there are intense pressures from both internal and external interests that challenge its efficacy as a multilateral trading organization. Evolution such as the occurrence of regional trade pacts and bi- and plurilateral pacts represents a potential shift in the trend in international trade, potentially undermining the universal applicability of the WTO rules. In the opinion of scholars, while GATT managed to establish certain rudimentary principles for trade, the current crises facing the WTO demonstrate the need for developing strategies in line with the multi-faceted nature of world trade relations in the modern age. The dialogue between GATTs initial blueprints and the new challenges of the WTO offers important lessons in the future direction of international trade regulation, and underlines the necessity of forcing legal frameworks to adapt in order to preserve effective multilateralism in a constantly changing world.

3.3.2. Agreement on Trade-Related Aspects of Intellectual Property Rights (TRIPS)

The TRIPS Agreement is a milestone shift in the international trade law, making intellectual property a key aspect of global commerce. Adopted at the conclusion of the Uruguay Round of negotiations, TRIPS established the minimum standards for protecting various intellectual property rights like copyrights, trademarks, and patents. TRIPS addresses issues about overprotection strangling innovation and slowing down access to essential products, particularly in the developing world. As the WTO seeks to harmonize the conflicting interests of its numerous member states, TRIPS graphically depicts the challenges in unifying intellectual property law and reconciling developing nations' needs. The TRIPS controversy highlights the intricate dynamics of trade, economic progress, and equitable access to knowledge, and underscores the necessities of rationalizing international law in the face of evolving conditions in the era of globalization. Furthermore, the TRIPS Agreement has provisions whereby member states can accommodate a degree of flexibility in enforcing these standards, particularly in the area of public health and access to medicines. Article 27.3(b) demonstrates this provision by stating the principle of recognizing nations like Kenya's right to derive local standards for biodiversity and farmers' rights. But a closer look at Kenya's compliance reveals a mismatch between international obligation asserted under TRIPS and national legal framework. Specifically, while Kenya tries to make use of the Article 27.3(b) flexibility to enhance distributive justice and public benefit, the country's adherence to the UPOV convention has somewhat limited its policy space. This trend reflects the challenges faced by states in attempting to reconcile national laws with international agreements which aim to promote equitable resource distribution and protect cultural expressions in an era of globalization (Rangnekar et al., 2008). An examination of the interplay between TRIPS and human rights involves an appreciation of how the agreement interfaces with broader regimes that govern intellectual property. Recent research points to a growing recognition of the need to take a human rights approach to intellectual property law, cited in UNESCO, WHO, and WIPO-driven policies. These models seek to find a balance between the relationship between the right to intellectual property and society's right to access knowledge and cultural expression. For instance, the General Comment on economic, social, and cultural rights creates a platform for questioning the exclusivity that is typically designed into intellectual property protection. This new human rights discussion not only faults present intellectual property regimes but also provokes debate about changing the agreements to be more humanitarian in nature (Helfer et al., 2007). As intellectual property law and human rights continue to develop in interaction with each other, the TRIPS Agreement continues to be at the center of addressing these pressing global issues (Figure 3.8).

Figure 3.8. Trade Related Aspects of Intellectual Property Rights (TRIPS).

Source: https://external-content.duckduckgo.com/iu/?u=https%3A%2F%2 Fblog-media.testbook.com%2Fblog%2Fwp-content%2Fuploads%2F2023%2F08%2Ftrade-related-aspects-of-intellectual-property-rights-1aec4d34.webp&f=1&nofb=1&ipt=b3b57eb34e7e0b4c8a739ba84d49ed6677cb8f70248b577f9480ad96bfe78ad1.

3.3.3. Agreement on the Application of Sanitary and Phytosanitary Measures (SPS)

The SPS Agreement is a vital component of the World Trade Organizations (WTO) law, whose role is to ensure human, animal, and plant life and health as well as the facilitation of trade. Through the establishment of standards that member states are required to put in place in regards to food safety as well as animal and plant health standards, the SPS Agreement attempts to balance the objectives of protection of health and the stimulation of international trade. This agreement addresses the oft-contentious intersection of trade policy and health, calling on countries to adhere to scientifically sound standards and not impose arbitrary standards that would disrupt trade flows. As countries make their way through these measures, the SPS Agreement underscores the importance of cooperation among countries to ensure that health needs are not unnecessarily closing off trade opportunities, paving the way for a safer and more open trading environment. The significance of the SPS Agreement also comes out vividly through its impact on national regulation and policy systems in member nations. Based on the principal-agent theory, governments have delegated the regulation to international standards in the SPS, which can alleviate the political cost associated with policymaking loss of control.

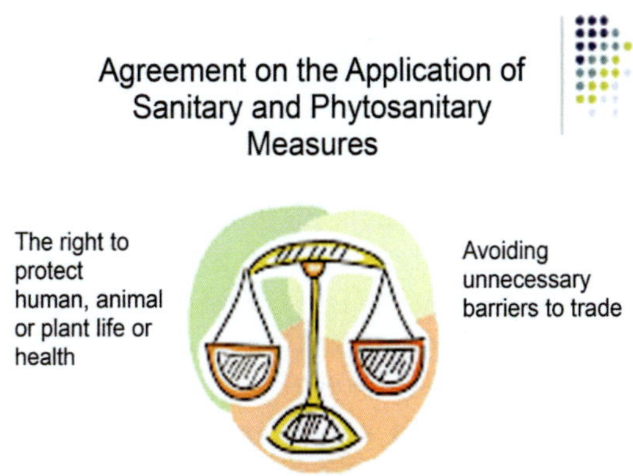

Figure 3.9. Agreement on the application of sanitary and phytosanitary measures (SPS).

Source: https://encrypted-tbn0.gstatic.com/images?q=tbn:ANd9GcTXDy7X3HGBsivZwHcTx_n6jmPIbz37i6EK2w&s.

Through the selection of institutionalized international cooperation outside the WTO framework, countries, especially developing countries, sought to synchronize local policy with global standards for improved competitiveness in trade. This delegation is assigned the problem of overestimation of the benefits of such standards compared to the underestimation of losses in sovereignty. When states face SPS measures, they must balance differential cost-benefit analyses by domestic interest groups in order to effectively balance international norms and protection of their own national interests (Buthe et al., 2008). The impact of the SPS Agreement is especially clear in developing countries, where compliance with strict SPS standards can be a daunting feat. For instance, Pakistan's experience is reflective of the difficulties involved in meeting these international norms, which can jeopardize the capacity of the country to export food and agriculture products correctly. Despite continued efforts aimed at reducing distortions in trade under the SPS Agreement, some of the key problems identified still exist to deter participation and adherence by nations like Pakistan. Compliance problems through the absence of resources and challenges with the international legal framework often render traded products from developing countries more limited. The problem raises questions about the fairness of the SPS Agreement as far as developing countries are concerned, and whether reform needs to be undertaken to ensure fair access to international markets (Mustafa, 2025) (Figure 3.9).

3.4. DISPUTE RESOLUTION MECHANISM (DRM)

The effectiveness of DRM under the World Trade Organization (WTO) is the cornerstone of global trade law. It is the core mechanism whereby member states can settle trade disputes arising from violations of WTO agreements. The mechanism is characterized by its ability to provide an organized and legally enforceable process that asserts members' rights and obligations. This is especially relevant with the high level of interdependencies generated by globalization. Of note is that the WTOs Dispute Settlement Understanding (DSU) has adapted to suit the complexity of issues facing modern trade, navigating between the imperative for adherence to fairness and transparency principles. In this way, the DRM serves not only as a means of conflict resolution but also ensures the rule of law in international trade, providing a more stable and foreseeable international trading environment. The interaction between the WTOs DRM and regional trade agreements (RTAs) has prompted much scholarly discourse, especially in light of the rising incidence of RTAs worldwide. The disputes that can be caused by duplicate provisions for dispute settlement call for scrutiny of the connection between such agreements and the WTO regime. For instance, the Appellate Body's ruling in Brazil Tyres refers to legal concerns that can occur when domestic regulation is subject to both WTO disciplines and regional commitments. In this, Brazil's application of MERCOSUR tribunal provisions to justify its import barriers was determined to be insufficient by the Appellate Body, illustrating the importance of adherence to the WTOs stricter standards. This case is a very good illustration of how conflicting obligations may create conflicts, illustrating the necessity for clarity in the international trade legal system to effectively address such conflicts and foster cooperation among trading nations (Hillman et al., 2009). Furthermore, incoherence of different mechanisms of dispute settlement challenges the future of global trade governance. Effective dispute settlement is not only crucial for sustaining trade relations but also to guarantee that economic arrangements yield concrete benefits across different parties. Failure by the Arab countries to accomplish economic integration signals the complex dynamics entailed as different legal traditions intersect. As has been explained in the context of the problems of Arab countries, structuring economic agreements demands structural reforms and harmonization of how disputes are settled (Malkawi et al., 2007). The harmonization would not only enhance mechanisms for settling disputes but also ensure more cooperation and trust among countries engaging in regional and international trade activities. It is crucial to solve these intricate issues in the development of the legal underpinnings of international commerce under the framework of emerging WTO agreements.

3.4.1. Overview of the Dispute Settlement Process

The World Trade Organization (WTO) dispute settlement process is a significant procedure for resolving trade disagreements between member countries. This process is guided by the Dispute Settlement Understanding (DSU), which prescribes the steps and procedures parties must follow when a trade dispute arises. Right from the start, the process centers on consultation as the initial line of approach, compelling parties to negotiate and find mutually acceptable solutions. Where consultations fail, the matter may be referred to a panel stage, where a neutral independent panel of specialists reviews the evidence and arguments presented by the parties in dispute. The complexity of this initial phase reflects the importance of effective preparation and presentation by member states, whose findings at these proceedings can carry long-term influences on patterns of trade and global relations. When a panel releases its report, the affected parties can appeal the decision to the WTO Appellate Body. In this regard, the appellate procedure plays a critical role since it provides a further review of the legal interpretations made by the panel and ensures that trade rules are consistently applied. The process of appeal is an essential factor in ensuring the integrity of the dispute settlement process since it seeks to rectify possible miscarriages of judgment that may be caused by the conclusions drawn by the first-tier panels. Recent issues like delay and controversy on the Appellate Body's operation have been questioning the success of this stage of judicial review. The ability of member states to engage in appellate proceedings highlights the importance of legal capacity under the WTO system so that they can vigorously defend their interests in the context of the prevailing legal constraints established by the agreements. In addition, the broader implications of the process of dispute settlement extend beyond the particular case; it informs WTO rule development and member relations in the system of global trade. As states navigate the complexities of the process, they do not simply seek to protect their trade interests, but are also participants in the collective development of international trade law. The reflexive nature of disputes generates interpretations and applications of agreements that have the ability to remake member obligations and rights. This dynamic process is central to shaping a member's regulatory autonomy, since nations are able to learn from their experiences and outcomes in order to reinforce their bargaining roles in subsequent interactions. Significantly, this evolving nature of this mechanism captures the ongoing interaction of power and policy within the world of international trade, illustrating how states are able to use legal instruments to advance strategic interests, as identified in Santos et al. (2012) (Figure 3.10).

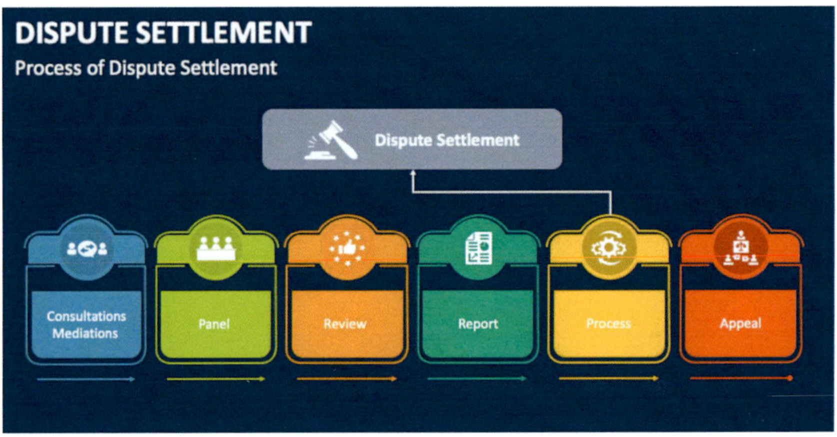

Figure 3.10. Dispute settlement.

Source: https://www.collidu.com/media/catalog/product/img/f/3/f3134c5113020d-821dc53cf0b00f7736bd4d1c9743b463d85d2ad1a65778a42d/dispute-settlement-slide1.png.

3.4.2. Role of the Dispute Settlement Body (DSB)

The World Trade Organization (WTO) DSB is a pillar of the international trading system, offering a formal mechanism for the resolution of disputes among member countries. Established under the Dispute Settlement Understanding (DSU), the DSB is tasked with ensuring the rule of law in international trade by ensuring that trade concessions do not remain theoretical but are effected through binding decisions. This formal process of dispute settlement is critical to ensuring that a peaceful trading regime is maintained, as it provides countries with an avenue to seek redress when they feel their rights under WTO accords have been infringed upon. In the midst of ongoing criticism for being unfair and ineffective, the DSB is a significant component of the multi-level legal framework that governs international trade, maintaining a promise of equitable and open practices in international commerce. Aside from arbitration, the DSB also plays a crucial role in the development of international trade law. Through its decisions, the DSB sets precedents that not only affect future disputes, but also inform the interpretation of WTO agreements themselves. This interpretive role is significant, especially in light of the complexity and evolving nature of trade relations. While member countries struggle with the complexity of competitive global markets, the DSBs adaptability, as it adjusts and responds to emerging trade practice, becomes even more essential. The conclusions and analysis derived through the DSB can possess the capacity to influence national trade practices and policies, thereby making it all the more indispensable to have a strong dispute settlement forum that can manage complicated issues in trade law effectively (Jackson et al., 2004). Even though it is important, the DSB is subject to huge criticism and questioning, i.e., its flexibility and effectiveness in the current global trade environment. Critics observe that the body has progressively been unable to handle the pressures of escalating nationalism and bilateral free trade agreements, which endanger the multilateral trading system post-World War II. Against the horizon of these pressures, it is important to observe that the legitimacy of the DSB depends on how effective the WTO as a whole is perceived to be. As states engage in fresh trade agreements, one must consider if the DSB can recast its role so that it is better equipped to address internal contradictions as well as external pressures. Acknowledging the shifting reality of global trade, it is essential that WTO members reconfirm their trust in the DSB so that it remains an essential tool for the application of the multilateral trading order (Bäumler et al., 2020) (Figure 3.11).

Figure 3.11. Role of the dispute settlement body (DSB).

*Source:*https://encrypted-tbn0.gstatic.com/images?q=tbn:ANd9GcQQYK5PamN6-cCpGDH3zMACExvseCx_07qvAQ&s.

3.4.3. Case Studies of Notable Disputes

The World Trade Organization (WTO) has been the hub institution for resolving international trade disputes, consistently bringing into relief important tensions in the international trading system. An important case is the United States imposition of tariffs on steel and aluminum imports, which precipitated a chain of retaliatory measures from a range of countries, including the European Union and Canada. This dispute raised the contradictions of weighing national security against international trade treaties, testing the validity of the use of national security as a justification for trade restrictions. The Dispute Settlement Body of the WTO ultimately played a central part in resolving the dispute, revealing the intricacies of WTO regulations in its response to unilateral trade practices. These cases are crucial in demonstrating the importance of the WTO framework in resolving disputes that could undermine international trade stability and economic cooperation.

China and the U.S. also have a long-standing dispute regarding intellectual property rights (IPR). Under the WTOs Agreement on Trade-Related Aspects of Intellectual Property Rights (TRIPS), the two countries have engaged in a bitter war comprising allegations of infringement and measures of enforcement. The U.S. accused China of not adequately protecting American patents, thus leading to economic loss to American companies. China, in turn, defended its move on the basis that American companies benefited from the same environment it established to promote technological advancement. The intervention by the WTOs highlighted the complexities of IPR in international agreements and the manner through which nations' interests compromise international trade standards. The consequences of such rulings are crucial to the world economy and multinational companies alike, which is reflective of why there has to be a clear policy within the WTO framework.

Ultimately, interference with trade and climate policy has been a contentious issue in a majority of WTO cases, particularly concerning whether environmental protection can restrict trade. In the case of the European Union's proposal to bring about a carbon border adjustment mechanism, many nations wondered if such policy constituted an acceptable trade barrier or necessary climate action. The debate around such a plan reflects underlying contradictions within environmental sustainability and trade liberalization, a problem that has never been so relevant in the wake of increasing global climate change. The WTO facilitation of such disputes sets the tone for the relevance of adopting a holistic stance that harmonizes trade agreements and climate pledges. With the globe exposed to twin imperatives of leveraging economic growth as a tool to meet economic aspirations while conserving the environment, this area of study through the case studies underscores the imperative necessity for adaptive legal systems that can address shifting global agendas (Ackerman et al., 2016; Anderson et al., 2013).

3.5. IMPACT OF WORLD TRADE ORGANIZATION (WTO) AGREEMENTS ON MEMBER STATES

The WTO agreements significantly influence the economic framework of member countries, promoting an open competitive world market. With the provision of rules-based solutions to trade policy, member states are compelled to adopt neoliberal economic policies that have the tendency to favor free trade and open markets. The change can stimulate national economies by enhancing access to foreign markets, foreign direct investment, and technological collaboration. However, their implementation has not been free of challenges. The less developed economies may struggle to adapt where the outcome can be adverse in the manner of increased competition that leads to the domestic industries as well as job security coming under threat. For instance, imposition of rigid standards can work in favor of large, technologically advanced countries at the expense of small economies where they lack the requisite resources needed to fairly catch up (Chang et al., 2004). Moreover, the WTO's dispute settlement process is a vital element in maintaining trade peace among members since it offers a legal avenue for settling disputes. The legal system operates to defuse tensions in trade and ensure compliance with agreed rules, thus stabilizing and equalizing trade relationships.

Nonetheless, the efficiency of this mechanism is occasionally challenged since member states are sometimes able to use loopholes in the agreements in order to protect their own interests. Trade-dispute-prone countries can experience severe economic consequences, both to their internal policies and diplomacy with other nations. The conflict between imposing compliance and providing exceptions for national interest usually leads to confrontation, triggering argument regarding the imperative of reform in the approach the WTOs mechanism responds to special needs of diverse economies (Howse et al., 2014). Apart from their economic impact, the WTO agreements also influence public policy among member countries, with particular mention of health, environment, and labor standards. Adherence to global trading requirements generally involves countries amending current legislation or developing new legislation to comply with global requirements. This can create conflict between domestic and foreign priorities, especially where public health or environmental concerns are at issue. For example, a government might prioritize public health measures over trade requirements, raising issues as to the impact of such measures on their status in the international trading community. Lastly, the interaction of WTO agreements and national policies illustrates the complexities of international trade governance and serves as testimony to the necessity for member states to navigate such complexities wisely, without having international necessities suppress their national interests (Chang et al., 2004).

3.5.1. Economic Implications for Developing Countries

The WTO agreements present both opportunities and challenges to developing countries, significantly altering their trajectories towards economic development. Historically, these nations have engaged WTO rules in ways that further or hinder their economic aspirations. The agreements are formulated in such manners that are most favorable to developed countries, which possess the resources and capacity to handle complex trade rules. However, the legal obligations established by the WTO can also be used as a platform upon which developing countries can negotiate for their economic interests. By employing interpretations of WTO rules, nations like Brazil and Mexico have shown how strategically litigation can enhance their policy independence in order to pursue targeted economic strategies within the limits of global regulations, ultimately in aid of their development goals (Santos et al., 2012). Implications of WTO agreements reach beyond traditional trade measures; they extend to influencing labor mobility and migrant labor management. The majority of developing countries are eager to benefit from labor service exportation but are significantly constrained by existing international legal frameworks such as GATS Mode 4. The mode primarily emphasizes temporary service supplier movement of high-skilled service providers with limited space for migration of low-skilled labor. Hence, the restrictive conditions of such contracts undermine the potential economic benefits gained from labor mobility and remittances for developing nations. In the absence of large-scale bilateral labor contracts and further integration of worker groups into multilateral arrangements, economies in most developing countries remain weak, thus undermining their growth prospects (Ramjoue, 2025). Furthermore, developing countries are confronted with complex regulatory systems that have a tendency to prioritize interest in developed economies. The ability to deploy WTO rules for purpose becomes a necessity for these nations since they possess the ability to reshape international economic policy to their development needs. The concept of "developmental legal capacity" thus enters the picture as a critical element in this regard, allowing developing nations to deploy legal weapons as instruments of growth while safeguarding their unique policy needs. By active participation in the negotiation processes and by playing their roles, such states can negotiate spaces of different economic methods that appeal to their specific aspirations. Thus, while the WTO arrangement would initially appear to be restrictive, it so happens that with close inspection, it can be a tool of economic empowerment, providing developing nations with an opportunity to protect their interests within an internationalized economy (Santos et al., 2012) (Figure 3.12).

Figure 3.12. World Trade Organization (WTO) agreements economic implications for developing countries.

Source: https://cdn.educba.com/academy/wp-content/uploads/2023/03/Advantages-Disadvantages-of-WTO.png.

3.5.2. Trade Liberalization and Market Access

Trade liberalization, facilitated by the World Trade Organization (WTO), is a core element of enhancing market access for countries around the globe. By reducing tariffs as well as non-tariff barriers, the WTO agreements encourage member countries to participate in fair competition, which, subsequently, contributes to economic growth. This liberalization provides developing nations the opportunity to make entry into more advanced markets, providing them with the opportunities to boost their exports. The experience of Costa Rica's trade liberalization indicates how countries can apply WTO rules on antidumping actions and safeguard measures to lay a solid legal foundation that protects local industries while developing market access. This dual focus encourages modernization within national industries in addition to acknowledging that enhanced foreign competition will be accompanied by problems but also provide room for economic growth (Monge-Arino et al., 2025). Despite the difficulty posed by the complexity of WTO rules, countries have immense room for discretion to interpret and apply these rules in a manner aimed at enhancing their competitive market position. This fine understanding is crucial for nations as they strive to make market access and national policy objectives a reality.

As an illustration, by applying good legal strategies, Brazil and Mexico have demonstrated that it is feasible to play around with their rule-setting structure within the parameters set forth by the WTO. Their observations show that while WTO obligations involve some type of limitation, they also provide opportunity for the use of legal mechanisms to support economic policy measures favoring domestic interests. In effect, the developmental legal capability which such countries leverage taps into the potential use of liberalization as both a market-opening tool and a protectionist tool for sensitive industries (Santos et al., 2012). In addition, the relationship between economic liberalization at the international level and national economic objectives creates core questions on how it is possible to balance world integration and national sovereignty. While nations dance this tango, safeguarding domestic industries against unfair trade practices becomes a priority. Inside Costa Rica, legal frameworks established under the WTO have allowed the government to balance challenges from increased foreign competition with safeguarding domestic market realities. This is an excellent illustration of how WTO arrangements can be employed not as restrictive means, but as channels whereby states can shape market access and pattern of trade. Thus, liberalization of trade comes across as an intricate juggling act, where the quest for access to markets is weighed against the imperatives of safeguarding home economic interests in the greater global trading world (Monge-Arino et al., 2025) (Figure 3.13).

Figure 3.13. Trade liberalization and market access.

Source: https://external-content.duckduckgo.com/iu/?u=https%3A%2F%2F1.bp.blogspot.com%2F-YRUFh0Hb4Ec%2FU_ykYDI_1OI%2FAAAAAAAAAyA%2FkVsSE0sehf4%2Fs1600%2FA%252B-%252BTrade%252BLiberalization.jpg&f=1&nofb=1&ipt=359b40217f160a564effd77dac24252be5785eb720aeff9bd876ab48956e1a2c.

3.5.3. Challenges Faced by Member States in Compliance

Member states' challenges in compliance with WTO agreements are diverse and typically imagined within the backdrop of the complexities of global affairs and economic interdependence. With increasing interconnectivity of the world economy, states are increasingly grappling with how to balance domestic policy harmonization in line with international standards. This harmonization can be particularly daunting for low-income countries that may not have the institutional ability or resources to adopt complete legal structures required of the WTO. The inability to obtain binding agreements at international levels is an indication of waning confidence in multilateralism and hence points to a lack of confidence in the existing structures of the WTO.

Since countries are experiencing these tensions, more support mechanisms to engender compliance are necessary, given the widening economic disparities and different national interests (Hillman et al., 2018). Moreover, the Doha Round talks freeze is proof of the complexity of achieving effective compliance between member countries. Trade liberalization negotiations have been stalled, casting doubts on the WTOs role in keeping up with the dynamics of global commerce today. Failure to make headway is an indication of the intricacies of national interests conflicting with shared ends. Most nations have focused on bilateral or regional arrangements at the expense of full-scale multilateral approaches, which has inadvertently undermined the WTOs role. In light of these contexts, it is critical that the WTO revisit its plans and create a more comprehensive approach to ensure the diverse interests of its member states are addressed. This may involve rewriting negotiation mechanisms or alternative areas of priority that are harmonic with the current economic landscape, such as trade facilitation mechanisms and non-tariff barriers, which would help support compliance practices (Dhar et al., 2013).

Further, the accelerated trend of the global production networks also complicate the problem of compliance within the WTO system. With intensifying globalizations, enterprises and countries have to face a reality of complicated supply chains and global cooperation. Such a reality demands a robust legal system that can effectively address and regulate these new economic forces. Most member states also lack appropriate legislation or mechanisms for implementing such complexities, leading to inconsistent compliance with WTO obligations. In addition, pressure from abroad to be compliant with international norms might cost local development goals, pitting national policy and international obligations against each other. To address these challenges, the WTO should promote capacity-building initiatives that enable member nations to enhance their legal systems and become more efficient in fulfilling international trade standards, thus promoting a more equitable and functional trading system (Hillman et al., 2018).

3.6. CRITICISMS OF THE WORLD TRADE ORGANIZATION (WTO) FRAMEWORK

The WTO has been under heavy criticism for its seeming inability to adequately address the interests of developing countries in its framework. According to its critics, the negotiating ground of the WTO is predisposed to favor the interests of the incumbent economic titans by undermining the voice and interests of developing countries. Such unevenness is particularly evident on major ministerial gatherings, such as the Cancun Ministerial Conference, where the lack of a more reflective bargaining process has been recognized as an systemic flaw. Neglecting to adequately incorporate the perspectives of these nations not only raises ethical issues about democratic legitimacy in the WTOs institutional structure but also suggests that perhaps new model for developing international trade regulation will be required, one that can better accommodate disparate needs and circumstances of global economic players (Macmillan et al., 2004).

The second source of dispute under the WTO framework relates to individual agreements, such as the Agreement on the Application of Sanitary and Phytosanitary Measures (SPS Agreement). The SPS Agreement, whose aim is to standardize food standards worldwide, has inadvertently favored the more developed nations, whose standards are higher and aligned to international levels. The third world, getting itself entangled into this complex web of standards, does not possess the institutional and technical capacity to take an active part in negotiations at a platform like CODEX. Their capacity to export agriculture produce is therefore significantly affected, as they are not in a position to adhere to the standards prescribed. This scenario is an indication of a larger criticism of the mechanisms of the WTO, that while theoretically liberalizing trade, could disproportionately advantage some nations over others and reinforce patterns of inequality in international trade (Chowdhury et al., 2008). In addition, the focus of the WTO on market-based principles is itself cause for considerable concern in terms of its compatibility with political and social imperatives within member countries. The critics say that the system prioritizes economic efficiency over social well-being and environmental sustainability. The WTO policies have a tendency to put free trade on a pedestal as an economic fix in disregard of the myriad of social ills arising from unregulated trade. Neoliberalism has a tendency to worsen poverty and inequalities, particularly in the developing world where socioeconomic conditions do not support aggressive liberalization. The need for a fairer system that reconciles the benefits of trade with protection of home industries and adherence to social standards is important in order to realize a fairer trading world and address issues facing the WTO (Macmillan et al., 2004).

3.6.1. Concerns Over Transparency and Accountability

World Trade Organization (WTO) has, over the years, come under criticism regarding its transparency and accountability mechanisms. As one of the significant players in global trade governance, the WTO's decision-making processes are often seen as closed, barred from the public by its limited access to information on negotiations and agreements. The situation undermines transparency immensely for those interested parties that would like to have a stake or hold the organization accountable. Amidst such worries, the calls for reform become stronger, calling for the establishment of more transparent communication channels and mechanisms that allow member states and civil society to understand and influence WTO actions. Such reform could not only enhance the legitimacy of the organization but also its general effectiveness in addressing global economic issues, thereby lending weight to the observation that transparency plays an essential part in trade fairness and justice (Brown et al., 2025). In answering charges of accountability problems, it is worthwhile to keep in mind the democratic deficit inherent in the WTO system. According to the critics, the organization lacks sufficient tools to involve national parliaments and civil society and, as a consequence, the distance between trade policymakers and people whose lives are affected by their policies grows.

By encouraging greater parliamentary involvement and creating transnational networks, the WTO would be better positioned to face the accountability challenge. Events such as the Parliamentary Conference on the WTO (PCWTO) illustrate the potential of parliamentary institutions to enhance democratic governance in global trade issues. Engaging national parliaments not only validates WTO decision-making but also initiates considerable discourse that weighs diverse interests of stakeholders, ultimately strengthening the argument for accountability as a key component of successful global economic governance (Krajewski et al., 2025). Moreover, greater accountability and transparency extends beyond institutional reform; it encompasses the broad promise of combating corruption and promoting ethical behavior in international economic governance. The G20 Summit, for instance, is now a platform for reorganizing global economic institutions, where anti-corruption measures and accountability mechanisms are emphasized in the WTO. Dialogue on these reforms recognizes the need to establish strict standards and processes for ensuring that all member countries adhere to fair trade practices. By integrating accountability and transparency into the fabric of its agreements, the WTO is able to not only create trust among its members but also reinforce its position as a facilitator of fair trade internationally, dispelling apprehensions that discredit it and neutralize its function in the international economic community (Brown et al., 2025).

3.6.2. Critiques Regarding the Influence of Developed Nations

The influence of the advanced world in the World Trade Organization (WTO) has been accompanied by several criticisms, most notably the issue of regulatory autonomy of less economically developed nations. It has been claimed that the WTO's legal regimes incline towards protecting the interests of the developed world at the expense of developing nations, thereby weakening the latter's ability to implement policies in line with their socio-economic environments. This disparity is further added to by the uneven legal and economic power of industrialized countries, which enable them to frame the negotiations and dictate the interpretation of WTO agreements. While others contend that these international legal obligations merely constrain states' regulatory freedom, careful consideration should take into account that developing nations also have avenues wherein they can articulate their interests and increase their policy space, as comparative analyses between Brazil and Mexico reveal. This reflective regard points to the prevailing tensions in the WTO setting with respect to equity and representation. Besides, structural advantages derived by developed economies extend beyond mere economic power, influencing organizational patterns at the WTO, too. Conventions that have become entrenched, i.e., that trade liberalization is always a good thing, are prone to neglect legitimate developing country concerns regarding food security, public health, and the environment.

These prescriptions tend to restrict the ability of nations to follow their own special development objectives as each of them chooses to do so and to apply protection whenever needed. For instance, measures that could favor domestic industries or conserve essential resources could be perceived as protectionism and could prompt legal response from powerful trading nations. This is so under the inherent power imbalances of WTO agreements under which developing nations struggle to voice their interests even if they explain their needs under the regime of international law and trade. The call for the reform of such power relations is important in establishing an even more equitable trading platform. Further, the intersection of trade law and human rights offers a new dimension to the reach of developed nations' influence on the world's regimes of governance. Intellectual property policies shed illumination on the manner in which developed nations design policies that are not necessarily suited for the developmental objectives of poorer nations. The squeeze for robust intellectual property safeguards is most commonly portrayed as a mechanism to spur innovation but can simultaneously prevent access to essential medicines and technology in the developing world. Legal institutions for advancing human rights, as debated in recent literature, emphasize weighting intellectual property rights against public health interests to ensure that the benefits of innovation are accessible to all. Such premises highlight the potential risk of dissonance between model-trailer trade agreements by advanced economies and the pressing social justice challenges facing less developed economies, and hence the need to critically examine how such influences virtually continue to perpetuate inequalities in the practice of international trade.

3.6.3. Debates on Environmental and Labor Standards

The debates regarding environmental and labor standards within the context of the World Trade Organization (WTO) agreements highlight the built-in tension among international trade liberalization and protection of social and environmental rights. Those who believe in strict labor and environmental standards argue that international trade is to be governed by standards that promote ethical interests, keeping the countries from resorting to lower standards for competitive reasons. This perspective presumes that without strict regulations, firms will be able to opt for maximizing profit at the cost of labor welfare and environmental integrity at the cost of a race to the bottom. Critics of the approach, however, argue that imposing high standards on everyone's plate has the danger of inhibiting economic progress, particularly among developing nations relying heavily on trade-exposed industries. The dilemma, thus, is to develop a framework that reconciles economic interests with the need to protect labor rights and environment. In the quest for global economic expansion, the intersection between labor standards and the environment creates a complex discourse. Some authors reason that a collective approach to these standards can be used to promote both social justice and environmental resilience. For instance, advancing labor standards can potentially lead to improved wages and conditions that provoke consumer demand, which can in turn benefit the world economy.

As constructed in arguments over global labor solidarity, workers in various regions of the planet need not be adversaries; their commonalities can lead to more balanced resource allocation and fairer labor practices across frontiers. This interdependence implies that improvements in labor practices can have repercussions for economic stability, which in turn can enable workers around the world to thrive rather than merely survive, justifying the argument that lower wages in one part of the world cannot be viewed in isolation from the global workforce dynamic (Athreya et al., 2000). Compounding the complexities of the debates are the differing views regarding democracy and governance practices in global trade scenarios, as highlighted by initiatives like the Rockefeller Brothers Fund Democratic Practice–Global Governance portfolio. The initiative aims to enhance democratic principles that serve as the foundation for negotiation processes around trade, climate, and development finance and highlighting the imperative of openness and accountability in the way these policies are formulated and implemented. By prioritizing participation and innovation in governance, advocates seek to ensure that all stakeholders, particularly those from marginalized communities, have a voice in the discussions shaping their futures. Investment in such governance strategies at the intersection of trade and environmental issues could encourage a more inclusive debate that addresses workers' rights and green issues concurrently in service to the higher purpose of equitable global governance in the market (Hite et al., 2016).

SUMMARY

A survey of the WTO Agreements and jurisprudence, it must be understood that these are the cornerstones of global trade regulation, offering a system based on rules that seeks to promote fairness and predictability. The triumph of the WTO depends on how it can enforce and interpret the agreements uniformly. As suggested in earlier analyses, responding to treaty interpretation calls for a composite approach, taking into account not just the text but also preparatory work and intent of the parties, and even the history of GATT practice. This interpretive critique is not merely abstract; it has tangible real-world consequences regarding the resolution of conflicts and the way member states deal with complex trade issues, ultimately deciding the effectiveness of the WTOs legal framework and how it develops over time according to shifts in global trade patterns (Jackson et al., 2004). Furthermore, the interplay among different legal principles guiding international agreements has gigantic consequences for the viability of multilateral cooperation. As mentioned, conditionality, separation, and open rules all represent different regimes for structuring cross-issue cooperation. Being familiar with these regimes is important to being able to comprehend how nations plan within the frameworks of the WTO agreements. For instance, conditionality can facilitate cooperation where environmental stakes are low so that trade agreements can proceed with reduced obstruction. However, environmental compliance intricacies can ruin such cooperation where stakes are high. Thus, how nations negotiate and uphold these principles directly affects the effectiveness of the WTO in solving not just trade but international problems as well (Conconi et al., 2001). Ultimately, the fate of the WTO depends on its adaptability and member states' commitment to negotiate in good faith. As the world evolves, so too must the legal frameworks governing international trade. The ongoing controversy over the interpretation of treaties, blended with the necessity for a pragmatic policy of cooperation, brings into focus the necessity for an evolutionary legal system that can fit in with diverse interests and encourage cooperation among states. In the coming future, the WTO must look into making its agreements more transparent and having more effective enforcement mechanisms so that it continues to stay relevant and credible in shaping the future of global trade law, and thus enhance its active contribution in developing equitable economic growth.

WTO agreements are valuable in that they are critical legal frameworks that facilitate international trade by restricting obstacles and promoting the openness of member nations. Through the establishment of a stable trading atmosphere, these agreements reduce uncertainty, allow firms to make plans accordingly, and spur competition, hence leading to improved economic growth. The harmonization of trading regulations not only benefits developed economies but also gives developing economies an opportunity to become part of the world economy. This open-ended framework has very important implications for sustainable development and poverty alleviation because the equal access to global markets has the potential to strongly empower economies that are looking for expansion. Moreover, the WTOs dispute settlement provisions ensure that trade disputes are settled in a neutral and effective manner, facilitating members' adherence to the agreements and enhancing their effectiveness. While helpful, the WTO agreements have been criticized and put under the spotlight, particularly in relation to how they can address issues of today's trade. As economies develop, there arise new challenges like geo-economic competition and subsidy wars among countries, which the current system is not adequately capable of addressing. For instance, the current system of categorizing subsidies into prohibited and actionable is now considered not sufficient to deal with the dynamism of modern markets. Hence, there has been a growing need to rebalance these regulations to accommodate the diversified nature of today's trading patterns. Such recommendations as the initiation of work programs at ministerial meetings, as suggested in the subsidy debate, aim to give new life to the agreements and render them relevant to the contemporary context (Hoekman et al., 2020). Such a realignment is essential in ensuring the WTO's position as an important player in economic global governance. In addition, new trade agreements and partners are a reflection of the need for the WTO to strengthen its frameworks so that it can keep up with the competition and remain effective. For instance, proposals such as the proposed China-Gulf Cooperation Council Free Trade Agreement, to be a comprehensive trade and investment agreement, test the WTOs existing frameworks and rules (Puig et al., 2017). They indicate the importance of WTO agreements in shaping international trade standards as well as the necessity for continuous review and adaptation. Through confronting these evolving challenges, WTO agreements can exert more impact on building a fair and balanced global trading regime. Finally, the success of the WTO lies in its ability to review and update its agreements so that they can be in the interest of all member states and sustainable economic growth across the borders.

REFERENCES

1. Ackerman, F., Bernasconi, N., Cabré, M. M., et al. (2016). Trade in the balance: Reconciling trade and climate policy: Report of the Working Group on Trade, Investment, and Climate Policy. https://open.bu.edu/bitstream/2144/22909/1/Pardee_TradeClimate_110316final.pdf (accessed on 30th October 2025).
2. Anderson, S., Aruaz, A., de Paula, L. F., Francis, et al. (2013). Capital account regulations and the trading system: A compatibility review. https://open.bu.edu/bitstream/2144/22903/1/_Capital-Controls-Eng_201303.pdf (accessed on 30th October 2025).
3. Athreya, B., Collingsworth, T., & Harvey, P. (2000). Developing effective mechanisms for implementing labor rights in the global economy. https://core.ac.uk/download/5129175.pdf (accessed on 30th October 2025).
4. Bäumler, J. (2020). Between a rock and a hard place. https://core.ac.uk/download/322846649.pdf (accessed on 30th October 2025).
5. Brewster, R. (2006). Rule-based dispute resolution in international trade law. https://core.ac.uk/download/62565363.pdf (accessed on 30th October 2025).
6. Brown, A. J., Strube, D., Oliveira, I., Joy, M., & Callaghan, M. (2025). G20 2014: Reform of the international organizations, financial regulation, trade, accountability and anti-corruption. https://core.ac.uk/download/pdf/30673851.pdf (accessed on 30th October 2025).
7. Buthe, T. (2008). The globalization of health and safety standards: Delegation of regulatory authority in the SPS Agreement of the 1994 Agreement Establishing the World Trade Organization. https://core.ac.uk/download/62553315.pdf (accessed on 30th October 2025).
8. Chang, S. W. (2004). Interaction between trade and competition: Why a multilateral approach for the United States? https://core.ac.uk/download/62547461.pdf (accessed on 30th October 2025).
9. Chowdhury, N., & Kumar, S. (2008). Technical capacity, policymaking and food standards: An overview of Indian experience. https://core.ac.uk/download/pdf/11481870.pdf (accessed on 30th October 2025).
10. Conconi, P. (2001). Conditionality, separation, and open rules in multilateral institutions. https://core.ac.uk/download/47559.pdf (accessed on 30th October 2025).
11. Dhar, B. (2013). The future of the World Trade Organization. https://core.ac.uk/download/18615812.pdf (accessed on 30th October 2025).

12. Engel, J., & Ghafele, R. (2025). Intellectual property related development aid: Is supply aligned with demand? https://core.ac.uk/download/pdf/6832324.pdf (accessed on 30th October 2025).
13. Gustafson, K. (2015). Boosting the private space industry: Extending NASA's duty-free import exemption to commercial space companies. http://scholarship.law.wm.edu/cgi/viewcontent.cgi?article=1089&context=wmblr (accessed on 30th October 2025).
14. Heath, J. B. (2020). Trade and security among the ruins. https://core.ac.uk/download/322820162.pdf (accessed on 30th October 2025).
15. Helfer, L. R. (2007). Toward a human rights framework for intellectual property. https://core.ac.uk/download/62563252.pdf (accessed on 30th October 2025).
16. Hillman, J. A. (2009). Conflicts between dispute settlement mechanisms in regional trade agreements and the WTO–What should WTO do? https://core.ac.uk/download/213034966.pdf (accessed on 30th October 2025).
17. Hillman, J. A. (2018). Multilateral economic institutions and U.S. foreign policy: Hearing before the Subcomm. on Multilateral Int'l Dev., Multilateral Insts., & Int'l Econ., Energy, & Envtl. Pol'y of the S. Comm. on Foreign Relations, 115th Cong., Nov. 27, 2018 (Statement of Jennifer A. Hillman). https://core.ac.uk/download/213035760.pdf (accessed on 30th October 2025).
18. Hite, K., & Dann, M. S. (2016). The Rockefeller Brothers Fund's Democratic Practice Global Governance Portfolio: Impact assessment, 2010–2015. https://core.ac.uk/download/86445418.pdf (accessed on 30th October 2025).
19. Hoekman, B. (2025). Proposals for WTO reform: A synthesis and assessment. https://core.ac.uk/download/pdf/6293366.pdf (accessed on 30th October 2025).
20. Hoekman, B., & Nelson, D. (2020). Rethinking international subsidy rules. *Bertelsmann Working Paper*, 28/02/2020. https://core.ac.uk/download/287647974.pdf (accessed on 30th October 2025).
21. Howse, R. (2014). Regulatory cooperation, regional trade agreements, and world trade law: Conflict or complementarity? https://core.ac.uk/download/62570443.pdf (accessed on 30th October 2025).
22. Jackson, J. H. (2004). International law status of WTO dispute settlement reports: Obligation to comply or option to buy out? https://core.ac.uk/download/70373714.pdf (accessed on 30th October 2025).
23. Krajewski, M. (2025). Legitimizing global economic governance through transnational parameterization: The parliamentary dimensions of the

WTO and the World Bank. https://core.ac.uk/download/pdf/6476957.pdf (accessed on 30th October 2025).

24. Macmillan, F. (2004). If not this World Trade Organization, then what? https://core.ac.uk/download/15005.pdf (accessed on 30th October 2025).
25. Malkawi, B. H. (2007). Regional integration: Whither Arab Free Trade Area? https://core.ac.uk/download/186331687.pdf (accessed on 30th October 2025).
26. Manero-Salvador, A. (2025). Special and differential treatments in world trade rules. https://core.ac.uk/download/pdf/7035252.pdf (accessed on 30th October 2025).
27. Monge-Arino, F., & Monge-Gonzalez, R. (2025). Anti-dumping policies and safeguard measures in the context of Costa Rica's economic liberalization. https://core.ac.uk/download/pdf/6615510.pdf (accessed on 30th October 2025).
28. Mustafa, K. (2025). Barriers against agricultural exports from Pakistan: The role of WTO Sanitary and Phytosanitary Agreement. https://core.ac.uk/download/pdf/7202794.pdf (accessed on 30th October 2025).
29. N/A. (2006). International legal instruments relevant to fisheries and fishing communities: A handbook. Introduction. https://core.ac.uk/download/16384872.pdf (accessed on 30th October 2025).
30. Nakatomi, M. (2013). Plurilateral agreements: A viable alternative to the World Trade Organization? https://www.econstor.eu/dspace/bitstream/10419/101201/1/770460968.pdf (accessed on 30th October 2025).
31. Ramjoué, M. (2025). How do people in Asia and the Pacific migrate legally for work? An overview of legal frameworks: GATS Mode 4, PTAs and bilateral labor agreements. https://core.ac.uk/download/pdf/6266473.pdf (accessed on 30th October 2025).
32. Rangnekar, D. (2008). Geneva rhetoric, national reality: Implementing TRIPS obligations in Kenya. https://core.ac.uk/download/105927.pdf (accessed on 30th October 2025).
33. Santos, A. (2012). Carving out policy autonomy for developing countries in the World Trade Organization: The experience of Brazil and Mexico. https://core.ac.uk/download/70374668.pdf (accessed on 30th October 2025).
34. Switzer, S. (2008). Environmental protection and the generalized system of preferences: A legal and appropriate linkage? https://core.ac.uk/download/9053220.pdf (accessed on 30th October 2025).

35. Villalta Puig, G., & Yee, A. T. H. (2017). Challenges and opportunities of the China–Gulf Cooperation Council Free Trade Agreement. https://core.ac.uk/download/151161890.pdf (accessed on 30th October 2025).
36. Von Soest, C., Calcagnotto, G., Wogart, J. P., & Hein, W. (2025). AIDS, access to medicines, and the different roles of the Brazilian and South African governments in global health governance. https://core.ac.uk/download/pdf/6862893.pdf (accessed on 30th October 2025).
37. Wolfe, R. (2018). Is World Trade Organization information good enough? How a systematic reflection by members on transparency could promote institutional learning. *Bertelsmann Stiftung GED Focus Paper*. https://core.ac.uk/download/287647949.pdf (accessed on 30th October 2025).

Chapter 4

Market Access for Goods

Contents

INTRODUCTION

The idea of access market is critical to promoting international trade and economic growth. Availability of markets allows goods and services to cross borders, leading to competition and innovation. With the increasing interdependence of economies, it is critical to learn the dynamics of market access to businesses that seek to exploit international markets. This undertaking entails maneuvering complex regulations, tariffs and trade agreements that determine the ease at which commodities can be availed to consumers in other regions. The importance of these aspects cannot be overemphasized, because companies who manage to take advantage of the market access strategies, may acquire a considerable competitive edge. More so, the advent of e-business has changed the game and it is very urgent that firms should adopt digital platforms that simplify cross-border operations and increase their coverage and this is to demonstrate the multidimensionality of market accessibility in the contemporary global economy (Lipych et al., 2020). The consequences of access to the market are not only limited to short-term gains of the business but also long-term economic factors, especially when it comes to developing nations. With these countries trying to integrate into the global market, their agricultural sector is exposed to special challenges which are shaped by external forces like trade policies to the nation.

Figure 4.1. Market access for goods.

Source: https://i0.wp.com/trade-access.eu/wp-content/uploads/2023/04/img_Market-access.jpg?resize=760%2C507&ssl=1.

The Common Agricultural Policy of the European Union (CAP) is a relevant case because the policy largely influences the competitive environment of the agricultural products that are traded on the international level. To countries that relied on the exportation of agricultural products, the intricacies in the CAP including regulations and subsidies offer a major challenge in market access and market survival. Furthermore, the unequal access to markets may amplify the susceptibility of the economies of the countries as they strike trade deals, which is why policy frameworks that facilitate equal trade relations are urgently required (Echessah et al., 2025). To sum up, having a discussion on market access means a logical study of the opportunities as well as the challenges that businesses are confronted with in a more complicated global trade environment.

The interaction of technology, regulation, and economic policies is one that can only be successfully negotiated with having a holistic picture of the interaction of these elements. Through these dimensions, the essay seeks to shed light on ways of improving market access to goods especially to the emerging economies that are struggling to grow. Moreover, the changing character of market access cannot be overlooked because the businesses must change with the increases in digital commerces, and, therefore, it is essential that research and policy changes must be made constantly. Finally, by promoting conditions that will encourage free and fair trade, it will not only help individual businesses thrive but will also help in global economic resilience since markets are becoming more interconnected than ever before (Figure 4.1).

Definition of Market Access

Market access concept constitutes a central area in the international trade field as it determines how goods and services are exchanged across the borders, and how the economies conduct international business. The ease with which a nation can sell goods and services to the market of another country without any major obstacles like high tariffs, quotas, or regulatory obstacles can be regarded as market access. This access is essential in facilitating competition, improving consumer choice, and economic growth. On the other hand, the restrictive measures may hinder the economic growth of a country by reducing its capability of engaging in global trade. This trade may be exemplified through trade negotiations where nations eliminate to reach agreements that are mutually advantageous and which will increase the market presence of the countries, which are the significance and sophistication of the global trading system. The implications of market access are not limited to just the trade statistics, they affect the agricultural sector which is often a center-stage when trade negotiations are involved.

When the access to the market is discussed, especially in the context of the Doha Round, its scopes of ambitions may differ, and it has a significant effect on the developing countries. In the case of African economies, what has been negotiated is a clear market access framework, which includes significant cuts in tariffs, is the key to unlocking potential growth. Nevertheless, as shown by recent studies, apparently small judgments on sensitive products may significantly compromise the general gains that come with extensive reduction of tariffs, thus, influencing the expected positive results of trade-sensitive economies. The sensitivity of products of production appears to be the obstacle on the way to maximizing profit of agricultural trade reforms, which confirms the necessity to carefully negotiate the dynamics (Hammouda et al., 2025). Moreover, climate policy/international trade brings another dimension of complexity to the discussion of market access. The frameworks that surround trade are sometimes seen to be inadequate in terms of environmental implications of trade practices which may have adverse effects on climatic objectives. Indicatively, new studies highlight the importance of trade agreements being conscious of the effects they have on the environment and that market access must also include aspects concerning climate change. With the struggle to define the goods and services that are eco-friendly in the organizations like the WTO, the definition of market access is highly intertwined with sustainability. The altering definition indicates the wider issue of balancing the processes of trade liberalization and environmental care, whereby, as nations attempt to improve their access to markets, they simultaneously maintain their own obligation on climate mitigation and adaptation (Ackerman et al., 2016).

Value of Market Access in Global Trade

Market access in global trade is an important factor that cannot be underestimated since it is an imperative factor in the national and international economic prosperity. By allowing foreign markets, countries especially developing countries would be able to increase their competitive advantages through exportation of goods and services that can match their production capabilities at home. As an example, an example of Chinese exports in the late 20th century shows how greater access to the market can trigger a fast pace of economic growth. During the period of 1987–1996, the Chinese export increased annually by an average of 14% which is an indication that the country was not only pursuing domestic production policies but also engaging in more global markets. Market access through trade creates a conducive environment to innovation and efficiency by facilitation of opportunities to trade and eventually leads to a more dynamic global economy although it also raises concerns on the even spread of benefits in economies, particularly in terms of processing trade dependence in China (Hu et al., 1999). In addition, trade barriers must also be eliminated in order to have a unified and effective global trading system. Non-tariff barriers, quotas, and tariffs tend to prevent free movement of goods thus killing economic interaction between countries. This scenario leads to the lack of accessibility to the market that can disproportionately impact the smaller or developing countries which fail to compete with the well-established economies. Reforms in policies that lead to an open trading system like those championed in the global trade talks are imperative in alleviating these problems. Such delinking of agricultural subsidies with production prices, coupled with promotion of open agricultural markets, may greatly improve access of countries between which agricultural exports are an important part of the total exports (N/A, 2003). Therefore, making markets free facilitates the maximization of economic potential and sustainable development of the regions. Lastly, the benefits of enhanced access to the market are not confined to economic measurements alone; they also have a larger social and political scope. Increased access can result in job creation, poverty reduction and better living standards as countries will be able to utilize their advantages and properly allocate resources via exports. There is also the possibility of building a good trading relationship, which can lead to diplomatic ties that ensure the world remains stable. But it is also important to note that there are different effects of market access on various sectors of each economy. Not every industry can be equally beneficial, which can cause socio-economic inequalities. Thus, as much as the benefits of access to global markets are obvious, it is important to implement policies that guarantee equitable growth. Open discussion of the trade practices will play a central role in shaping the future of the world markets and will guarantee that all the involved countries will benefit (Hu et al., 1999; N/A, 2003) (Figure 4.2).

Figure 4.2. Importance of market access in global trade.

Source: https://external-content.duckduckgo.com/iu/?u=https%3A%2F%2Fwww.superdisty.com%2Fwp-content%2Fuploads%2F2021%2F05%2FCopy-of-Untitled-11-2-915x610.jpg&f=1&nofb=1&ipt=a210c6a16abe6b22de6af4f6b07027d4628e19611247183ce26063ff4487f978.

4.1. HISTORICAL CONTEXT OF MARKET ACCESS

Historic background of market access illustrates the intricate interaction between economic systems and social organization, especially against the context of peasantries. Economic development has followed different paths in different regions and cultures, depending on the local resources, the governmental policies, and the world tendencies. As an example, peasant societies have been forced to endure changes in the needs of the market, contending with changing production methods in order to remain relevant in a more competitive world. As explained in the analysis of peasant labour and change, the functions of these communities are by no means monolithic. They represent various methods of market access, which include the adaptation, accommodation, and resistance strategies that underline not only their historical backgrounds but also the current economic issues. These patterns remain important in the analysis of the market access functioning in contemporary times, especially in developing economies where the smallholder farms are of a major contribution to the feeding of the growing populations and in the development of the local economies (Cottyn et al., 2017).

Furthermore, the development of market access is impossible to be complete without the effects of intellectual property (IP) and globalization. The two opposites observed in modern discourse present two opposite views on the role of IP as a determinant of economic growth and markets. On the one hand, there is passion regarding the knowledge economy because innovations and ideas can trigger major developments, and thereby promote market accessibility to goods. On the other hand, critics point out that the IP system tends to give preference to large multinational corporations at the expense of the local businesses especially in developing countries. These companies can take up monopoly of key markets charging consumers more and leaving the small and medium-sized businesses out of the competition. This opposition highlights the necessity to take critical insight into the way historical trends in IP and globalization have instilled current market access, providing diverse socioeconomic groups with opportunities and barriers (Bashi et al., 2008). In this perspective, the historical background of market access may finally be considered a dynamic story subject to socioeconomic transformations and policy variations that may indicate the broader historical movements. The progress of international trade relations, changes in agricultural policies, the development of digital economies are all aspects that keep changing the market access landscape. Through these historical influences, we are able to appreciate the existing structural inequalities and opportunities that are available in the existing markets. In addition, knowledge about the historic trends of resistance and adaptation of peasant communities can provide us with information about the means that can be used to increase equitable accessibility to markets in the future. The study of these dimensions leads to a holistic understanding of market access that does not only look at the economic indicators, but also reflects the actual experience and past consequences of the people affected by the transformation of markets (Cottyn et al., 2017).

4.1.1. Evolution of Trade Agreements

Trade agreements have evolved greatly over the historical context, and it is indicative of more widespread economic and political developments in the international environment. These agreements were initially more concerned with tariffs and quantitative restrictions which were used to control international commerce and safeguard local industries. But in the late 20th century, with the increased rate of globalization the terms of the trade agreements broadened to include more and more issues such as intellectual property rights, labor standards, and environmental safety. This has been brought about by the fact that it has come to light that trade is not only associated with the exchange of goods, but also the establishment of economic interdependence and cooperation among countries. As a result, current trade agreements do not only ensure access to markets by goods but also attempt to create frameworks which ensure sustainable growth and equitable trading behaviors. The effect of trade agreements on market access has been immense, especially in areas where economic transitions have been so severe. An example is the introduction of free trade agreements (FTAs), which has given remarkable growths in trade flows, which have had positive effect on the trade balance of most of the participating countries. Recent research using the gravity model, such as detailed examination of agreements between the EU and Central and Eastern European nations, show a significant positive impact on trade of FTAs, but with differing results on imports and exports across countries.

This kind of disparities underscores the intricate dynamics at work where not every nation is equally benefiting in the increased market access these agreements offer. Since countries will still be negotiating on trade agreements, it is important to comprehend these asymmetric effects so as to formulate policies in ways that fairly share the advantages of improved market access (Caporale et al., 2009). More so, the development of trade agreements can be illustrated by the current activities of the European Unions to enter into Economic Partnership Agreements (EPAs) with the Southern hemisphere nations. Based on the Cotonou Agreements, these negotiations represent a promise to develop economically and integrate the region by the African, Caribbean, and Pacific (ACP) countries. EPAs help these developing countries to become more competitive in the global marketplace by enabling them to gain more access to the market and to bring more investment into the country. Nonetheless, the effectiveness of such efforts depends upon a variety of circumstances, with one of them being the capacity of ACP nations to negotiate and apply the agreements successfully. Empirical data indicate that these arrangements constitute great opportunities to expand the level of trade, though need to be carefully planned and firms institutional structures to secure sustainable results (Nicolò Tomaselli, 2025) (Figure 4.3).

Figure 4.3. Historical context of trade agreements.

Source: https://fastercapital.co/i/Trade-agreements--The-Impact-of-Trade-Agreements-on-Economic-Integration--Historical-Context-of-Trade-Agreements.webp.

4.1.2. Impact of Globalization on Market Access

Globalization has had a dual effect on the accessibility of markets that have opened up opportunities as well as challenges to international trading. With globalization promoting interconnectedness, goods flow across borders and businesses can penetrate new markets with relative ease. This has improved access to the market which allows companies to diversify their consumer markets and work with economies of scale by placing themselves in a competitive position to compete globally. These possibilities, however, come with complexities; as businesses operate in different areas, they are bound to deal with different regulations, standards and consumer preferences. Also, the processes of globalization introduce the increased competition with the foreign actors, which forces local companies to evolve or face the threat of becoming obsolete. The interconnectedness brought about by global networks explains how subtle the impacts of globalization may be and as such, businesses and policymakers have adopted strategies that best address the opportunities as well as challenges posed by tapping into the global markets (Wells et al., 2001). In addition, the impact of globalization on market access can be seen through the immense increase of trade and investment flows especially in such regions as the European Union. An analysis of globalization indicators in 2001–2006 in the EU-27 showed that on the basis of expanded trade openness and foreign direct investment (FDI), most areas gained a lot due to globalization (Sellner et al., 2025). This development in the region highlights the critical significance of globalization in intensifying market penetration and general economic wellbeing of countries. The details of growth dynamics, however, suggest that there is not an even distribution of the gains of globalization; those areas with already large GDP per capita are facing diminishing returns to globalization than their poorer ones. Therefore, in as much as there are geographical regions that are doing well, others might be lagging and some targeted policies to see to it that global markets are equally accessible to everyone, as well as to reduce any possible differences that globalization may bring about. In conclusion, the interaction between globalization and access to the market highlights the necessity of adaptive strategies that would consider changing consumer trends and technological progress. With the continuous development of globalization, companies should be cautious of the new trends and changes in global markets. As an example, digital globalization will provide new avenues of accessing markets through e-commerce and using technology to access consumers directly. With data analytics and digital marketing tools, businesses are able to gain a better idea of local market dynamics, enabling them to appeal more to local areas. However, the high dynamic rate may also be dangerous, with volatility and the disruption of traditional supply chains being one of them. As a result, efficient interaction with the globalized economy necessitates continuous evaluation and responsiveness, so that the business can exploit new opportunities and respond to the challenges that come with the increased access to markets (Wells et al., 2001) (Figure 4.4).

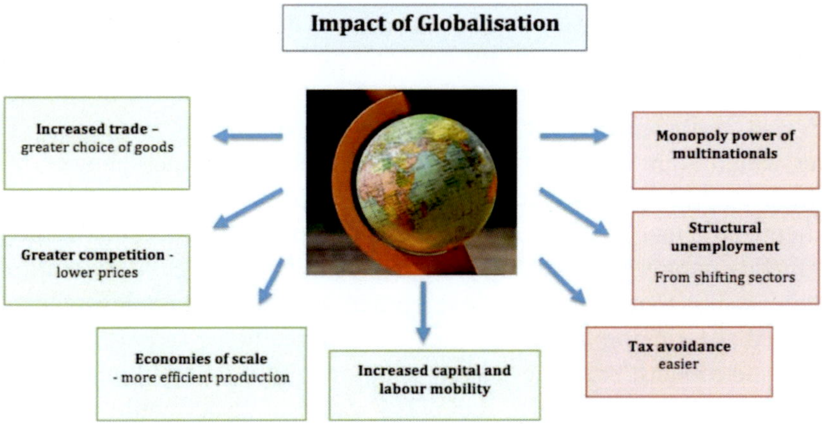

Figure 4.4. Impact of globalization on market access.

Source: https://external-content.duckduckgo.com/iu/?u=https%3A%2F%2Fwww.economicshelp.org%2Fwp-content%2Fuploads%2F2012%2F11%2Fimpact-of-globalisation.jpg&f=1&nofb=1&ipt=ebf1cbc242075b8b694be1a5baec4878cd8940823d5342281753e39e29b5f655.

4.1.3. Key Historical Events Influencing Market Access

Historically, there are critical events, which influenced the situation in markets access and changed the definition of the nature of goods exchange on the cross-border level. The formation of trade routes in the old civilizations had laid the foundation of basic networks that came in trade of commodities. Nevertheless, the creation of the Silk Road and other trade routes was what actually transformed the economic exchange between the West and the East. These initial trade routes that were in place not only facilitated the exchange of tangible commodities, but also made it possible to spread culture and technology. The latter emergence of maritime trade in the Age of Exploration further broadened the market access, introducing remote markets into a contact interaction. As ships started crossing between oceans and continents, the economic integration that ensued provided a fundamental foundation to modern-day global trade, which just goes to show how historical events may expand the boundaries of markets. Another crucial date in the history of market access was the Industrial Revolution, which has dramatically changed the paradigms of production and consumption. Technology and transport inventions like the steam engine and railroads reduced the cost of transporting goods drastically.

This not only enabled the domestic market to grow but also made international avenues available to trade. Flexibility in transporting goods facilitated manufacturers to access consumers at a distance and in the process, expanding the market accessibility boundaries. Moreover, the creation of the regulatory frameworks, including the tariffs and trade agreements, in this period also contributed a lot to the formation of market dynamics. These policies which were informed by the political and economic changes opened new market opportunities where goods could move to new markets even as they affected the local economies and the whole trade influence, this depicts the simultaneous nature of technological advancement and regulatory controls in improving access to markets. The development of the World Trade Organization (WTO) and the signing of diverse free trade agreements as part of historical events in the modern era have played a major role in determining the market accessibility to goods. In 1995, the WTO was established with objectives to establish a more predictable and orderly world of trade in order to minimize trade barriers and allow countries to leverage on comparative advantages. On the same note, free trade agreements such as NAFTA have helped to enable the free movement of goods across the boundaries, which has further merged the economies. These programs are indicative of a shared perception of the contribution of collaborative interaction towards improving access to the market. Moreover, the modern problems like cultural tourism, which has been debated in academic reviews, have transformed market dynamics in presenting relevance of cultural interactions in determining the market attractiveness and sustainability. The combination of all these historical forms of development has remained influential in the ways of entry into markets and exchange of goods in the international economy (Beckert et al., 2025; Tur et al., 2017).

4.2. BARRIERS TO MARKET ACCESS

Market access barriers may pose a serious impediment to the possibility of goods being brought to consumers especially when dealing with the international trade. This is because, as nations progress in bilateral and multilateral trade, trade relations are usually complicated by the imposition of tariffs and non-tariff barriers. The example of a study of QUAD countries (Canada, USA, Japan, and the EU) shows that policy barriers such as tariffs are important but other factors have an equally significant impact on the market access. These are the cultural distance and domestic product preferences of consumers that may cause effects on trade reduction that are frequently undervalued. All these complications in trade barriers indicate that the very notion of accessing markets is a subtle one, not only in the form of explicit policy barriers but implicit consumer preferences and behavior, which can be multiple times more effective than actual policy barriers themselves (Olper et al., 2025).

Also besides the obstacles of cultural inclination and tariffs, the dynamic nature of trade agreements also influences the dynamics of market access. In the analysis of the impacts of trade policies on small developing nations, it is observed that external trade barriers are also a significant factor in market accessibility problems. In the case of such countries, it may be more helpful to engage in agreement on regional integration as well as liberalize the trade regimes to have an opportunity to enter bigger markets. Nevertheless, the undermining of positive trade relation witnessed in the scenario of Cotonou Agreement of African, Caribbean and Pacific (ACP) states and the EU state highlights the need to establish stronger trade policies. These policies involve encouraging South-South cooperation and providing technical support to reforms that can support the improved integration into the global markets (Schiff et al., 2025). In conclusion, to overcome the barriers to market access, it is a multifaceted approach which involves policy reform and consumer behavior. The lessons during the analysis of the QUAD countries help to not only describe the complexity of the effects on trade but propose that countries should review their trade policies in the context of cultural and economic interactions. Similarly, in the case of small states operating under the framework of the prevailing agreements, aggressively seeking free trade agreements and regional integration may be a channel through which market access is improved. This interaction of policy changes, international cooperation, and consumer interaction is going to be essential in enhancing access to goods in the market hence leading to economic growth and sustainability at a global level (Figure 4.5).

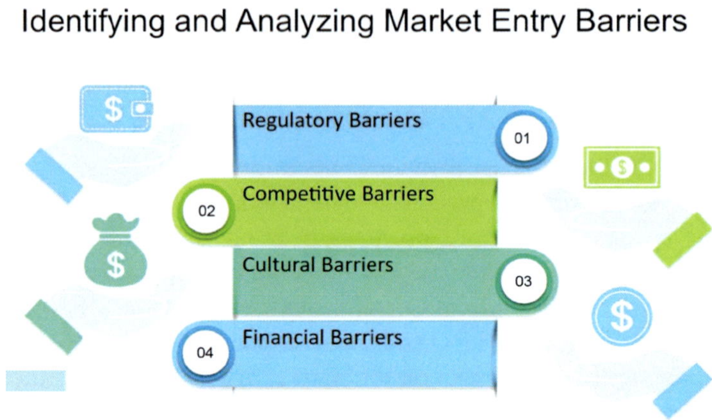

Figure 4.5. Market entry barriers.

Source: https://fastercapital.co/i/Breaking-Down-Barriers--Overcoming-Market-Entry-Barriers-with-Cultural-Understanding--Identifying-and-Analyzing-Market-Entry-Barriers.webp.

4.2.1. Tariffs and Trade Barriers

Tariffs and trade barriers have a crucial role to play in defining market accessibility of goods in the modern environment of global trade. Tariffs are taxes levied on imported goods and increase the prices and may limit the movement of goods across the borders. Nations tend to defend these responsibilities by a need to protect their home industries, to develop new industries and protect jobs against foreigners. Nevertheless, though these are meant to be protective, the tariffs may also result in retaliation, starting trade wars, which have negative effects on both the importing and exporting countries. The delicate nature of encouraging local industry and encouraging the open markets complicate the matters, when the trade barriers change depending on the domestic political reasons and international relations. Another important phenomenon of trade barriers is non-tariff barriers (NTBs), which is commonly viewed as more insidious than tariffs as being complex and subtle. The barriers are regulations and standards, which countries build to ensure consumer safety and ensure environmental sustainability. Nevertheless, under abuse, NTBs may impose barriers that will discriminate against the foreign goods unfairly, which will result in an uneven playing field. As an example, when the regulations are excessively strict or not fully or consistently implemented, it will inadvertently put the domestic products in a disadvantaged position, which will lead to trade disputes. According to the research covered under the topic of trade relationship between EU and U.S., the regulatory dialogue is urgently required to ensure that NTBs do not escalate to become serious barriers to market accessibility (Vandenbussche et al., 2002). The strategic significance of tariffs and trade barriers in promoting or making bilateral relations difficult is demonstrated by the economic costs of the trade agreements such as the U.S. South Korea Free Trade Agreement (KORUS FTA). KORUS agreement will remove tariffs on the majority of manufactured products and will provide regulatory reforms that will accelerate trade flows between the two countries. But the future of true market opening depends on the discussion of sensitive areas like autos and agriculture where trade barriers were issues of contention in the past. Although it is widely supported by important quarters, there are worries against it because of the lack of sufficient market openness. The dichotomy of support and opposition explains the decisive influence of tariffs and trade barriers in determining the outcomes of trade negotiations, and thus, the impact on economic performance of both parties (Cooney et al., 2008) (Figure 4.6).

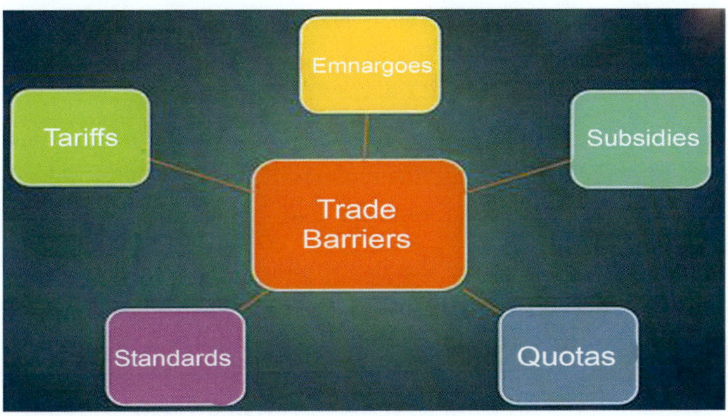

Figure 4.6. Tariffs and trade barriers.

Source: https://external-content.duckduckgo.com/iu/?u=https%3A%2F%2Fthfvnext.bing.com%2Fth%2Fid%2FOIP.Iqjp3P_Vl6FJnr2z4ErQXwHaEK-%3Fcb%3Dthfvnext%26pid%3DApi&f=1&ipt=5c1cc8babefe0dc54c1a30fc795643c853ce4f80ae4e4564590d14efa99a70df.

4.2.2. Non-Tariff Barriers (NTBs) and Regulations

The issue of complexity of NTBs presents a big challenge in ensuring that there is an equitable access to goods within the international trade. Compared to the traditional tariffs, which provide a simple approach of applying restrictions to trade, NTBs are quite extensive and cover a wide variety of regulation tools that may cause the blockage of trade flows even when the tariffs are reduced. Such obstacles are high quality standards, licenses and country-specific customs. Although significant steps have been made towards the removal of explicit trade barriers, numerous domestic measures still hamper trade and foreign direct investment (FDI), so that as Golub et al. (2003) point out, NTBs can as well impose as strong a pull on market access as traditional tariffs. Therefore, the need to discuss these regulatory differences is to create a more integrated global economy and providing all market participants with equal opportunities to participate in trade.

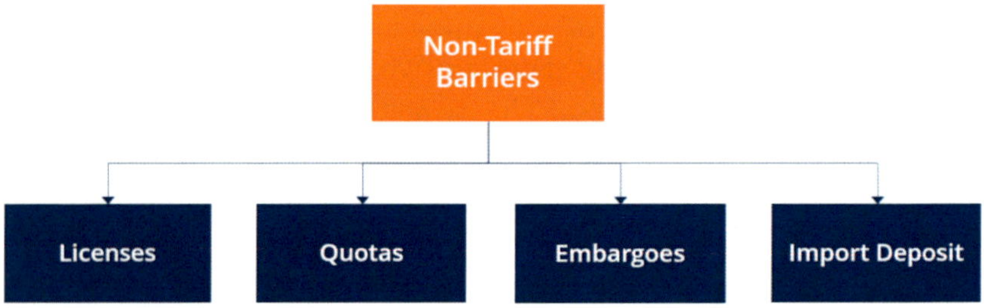

Figure 4.7. Non-tariff barriers.

Source: https://cdn.corporatefinanceinstitute.com/assets/non-tariff-barriers-1024x332.png.

This has been as a result of the elimination of non-tariff barriers which not only has become a priority towards the improvement of trade relation but also has become a priority towards the economic growth of different regions. Research of the European Union and its neighbors reveals that decreased NTBs may create a considerable boost in welfare and GDP growth in countries that are partners (Orlova et al. 2025). As an example, the welfare gain potential among CIS countries in case NTBs are reduced is analyzed, which will transform into an increase in GDP and real wages. These lessons highlight the importance of integrating regulations and standards with the aim of minimizing compliance requirements to exporters. These measures do not only support trade growth, but also economic integration as it makes the trading environment more predictable and transparent thereby supporting investment and innovation. Besides, the interaction between regulatory systems and market accessibility is becoming a more pressing issue in an age of profound economic integration and globalization. Non-tariff barriers may act as protectionist, or restrictive, policies, making the current situation in the international trade more complicated. With the countries aligning their regulations under a trade agreement, it can be seen that collaborative efforts are necessary in order to solve NTBs. Golub et al. (2003) notes that it is only through thorough measures that go beyond lowering tariff rates to entail domestic market reforms that significant cuts in policy barriers can be reached. Therefore, they need to focus on policies that will simplify customs procedures, rationalize product rules, and create competitive markets, which, in combination, will enable an easier entry to the market and lead to economic growth in a globalized world (Figure 4.7).

4.2.3. Political and Economic Factors Affecting Access

The interdependence between political and economic forces is a decisive factor on the access of goods in the market, especially in the developing nations. One of the primary themes in this discussion is the effect of government policies and regulatory frameworks on accessibility. As an example, the privatization of animal healthcare in sub-Saharan Africa can explain the impact of ill-timed policy reforms. The accessibility of the relevant services to many livestock owners, especially the remote rural ones, presents insurmountable obstacles to the unaffordability of the required services and the lack of proper infrastructure. This scenario emphasises how political choices in privatization processes may unintentionally enhance a state of existing inequalities restricting the capability of marginalized groups to engage in market opportunities. Accordingly, it would be crucial to insight into the systems of governance and politically driven decisions toward such policies when resolving the efficiency and effectiveness of services aimed to promote economic growth (Riviere-Cinnamond et al., 2025). Also, the importance of intellectual property rights (IPR) in promoting trade and investment is highlighted by economic theories about market access. An example is in China where adherence to treaties such as the TRIPS has significant effects on entry into the market and legitimacy of a business activity. By ensuring the innovation protection, IPR can also help to stabilize the business environment which promotes foreign investment. The assessment of whether Chinas conforms to these standards, however, makes it clear that the situation is not as easy as it seems, with domestic economic policies and international pressure being among the factors to consider. These may influence the views toward market viability and investor confidence. The analysis of the interrelation between political choices and the economic theories can help to understand more the role of IPR protection in influencing access to foreign markets and the equitable development of an economy (Fojtíková et al., 2018). This makes a connection between political governance and the ease of accessing an economy a very crucial factor in defining the dynamics of international trade. Policies on trade tariffs, subsidies, and regulatory practices affect entry into the market of goods in diverse manners. In most instances the inability to listen to the voices of the local stakeholders may result in distortions of policy outcomes and end up hindering access by the most needy. In addition, these disparities also need a delicate approach in terms of the larger economy such as the implication of globalization and market liberalization. Proper governance which is transient and inclusive plays a crucial role in promoting a fair market. Not only will it ease the access to goods, but it will also lead to sustainable economic growth, which will ensure that the advantages of trade can be distributed between all layers of the population and eradicate historical injustices that were embedded by decisions of the past political authorities (Riviere-Cinnamond et al., 2025).

4.3. ROLE OF INTERNATIONAL ORGANIZATIONS

International organizations also serve the crucial role of easing access to the market of goods, as they are the ones who create and ensure the existence of the regulatory mechanisms under which international trade is conducted. These organizations, including the World Trade Organization (WTO) and regional trading accords, attempt to minimize trade protection, smooth customs processes, and harmonize standards. International organizations allow countries to compete fairly by establishing a consistent body of rules and therefore, economic efficiency and growth. The structures established by these bodies not only enable the developed countries to carry on with their trade endeavors, but also offer important help to the developing economies that may be having considerable entry barriers into the world market. With the changing nature of these organizations, they still continue to influence the dynamics of international commerce such that the access to markets is equitable and inclusive. Also, the role of international organizations in enhancing co-operation between governments and the private sector is significant particularly in sectors such as agriculture and infrastructure. These organizations facilitate investments and innovations by involving stakeholders in different initiatives, which are critical in opening the market outreach. As an example, international partnerships that enhance technological advancements and the promotion of sustainable practices have a great influence on irrigation management in agricultural sectors. Such partnerships have the potential to strengthen productivity and resource management, which eventually transforms the lives of farmers and their families. The combination of state and privatized initiatives plays a crucial role in making sure that agriculture is sustainable in the developing countries and should therefore be an important element in the quest to expand market access to basic commodities in a globalized economy (Inocencio et al., 2014). Additionally, the international organizations are also avenues in which professional standards are created which can greatly affect the mechanisms of market access. An example of such efforts is the International Bar Association (IBA) that has contributed significantly towards unifying Mutual Recognition Agreements (MRAs) in legal profession. These type of MRAs that enable international lawyers to move and practice serve as examples of how entirely non-state actors can develop rules that can guide governmental and organizational policy. IBA participation highlights the significance of working with professional bodies in building and overseeing structures to regulate market access. Nevertheless, problems still exist, particularly when it comes to developing countries that are not successful in adopting MRAs. The IBA is not only assisting legal professionals but also improving the general scheme of market access, which helps create a more integrated global economy (Collins et al., 2019) (Figure 4.8).

Figure 4.8. Role of international organizations.

Source: https://fastercapital.co/i/Bank-secrecy--Bank-Secrecy-and-Capital-Control--Finding-the-Right-Balance--The-Role-of-International-Organizations.webp.

4.3.1. World Trade Organization (WTO) and Its Functions

The WTO is playing a central role in the facilitation of international trade by setting and implementing a system of trade agreements between the member countries. The fundamental purpose of its activity is to make trade as free and predictable as possible and to increase access to goods. The WTO has been able to negotiate trade agreements through which it plays a very important role in harmonizing the regulations and cutting down the tariffs between member countries. This institutionalization is of great importance especially in relation to trade liberalization where nations seek to reduce restrictions that might deter the free movement of products. The WTO facilitates the establishment of a favorable environment that supports international trade by ensuring the observance of trade rules, leading to economic growth and development of its members. The WTO, in a way, is instrumental in the formulation of the regulations that govern international trade, which have a direct effect on market access. The decision of nations like Jordan to join WTO is a classic example of the issues and implications of becoming a member of this multilateral trading system. The experience of the Jordans shows the strict obligations which are to be taken by newcomers and which usually presuppose some serious legal and economic changes aimed at meeting the requirements of the WTO. An example is that Jordan accepted to cut tariff and liberalize its services market besides amending its intellectual property regime. Nevertheless, the circumstances of such accedences are usually unique which will result in imbalanced responsibilities and benefits where new members are expected to put in more dedication than existing ones. Thus, the time-consuming and expensive nature of the accession process of the country by Jordans explains why WTO provides the country with access to the markets- although sometimes with long-term effects on the economies and trade relations (Malkawi et al., 2010). The role of WTO is not that of facilitation of trade agreements only; it also acts as an arbitrator to disputes that may occur between member states. The resolution of disputes is an important organizational role that tends to create a stable trading environment. The WTO is a well-organized system through which countries can solve their trade disputes whilst ensuring that the members stick to agreed rules. This especially matters when it comes to the accessibility of goods in the market because disagreements may present themselves with regards to tariffs, subsidies or trade barriers which influence competitiveness of goods in global markets. These activities by the organizations in their oversight and enforcement work to ensure that conflicts do not escalate, hence ensuring that there is a more collaborative trade environment. Also, the WTO, based on the discussions at the Doha Round, is still engaged in numerous issues of the trade relations among countries such as trade liberalization and balance of interests between developed countries and developing countries, and this says a lot about its multifunctional approach to the global trade (Ahearn et al., 2010).

4.3.2. Regional Trade Agreements (RTAs) and Their Significance

These RTAs are critical in defining access to goods in the market by promoting trade among the member states by eliminating tariffs and simplifying trade policies. They tend to come about as a reaction to the strains of the global trade processes as countries are trying to strengthen their economies, without the burden of the slow moving international bargains. It is important to note that RTAs may be used as the tool of economic development as they allow the involved countries to utilize their comparative advantages and therefore increase productivity and promote regional collaboration. The importance of RTAs is not limited to supporting trade, RTAs can create political linkages as a result of which, stability and development in the region can increase. Consequently, the general knowledge of RTAs is essential to the analysis of their implications on the accessibility of goods to the market globally. Within the European Union (EU) and its Economic Partnership Agreements (EPAs) with African, Caribbean, and Pacific (ACP) countries, RTAs are an attempt to facilitate economic integration and development.

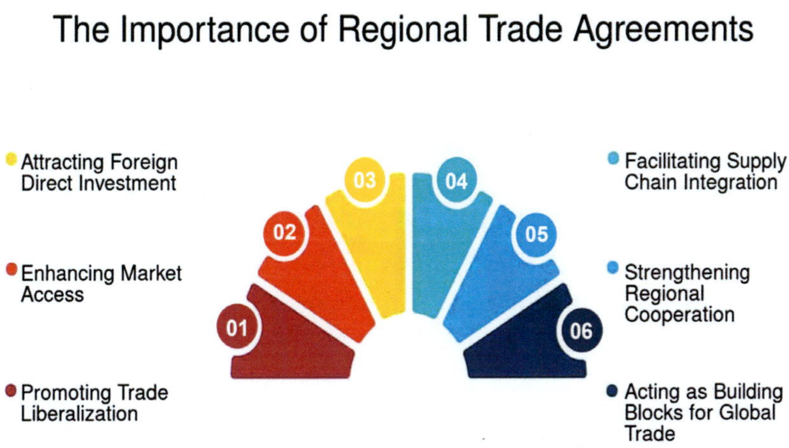

Figure 4.9. Regional trade agreements and their significance.

Source: https://fastercapital.co/i/International-economic-integration--How-to-Benefit-from-International-Economic-Integration-and-Regional-Trade-Agreements--The-Importance-of-Regional-Trade-Agreements.webp.

These EPAs represent a natural extension of the previous trade agreements that were geared towards improving the insertion of the ACP countries into the world trading system. Through preferential trade conditions, the EU aims at supporting the economic development of these areas and contributing to their conversion to sustainable economic growth. But the effectiveness of such arrangements depends on the good faith of both parties to respect the terms contained in the agreements. Consequently, there have been a lot of empirical studies on the conditions that have to be met to have these agreements work such as institutional capacity, development of infrastructure, and compliance with trade regulations. The achievements and difficulties encountered in the EU-ACP EPAs finally give much knowledge on the general implication of RTAs on the access to goods. The interaction between trade and migration also creates a complex picture of regional trade agreements. It is noteworthy that although the main emphasis of RTAs has been on tariff cuts and facilitation of trade, there is increased appreciation of interrelation of trade and migration policies. Liberalization of trade in services and the free flow of people may have immense economic advantages that cannot be underrated with the standard traditional trade agreements. Migration policies that promote transient movement as observed in the literature are increasingly being incorporated into trade negotiation, and this is a good indication that there is a move towards appreciating the value that skilled labor mobility contributes to economic growth. Nevertheless, the idea of progress in multilateral structures is a complicated task, as in the case of the little progress made on Mode IV of the General Agreement on Trade in Services (GATS). Hence, it is important to know these interdependencies when grasping the overall effects of RTAs on access to goods in the market and the macroeconomic environment (Figure 4.9).

4.3.3. Impact of International Organizations on Market Access

The international organizations are instrumental in promoting the access of the market in standardizing the trade regulations and practices internationally through the formation of the frameworks to promote trade rules and practices on international borders. These agreements like World Trade Organization (WTO) and regional trade agreements give the member states guidelines that assist them overcome hurdle to trade like tariffs and non-tariff barriers. International organizations can help achieve a more predictable marketplace through agreements which deal with technical barriers and trade facilitation. As an example, the improvement of the connectivity through transport infrastructure and the streamlining of customs procedures have been recorded. This does not just strengthen the effectiveness of the cross-border trading, but also improves the competitiveness of the national business among the member states encouraging the growth of economy in member states. These organizations have the ability to influence the ability of a country to access and navigate the international markets since they establish clear norms and standards. In addition, the role of international organizations is also seen in the institutional and organizational structure that regulates trade. These institutions usually offer technical and capacity building aid to developing countries to ensure that they meet international standards which allow them to gain access to market. This is especially important in areas where institutional vulnerabilities exist as witnessed in numerous researches pointing at the barriers that are associated with customs procedures and border crossings. Implementation of unified transport documents and enhancement of electronic communication have been cited as being effective measures in mitigating these issues. As an example, the parallel implementation of technical and institutional innovations is essential in ensuring the creation of an environment that promotes efficient cargo transport, which eventually drives goods accessibility to the market. Thus, international organizations actively participating in both structural and procedural barriers are the keys to improving the global trading system. The international organization influence on the access to markets also includes the cooperation of the state and the business in their resources distribution and investment policies. As an instance, the programs, which enable the formation of the partnership between the government and the corporations, may result in the improvement of infrastructure and the efficiency of the supply chains. The feasibility of the involvement of the private sector in activities like irrigation management is an illustration of how diversified investments can solve the problem of localized market accesses especially in the developing economies. The international organizations help to empower farmers and local communities by promoting new financing models and participatory management practices, which increases their market accessibility. The involvement of private investment in such regions, as mentioned in the above research, would have significant payoffs, creating economic growth and stability among households. Therefore, the partnership between international organizations and both state and non-state bodies actively changes the terrain of market accessibility, and it allows more inclusive economic space.

4.4. CASE STUDIES OF MARKET ACCESS

Case study analysis of market access offers important insights into the success of trade agreements especially in comprehending the effects of Rules of Origin (RoO). In the North American Free Trade Agreement (NAFTA) environment, it has been seen in research that although preferential access was meant to ease trading, the real gains might not have been massive. A study that compares Mexican exports to the U.S. in 2001 reveals that costs of RoO may be high, whether in final or intermediate goods. The results show that the need to revise tariff classification is more likely to issue high cost on final goods rather than intermediate goods, indicating that there are more layers of complexities that might discourage the best access to the market. In this way, this information demonstrates that although trade agreements are designed to lower barriers, the underlying needs might unintentionally limit but not promote integration of the market, questioning the effectiveness of these models in terms of improving trade flows (Céline CARRERE et al., 2025). However, differently, the aspects of market access can be addressed within the framework of differentiation of the product quality between similar economies. To elaborate the idea of vertical product differentiation, there is some empirical evidence that trade among nations with similar economic status leads to significant differences in the quality of products. According to a theoretical model, the quality of goods exported is usually higher than the quality of goods sold in the domestic market, and larger economies tend to be exporters of high-quality goods, as opposed to their smaller counterparts. This complexity underlies the role played by trade relations not only through tariff barriers but also through the intrinsic characteristics of traded goods. Thus, when the nations are negotiating their entry into the market, it is essential to make sure that the products fall to the high-quality standards. This interaction between quality and access complexifies the pattern of trade internationally, exposing strata of rivalry that disrupt easy presumptions on market competences and access pathways (Helble et al., 2025). Finally, the interpretation of case studies of market access shows a complex environment in which different factors operate together to determine trade results. The NAFTA debate shows that although trade agreements are meant to make this an easy task, the plethora of compliance requirements, including RoO and quality standards, may make access more challenging and reduce expected gains. Conversely, a review on quality trade dynamics among similar economies illuminates on how product differentiation is central in determining competitive advantages. These two positions, regulatory restrictions and quality-based competitiveness, highlight the complexity of the market access. What becomes more apparent is that, as the countries seek to increase their presence in global commerce, they must manoeuvre around these complexities, using both regulation regimes and product innovation, to effect sustainable entry into the marketplace and economic prosperity.

4.4.1. Success Stories in Market Access

Transformative potential of the collaboration between businesses and stakeholders in strategic form is often emphasized in the success stories in the market access. A good example is that of the water management industry where firms have come to realize the need to adopt sustainable practices. Through the interaction with other non-business actors, companies have been able to come up with creative solutions that are not only able to strengthen their market existence but also help in making the environment sustainable. This paradigm of partnership does not only help to explain the primary problems of water scarcity, but also coincides with the increasing consumer desire of responsible business approaches. According to N/A (2006) promoting understanding between the stakeholders has become one of the key elements in managing water and this illustrates how corporations can maneuver and succeed in the confusion of contemporary market entry. The other interesting success story is formed where there is a union between economic empowerment and social responsibility with special interest to women with disability. Programs like the International Symposium on Microcredit to Women with Disabilities have highlighted the necessity of special support mechanisms to respond to the special needs of this population. These programs empower women with disabilities to navigate and access markets that they previously could not, through empowering them with the necessary knowledge and skills.

Figure 4.10. Success stories in market access.

Source: https://fastercapital.co/i/Social-entrepreneurship-market-access--Breaking-Barriers--Social-Entrepreneurs-and-Access-to-Markets--Success-Stories-of-Market-Access.webp.

Another important lesson of this initiative is the role of leadership in the marginalized communities, in order to speak on their behalf at the economic table. The fact that these women must actively participate in economic development, as noted by Mobility International USA (MIUSA) (1998) underscores a critical factor in the marketplace accessibility of ensuring that the voices of different communities are not merely heard but also empowered. The climax of these success stories shows that market access does not constitute only a transactional effort but a multi-layered challenge that needs profound involvement and novel strategies. The two illustrate how dealing with environmental and social concerns may result in efficient market tactics and policies that would advance equity and sustainability at the same time. Those companies, which are interested in cooperation with the variety of stakeholders, not only increase the operational sustainability but also make a valuable contribution towards the societal objectives. When considered in the light of market demand to goods, these stories are effective aids to remembering how the aligning of business goals with the wider social responsibilities can provide a new platform of opportunities, creating an economic environment that is more accommodating and sustainable (Figure 4.10).

4.4.2. Challenges Faced by Specific Countries

Nations which have open trade lines can also encounter significant hurdles which hinder access to markets of goods especially when the economies are developing. The existence of tariffs and trade barriers, introduced by more powerful countries, is one of the major obstacles as it may inhibit the movement of goods and reduce the chances of export. Indicatively, the agricultural products in the developing nations often face high tariffs which hurt their competitiveness in the international markets. As a result, the smallholder farmers in these areas find it difficult to make profitable sales and this restricts them in enhancing production. According to Dammert et al. (2014), whereas Fair Trade programs are designed to stimulate the well-being of the rural farmers by offering them high prices, the intricate nature of the market access is laden with constraints that stifle their economic and social progress. This demonstrates how essential trade policies are to the socioeconomic status of countries that are exporting. Moreover, the issue of reaching international markets is aggravated by the fact that it is a task to comply with the regulatory specifications of the importing nations. These conditions are usually standards of high quality, certifications and adherence to safety and environmental regulations, which is especially cumbersome to small producers in third world countries.

These constraints are further aggravated by the absence of infrastructure and technical expertise resulting in decreased competitiveness in the global markets. According to the themes discussed in Cooper et al. (2014), nations like those involved in Trade in Services Agreement (TISA) negotiations face policy problems that are not related to merely reducing tariffs. They have to deal with elaborate regulation systems, which will suffocate the chances of local companies to freely participate in global trade. This interaction between compliance needs and access to markets hence points out the complex issues surrounding certain nations in their effort to achieve economic development. In addition, the world market demand changes and instability of commodity prices pose further barriers to goods accessibility in markets. The effects of changing consumer tastes and market dynamics are especially likely to affect countries that depend considerably on the export of particular products, especially agricultural products. Such instability in the market may lead to dwindled revenues affecting the economies of the nations and causing the producers to continue their cycle of poverty. Some countries have attempted to diversify and create new forms of industries as a response to these challenges, but the introduction of a new industry is usually sluggish and is accompanied by difficulties of its own. The knowledge of Dammert et al. (2014) points to the idea that such efforts as Fair Trade help to alleviate some of the pressure, but not enough to solve the overall problem of restricted market access and the shifts in productivity. These underlying issues are a critical aspect in promoting sustainable development and resilience of nations to the dynamics of international trade.

4.4.3. Lessons Learned from Case Studies

Case studies are rich in giving insights on the complexities and problems of accessing goods in the market. Through weighing various real-life cases, scholars can extract general impediments that include regulatory challenges, logistical flaws, and customer tastes influencing market penetration. As an example, those countries that have strict agricultural importation controls tend to restrict entry of foreign produce, which may prevent diversification in the market and economic development. Experiences of such situations point to the need of policymakers to ensure that the regulatory frameworks are more inclusive so that they can allow trade without compromising on the safety and quality of trading. Also, according to case studies, it is important to observe local market dynamics and consumer behavior, which forces businesses to modify their strategies to increase market penetration and sustainability to ensure that approach to market access is more complete (Armenteras et al., 2011). An important lesson gained after conducting different case studies is the need to involve stakeholders in the market access process. The key to effective case studies is often cooperation of governmental bodies, the players of the private sector, and the local communities.

The involvement of the stakeholders instills trust and the market strategies are considered to be in line with the needs and aspirations of the affected populations. As an illustration, the involvement of local farmer cooperatives in supply chains has been successful in improving agricultural product accessibility to markets. This partnership does not only assist in the development of local economies but also makes market solutions sustainable and socially fair. The lessons learned point out that the active involvement of the stakeholders can help avert possible conflicts, decrease the risks of implementation and ultimately help the market access programs to be more in line with the modern objectives of inclusivity and sustainability (Beria et al., 2010). Besides, the analysis of case studies highlights the importance of sustainability towards the realization of long-term market access. It is becoming increasingly accepted that market access strategies have to have environmental considerations in addition to the economic goals in mind. To explain, market models that combine ecosystem service indicators and environmental services payments overlook successful approaches. These twin-tiered systems provide financial incentives to the conservation of natural resources and the encouragement of products that have their values based on sustainable practices. The lessons that are learned in these cases would show that companies are able to reduce their exposure to climate change and resource depletion by adopting sustainable practices, which will appeal to environmentally conscious consumers. This will help not only to increase market access but also to increase the financial stability of supply chains against the future uncertainties, hence being beneficial to both environmental integrity and economic success (Armenteras et al., 2011).

4.5. TECHNOLOGICAL ADVANCEMENTS AND MARKET ACCESS

Technological developments are very critical in determining markets access of goods and this aspect has greatly changed the way business is conducted in the global markets. The expansion of digital tools and platforms has provided opportunities to companies as never before to reach consumers, automate processes, and streamline supply chains. These technologies allow small and medium-sized enterprises (SMEs) to act at a global scale, which was previously done by large companies. Furthermore, the incorporation of data analytics enables companies to learn about market trends and customer preferences and make marketing and product development more targeted. This is responsive in multiple industries whereby technology is becoming a trigger in a fast-track adaptation and innovation whereby firms are willing to expand their scope beyond the local borders and improve their competitive factors in a fast-interconnected world market. VUCA (volatility, uncertainty, complexity, and ambiguity) has become a part of the modern business environment, and companies are encouraged to reevaluate their business practices in the context of technological improvements. The example of emerging market companies, including Chinas Haier Group, demonstrates how these firms can take advantage of management innovations to overcome obstacles in the VUCA environment. Through the practice of agile management in the framework of Rendanheyi Haier had managed to change their organizational structure that was a traditional hierarchical structure to a responsive and customer oriented enterprise. This turnaround highlights the significance of technology in increasing product availability as well as the adaptive culture that is able to survive in the volatile and dynamically changing market. These strategic changes help companies to optimize their market access approaches so that they are sensitive to the changing customer requirements as well as competitive forces. Moreover, the globalization process coupled with the interconnectedness points to the importance of technology in enlarging the market access. Globalization encourages interdependent structures that cut across geographical borders allowing firms to take advantage of different markets to develop. Technological advancements also play a role in this phenomenon where it improves communication, the cost of transactions and provides platforms to work with others across countries. Nonetheless, growth of these networks also creates issues on the implication of globalized trade especially on the aspect of policy implications and unintended impacts of globalized trade. When operating within these complicated networks, companies should be keen to change their strategies to reduce the risks they may face and to exploit the opportunities they get to enter the market. After all, technological advances are rather a two-sided sword that offers companies opportunities to develop, yet also asks them to be quick and forward-looking in the market (Wells et al., 2001).

4.5.1. E-Commerce and Its Impact on Market Access

E-commerce has changed how people can access goods in the market fundamentally and this has opened up more opportunities to businesses all over the world. Firms are now able to reach consumers in remote markets with relative ease as this was previously limited by geographical barriers and infrastructural limitations. This has increased access to markets and hence competition enabling smaller businesses to venture into markets that were once dominated by large firms. New entrants have made the marketplace to be more diverse considering that businesses are able to create an online presence at a minimum investment. Nevertheless, also comes with this augmented accessibility are challenges of companies having to adapt to diverse regulatory environments and consumer tastes and preference that vary widely across several regions. Therefore, e-commerce provides a fresh opportunity to engage in the market through better participation, but on the other hand, companies need to maintain flexible strategies when entering the dynamics of international trade. Moreover, the development of e-commerces affects dynamics of international trade and regulation. Governments have the challenge of adjusting their policies to the reality of a digital economy, and this can require provisions to change rules on data privacy, payment systems, and consumer protection. E-commerce is progressively being discussed as an essential element of market access in trade agreements, compelling countries to cooperate on standardizing e-commerce laws. International collaboration is essential to deal with cross-border impediments that might interfere with the free movement of goods and services in the digital environment. As observed in the discussion of the steel industry in China, there are complexities in the global trade dynamics whereby countries have to negotiate on the rules that would create a level playing field whereby e-commerce would play a positive role in ensuring that global trade relations are healthy (Tang et al., 2010). In addition, the increasing awareness is that e-commerce does not only influence the access of the market, but also the competitive environment itself. As online markets and online infrastructures continue to populate the market, companies face novel competition that is disrupting traditional market configurations. This may cause major changes in pricing, supply networks, and consumerism. With firms engaging in competition in the digital arena, concerns on domestic subsidies and its spillover effects are brought to the centre stage of trade talks. Existing World Trade Organization (WTO) regulations might be inadequate to handle the intricacies of e-commerce and subsidy policy and a call to reform the rules to facilitate fair competition and good regulations has been raised. To overcome these challenges, governments should work together to formulate guidelines that promote an even playing field in the physical and digital market, thus improving market accessibility and economic stability (Hoekman et al., 2020) (Figure 4.11).

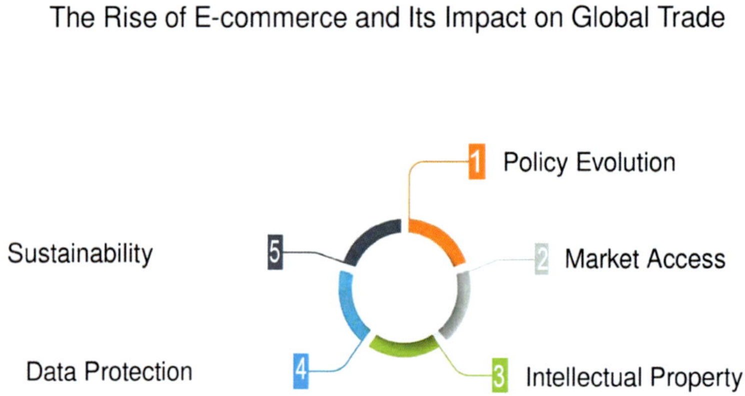

Figure 4.11. E-commerce and its impact on market access.

Source: https://fastercapital.co/i/International-trade-policy--International-Trade-Policy-and-E-commerce--A-Game-Changer-for-Businesses--The-Rise-of-E-commerce-and-Its-Impact-on-Global-Trade.webp.

4.5.2. Role of Technology in Reducing Barriers

Technology is being used in the current global economy to break the demarcations that have been traditionally used to limit market access to goods. The digital developments more especially in information communication technology (ICT) enable a smooth flow of transactions and interactions among different geographic regions. These technologies can help businesses to be more efficient, minimize the cost of operation, and increase their market beyond the locality. ICT has transformed conventional market accessibility by closing the divide between producers and consumers. Nevertheless, there is a correlation between greater ICT infrastructure and economic growth but the causative aspect of this correlation needs to be investigated further. Such complexity implies that, although technology has a transformative potential, it does not equally apply to every region but can be extremely different depending on the socio-economic conditions (Faith et al., 2016). Furthermore, new technologies like digital twins are pushing the boundary further in minimizing the barriers further, particularly in those areas where human connection and subjective information play a vital role. Making the virtual representations of the physical assets will enable the businesses to optimize their activities in real-time, which will enable them to react more appropriately to market demand and consumer behavior. This would be useful especially in the operational and maintenance period of complex systems. Visualization and analysis of large volumes of data allows improving the decision-making process, which ultimately results in a more efficient allocation of resources. As organizations exploit the opportunities of such advancements, they can not only enjoy a competitive advantage, but also make the market a leaner place, helping smaller businesses that, in the past, could not overcome the overwhelming odds (Berntsson et al., 2023). As much as the advantages of technology in market entry are very clear, it is vital to note that there are challenges that are associated with its implementation. The digital divide may be worsened with the introduction of digital technologies, especially in those areas where the infrastructure and digital literacy are not widespread. With markets becoming more reliant on technological systems, access inequalities can give rise to new barriers. Consequently, policymakers and stakeholders should take into account fair policies that would facilitate equal access to technology. These programs have the potential to empower the underrepresented firms and eventually result in a more even-handed market. With these issues resolved, the potential of technology as a means of minimizing barriers can be achieved in its entirety, and opportunities to create a more equal global economy will open up (Faith et al., 2016).

4.5.3. Future Trends in Technology and Market Access

The geography of market accessibility of goods will be changed by technological developments, especially regarding the digital platform. With e-commerce steadily entering the international marketplace, companies are turning to artificial intelligence and data analytics to empower market penetration and consumer interaction. Not only does this democratize market access, previously controlled by bigger companies, but it also allows small and medium-sized enterprises (SMEs) to access international customers with relative ease. Transparency in supply chain enhanced by blockchain further improves trust and efficiency which is important elements of entering new markets. Through these technological innovations, businesses are able to streamline their businesses, which eventually leads to a wider market base and financial strength. This synergy of these breakthroughs does not just create competition but also points to a wider move towards inclusiveness in markets as highlighted in the ideas presented in Shaping Inclusive Markets. It is also critical to note the significance of collaborative platforms that unite suppliers and consumers within geographical limits. This tendency is changing the traditional approach to accessing markets where intermediaries usually dominated distribution channels. Rather, companies are currently dealing with consumers directly and reducing overheads, which consequently, decreases consumer prices and enhances access of products. E-media, including social media and influencer marketing, contribute more to product visibility and participation of consumers in the market.

Figure 4.12. Future trends in technology and market access.

Source: https://imageio.forbes.com/specials-images/imageserve/65c9c44ac205195ae02e22ec/0x0.jpg?format=jpg&height=900&width=1600&fit=bounds.

Consequently, the future of access to the market will be more focused on direct interaction and community-specific approaches, creating a feeling of connectedness between manufacturers and customers. This direct access is not only a loyalty-building move but also a sign of a paradigm shift in consumer expectations since people want to see the inner workings and a real relationship with the brands they decide to work with, which is essential in the framework of economic inclusion outlined in the corresponding studies. The effects of these technological developments in regard to market access are profound especially in areas where the economy is undergoing change as is the case in the Chicago metropolitan area. In the past, Chicago has been able to transform itself out of an industrial economy to a diverse knowledge and service based environment, one that is innovative and highly endowed in human capital. Nevertheless, growth rates are slowing down and thus adaptive strategies are required in order to take advantage of technology in order to maintain economic prosperity. The exercise of regional planning such as the GO To 2040 is intended to capitalize on these trends to boost productivity and employment through innovation and by making sure that sectors that grow at high rates are promoted. This is a strategic move that emphasizes the need to match technology to market access programs to generate a long-term economic growth and resilience. The overlap of these trends underscores the importance of the strategic planning and creative responses to have future market access principles to benefit wider sections of the economy in addition to resolving the new challenges in urban management and space-efficientness, which have been stressed in the recent evaluations of regional economic potential (Figure 4.12).

4.6. POLICY RECOMMENDATIONS FOR IMPROVING MARKET ACCESS

Enhancing market access to goods requires a complex solution that deals with tariffs as well as non-tariff barriers. To establish relations that would minimize or completely remove tariffs and yet at the same time streamline non-tariff barriers (complicated customs regimes and strict regulations) strategic trade agreements should be prioritized. These agreements should not only wish to streamline the present short-term economic gains, but also look at the long-term sustainability and mutual development among the partners in the trade. This is especially important to developing economies that tend to have barriers to entry to the market. Due to the simplification of regulations and the number of transparency, a country will be able to make the environment in which the trade can take place, thus improving its competitive advantage and giving people more options among various goods. This should be geared towards providing a fair trading environment that will enable market accessibility and economic stability as highlighted in the guidelines established in detailed economic strategies like GO TO 2040 (Kosarkoet al., 2011). When dealing with agricultural and industrial products, there is need to have strong policies that will have the developing countries have better access to the market and especially when it comes to the Doha Round talks. It is important that the needs of these countries be addressed in the context of the World Trade Organization so that the countries can enjoy their needs and that the benefits of the trade are shared fairly. Doha Round recommendations also focus on special treatment, such as better access to global markets, that may assist developing countries in strengthening their economies. These actions are not only important in the development of an economy, but also in ensuring equity in international trade. It will not only help developing countries to grow their economies as they will be able to enter into the global markets on an equal footing but will also help to ensure that the world economy grows in the long term as the economic growth of individual countries will be interconnected (Deardorff et al., 2025). Trade facilitation measures can contribute greatly to improved market access of goods at a global level. Nations must invest in infrastructure enhancement, including logistics network and port infrastructure, not to mention, which are essential to trade. Trade facilitation ensures that delays are minimized, costs are minimized and eventually the domestic producers become more competitive. Also, transfer of technology and capacity building programs can empower local businesses so that they can meet international standards. There will be improved cooperation among governments, the private sector, and international organizations, which will contribute to the sharing of the best practices and innovative solutions. This would not only enhance market access but also make the fruits of trade more distributed, to make the economic environment more inclusive and within this economic environment, growth and innovation in various areas will be fostered (Kosarko et al., 2011).

4.6.1. Strategies for Reducing Tariffs and Barriers

In order to make goods more accessible to the market, the reduction of tariffs and barriers is a decisive solution that nations can implement to make trade easy. The tariffs being the taxes imposed by the government on goods imported to a country affect the entry into the market greatly thereby raising the price to the consumers eventually lowering the competitiveness of the local industries. The lowering of these tariffs will prompt imports thus enhancing consumer choice and fostering competition among the local businesses. Studies have shown that the impact of tariff reduction in an exporting country is positive on exports as compared to a reduction in the importing country. It would imply that active policy responses leading to the reduction of the tariffs can not only positively impact the exporters and their ability to reach more markets but contribute to the improvement of the general economic environment, which would be a win-win situation in terms of the trade partners (Fang et al., 2015). Market access is also challenged by non-tariff barriers (NTBs) that contain a range of regulatory and policy actions. These obstacles are normally presented as import quotas, technical standards, and discriminatory licensing procedures which are more barricading than tariffs. The harmonization of the standards and regulations in tackling NTBs will also help ease the cross-border flows of goods. Indicatively, reduction of NTBs can greatly increase imports of environmental goods, which demonstrates how environmental factors can also be consistent with trade facilitation. A study represents that the reduction of tariff barriers in the countries of importation results in more environmental goods, which is why regulations can be well-implemented to facilitate both trade liberalization and environmental sustainability (Fang et al., 2015). Moreover, effective minimization of trade barriers requires an all-inclusive strategy, which involves complementary policies. Such policies ought to encompass macroeconomic stability, flexible labor market and competitive markets, which are mandatory in the alleviation of the negative impacts of trade liberalization. Notably, the World Bank highlights the importance of a coherent trade policy structure in reducing poverty and improving market accessibility to the developing countries. Countries can use tools like export subsidies and duty drawback to help establish a more favorable environment to traders. Notably, adjustment costs could be resolved by safety nets and retraining programs that can make sure that advantages of trade reform are widely distributed and hence help to create a more inclusive economic environment that facilitates sustainable growth (Figure 4.13).

Figure 4.13. Strategies for overcoming tariffs and trade barriers.

Source: https://fastercapital.co/i/Tariffs-and-trade-barriers--Overcoming-tariffs-and--Strategies-for-Overcoming-Tariffs-and-Trade-Barriers.webp.

4.6.2. Importance of Regulatory Harmonization

Regulatory harmonization is a very important aspect to increase market access to goods in an economy that is becoming more and more globalized. By harmonizing the rules and standards of the countries, the barriers commonly hindering the free movement of items across the borders are minimized. This does not only help in trade, but also improves consumer protection, safety and environmental sustainability. As an example, in industries such as pharmaceuticals and medical equipment, coordinated policies have guaranteed that goods are of the same quality and effectiveness, hence protecting the health of the population.

Furthermore, such harmonization can foster innovation, because other companies are likely to invest in research and development in a situation where they better understand the regulatory environment in various markets. Therefore, regulatory harmonization may be the key to the development of an efficient and more dynamic global market. Besides encouraging innovation, regulatory harmonization helps in economic growth by allowing small businesses to enter into foreign markets. The small companies that might not have the resources to overcome the complex and differing national regulations find it easier to export their products when they are standardized. These businesses are able to spend more on production and less on coming out of regulatory hurdles by simplifying the compliance processes. This is especially essential in emerging economies where small businesses are part of the economy and workforce. With such firms getting access to bigger markets, they are also able to scale their operations, enhance their product offerings and eventually lead to the entire economic development of their regions. Hence, regulatory harmonization is not only pertinent to trade facilitation but also a source of growth and its non-discriminatory inclusion in international commerce. Finally, regulatory harmonization may be important in solving global issues which affect the world beyond national boundaries like environmental problems and pandemics. When nations work together to create similar regulatory measures, they are better able to address such issues which demand a concerted effort. To illustrate my point, harmonized regulations will help immensely in the development of initiatives that seek to curb carbon emissions or the transmission of infectious diseases. The standardization of standards and practices allows countries to exchange information and resources, which increases their overall ability to respond to global crises. The harmonization of regulations presents an opportunity to increase broader cooperation as demonstrated by the development of technologies and practices that are geared towards sustainability such as the introduction of hybrid systems in environmental management Dunér et al. (1992). Therefore, the importance of regulatory harmonization is not the only one that is economically defined, but also in its prospects of creating joint solutions to urgent global issues.

4.6.3. Role of Government and Private Sector Collaboration

The interaction between the collaboration of the government and the private sector considerably influences the access to the goods on the market, which makes it possible to exchange resources and experience that potentially might contribute to efficiency and innovation. Governments have been known to liaise with the private entities in the effort to uplift infrastructure and simplify the regulatory procedures which are highly important in facilitating a business friendly environment. As an example, removal of government bureaucracy by government restructuring, as well as investment in logistics and technology by the private sector, can directly affect the competitiveness of exports. The partnership is also able to determine areas that are potentially open to growth, which is demonstrated by studies on major sector supply chains, which indicate current barriers and possible growth prospects in different areas like those reported in Greater Lincolnshire (Bosworth et al., 2012). Moreover, the so-called public-private partnerships (PPP) tend to become one of the effective strategies of enhancing market access to goods, especially in the developing economies. Such partnerships enable sharing of resources and experience to overcome the infrastructure gaps and service delivery issues that can impede trade. Through the synergy of the two industries, including the regulatory power of the government and the innovation ability of the private industry, it is possible to implement an initiative together as a result of which stronger supply chains may be achieved. This dynamism is not only favourable to the immediate stakeholders, but also leads to the overall economic stability and growth since this provides a conducive environment in which goods can be manufactured and distributed effectively. The lessons learned in studying the service provision arrangement in different settings show the relevance of such partnerships in the attainment of viable market access remedies (David-Barrett et al., 2015). Furthermore, the importance of government in enabling and controlling the activities of the private sector cannot be underestimated when it comes to market access. Governments should put in place clear policies and frameworks that will promote the participation of the responsible private sector besides protecting the population and promoting fairness. This is an essential balance because excessive dependence on the private organism may result in unfairness and inefficiency in the market. Successful teamwork involves continuous communication and negotiation, which may be promoted by the use of stakeholder engagement programs and comparable goals. Through harmonizing of the interests between the people and the business, the stakeholders will be able to pull together towards the promotion of market access strategies which will eventually lead to the consumer benefiting and thus sustainable economic development. Finally, the combination of the government and the power of the nongovernmental organizations encourages the existence of an active market where the resources can easily reach the populace, which is why the collaboration of the two sides is so significant (David-Barrett et al., 2015).

SUMMARY

A market access analysis of goods, it is clear that the role of e-business is vital in contemporary economic models. Digitization of commerce has not only transformed the manner in which goods are sold and marketed but also the way in which businesses engage with consumers anywhere around the world. As shown in the recent research, organizations that adopt e-business practices can highly improve their competitive advantage and efficiency. In some economies, especially in emerging markets like Ukraine, e-commerce has prompted the growth of the economy and this has emphasized the importance of businesses adjusting to digital market places. This is in line with the conclusion that without strategic approach to e-business, firms will stand to lose their market positions. Therefore, to enhance the e-business structures to achieve sustainable development in competitive global markets, policies and support systems should be established as pointed out by Lipych et al. (2020). Moreover, the quality of the market access structure depends on the alignment of regulations and standards among the borders. Lack of alignment of laws associated with e-commerce means that businesses are hampered by obstacles that prevent their growth and expansion in foreign markets. This highlights the need to have businesses work in alliance with policy makers to provide an enabling environment where the market can be accessed.

The adoption of e-business models would entail large-scale investment in technology and development of sound digital infrastructures since this is a precondition to exploiting emerging market opportunities. Therefore, effective e-business model can only be realized through the adoption of favorable regulatory measures that will reflect the dynamic nature of global trade. Going ahead, strengthening global collaboration on regulatory matters is one of the crucial measures towards enhancing accessibility to goods in the market, which should be seen in the light of the considerations outlined by Dale et al. (2013). In conclusion, the point of e-business and access to markets shows a multitude of opportunities yet to be exploited. It is apparent that organizations are forced to incorporate new strategies that embrace digitization in their operation in order to maximize efficiency and reach customers. This is necessitated by the historical legacies of trade systems that have been depicted in preceding studies that emphasized the fluidity of markets and the significance of flexibility. Globalization creates competitive environment that requires proactive approach in the area of e-business integration in which firms are no longer just concerned about the quality of the product but also on the creation of sustainable e-commerce practices. Therefore, future studies may shed more light on the effectiveness of different e-business models and their effects on accessing the market with goods such that businesses are adequately prepared to face the present and upcoming challenges within the global market environment. The strategic insight, as well as systemic support, can be crucial in this case to allow the successful engagement in international trade, as proposed by Dale et al. (2013) and Lipych et al. (2020). When analyzing the market access of goods, there were some important points that came out highlighting its complexities and implications in different sectors. A key area that is repeatedly brought up in discussions is the significance of the concept of backcasting as one of the strategic instruments that can be used to create both the long-term and short-term policy actions. The approach helps the stakeholders to consider where they want to be in the future as well as work backwards to find out steps that can be taken to access the market. This would be more effective in ensuring that the present and future market dynamics are considered and eventually come up with more robust and adaptive strategies of improving the market opportunities. With the incorporation of the concept of backcasting into the policy-making process, the stakeholders can manage to align their ambitions with realistic measures that can be taken to respond to the changing market conditions and establish a basis on sustainable economic growth and competitiveness in international trade (Bärlund et al., 2010).

Also, the importance of the regional cooperation was pointed out as a necessity to improve the market access to goods. The Delaware River ports case study illustrates that maritime trade can be used to develop an economy when ports authorities and stakeholders collaborate. A comparison of the port condition in the region will show that not only can efficient operation be enhanced but also a synergy is formed to promote economic activity in the region as a whole. The results demonstrate that regional port activity sustains high numbers of employment opportunities with each port job leading to other jobs because of flow of economies and spending by employees. This inter-relationship spells out the importance of ports strategically investing in infrastructure facilities to enhance their positioning in the competitive environment as an avenue of effectively realizing their potential as critical channels of accessibility to the market (N/A, 2008). Finally, conclusions on the discussions were summarized into the overall implications of market access to goods in the global world, especially in relation to breaking the barriers and maximizing the trade networks.

The results echo the theory that policy frameworks and operational logistics need to adapt to maintain and increase market access in a growing global economy that is becoming more and more interconnected. The stakeholder engagements have proven that a holistic strategy, integrating technology, infrastructure, and regional collaboration, is critical in resolving the current trade barriers and opening new markets. This integrated approach is not only aimed at supporting the local economies but also the regional markets are placed in the global order that focuses on the competitiveness and innovation. The constant communication and readjustment as the stakeholders maneuver through these complexities will definitely be important in ensuring that market access is a priority agenda in economic development considerations (Bärlund et al., 2010).

REFERENCES

1. Ackerman, F., Bernasconi, N., Cabré, M. M., Corbett, et al. (2016). Trade in the balance: Reconciling trade and climate policy: Report of the Working Group on Trade, Investment, and Climate Policy. https://open.bu.edu/bitstream/2144/22909/1/Pardee_TradeClimate_110316final.pdf (accessed on 30th October 2025).
2. Ahearn, R. J. (2010). Trade primer: Qs and as on trade concepts, performance, and policy. https://core.ac.uk/download/5128324.pdf (accessed on 30th October 2025).
3. Ahmed, I., Brown, A., Dayal, A., Koh, H., Agarwal, R., & King, S. (2017). Shaping inclusive markets: How funders and intermediaries can help markets move toward greater economic inclusion. https://core.ac.uk/download/86445450.pdf (accessed on 30th October 2025).
4. Ahmed, Z., Bacarreza, G., Bedford, R., Beets, N., Bhagwati, J., Borjas, G., et al. (2009). International trade agreements and international migration. https://core.ac.uk/download/29196183.pdf (accessed on 30th October 2025).
5. Armenteras, D., Ash, N., Barano, T., et al. (2011). Developing ecosystem service indicators: Experiences and lessons learned from sub-global assessments and other initiatives. https://core.ac.uk/download/55724599.pdf (accessed on 30th October 2025).
6. Artal Tur, A. (2017). Culture and cultures in tourism. https://core.ac.uk/download/199454604.pdf (accessed on 30th October 2025).
7. Bärlund, I., Dubel, A., Kok, K., et al. (2010). Pan-European back casting exercise, enriched with regional perspective, and including a list of short-term policy options. https://core.ac.uk/download/pdf/29235489.pdf (accessed on 30th October 2025).
8. Beckert, J. (2025). Where do prices come from? Sociological approaches to price formation. https://core.ac.uk/download/pdf/6722787.pdf (accessed on 30th October 2025).
9. Ben Hammouda, H., Karingi, S., Lang, R., et al. (2025). Can market access help African agriculture? https://core.ac.uk/download/pdf/7304804.pdf (accessed on 30th October 2025).
10. Beria, L., & van Noordwijk, M. (2010). Principles for fairness and efficiency in enhancing environmental services in Asia: Payments, compensation, or co-investment? https://core.ac.uk/download/pdf/29238296.pdf (accessed on 30th October 2025).
11. Berntsson, A., & Sandström, E. (2023). Digital twins for sustainability

in building operations–How a large commercial real estate firm can use digital twins to generate sustainable values in the O&M phase. https://core.ac.uk/download/620667259.pdf (accessed on 30th October 2025).

12. Bosworth, G., Hingley, M., Price, L., et al. (2012). Opportunities for Greater Lincolnshire's supply chains: Full report. https://core.ac.uk/download/9553358.pdf (accessed on 30th October 2025).
13. Caporale, G. M., Rault, C., Sova, A., et al. (2009). The impact of association agreements on trade flows and the trade balance: Evidence from the CEEC-4. https://core.ac.uk/download/336037.pdf (accessed on 30th October 2025).
14. Carrère, C., & de Melo, J. (2025). Are different rules of origin equally costly? Estimates from NAFTA. https://core.ac.uk/download/pdf/6515484.pdf (accessed on 30th October 2025).
15. Collins, D. A. (2019). The International Bar Association and trade in legal services: Meta law-making in international economic law? https://core.ac.uk/download/169434481.pdf (accessed on 30th October 2025).
16. Cooney, S., Cooper, W. H., Jones, V. C., et al. (2008). The proposed U.S.-South Korea Free Trade Agreement (KORUS FTA): Provisions and implications. https://core.ac.uk/download/5129465.pdf (accessed on 30th October 2025).
17. Cooper, W. H., & Nelson, R. M. (2014). U.S. foreign trade in services: Trends and U.S. policy challenges. https://core.ac.uk/download/20537776.pdf (accessed on 30th October 2025).
18. Cottyn, H., & Vanhaute, E. (2017). Into their land and labors: A comparative and global analysis of trajectories of peasant transformation. https://core.ac.uk/download/84046793.pdf (accessed on 30th October 2025).
19. Dale, G. (2013). Market less trading in Hammurabi's time: A re-appraisal. https://core.ac.uk/download/29140805.pdf (accessed on 30th October 2025).
20. Dammert, A. C., & Mohan, S. (2014). A survey of the economics of fair trade. https://www.econstor.eu/dspace/bitstream/10419/98935/1/dp8167.pdf (accessed on 30th October 2025).
21. David-Barrett, E. (2015). The state-private interface in public service provision. https://core.ac.uk/download/30613585.pdf (accessed on 30th October 2025).
22. Deardorff, A. V., & Stern, R. M. (2025). Enhancing the benefits for India and other developing countries in the Doha Development Agenda negotiations. https://core.ac.uk/download/pdf/7053651.pdf (accessed on 30th October 2025).

23. Dunér, V., & Myhrberg, T. (1992). The Second Banking Directive: Conflicts, choices, and long-term goals. https://core.ac.uk/download/62547860.pdf (accessed on 30th October 2025).

24. Echessah, P. N. (2025). Effects of EU's Common Agricultural Policy reforms on prospects for Eastern and Southern Africa's trade with the EU under the Economic Partnership Agreements. https://core.ac.uk/download/pdf/6505687.pdf (accessed on 30th October 2025).

25. Faith, B., Hernandez, K., Prieto Martín, P., et al. (2016). The impact of digital technology on economic growth and productivity, and its implications for employment and equality: An evidence review. https://core.ac.uk/download/286047706.pdf (accessed on 30th October 2025).

26. Fang, H., He, Q., Peng, B., et al. (2015). Trade liberalization and trade performance of environmental goods: Evidence from Asia-Pacific Economic Cooperation members. https://core.ac.uk/download/213088391.pdf (accessed on 30th October 2025).

27. Fojtíková, L. (2018). China's intellectual property rights commitments in the WTO: Legal and economic implications. https://core.ac.uk/download/161960388.pdf (accessed on 30th October 2025).

28. Frynas, J. G., Mellahi, K., & Mol, M. J. (2018). Management innovation made in China: Haier's Rendanheyi. https://core.ac.uk/download/160275675.pdf (accessed on 30th October 2025).

29. Ghafele Bashi, R. (2008). Perceptions of intellectual property: A review. https://core.ac.uk/download/28970391.pdf (accessed on 30th October 2025).

30. Golub, S. S., Hajkova, D., Mirza, D., et al. (2003). Policies and international integration: Influences on trade and foreign direct investment. https://core.ac.uk/download/153166346.pdf (accessed on 30th October 2025).

31. Helble, M., & Okubo, T. (2025). Heterogeneous quality firms and trade costs. https://core.ac.uk/download/pdf/6616191.pdf (accessed on 30th October 2025).

32. Hoekman, B., & Nelson, D. (2020). Rethinking international subsidy rules. *Bertelsmann Working Paper*, 28/02/2020. https://core.ac.uk/download/287647974.pdf (accessed on 30th October 2025).

33. Hoekman, B., Michalopoulos, C., Schiff, M., et al. (2025). Trade policy reform and poverty alleviation. https://core.ac.uk/download/pdf/6373301.pdf (accessed on 30th October 2025).

34. Howse, R. (2014). Regulatory cooperation, regional trade agreements, and World Trade Law: Conflict or complementarity? https://core.ac.uk/download/62570443.pdf (accessed on 30th October 2025).

35. Hu, A., Barshefsky, C., Jin, B., Chan, A., Cheung, K. Y., Dale, H., et al. (1999). The politics of Chinese trade and the Asian financial crises: Questioning the wisdom of export-led growth. https://core.ac.uk/download/49114.pdf (accessed on 30th October 2025).
36. Inocencio, A., Penning de Vries, F., & Sally, H. (2014). Opportunities for private sector participation in agricultural water development and management. https://core.ac.uk/download/pdf/6352701.pdf (accessed on 30th October 2025).
37. Ionicheva, V. N., Medkov, A. A., Tsvetkov, V. A., et al. (2015). Institutional and organizational features of cross-border cargo traffic in the post-Soviet space integration terms. Part I. https://elar.urfu.ru/bitstream/10995/47448/1/r-economy_2015_v1_3_05.pdf (accessed on 30th October 2025).
38. Kosarko, G., & Weissbourd, R. (2011). Economic impacts of GO TO 2040. https://core.ac.uk/download/71345969.pdf (accessed on 30th October 2025).
39. Lipych, L. H., & Mokhniuk, A. M. (2020). E-business in Ukraine: Peculiarities, tendencies, prospects. https://core.ac.uk/download/pdf/323228985.pdf (accessed on 30th October 2025).
40. Malkawi, B. H. (2010). Jordan's accession to the WTO: Retrospective and prospective. https://core.ac.uk/download/186331686.pdf (accessed on 30th October 2025).
41. N/A. (1998). Loud, proud and prosperous! Report on the Mobility International USA International Symposium on Microcredit for Women with Disabilities. https://core.ac.uk/download/5119930.pdf (accessed on 30th October 2025).
42. N/A. (2003). Promoting U.S. economic growth and security through expanding world trade: A call for bold American leadership. https://core.ac.uk/download/71356602.pdf (accessed on 30th October 2025).
43. N/A. (2006). Business in the world of water. https://core.ac.uk/download/71345777.pdf (accessed on 30th October 2025).
44. N/A. (2008). Maritime commerce in Greater Philadelphia: Assessing industry trends and growth opportunities for Delaware River ports. https://core.ac.uk/download/71342612.pdf (accessed on 30th October 2025).
45. Olper, A., & Raimondi, V. (2025). Explaining national border effects in the Quad food trade. https://core.ac.uk/download/pdf/6653387.pdf (accessed on 30th October 2025).
46. Orlova, I., Maliszewska, M., & Taran, S. (2025). Deep integration with

the EU and its likely impact on selected ENP countries and Russia. https://core.ac.uk/download/pdf/6704175.pdf (accessed on 30th October 2025).

47. Riviere-Cinnamond, A. (2025). A public choice approach to the economic analysis of animal healthcare systems. https://core.ac.uk/download/pdf/7055427.pdf (accessed on 30th October 2025).
48. Schiff, M. (2025). Regional integration and development in small states. https://core.ac.uk/download/pdf/6644694.pdf (accessed on 30th October 2025).
49. Sellner, R., & Polasek, W. (2025). Does globalization affect regional growth? Evidence for NUTS-2 regions in EU-27. https://core.ac.uk/download/pdf/6580289.pdf (accessed on 30th October 2025).
50. Tang, R. (2010). China's steel industry and its impact on the United States: Issues for Congress. https://core.ac.uk/download/5132159.pdf (accessed on 30th October 2025).
51. Tomaselli, N. (2025). *Economic Partnership Agreements: Redesigning Trade and Development Among EU and ACP Countries*. https://core.ac.uk/download/pdf/6972987.pdf (accessed on 30th October 2025).
52. Vandenbussche, H., Venables, A. J., & Wooton, I. (2002). Enhancing economic cooperation between the EU and the Americas: An economic assessment. https://core.ac.uk/download/9019704.pdf (accessed on 30th October 2025).
53. Wells, G. J. (2001). The issue of globalization—An overview. https://core.ac.uk/download/5121958.pdf (accessed on 30th October 2025).

Chapter 5

Trade in Services (GATS)

Contents

INTRODUCTION

The global trade landscape has been radically transformed, most notably by the coming of the General Agreement on Trade in Services (GATS). A key component of the World Trade Organization (WTO) framework, GATS attempts to promote cross-border trade in services, which now have a burgeoning share of international economic activity. This agreement is significant as services now constitute a major proportion of GDP and employment in most nations, particularly developing nations. While conventional trade agreements have addressed goods primarily, GATS recognizes the importance of services and therefore considers the complexities that are associated with this sector. By encouraging a formal approach to trade in services, GATS offers member countries a platform on which to negotiate commitments having the potential to increase market access and stimulate economic growth and directly impact their development courses. The significance of GATS is also highlighted by its potential effects on developing countries. As technological advancements and globalization keep unfolding, spillover of information technologies has opened avenues for these nations to take part in the services market, particularly the IT services market. The GATS framework encourages these countries to open the service imports, an exercise that would see the sectors increase efficiency and competition. However, with opportunities come obstacles that must be navigated with caution. The developing nations must balance their commitment under GATS with local priorities, especially concerning general services such as health care and education. The Doha Development Round talks bring to the forefront this balance since the developing nations are being urged to raise their level of engagement in service imports, most notably in producer services where liberalization is more productive (Lücke et al., 2025). Although there might be positive aspects, the consistency of GATS with host policy frameworks is a predominant issue for the majority of nations. The interplay between the opening of trade and regulatory autonomy becomes extremely apparent when looking at CARs and financial stability. As noted by the Pardee Center Task Force, existing trade and investment arrangements threaten to limit the potential of countries, especially developing countries, to optimally take advantage of CARs, depriving them of economic sovereignty. Financial volatility threats highlight that liberalism in the services sector must be exercised with caution. Policy-makers are required to walk the delicate tightrope between facilitating an open trading environment and safeguarding national interests, in a manner that commitments undertaken under GATS would not eviscerate the ability to make policies that are critical to sustainable development (Anderson et al., 2013).

Definition of Trade in Services

The definition of trade in services is a key one in the comprehension of the framework offered by the GATS. Service trade is a form of trade involving a wide range of economic activities that are not physical but focus on offering services. Services can include such industries as finance, telecommunication, education, and health, among many others. Service trade is more complex compared to merchandise trade since services are intangible, and where there often needs to be a direct interaction between service providers and consumers. Such diversity brings out the importance of rules such as GATS, which aims to facilitate the trading of services by overcoming some issues, such as the constraints of cross-border delivery and inconsistencies in national rules. The GATS system aims to liberalize international trade in services by establishing rules and commitments that member countries would need to abide by. One of the pillars of GATS is its categorization of supply modes and service industries. The agreement identifies four broad modes of supply: commercial presence, presence of natural persons, consumption abroad, and cross-border supply. The categorization is central to the definition of how services are traded and in what circumstances they may be supplied across borders.

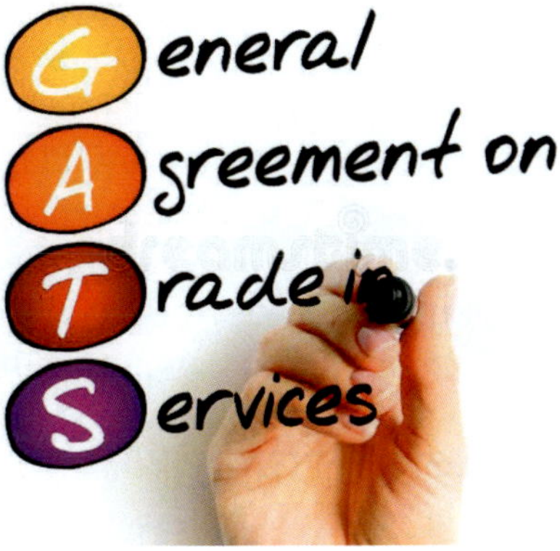

Figure 5.1. Trade in Services (GATS).

Source: https://thumbs.dreamstime.com/b/gats-general-agreement-trade-services-acronym-business-concept-background-gats-general-agreement-trade-services-254162816.jpg.

For instance, the cross-border supply mode supports services to be supplied from a country to another without physical presence, which is crucial for industries like information technology and consultancy. Awareness of these modes does not only reveal the operational processes of services trade but also its effects on international economic exchanges. Service trade, as outlined in the context of GATS, is also rendered more intricate by the trend towards offering total solutions rather than individual services. As noted, companies are increasingly departing from offering services on an individual basis to offering holistic solutions that are meant to cater to customers' needs, which necessarily affects the way services are packaged and delivered. This new way of service delivery renders channel management strategies requiring a review, especially in competitive settings. The connections between customers and providers strengthen as end-to-end solutions require an increased level of collaboration and tailoring. Therefore, policymakers and corporations both need to travel through the hurdles presented by these developments while remaining in line with GATS obligations so that they can respond to the dynamic nature of services trade without obstructing compliance with global standards (Anderson et al., 2013; George et al., 2025) (Figure 5.1).

Overview of the General Agreement on Trade in Services (GATS)

The GATS is a milestone in global trade, which was primarily launched to offer a comprehensive framework for services trade liberalization. Negotiated within the Uruguay Round in 1995, GATS was the first multilateral agreement that attempted to advance trade in services by enshrining member countries' commitments. This agreement covers an extensive set of services ranging from financial and telecommunication services to tourism and transport. By making it possible for nations to make particular commitments toward opening up their service markets, GATS aims to encourage competition and foreign direct investment, ultimately fueling economic growth and consumer choice. But the sophistication of GATS also reflects the challenge of balancing national interests with international trade commitments, as countries seek to balance the complexities of subjecting their domestic regulation to multilateral frameworks. One of the key aspects of GATS is that it classifies service sectors into four distinct modes of supply, which is used to mark the way services can be provided across borders. Mode 1 refers to the cross-border supply of services, Mode 2 refers to the consumption of services outside a country, Mode 3 refers to foreign commercial presence by suppliers of services, and Mode 4 refers to the movement of natural persons supplying services.

Each mode has significant implications for how countries approach trade negotiations, as they must consider not only the economic impact of liberalizing specific sectors but also the social and regulatory dimensions associated with service provision. For instance, in Mode 4, governments have been discriminating in their engagements, sometimes articulating the interests of domestic labor markets as well as immigration policies, particularly in the context of mixed skill requirements in different industries of services (Ramjoue, 2025). Moreover, evolving patterns in world trade lay greater importance on financial services and including the same in preferential trade agreements, a consideration that is most relevant to the context of GATS. As more nations recognize the importance of financial services in promoting economic development, the makeup of such agreements is most important. An example would be examining how financial services can be integrated into the trade arrangements of nations such as China, which will reveal global economic policy trends generally (Stephanou et al., 2025). The crossroads of domestic regulation and cross-border obligation under

GATS pose unique challenges and opportunities for countries hoping to gain competitive edge in the new, rapidly emerging world market. Through these complexities, GATS implications in services provision will continue evolving, charting the destiny of the future world of international service trade.

Importance of General Agreement on Trade in Services (GATS) in the Global Economy

Within the global economy environment, the GATS plays a unifying role by promoting the opening up of service sectors across borders. Since services form a significant portion of world economic activity, they need to be incorporated into world trade agreements in order to promote economic growth and development. Since the inception of GATS, there has been collective action towards convincing member countries to drop barriers long-standing in the way of trade in services. This liberalization has ushered in substantial increases in the levels of trade, competition, and the standard of services. Moreover, GATS not only serves as a driver of economic activity but also stimulates technological advancements and knowledge transfer between countries, which can drive innovation in service sectors. A key sector where GATS proves to exert its impact is the electricity and water sectors.

The structure allows for investment and collaboration between member states to aid in the sharing of know-how and resources needed in the development of these fundamental services. The system of liberalization under GATS allows countries to engage in actual discussions on regulatory measures and standards, which is crucial in industries that are often marred with excessive regulation and monopolies. By determining the organization of these sectors, GATS makes them cost-effective and responsive to consumers' needs, thus furthering overall development objectives. It has been found in studies that such cooperation, thanks to GATS, can deliver outstanding enhancement of infrastructure and delivery of services, ultimately making the global economy more affluent (Hall et al., 2006). Finally, the literature on trade in services highlights the importance of GATS to ensure that the determinants and advantages of international trade and investment in services are fulfilled. While research indicates the economic benefits obtained from increased trade liberalization, it also states the potential welfare gains derived therefrom. The acknowledgment of such gains has prompted governments and policymakers to consider the establishment of strategic trade agreements that would prioritize the service sector. Through the facilitation of an environment that is conducive to cooperation, GATS can stimulate development and enhance the competitive strengths of nations, particularly those with developing service sectors. Since there is increasing evidence of positive economic impacts of services liberalization, GATS is an essential framework for promoting world competitiveness and economic resilience building (Hoekman et al., 2025) (Figure 5.2).

Figure 5.2. Importance of General Agreement on Trade in Services (GATS) in the global economy.

Source: https://external-content.duckduckgo.com/iu/?u=http%3A%2F%2Fwww.simplynotes.in%2Fwp-content%2Fuploads%2F2016%2F03%2FGATS_001.jpg&f=1&nofb=1&ipt=f14f0e42e19d83f129078929024d61f4d0ff1f4cfcc08ddd69334c0d4fd31717.

5.1. HISTORICAL CONTEXT

The institution of the General Agreement on Trade in Services (GATS) marked a significant milestone in the evolution of international trade frameworks, particularly in the context of growing globalization and market interdependence. The GATS emerged from the Uruguay Round negotiations of the late 1980s and early 1990s, wherein the need for a systematic approach to service trade increasingly became apparent. Prior to GATS, international trade was largely goods-based, and the services sector was all but unregulated. In the realization that services are a key driver of economic development and growth, negotiators endeavored to create a general agreement that would facilitate trade and investment in the various service sectors. As governments began to deregulate markets, GATS attempted to provide legally binding commitments to provide access and draw foreign investment, resulting in a more stable trading atmosphere and improved competition in the services sector across the globe. There have been many factors that have shaped and broadened the GATS framework over time. The advent of information and communication technologies has changed the delivery of services, leading to greater cross-border service transactions. The transformation necessitated that regulatory approaches be realigned because existing barriers to trade in services, such as entry barriers and national regulations, could hamper growth and innovation. Countries faced the challenge of balancing domestic regulatory demands with international commitments towards liberalization (Mattoo et al., 2025). The GATS regime has now come to evolve provisions to address these challenges in the form of rules governing domestic regulations intended to guarantee fairness and efficiency and safeguard national interest. Through a combination of binding obligations and continuous negotiation, GATS is an anchor instrument to understand the complexities of modern service trade. Further, the history of GATS is shaped by differential participation by countries under the agreement, particularly in the contrast between developed and developing countries. The negotiations have also brought to light stark contrasts in the perception of the advantages and challenges of service liberalization by countries. Developed nations should have well-developed services sectors that can easily adapt to international competition, while most developing countries are plagued by regulatory and capacity constraints (Stephanou et al., 2025). This divergence has created controversy surrounding reciprocity and fairness in trade negotiations because developing countries seek to ensure their interests, particularly in industries like finance and telecommunications, are properly catered to. As GATS unfolds, the ongoing development of such prior history reflects the need for constant dialogue and reform, inviting wider participation that benefits more countries in the world service economy.

5.1.1. Development of General Agreement on Trade in Services (GATS) in the Uruguay Round

The GATS became a major template in the Uruguay Round, taking place between 1986 and 1994. It was a new innovation in world trade where services, an important segment of the economies in the modern world, were treated with special consideration within a global trading environment. Increased acknowledgement on the part of developing countries of the necessity for liberalization of the domestic markets for services was one of the major drivers towards the establishment of GATS. It was during the late 1980s that the majority of these nations began adopting more market-oriented policies, believing that they were able to increase the efficiency of their service industries through liberalization. It was not only a move in response to domestic economic stresses but also triggered collective effort by developing countries towards the negotiation of a multilateral agreement, ultimately leading to the draft GATS that would shape the terms of international service trade (DEC et al., 2025). The GATS negotiations exposed the complexity in addressing non-tariff barriers (NTBs), which have a tendency of discouraging service providers from foraying into foreign markets.

Figure 5.3. Development of General Agreement on Trade in Services (GATS) in the Uruguay round.

Source: https://i0.wp.com/www.ppesydney.net/content/uploads/2016/06/uruguay-round.jpg?resize=420%2C267&ssl=1.

Government administrative regulations, although unavoidable in controlling domestic markets, ironically pose to foreign entrants obstacles and thereby trigger calls for their liberalization. The Uruguay Round negotiations put this conflict in the limelight as nations grappled with achieving a balance between domestic regulatory interests and international market access commitments. It was then made clear that it would require a complete appreciation of the motivations behind various national regulations in order to obtain substantial concessions in areas of services. The negotiations were intended to dismantle such obstacles with consideration of the domestic context, observing numerous of the regulations had originated as a response to home market failure motivations rather than merely to exclude foreign competition (Lejour et al., 2025). Ultimately, the establishment of GATS was a milestone in the worldwide services explosion since it not only brought trade in services into international law but also laid out a framework to keep negotiating. The GATS framework enables regulatory coherence and attempts to support reform efforts for members. The majority of developing countries, motivated by their unilaterally changed policies, view accession to GATS as a method of enshrining reforms and enhancing efficiency within their services sectors. However, the challenge is ensuring that such agreements are not cosmetic commitments but rather drivers towards real opening up of markets and enhanced competition. Membership in a binding multilateral agreement has been considered critical to maintain momentum in liberalization, providing incentives against retrenchment of so far agreed policy, and ultimately building a more dynamic global services trade climate (DEC et al., 2025) (Figure 5.3).

5.1.2. Key Milestones in the Evolution of Service Trade

The evolution of service trade has been characterized by a string of milestone developments that record the increasing significance and sophistication of services in global business. Arguably the most important development was the creation of the General Agreement on Trade in Services (GATS) in 1995, an outcome of the Uruguay Round of multilateral trade negotiations. This treaty was a milestone shift in thinking about international trade, with the establishment of a legal framework for the trade in both goods and services. It officially established the services sector as a distinct sector for the first time, and promoted principles such as most-favored-nation treatment and national treatment. This framework not only encouraged member countries to lower trade barriers but facilitated easier negotiation on alternative delivery modes of services, hence generating the possibilities for more international integration of services. These initial efforts paved the way for subsequent developments in service trade relations. Still another important step in the evolution of service trade came with the emergence of regional trade arrangements (RTAs) that are targeted on services. More recently, various regions of the world have pursued such agreements to facilitate integration and cooperation between members and liberalize their own service industries as well. For instance, the Association of Southeast Asian Nations (ASEAN) has come very close to establishing its own Free Trade Agreements (FTAs) with a primary emphasis on trade in services. As emphasized by Chirathivat et al. (2013), the historical evolution of ASEAN FTAs both reflects the achievement of the ASEAN Free Trade Agreement and draws such agreements into greater economic initiatives, such as the ASEAN Economic Community (AEC). By promoting smooth trade relationships through RTAs, states have enlarged their service industries, thus deepening their roles in international supply chains. Lastly, the push for digital services in the 21st century has redefined the complexion of service trade, presenting opportunities along with difficulties. The rapid advance of technology has spurred the development of e-commerce, which has expanded the reach of such sectors as finance, education, and professional services. This transformation of the digital age has forced nations to rethink regulatory frameworks and implement provisions that enable digital trade to flourish. Together with the evidence in Kolesnichenko et al. (2025) regarding the importance of economic cooperation between neighboring countries, the influence of the digital economy underscores responsive policies that can sustain service trade in a setting under constant transformation. The need for international cooperation in such areas as data protection and international electronic transactions has grown to a top-level priority, which, thus, indicates an ongoing process of how service trade is carried out and regulated across the world.

5.1.3. Impact of Globalization on Service Industries

Economic globalization has significantly transformed service industries, creating opportunities and challenges for countries involved in international trade. With nations becoming more integrated into the world economy, liberalization of service sectors has been a significant area of concern in trade negotiations. In particular, the General Agreement on Trade in Services (GATS) has tried to facilitate this process by promoting the movement of services across borders. Leveraging the comparative advantage of a nation's service sector could lead to higher economic growth and development. But whereas globalization accelerates the transmission of services and technical know-how, it also imposes new competitive forces on domestic firms that can fall unevenly on them. Thus, the tension between benefiting from the spoils of globalization and protecting domestic service sectors has been a contentious one, particularly in developing countries. The interplay between worldwide migration and service trade goes to further amplify the richness of complexity of globalizations impact on service sectors. Movement of skilled human capital has come to be increasingly regarded as essential to the competitiveness of service sectors. For instance, while GATS allows the temporary movement of service professionals, these measures have been limited in application, resulting in lost potential for economic progress in the majority of nations. Since in most countries trade and migration policies are determined independently of one another, failure to harmonize these disciplines can undermine benefits. This limitation puts into focus the need for more labor mobility-conducive policies, which potentially could be a stronger driver for the economy than pure trade liberalization on its own. By understanding the interconnection between migration and trade, policymakers would be in a position to build a framework that is supportive of not just better service delivery but also economic stability across borders (Ahmed et al., 2009). To developing countries, globalization presents a unique package of challenges and opportunities in their service economy. With the introduction of information technologies, windows have been opened to such countries for them to export IT and other services to global markets. The ongoing negotiations on the Doha Development Round, however, have raised skepticism on the liberalization of imports of services, which are not necessarily aligned with national priorities. Whereas promises to open up producer services are likely to increase competition and service quality, consumer services are more challenging in that they deal with limited-demand areas and where monopoly conditions exist. Therefore, developing countries have to think carefully about which sectors to first target in negotiations under GATS. Ensuring that trade commitments are aligned with national development needs is important. Secondly, increased prospects for temporary labor migration would greatly benefit developing countries, as they enhance capability and strengthen the service industry in the international economy (Lücke et al., 2025) (Figure 5.4).

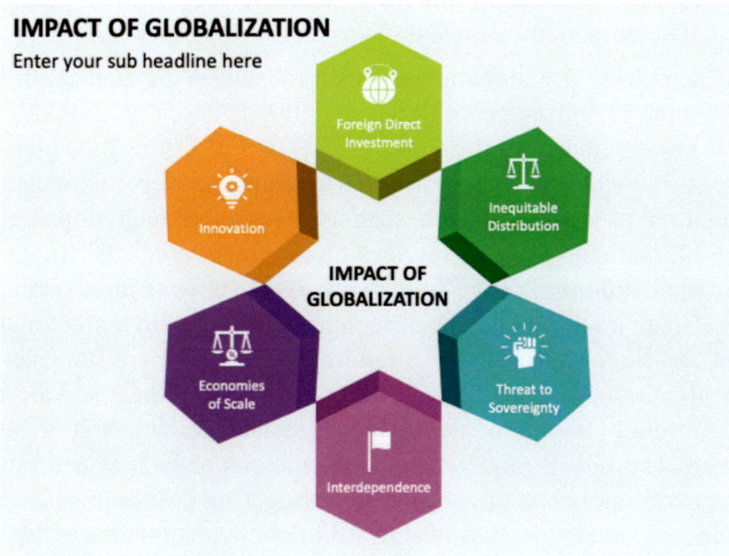

Figure 5.4. Impact of globalization.

Source: https://external-content.duckduckgo.com/iu/?u=https%3A%2F%2Fcdn.sketchbubble.com%2Fpub%2Fmedia%2Fcatalog%2Fproduct%2Foptimized1%2F5%2Fc%2F5cd8ae5b8b39e243a4bc5407591fce9e87c6f5fca125b051079ffe9197b56b63%2Fimpact-of-globalization-mc-slide1.png&f=1&nofb=1&ipt=4337826aefd148a471a58bcc89a34e6e9a1e20635eec69cd78040fa8b2b13f42.

5.2. STRUCTURE OF GENERAL AGREEMENT ON TRADE IN SERVICES (GATS)

The framework of the GATS is basically that which will facilitate international trade in services by establishing a comprehensive and open structure. In essence, GATS provides for commitments that member states make regarding the treatment of foreign providers of services. This framework is segregated into various modes of supply, such as cross-border trade, consumption abroad, commercial presence, and presence of natural persons. Each mode reflects different manners in which services are delivered and highlights the different manners in which countries engage in services trade. From the definitions of the modes, GATS attempts to provide definition to agreements of trade as well as enhance the predictability of service markets, a step that eventually benefits both the importers and exporters of services, resulting in an integrated world economy. Under the GATS framework, scheduling and negotiating commitments are essential features that represent each country's policy stance towards liberalization. The member states analyze their own service sectors and determine what areas of services they will expose to international competition. The self-declared scheduling provides variable degrees of commitment, resulting in a heterogenous service trade pattern among members.

While countries are negotiating, such obstacles as non-tariff barriers (NTBs) slow the liberalization of trade, as policy is based on domestic market failure and not explicit protectionism. The system of GATS thus includes the commitments but states that to these are also examples of continuous dialogue and negotiation procedures which seek to overcome such impediments to render the international trade in services more effective in total (Lejour et al., 2025). The implications of GATS framework extend beyond mere facilitation of trade; it is also an important means of regulatory reform and market integration within the developing world. By aligning their regulations to meet GATS commitments, countries can more effectively advance their service sectors, mobilizing foreign investment and technical assistance, which are essential to development. The GATS model encourages nations to look at and repeatedly modify their commitments, thereby perhaps triggering development in markets such as telecom, education, and health. Additionally, as evidenced by studies, removing trade barriers can create enormous welfare benefits, testifying to the contribution of GATS towards efficient service delivery and consumer preference. This connection between commitment schedules and regulatory regimes ultimately shapes the context of service trade in the global economy, offering prospects and challenges to the participating countries (Hall et al., 2006).

5.2.1. Four Modes of Supply

The Four Modes of Supply of the General Agreement on Trade in Services (GATS) provide an aggregate coverage in learning delivery across borders of services. These modes—cross-border supply, consumption abroad, commercial presence, and presence of natural persons—indicate the various ways service suppliers engage with foreign markets. All the modes address various types of service transactions as well as spot the international trade in services dynamics. Cross-border supply facilitates the delivery of services from one country to another without the physical presence of the provider, a clear illustration of the growing influence of technology and online platforms in facilitating trade. This is particularly evident in sectors like education and finance, where remote transactions can enhance market access and efficiency, creating more opportunities for the consumer as well as the provider. The implications of the Four Modes of Supply extend beyond definitional boundaries; they raise serious policy challenges with international trade negotiations. For instance, cross-border supply and consumption within or outside a country are generally subject to non-tariff barriers (NTBs) that may limit market access in foreign markets. NTBs can vary from licensing processes, certification procedures, to other regulatory measures that can disproportionately affect foreign service providers.

As in recent negotiation debates surrounding the Trade in Services Agreement (TISA) and the Trans-Pacific Partnership (TPP), the nuances presented in these barriers necessitate subtle methods of trade negotiation. The challenge is to balance the need for domestic regulation—sometimes justified as means of combating market failure—against the requirement to guarantee fair access for foreign services providers, a duty that can be both politically sensitive and technologically demanding (Cooper et al., 2014). In negotiating these problems, an understanding of the Four Modes of Supply also sheds light on the economic benefits of liberalization in services. Literature argues that removal of the obstacles associated with these modes can produce important welfare gains for countries engaging in international service trade. However, the negotiation process is protracted and complicated, as governments grapple with domestic regulations that do not necessarily align with international trade. Reform proposals such as the inclusion of economic necessity tests to determine the merits of individual regulations take cognizance of growing realization that regulatory regimes must be responsive to the changing terms of trade agreements. The implementation of such a measure, while challenging, would make domestic and international objectives more harmonious with one another, ultimately leading to stronger and more equitable trade in services among member nations (Lejour et al., 2025) (Figure 5.5).

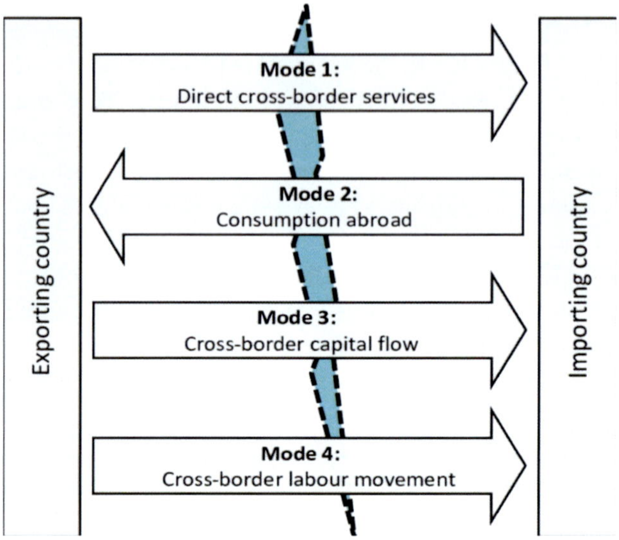

Figure 5.5. General Agreement on Trade in Services (GATS) 's four modes of supply.

*Source:*https://www.researchgate.net/profile/Lucian-Cernat/publication/264194417/figure/fig3/AS:616391082266624@1523970494061/GATSs-four-modes-of-supply.png.

5.2.2. Schedule of Commitments

Schedule of Commitments is a key component of the General Agreement on Trade in Services (GATS), establishing the framework for member states to outline their commitment to liberalizing trade in services. Every member state submits its Schedule, detailing specific commitments to market access and national treatment for various sectors of services. This positive-listing process demands that obligations be precisely articulated, thus leaving a listed service unbonded and allowing countries considerable room to maintain protectionist measures. The Schedules thereby specify the degree of liberalization by a member and those areas where protections remain. The implication of these commitments is highlighted in that they could enable transparency, but the success of such transparency differs considerably among various member countries, especially when examining the coverage and limitations in their own Schedules (Malkawi et al., 2019). Furthermore, the material included in the Schedules is important in determining the inequality between developed and developing countries in signing commitments to freer trade in services. Rich nations generally schedule a wider variety of service sectors than their developing nations, and in most cases, they are preceded by fewer market-access restrictions. For example, data reveal that whereas high-income nations approved about half of their service sectors, developing nations as a group scheduled only 11% (Hoekman et al., 2025). This imbalance raises concerns about equity and poses challenges to developing nations aiming to build strong service sectors through foreign trade. The limited scope of activities not only constrains foreign service suppliers' entry but also can retard domestic firms' growth relying on foreign partners and technology. As such, the imbalance in commitments has far-reaching effects on global trade flows, reflecting underlying economic imbalances. Finally, the development and reform of the Schedule of Commitments require consultation between member nations to address its substantive flaws. Current criticism suggests the need for better transparency regarding unbound sectors, which are most frequently loaded with sensitive trade restrictions. Finally, the current framework lacks uniformity of rules across commitments, suggesting that an integrated system can assist in liberalization across the board (Hoekman et al., 2025). Stronger GATS architecture with enhancements such as the shift towards negative-listing would introduce enhanced transparency on the fields of restriction and their economic implications. Facilitating such reforms, member countries can unlock more service trade potential, enhance competitiveness, and benefits from globalization penetrate a wider range of service sectors, leading to more equitable economic growth.

5.2.3. General Obligations and Specific Commitments

General Agreement on Trade in Services (GATS) has an arrangement for negotiating specific commitments that govern trade in services across borders. Through this arrangement, general obligations are the main guiding principles that see member states conduct their trade according to these guidelines. General obligations consist of transparency, non-discrimination, and progressive liberalization of service markets. Through ensuring that all member states play by the same rules, GATS ensures a level playing field for trade. Interestingly, such general pledges are not necessary to eliminate all trade barriers simultaneously but rather call for gradualism that is sensitive to the different capacities and needs of individual countries. This flexibility is crucial in helping countries mold their commitments in a way that accommodates their specific economic circumstances and priorities but within the framework of general GATS principles. National commitments in GATS act as binding agreements that outline the exact conditions and services a country will offer foreign suppliers. Individual commitments will vary considerably from one industry to another as governments retain the discretionary authority to approve special obligations depending on national interests and the diversity of sectors. For instance, while some countries open up sectors like finance and telecommunications, they can prefer tighter regulation that favors domestic industries and employment. Jordan, for example, has been able to navigate this by creating a list of binding commitments that address commercial agency regulations in compliance with GATS, according to some analyses of its trade climate (Malkawi et al., 2019). By achieving a balance between these commitments and general obligations, states can adequately balance their integration of service sectors in the international economy with the safeguarding of domestic priorities. The interplay between specific commitments and general obligations in GATS captures the fine balance that governments must achieve in negotiations. While as much as general obligations impose broad standards of behavior, the specific commitments allow for specific solutions that take into account country-specific conditions. This twin design enables governments to attract foreign investment and services suppliers while also protecting their national interests. As learnt through various trade agreements, GATS flexibility can lead to substantial differences in taking and applying commitments, as discovered with certain bilateral investment treaties (BITs) with lower transparency and legal clarity (Adlung, 2009). Lastly, a successful use of GATS involves a careful understanding of how these general obligations and specific commitments interact with each other, defining the present and future situation in international trade in services (Figure 5.6).

Figure 5.6. General Agreement on Trade in Services (GATS) 's general obligations and specific commitments.

Source: https://www.transnationalmatters.com/wp-content/uploads/2024/05/users_7dd1dc79-7cb9-40c2-b5f8-d0e040fa311b_generations_7b19ba9c-dfb6-48f4-8c85-3c21ff27cf02_Default_a_group_of_lawyers_gathered_around_a_large_clutterfree_0-1.webp.

5.3. ECONOMIC IMPACT OF GENERAL AGREEMENT ON TRADE IN SERVICES (GATS)

The GATS is a watershed moment for international trade policy in that it covers a range of different service industries, which have come to dominate the world economy in recent years. The service industry has grown to become the largest and most dynamic sector of world output, responsible for over 60% of total economic production and generating enormous jobs opportunities across the globe. Between 1990 and 2003, services trade experienced growth rates consistent with that of goods, highlighting its increasing role in cross-border economic activity. Even as GATS was being negotiated during the Uruguay Round, the advent of regional trade agreements has further complicated it from being effective, as many countries increasingly place more emphasis on bilateral or multilateral arrangements better capable of addressing some service needs. The ongoing growth of GATS participation is indicative of the potential and challenges involved in liberalizing services trade while maintaining level access and competitive levels globally (De et al., 2025). Perhaps the greatest economic impact of GATS has been its regulatory framework, which facilitates liberalization in services trade and consequently enhances consumer access and intensifies competitive forces among providers. This has specific relevance for such sectors as the tourism sector, which have been long enjoying liberalized transactions. GATS targets the simplification and harmonization of rules for cross-border transactions in services, including sectors that have high development potential in the developing economies.

For instance, such economies as Korea have begun viewing GATS as an economic development stimulus for the tourism sector, provoking strategic policymaking to support liberalization as a strategy for stimulating economic development. The examination of tourist services in GATS not only reveals its role in global economic integration but also addresses the shortcomings between private and public views of the benefits of such an agreement (Lee et al., 2025). The proper utilization of GATS and its effects on the economy are, however, multifaceted and plagued by problems, particularly for developing countries aiming to break into international service markets. Compliance standards such as acceptance of some regulatory standards and openness programs create obstacles that are particularly burdensome for less developed economies of services. The majority of service industries still face strict regulation in the form of compulsory licensing and citizenship to limit their international market competitiveness. Developing nations, therefore, approach the negotiations cautiously, fearing lack of adequate market access in the industrialized world may quash their growth potential. Thus, the economic implications of GATS involve not just the possibility of increased trade but also the need for developing countries to engage responsibly in service negotiations that acknowledge their own unique challenges and opportunities in a globalized economy (De et al., 2025) (Figure 5.7).

Figure 5.7. Economic impact of General Agreement on Trade in Services (GATS).

Source: https://external-content.duckduckgo.com/iu/?u=http%3A%2F%2Fwww.moneylenderpro.com%2Fwp-content%2Fuploads%2F2018%2F01%2Feconomic-impact.jpg&f=1&nofb=1&ipt=eeb2a4a095be62b284ef41c27a858759e97419f38df380ff5457cd3ce37bea5e.

5.3.1. Growth of the Service Sector

The face of the world economy has witnessed a significant change with the speedy growth of the service sector, which has become the biggest and fastest-growing sector in the last few decades. This increase is evident from the contribution of the service sector to more than 60% of world output and a substantial proportion of jobs in many countries. Throughout the 1990–2003 period, growth rates of services trade were comparable to that of merchandise at an average rate of around 6% per year (De et al., 2025). These trends depict a paradigm shift in which services, once viewed to be peripheral to trade discourse, have become frontline drivers of economic growth and international negotiation. The trend that persists is the fact that liberalization of services is needed not only to enhance economic production but also to facilitate broader trade agreements between nations. International trade agreements have increasingly focused on the service sector, and the General Agreement on Trade in Services (GATS) offers a framework for negotiation and liberalization. The GATS has given rise to numerous regional trade agreements (RTAs) with specific provisions pertaining to services, in line with the new economic currents on a global level (De et al., 2025). All of the above RTAs, including those between the United States and countries in the Asia-Pacific region, have had substantive chapters dealing with services, thereby creating further doors of opportunity for trade in services. These endeavors reflect clearly an awareness of the importance of services in global patterns of trade. In addition, as observed with numerous regional agreements, such as the ASEAN Framework Agreement on Services, the focus on service liberalization gathers pace, setting up a competitive benchmark for nations looking to deepen economic relations through service trade. However, the growth of the service sector is not without its challenges, particularly in the form of regulatory impediments to international trade. Although liberalization of the trade in services under frameworks like GATS has been underway, many service sectors continue to be rigidly regulated and subject to constraints on market access. The problem in measuring the output and development of the services sector even makes it hard to negotiate, as the less-developed countries lack information that they need to overcome these challenges. Consequently, there is a genuine fear among these nations regarding North-South negotiations due to perceived imbalances of power and information asymmetry. In the future, managing these challenges will be crucial to ensure that the benefits of service sector growth are enjoyed equally and that trade agreements really contribute to economic development and cooperation that is inclusive across borders (Figure 5.8).

Figure 5.8. Growth of the service sector.

Source: https://static.investindia.gov.in/s3fs-public/2019-05/Servicessec_1.jpg.

5.3.2. Effects on Employment and Labor Markets

General Agreement on Trade in Services (GATS) has significant implications for employment and labour markets across most industries since it fundamentally reverses the cross-border service trade dynamics. By opening markets to international competition, GATS enhances efficiency and productivity, leading to economic growth as a whole. But this cross-border supply of services will also exert downward pressure on domestic wages and job security, particularly where labor costs are a critical factor. With ongoing trade liberalization, workers in regions unable to compete with cheaper foreign services will find themselves losing their jobs, which will result in calls for stronger labor protections and retraining. The balance between preserving the worth of trade and safeguarding home jobs is a fragile one, and underlines the need for inclusive policies that balance out detrimental impacts on vulnerable employment streams. Furthermore, labor mobility across borders, facilitated by GATS, establishes a complex interaction between employment dynamics and migration flows. While GATS primarily addresses trade in services, mobility of service workers through Mode IV has been limited in scope and has yielded incremental success only in terms of labor mobility. Such restraint can inhibit countries from being in a position to reap maximum potential economic gains because skilled labor can move anywhere there is greater demand for their expertise. The link between labor migration and trade negotiations has been neglected in significant measure, as evidence indicated rising labor mobility as a source of great benefits for both sending and recipient countries. Therefore, the inclusion of labor migration in trade negotiations can be crucial to ensuring the full potential of GATS in relation to employment and labor market arrangements and fostering a more flexible and adaptive labor environment. Lastly, solving labor issues in light of GATS requires the rethinking of labor standards and the rules that govern service trade. Recent trade agreements integrate more labor standards to prevent worker rights from being compromised with increasing competition and liberalization of the market. This indicates an acknowledgment of the fact that sustainable economic growth must not be achieved at the cost of labor rights and working conditions. Appeal to international labor standards can be used as the foundation of ensuring employment generation under GATS does not lead to exploitation or labor condition depreciation. The dynamics between occupational safety, wage level, and job security reinforce the importance of congruence of trade agreements with robust labor policies. As arguments on labor and trade evolve, market players must give high priority to using effective measures in utilizing effective strategies that promote economic development and uphold respect for workers' rights to secure the effects of GATS on the employment sector and the labor markets as positive and equitable to all parties.

5.3.3. Influence on Foreign Direct Investment (FDI)

The link between FDI and service trade, particularly in relation to the General Agreement on Trade in Services (GATS), is key to understanding economic growth processes in developing countries. FDI is a significant means of technology transfer, managerial expertise, and capital flow into countries, stimulating home economies and moving service sector capabilities forward. Specifically, the health services sector, often highlighted in discussions about investment liberalization, stands to benefit significantly. The experiences from selected developing countries provide valuable insights into how liberalization practices can attract FDI, creating a more competitive environment while simultaneously improving service quality. This. It reflects a greater acceptance that liberalization strategically in services can stimulate growth and innovation, regardless of more traditional manufacturing-based means of development, which is in line with the objectives of GATS (Sharma et al., 2025).

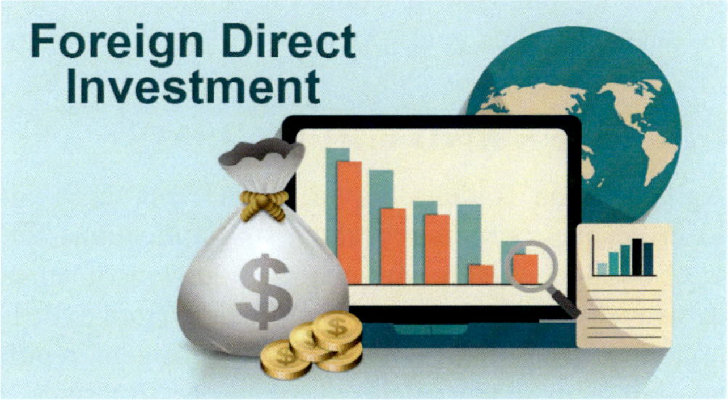

Figure 5.9. Foreign direct investment (FDI).

Source: https://external-content.duckduckgo.com/iu/?u=https%3A%2F%2Fwww.biatconsultant.com%2Fblog%2Fwp-content%2Fuploads%2F2021%2F05%2FForeign-Direct-Investment.jpeg&f=1&nofb=1&ipt=0f06a0af020b6d092acd8414cdde5ab884f840882387d98f68a9bce8061900e4.

In addition to this, trade liberalization in services has also been ranked as one of the key drivers of increasing FDI flows, particularly in sectors where local capacity is weak enough to meet international standards. In the past, there have been detailed examinations mapping out the immediate nexus between liberalization of the services sector and FDI, with the outcome that the reforms unleash dormant economic potential in often overlooked sectors. The debate surrounding the GATS highlights the necessity of countries embracing a process of gradual liberalization in harmony with their own economic circumstances and ability. Recent literature emphasizes the fact that while potential welfare gains of liberalization of services are likely to be high, there must be careful thinking while formulating guidelines to convert these benefits into optimal gains and to support national development priorities, hence advocating a case for a strategic approach to FDI (Hoekman et al., 2025). In addition, the emphasis on sector-specific FDI incentives that are suited to the specific challenges that country like Nepal faces is a critical element of successfully implementing liberalization policies using the GATS framework. In exploring the policy processes of selected developing countries, it becomes clear that suitable incentive frameworks could not just attract FDI but also transfer knowledge and improve local human capital. Lessons from these countries teach the importance of having a positive regulatory environment that serves both local interests and international obligations. While the debate concerning FDI continues, the insertion of focused investment incentives into national policy-making indicates that there needs to be an informed understanding of how such investments are able to spur growth within the service sector and, indirectly, help achieve national economic goals (Sharma et al., 2025) (Figure 5.9).

5.4. CHALLENGES AND CRITICISMS

The General Agreement on Trade in Services (GATS) is faced with very high challenges and criticisms, particularly about its implications for developing countries. The critics link GATS with the continuation of an unjust global economic order where richer nations reap significantly from trade liberalization while poorer nations struggle to live up to its stringent regulations. This process leaves a sense of disenfranchisement, especially since the majority of developing nations lack administrative capacity to apply the domestic regulations that GATS mandates. As became apparent in the controversy that ensued following the WTOs Cancun Ministerial Conference, these nations lamented the existence of a free trade regime that benefits multinational firms and exploits national economies, in effect showing the complexity of negotiating a justly fair system of trade in services (Macmillan et al., 2004). Another major challenge is the regulation of rules over services, particularly in service sectors that have implications on public welfare, such as education and healthcare. The GATS model encourages the takeover of services by the private sector and involvement of private enterprises, which has the effect of increasing the cost of such services to consumers. In the majority of developing countries, the move towards such privatization can not only erode access to public services, but increase inequalities in societies. It is argued by critics that while GATS aims to promote development and efficiency, the very frameworks on which these are based favor economically advanced nations, with developing nations having to navigate a system of rules that are at once complex and cumbersome (Finger et al., 2025). The governance structure of the GATS has also been criticized as being non-democratic and opaque. The decision-making procedure of the WTO has been criticized for excluding diverse voices, particularly Global South voices, which taints the legitimacy of the agreed-upon agreements. This lacuna generates an impression that trade policy is being dictated by an elite rather than being negotiated equally among all member states. Addressing such governance issues can call for a fresh conceptual thought in constructing trade agreements, based on inclusiveness and fair representation to counteract the asymmetries of global trade systems (Macmillan et al., 2004) (Figure 5.10).

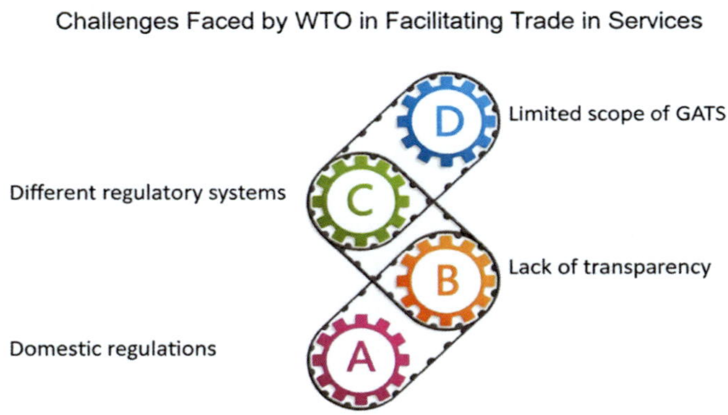

Figure 5.10. Challenges and criticisms of the General Agreement on Trade in Services (GATS).

Source: https://fastercapital.co/i/Beyond-Goods--Exploring-WTO-s-Role-in-Facilitating-Trade-in-Services--Challenges-Faced-by-WTO-in-Facilitating-Trade-in-Services.webp.

5.4.1. Concerns Over Regulatory Autonomy

International trade agreements, on the other hand, are prone to give rise to profound regulatory autonomy issues. GATS, in particular, presents a dual dilemma: while promoting a culture of liberalized trade, it simultaneously places constraints on the freedom of nations to adopt and implement regulation to protect domestic interests. An excellent illustration of this tension is found in the U.S.-Gambling case before the WTO Appellate Body, where the application of GATS highlighted the tension between upholding national regulatory control and international trade obligation compliance. The ruling raised issues of how far states are entitled to follow their regulatory powers without intruding on foreign service suppliers' interests, a dilemma which raises the more abstract issues of reconciling trade liberalization with the requirements of domestic governance (Kalupahana et al., 2007). The search for one-stop-shop solutions in service delivery, which is being witnessed in contemporary market trends, also complicates the arena of regulatory autonomy under the GATS regime.

Firms now wish to deliver integrative solutions rather than normal standardized services, leading to sophisticated supply chains and dependencies among various service providers. This paradigm of service delivery is disturbing to the existing regulatory regimes, particularly when these regimes are not designed to deal with the complexity of bundled solutions. As companies make the transition to providing bundled services, regulators must grapple with the demurrage of maintaining a level playing field, protection of consumers, and quality of services against the background of fulfilling GATS requirements. Therefore, it is imperative that regulatory systems are adapted to reflect the evolving character of trade in services to protect market access and regulatory sovereignty (George et al., 2025). Last but not least, addressing the problem of concern under the scenario of the GATS involves a judicious review of existing systems and existing negotiations. As international trade geography of services widens and evolves, there is a pressing debate that must be engaged in regarding the necessity to shape GATS rules in a way that they will be more conformable to the domestic economy's regulatory requirements. There must be undue restrictions minimized that are impediments to trade while recognizing regulatory mechanisms as guarantees of public interests like health, safety, and environmental standards. Proposals to guide this process of negotiation need to work towards securing a balance that fosters liberalization without jeopardizing the autonomy necessary for nations to regulate in light of burgeoning cross-border e-services. It is only through such a balanced approach that tensions inherent in GATS are best managed and scope is provided both for trade prosperity and the protection of domestic regulatory prerogatives (Kalupahana et al., 2007).

5.4.2. Issues of Equity and Access to Services

General Agreement on Trade in Services (GATS) aims at enhancing global trade by liberalizing services across member states. But the intention driving this objective is provoking heightened concerns over equity as well as accessibility, particularly among emerging economies like Bangladesh. While GATS provisions guarantee economic growth with untrammeled access to the market, they derogatively preclude nations with poor infrastructural and regulatory systems. For instance, Bangladesh's determination to accede to GATS commitments in the liberalization of financial services, as introduced by Dr. Raihan (2025), indicates the imbalance between the developed and developing world. An unbalanced playing ground has a propensity to promote limited access to essential services, enhancing prevailing socio-economic inequalities as well as curbing the ability of nations to achieve balanced development in key sectors. Moreover, the lack of universally applicable rules in GATS further increases discrepancies in the provision of services. Unlike GATT, GATS does not accord priority to regulatory instruments which would provide level playing field competition for the providers of services. Such a regulatory gap may introduce inefficiencies and entry barriers detrimentally affecting the small nations, rendering them vulnerable to large, industrial economies for exploitation. As Mattoo et al. (2025) have suggested, the firming up of multilateral rules and the demystification of commitments can foster fair access to services for all nations. This calls for a focused effort towards reconciling market access with the support of a more inclusive orientation, especially for low-resource and enforcement-constrained countries. Compounding the predicament are the anti-competitive practices that may emerge in service areas such as transport and communications. These procedures can to a great extent operate beyond the ambit of national competition legislation, leaving small countries like Bangladesh in a helpless situation where they are unable to utilize legislative measures to safeguard their interests. The present framework of GATS fails to address these concerns effectively, leaving the majority of countries open to possible market distortions that curb fair access to essential services. To address such issues, the introduction of stronger multilateral regulations is necessary, which would not only allow the smaller countries to gain from liberalization but also protect their interests against potential control by international cartels, as noted in Mattoo et al. (2025). This would allow making the trading system more equitable under the banner of GATS.

5.4.3. Critique of the Effectiveness of General Agreement on Trade in Services (GATS)

GATS aims at expanding international trade in services by establishing a multilateral framework of rules that regulate such trade. The criticism is typically that the agreements had limited success in achieving its key goals. Critics contend that GATS excessively benefits developed nations by gaining them expanded access into developing world markets without granting similar concessions in return. This imbalance has the potential to widen in place inequalities, allowing richer nations to capture poorer nations' service economies. Most importantly, the emphasis on liberalization as a solution for the future threatens to obscure the necessity for the richness of developing economies that involves in support of local capacity building and provision of sustainable development. As such, the GATS model has been regarded as having greater sympathy towards mature economies' interests than towards the aspirations of emerging markets, and hence subject to criticism at its very foundation about its overall efficacy in ensuring equitable global trade in services. Furthermore, GATS is also facing difficulties in applying Mutual Recognition Agreements (MRAs), particularly in legal services. The IBA plays a significant role in the formation of such

MRAs, but their adoption in developing economies is far from satisfactory. Not only does this inhibit the ability of international legal practitioners to function optimally, but also reflects on the structural impediments of emerging economies. If destinations like the IBA are unable to relate with the realities of developing nations, then the likelihood of GATS facilitating significant trade exchanges is extremely slim. As noted, the low inclusion of developing countries in MRAs can limit their legal communities from taking advantage of the global standards, thus limiting their capacity to engage in international legal practice in an effective manner, thus exposing a major weakness of the GATS model. Moreover, the success of GATS in advancing service delivery, particularly in vital services like electricity and water, occasions an inherent criticism of the model it advocates. The GATS advocates for privatization, but evidence suggests that private provision of public services is often not adequate to meet the needs of marginalized people. As noted, performance gains generally touted by pro-privatization proponents can be overpowered by increasing inequities and risks, particularly for those areas with poor institutions. Policymakers may be making commitments, like those of GATS, without realizing their ultimate effects on affordability and access to essential services by low-income communities. The emphasis on market opening can come at the cost of the necessity for large-scale planning and proper regulatory frameworks, with attendant ineffective provision of services in the face of theoretical improvement. The GATS model therefore appears to be inherently flawed in securing equitable and sustainable provision of services in various socio-economic environments, requiring a review of its overall effectiveness (Figure 5.11).

Figure 5.11. Critique of General Agreement on Trade in Services (GATS).

Source: https://fastercapital.co/i/Beyond-Goods--Exploring-WTO-s-Role-in-Facilitating-Trade-in-Services--Criticisms-and-Reforms-of-WTOs-Role-in-Facilitating-Trade-in-Services.webp.

5.5. CASE STUDIES

Case study analysis in the framework of the General Agreement on Trade in Services (GATS) seeks to illuminate the complexities and practical applications of trade in services. Case studies offer a valuable methodological tool, allowing academics and policymakers to research specific instances of GATS application in various sectors and geographical locations. Through examining real cases, such studies can elicit the nuances of how policies in international service trade interact with domestic policies, especially health and safety measures. For instance, examining alcohol trade disputes elicits the balance that countries must achieve between international commerce commitments and public health objectives. This is a critical analysis, as it indicates the dangers that WTO agreements pose for national policies to minimize alcohol harm, which can lead to increased society costs in the long term if protectionist measures are found not to be GATS compliant (Gould et al., 2008). Apart from pointing to the contradiction between trade agreements and domestic policies, case studies can provide information on the regulatory systems for diverse service sectors. The Pardee Center Task Force reports point to the importance of establishing the compatibility of trade and investment treaties and policy effectiveness. For example, examination of the impacts of bilateral investment agreements (BITs) and Free Trade Agreements (FTAs) on capital account regulations marks critical shortcomings in developing nations' ability to exercise economic sovereignty. According to the reports, many countries are put in check by international agreements, preventing them from implementing measures that are vital for long-term economic growth. By examining these regulatory concerns through case studies, academics can potentially contribute to a general insight regarding how nations address the complexities of GATS and thereby enhance the debate on the future of services trade (Anderson et al., 2013).

Case studies can also provide grounds for proposing pragmatic strategies which policymakers can adopt in addressing the adverse effects of GATS. For instance, learning from the examples in which health-oriented policies successfully deflected WTO cases can teach best practices. These examples indicate that specificity in operationalizing differences between protectionist and health-centered regulations can enhance countries' capacities for promoting policies based on public health without infringing on trade obligations. Besides, it emphasizes the necessity of states acting together to create an environment in which trade regulations do not hamper efforts to address urgent health issues. Such meticulous analyses not only add to our understanding of the nexus between domestic policy and trade but also provide policymakers with critical guidance on how to protect public interest under international trade commitments (Gould et al., 2008).

5.5.1. General Agreement on Trade in Services (GATS) and the Telecommunications Sector

GATS has significantly affected the telecommunications sector by establishing a framework for international trade that promotes liberalization and competition. In effect, GATS aims at guaranteeing trade among various service sectors, including telecommunications, by reducing the barriers to foreign investment and opening up the market. This has encouraged entry by various international players, with the encouragement of technological advancement and better delivery of services in many countries. More competition as a result of GATS obligations has led to enhanced efficiency and quality of telecommunication services, with consumers enjoying better options. Besides, the agreement states specific modes of supply of services, thereby bringing clarity and order that has encouraged investment in telecommunication infrastructure, thereby transforming communication environments worldwide. In developing countries, GATS participation has been particularly vital since it is part of broader economic reforms initiated during the late 1980s. The majority of these nations viewed liberalizing the access of service markets as a great step towards enhancing domestic telecommunication sectors' quality and efficiency.

The GATS negotiations represent the movement towards market reforms, providing a forum for such nations to advance their interests while receiving global economic challenges in return. The advent of GATS, therefore, was a momentous occasion for developing nations to participate in multilateral talks, whereby they could leverage the pressures of the outside world for regulation reforms and liberalization of the marketplace, finally focusing on bringing their telecommunication infrastructure up to date and increasing access among their citizenry (DEC et al., 2025). The effects of GATS on the telecommunication industry, however, have not all been positive, calling for a critical review of its consequences. While the deal has led to competition and investment, it has also been in the middle of controversy regarding the equitable sharing of benefits and dependence on external telecommunications corporations. Its critics argue that the pressures exerted by GATS can be so intense that corporate interests sometimes become more important than local community interests at the cost of providing vital services to rural and poor communities. Also, the risk of regulatory reversal is one that would have to be countered, as commitments under GATS can be in variance with national policy goals toward safeguarding domestic interests. Hence, while GATS offers a formal process to liberalization, implications on the telecommunication industry have to be critically evaluated to ensure that benefits from globalization are not achieved at the expense of domestic requirements and development (Cooper et al., 2014).

5.5.2. General Agreement on Trade in Services (GATS) in the Context of Financial Services

GATS is at the heart of financial services liberalization worldwide. When nations engage in trade negotiations, that is, regional trade agreements (RTAs) under GATS Article V, welfare gains are high both in the services and goods markets. The financial industry, being one of the most important areas of GATS, embodies such economic growth potential to its fullest capacity. Notably, the effects of the arrangements do not flow equally across industries; the business services sector is the most impacted by growth in trade, hinting that the financial services are not standalone but complement other service industries. Besides, the quantitative emphasis narrowed by earlier studies presents a demand for cautious scrutiny to comprehend the implications of the RTAs more conclusively (Park et al., 2025). Identifying the sectorial responses to the arrangements will be instrumental in so far as countries cope with the complexity of trade in services across borders. Liberalization of financial services, facilitated by ease through the GATS framework, has policy implications of far-reaching effects on member countries. Experiences from crises such as the 1997 Asian crisis demonstrate how financial liberalization, if left unchecked, can result in serious economic repercussions. Countries need to have responsible policies that combine the commitments entered into GATS with the broader objectives of economic stability. For instance, countries like China are leading their financial opening while balancing obligations so that liberalization will not undermine economic resilience. A close look at other nations' financial liberalization policy that has run into crisis, such as Indonesia and Malaysia, places particular stress on adhering to macroeconomic stability considerations in seeking growth (Kim et al., 2002).

Financial system interconnectedness requires that nations move towards liberalization with prudence and understanding, aware of the fact that financial stability comes first even when confronted with pressure from global markets. Further, the link between liberalization of capital accounts and liberalization of financial services must be closely examined under the GATS framework. As the financial sector continues to evolve, the integration of the liberalization processes could promote development but also increase vulnerabilities if not handled carefully. GATS-participating nations must ensure to give top priority to mobilizing resources for sustainable economic development in a way that their financial systems still remain robust and competitive amidst a rapidly changing global environment. It is the precept of financial stability and competition that should guide nations to open their markets in a way that economic well-being is not sacrificed but benefits accrue from liberalization. The detailed calibration of such policies will not only support national economic objectives but also add to the total efficacy of cross-border trade in financial services, establishing a healthy basis for future economic transactions (Kim et al., 2002) (Figure 5.12).

Figure 5.12. General Agreement on Trade in Services (GATS) in the context of financial services.

Source: https://external-content.duckduckgo.com/iu/?u=https%3A%2F%2Fwww.digitalauthority.me%2Fwp-content%2Fuploads%2F2018%2F12%2Ffinancial-services-marketing.jpg&f=1&nofb=1&ipt=197d03ef4147ad42c71106f0879f8dc457a9aad43259151c16b1978e4b12a827.

5.5.3. Impact of General Agreement on Trade in Services (GATS) on Healthcare Services

General Agreement on Trade in Services (GATS) has had a very great impact on healthcare services across the world, with both opportunities and challenges. With healthcare sectors being liberalized in countries, foreign investment and provision of services have risen, tending to increase access to highly developed medical technology and expertise. This transformation can be seen especially in nations like Asia, whose entrance by multinational health service providers has favored competition and service quality. However, according to Lethbridge et al. (2004), the transformation initiated by GATS has also extended to the roles of local healthcare systems, corporate interests, and labor unions, unleashing tensions that may undermine the integrity of public health services. The consequences of GATS extend beyond mere market forces; they also encompass significant health policy issues. As healthcare services are opened up to liberalization, countries must balance economic interests and the basic principles of equity and access in the field of healthcare. The GATS structure encourages private sector investment and the incentives of profit, which could tilt towards successful populations at the expense of disadvantaged groups. Despite the hope of increased quality and efficiency, there are substantial hurdles to effective regulation and implementation of health services based on public interest, highlighted in Lethbridge et al. (2008). This paradox relates to the difficult relationship between trade agreements and access to health care, raising fundamental questions about prioritizing profit over population demand for health. Furthermore, the GATS-style regulatory regime impacts the governance structure of healthcare systems, particularly regarding occupational health and safety. With occupational health provision included in trade agreements, the aim is to render workplaces safe for healthcare providers as well as patients. The effect of the regulations is, however, diminished by insufficient enforcing capacity and a general lack of political will to place such important sectors at the forefront. The complexity of compliance and the heterogeneity of regulatory requirements across countries also contribute to the complexity, undermining the quality and safety of health services globally. As discovered by Lethbridge et al. (2008), without a high level of political commitment and arrangements for accountability, the likelihood of improved health outcomes through GATS remains precarious, calling for the implementation of a prudent trade strategy for healthcare services.

5.6. FUTURE OF GENERAL AGREEMENT ON TRADE IN SERVICES (GATS)

The future of the General Agreement on Trade in Services (GATS) depends upon its capacity to adapt to emerging new trends in the global economy and the shifting world trade environment. While nations increasingly come to appreciate the role of services in their economic foundations, the GATS has a serious challenge to adapt in order to protect and enlarge these industries. Rise of electronic services, say, has brought in a new area of business which GATS must keep pace with, hence the necessity to have changes in its regulatory frameworks. Moreover, international negotiations such as the Trade in Services Agreement (TISA) bring opportunities and tests to GATS, provoking it to adapt to the contemporary market realities without compromising on being beneficial to the interests and development intentions of member countries, as indicated by ongoing reviews of U.S. foreign trade in services which give significance to effective international disciplines in service trade (Cooper et al., 2014). Moreover, it is necessary that the GATS scheme contains provisions under which countries, particularly developing countries, can navigate the complexities of service trade across borders. With persistent financial fragilities continuing to emerge in the world, the ability of countries to impose capital account regulation (CARs) becomes increasingly vital. Through the support of compatibility between domestic regulatory flexibility and trade obligations, GATS can stabilize economies without undermining international cooperation (Gallagher et al., 2012). This architecture balances power relations, providing the policy space that nations require to pursue national agendas, with a thrust towards a participatory paradigm of international trade negotiations. Channels of debate of GATS in the future will therefore have to draw upon the wisdom and expertise of developing countries in negotiating a comprehensive service trade regime focused on equitable development and sustainable development. In this context, the GATS will also need to incorporate technology and innovation into its foundational principles. The fast pace of technological change in the digital era has seen service delivery models not only change but also go global, so much so that a sophisticated approach to regulating trade is warranted. GATS needs to deal with challenges concerning e-commerce, data flows, and cybersecurity and provide regulations that facilitate growth while protecting consumer interests. As the member states confront these developments, the necessity of international cooperation becomes apparent, as it creates avenues for information sharing and best practices necessary in creating an efficient service trade environment. Thus, the future direction of GATS will be guided by its determination to realign itself with the needs of participants in an increasingly integrated world economy, leading the way towards a comprehensive and responsive global trade in services (Figure 5.13).

Figure 5.13. Future of the General Agreement on Trade in Services (GATS).

Source: https://www.transnationalmatters.com/wp-content/uploads/2024/05/users_7dd1dc79-7cb9-40c2-b5f8-d0e040fa311b_generations_f2130756-2b40-4b0e-a9ed-91a40b6efc8a_Default_a_diverse_group_of_professionals_standing_around_a_glo_0-1.webp.

5.6.1. Potential Reforms and Updates

The General Agreement on Trade in Services (GATS) is a significant architecture for regulating trade in services across borders, yet numerous potential reforms would render it more efficient. Among them is this key aspect of reform: to address the imbalances between GATS commitments and member countries' real policy. For instance, the measure to which commitments touch upon policies of quality of services is as diverse as indicated by the variation seen between economies. The disciplines in GATS can be strengthened to increase compliance and close the imbalance between commitments and practices. Through promoting greater transparency among member states, the agreement would assist in driving enhancements in service quality and availability, targeting grievances made against such domains as electricity and water, that have hitherto struggled under GATS rules (Hall et al., 2006). Another reform path would be for GATS to be aligned with overall economic and policy goals, including the United Nations Sustainable Development Goals (SDGs). Applying sustainability principles to GATS can improve the provision of services across many industries while facilitating access to all member nations. As more global attention is put on sustainability, environmental, social, and governance concerns being incorporated into trade architectures may result in more legitimacy and acceptance of GATS. This integration would provide countries with the bargaining power to prioritize sustainability in the pursuit of trade liberalization, a necessity for reconciling economic growth with environmental purity. As the world continues to move towards more enlightened economic action, GATS must evolve to capture such necessities, such that trade liberalization does not undermine efforts towards sustainability (Eschenbach et al., 2025). Finally, GATS reform needs to be advised on the idiosyncratic challenges of small economies, which typically struggle to leverage GATS in order to commit significantly. The commitment horizon of trade agreements is considerably compromised by reduced enforcement incentives and external pressure in small markets. Collective action among WTO members to enhance the capacity of these countries to engage actively within the GATS framework is necessary. This could involve direct support in the form of capability formation and building skills. Through the establishment of a culture of more cooperation and help, GATS could fulfill its potential as a device of economic empowerment, allowing small nations to cope better and more equally with the complexities of cross-border service trade (Eschenbach et al., 2025).

5.6.2. Role of Emerging Economies in General Agreement on Trade in Services (GATS)

Emerging economies become the key element in the General Agreement on

Trade in Services (GATS) that maps out international trade through increased participation and opening up of their own service markets. When such nations become part of the global marketplace, they bring diverse services, from IT and consultancy to healthcare and education, until now the domain of the developed economies. Their accession facilitates greater competition and innovation and enhances the quality and supply of services around the globe. The GATS mechanism calls these new economies to commit to the opening of their service economies, which can assist in domestic development via foreign direct investment (FDI) and technology transfer. This is consistent with their broader economic agendas of development and modernization and assists them in deepening their positions within the international economy. Furthermore, reforms in emerging economies usually harmonize with other regulatory and financial reforms. According to recent studies, the link between these nations long-run economic development and facilitating financial sector reforms is absolute. The Deputy Treasury Secretary Kenneth Dam has stated that reforming domestic financial systems can serve as an economic growth engine, highlighting the institutional capacity in the services sector. To such economies, it is imperative to build a robust regulatory structure not only to enhance the ability to comply with GATS obligations but also to enhance their ability to negotiate favorable terms in service trade. Subsequently, as developing economies strengthen policy frameworks, they become better placed to utilize the benefits inherent in GATS and hence enhance their voice in multilateral service trade negotiations. Finally, the strategic role of the rising economies in GATS involves not only economic growth and regulatory adaptation but also geopolitical changes in service trade talks. Since the rising markets have grown even more powerful in global discussion, they are included in the discussion of global trade agreements such as the Trade in Services Agreement (TISA) and the Trans-Pacific Partnership (TPP). These negotiations reflect the sophistication and difficulty of the rising presence of these countries for established economies as they cope with it. Emerging economies are pivotal in developing holistic standards that accommodate various development trajectories because of their different ideas and interests. Their engagement thus not only adds depth to existing debates but also works as a counterbalance to interests, and thus the GATS structure is an increasingly inclusive and balanced instrument for international trade (Cooper et al., 2014). This emerging scenario serves to recognize new economies as significant stakeholders in the GATS model, thus transforming the landscape of global trade (Dobson, 2025).

5.6.3. Predictions for the Evolution of Service Trade

Service trade growth has been of interest to economists and policymakers since the mid-1980s, mainly due to leadership initiated by the World Trade

Organization (WTO) and regional trade agreements. Focus on liberalization of the services sector has stimulated an enormous body of literature on determinants of international services trade and potential benefits of such liberalization. As countries become more aware of the key role that services have to contribute to their economies, forecasts are for the trend towards further integration of service markets to gain pace. Studies have shown that greater trade and investment in services can bring about major welfare benefits, which have further emphasized the significance of global cooperation and trade agreements in promoting these advancements (Hoekman et al., 2025). The challenges presented by the complexity of service regulation can lead to innovations in policy-making and thereby affect the future shape of global trade in services. Though the optimistic expectations of the liberalization of service trade are adequately argued, the process is not free from controversies. Critics refer to the intrinsic risks involved in depending on international trade rules for the regulation of public services and demanding intense examination of the implications of market-driven reforms. Specifically, the trade agreement exemption provisions, including those of WTO and NAFTA, produce a compound context for public health services.

The debate is over the interpretation of the provisions, where opposing views on both sides have been expressed on whether or not they are helpful in protecting local sectors from stringent trade obligations. This dialectic suggests that while the defenders of trade agreements may appeal for a liberal reading of such safeguarding, the onus ultimately rests with policymakers to navigate these waters carefully. In the context of services reform being in motion, policymakers have to weigh the dangers of market aspects opening up against the requirement of protecting public welfare (Crawford et al., 2011). Lastly, projections regarding the expansion of service trade are strongly linked to ongoing technological innovations, regulatory measures, and international bargaining. The evolution of electronic services and rapid developments in communication technologies are transforming the delivery and trade of services and are creating new channels for growth and innovation. With service industries becoming more and more integrated with technology, cooperation between nations will become crucial in overcoming the hurdles of regulation and competitiveness. The future development of service trade will understandably include responsive policies that guarantee not just free trade but also the safeguarding of social interests. Emphasizing the need for integrated frameworks will facilitate sustainable development in the context of increased globalization so that developing economies can join the service trade field meaningfully and mitigate consequential risks (Hoekman et al., 2025).

SUMMARY

A critique of the GATS lays bare the complicated interplay between international trade policy and economic domestic interest. As nations increasingly engage as active actors in global markets, the need for structured frameworks like GATS becomes overwhelming. These accords not only encourage cross-border services exchange but also provide guidelines on negotiations that cater to the unique challenges that the services sector presents. The United States, in this regard, faces policy challenges that have their origins in the intricacies of negotiating international accords, addressing issues such as regulatory harmonization and open measurement of services trade. This is highlighted in U.S. foreign trade in services research, especially with regard to ongoing agreements like the Trade in Services Agreement (TISA), which attempts to institute overarching principles of rules for trade in services as a reaction to evolving global needs (Cooper et al., 2014). Furthermore, GATS implications extend to essential sectors like utilities, for example, electricity and water, as in being considered for service trade liberalization debates. The effect of GATS on such essential service sectors is concerning with respect to access, price, and quality of services provided to the consumer. Through provision of foreign investment opportunities and access into local markets, GATS aims at enhancing competition and efficiency. However, it is crucial to subject this competitive market to critical examination of whether it serves the public interest or primarily promotes multinational corporations. The experience of countries grappling with the consequences of GATS in public utilities is a tale of caution about the nexus between trade liberalization and the very elementary needs of citizens and the environment (Hall et al., 2006). In summary, the GATS model presents opportunity and challenge demanding cautious attention by policymakers and other interested parties. Overall success of GATS in enabling expanded service trade hinges on the ability of negotiating nations to navigate through the contentious field of domestic compared to foreign interests. As the terrain of global trade models continues to evolve, any controversies surrounding implications of GATS will continue to characterize trade policy discourse. The adaptability of such agreements will determine their viability in addressing the prevailing economic realities so that they may be in harmony with the greater objectives of sustainable development and equitable trade practices. Lastly, one should comprehend GATS and its possible impact to facilitate a balanced approach towards international trade in services.

The GATS was a dramatic and revolutionary shift in the global trading landscape, particularly for developing countries. In the late 1980s, most of these nations started more market-oriented domestic policies, observing that opening service markets to access could enhance the quality and efficiency of their service sectors. This very important turn gave common impetus to developing countries to seek multilateral negotiations for service trade liberalization. As a result, the draft GATS was conceived out of the Uruguay Round negotiations as the sum of these changing perspectives, an amalgamation of unilaterally driven policy reforms with a view toward integrating services into the global economy, recharting national and regional development strategies (DEC et al., 2025). Yet the more protectionist negotiating tactics utilized by developing countries throughout the GATS talks engender serious questions regarding the soundness of their liberalization commitment. Although the intention was to shore up domestic services via international commitments, there is a paradox: numerous policy reforms in these nations were prompted by foreign pressures instead of domestic industry pressures. Such disparity can undermine the credibility of liberalization efforts and trigger doubts about the sustainability of such reforms. However, being part of a binding multilateral system like the GATS might enable them to stay committed to efficiency in the service sector by having better chances of higher costs from the reversal of committed reforms, thereby serving as a catalytic agent towards further regulatory change (DEC et al., 2025). The context of GATS negotiations also leads to a broader debate that is centered on the relationship between developing countries' economic policy sovereignty and trade agreements. It has been established in the studies that the majority of developing countries are significantly hindered from using necessary capital account regulations by being obligated under other trade and investment agreements. Such contracts, based on the Pardee Center Task Force report, can limit the flexibility required for effective policy intervention and, therefore, limit economic resilience. Thus, the current controversy surrounding GATS necessitates a serious examination of how such global frameworks can be made to coincide with the national agendas of developing countries so that a way of integration is pursued which meets international trade involvement and the national imperatives of regulation and development of the market.

REFERENCES

1. Adlung, R. (2009). Trade in healthcare and health insurance services: WTO/GATS as a supporting actor (?). https://www.econstor.eu/bitstream/10419/66559/1/730076229.pdf (accessed on 30th October 2025).
2. Ahmed, B., Bacarreza, J., Bedford, R., Beets, G., Bhagwati, J., Borjas, G., Carmichael, G., et al. (2009). International trade agreements and international migration. https://core.ac.uk/download/29196183.pdf (accessed on 30th October 2025).
3. Alexander, N., & Kessler, T. (2025). Assessing the risks in the private provision of essential services. https://core.ac.uk/download/pdf/7043216.pdf (accessed on 30th October 2025).
4. Anderson, S., Aruaz, A., de Paula, L. F., Francis, D., et al. (2013). Capital account regulations and the trading system: A compatibility review. https://open.bu.edu/bitstream/2144/22903/1/_Capital-Controls-Eng_201303.pdf (accessed on 30th October 2025).
5. Baumert, J., Heuschel, D., Johnson, K., Lynch, L., et al. (2008). International cooperation on trade and labor issues. https://core.ac.uk/download/5118835.pdf (accessed on 30th October 2025).
6. Chirathivat, S., & Srisangnam, P. (2013). The 2030 architecture of Association of Southeast Asian Nations Free Trade Agreements. https://www.econstor.eu/dspace/bitstream/10419/101210/1/745215807.pdf (accessed on 30th October 2025).
7. Collins, D. A. (2019). The International Bar Association and trade in legal services: Meta law-making in international economic law? https://core.ac.uk/download/169434481.pdf (accessed on 30th October 2025).
8. Cooper, W. H., & Nelson, R. M. (2014). U.S. foreign trade in services: Trends and U.S. policy challenges. https://core.ac.uk/download/20537776.pdf (accessed on 30th October 2025).
9. Crawford, M. (2011). No watertight compartments: Trade agreements, international health care reform, and the legal politics of public sector exemptions. https://core.ac.uk/download/58776524.pdf (accessed on 30th October 2025).
10. De, D., & Nag, B. (2025). Services in regional trade agreements: Implications for India. https://core.ac.uk/download/pdf/6799070.pdf (accessed on 30th October 2025).
11. Dobson, W. (2025). Further financial services liberalization in the Doha

Round? https://core.ac.uk/download/pdf/6454319.pdf (accessed on 30th October 2025).

12. Eschenbach, F., & Hoekman, B. (2025). Services policies in transition economies: On the European Union and the World Trade Organization as commitment mechanisms. https://core.ac.uk/download/pdf/6242833.pdf (accessed on 30th October 2025).
13. Finger, J. M., & Nogués, J. J. (2025). The unbalanced Uruguay Round outcome: The new areas in future WTO negotiations. https://core.ac.uk/download/pdf/9310972.pdf (accessed on 30th October 2025).
14. Gallagher, K., & Stanley, L. (2012). Global financial reform and trade rules: The need for reconciliation. https://open.bu.edu/bitstream/2144/22732/1/Pardee-IIB-024-Sept-2012.pdf (accessed on 30th October 2025).
15. George, C., Kirkpatrick, C., & Scrieciu, S. S. (2025). Enhancing the contribution of trade liberalization in environmental services to sustainable development. https://core.ac.uk/download/pdf/6674653.pdf (accessed on 30th October 2025).
16. Gould, E., Grieshaber-Otto, J., Grieshaber-Otto, J., Ziegler, D., Gould, R., Bloche, M. G., Shaffer, E. R., et al. (2008). Trade and health: How World Trade Organization (WTO) law affects alcohol and public health. https://core.ac.uk/download/16268371.pdf (accessed on 30th October 2025).
17. Hall, D., & Thomas, S. (2006). GATS and the electricity and water sectors. https://core.ac.uk/download/67097.pdf (accessed on 30th October 2025).
18. Hoekman, B. (2025). Liberalizing trade in services: A survey. https://core.ac.uk/download/pdf/6373353.pdf (accessed on 30th October 2025).
19. Hoekman, B. (2025). Tentative first steps: An assessment of the Uruguay Round agreement on services. https://core.ac.uk/download/pdf/6521953.pdf (accessed on 30th October 2025).
20. Hoekman, B. M. (2025). *Developing Countries and the Uruguay Round: Negotiations on Services*. https://core.ac.uk/download/pdf/6616128.pdf (accessed on 30th October 2025).
21. Kalupahana, K., & King, N. J. (2007). Choosing between liberalization and regulatory autonomy under GATS: Implications of U.S.-Gambling for trade in cross-border e-services. https://core.ac.uk/download/539447752.pdf (accessed on 30th October 2025).
22. Kim, Y. H. (2002). Financial opening under the WTO agreement in selected Asian countries: Progress and issues. https://core.ac.uk/download/39426743.pdf (accessed on 30th October 2025).
23. Kolesnichenko, A., Roberts, J., Jakubiak, M., Ülgen, S., & Paczynski,

W. (2025). *The New EU Frontier: Perspectives on Enhanced Economic Integration*. https://core.ac.uk/download/pdf/6704182.pdf (accessed on 30th October 2025).

24. Lee, M. (2025). The implementation of the GATS and its impact upon tourism development. https://core.ac.uk/download/77067.pdf (accessed on 30th October 2025).
25. Lejour, A., & Kox, H. (2025). A different approach to WTO negotiations in services. https://core.ac.uk/download/pdf/6670638.pdf (accessed on 30th October 2025).
26. Lethbridge, J. (2004). Changing healthcare systems in Asia. https://core.ac.uk/download/67058.pdf (accessed on 30th October 2025).
27. Lethbridge, J. (2008). Occupational health regulations and health workers: Protection or vulnerability? https://core.ac.uk/download/67329.pdf (accessed on 30th October 2025).
28. Lücke, M., & Spinanger, D. (2025). Liberalizing international trade in services: Challenges and opportunities for developing countries. https://core.ac.uk/download/pdf/6796290.pdf (accessed on 30th October 2025).
29. Macmillan, F. (2004). If not this World Trade Organization, then what? https://core.ac.uk/download/15005.pdf (accessed on 30th October 2025).
30. Malkawi, B. H. (2019). Reflection on exclusivity and termination of commercial agency in Jordan: The intertwining of domestic regulation and international trade law. https://core.ac.uk/download/186331798.pdf (accessed on 30th October 2025).
31. Mattoo, A. (2025). Shaping future GATS rules for trade in services. https://core.ac.uk/download/pdf/6615527.pdf (accessed on 30th October 2025).
32. Park, I., & Park, S. (2025). Regional liberalization of trade in services. https://core.ac.uk/download/pdf/6586034.pdf (accessed on 30th October 2025).
33. Raihan, A. (2025). Ongoing negotiations on the GATS FSA: Bangladesh's concerns and position. https://core.ac.uk/download/pdf/9305554.pdf (accessed on 30th October 2025).
34. Ramjoue, M. (2025). How do people in Asia and the Pacific migrate legally for work? An overview of legal frameworks: GATS Mode 4, PTAs and bilateral labor agreements. https://core.ac.uk/download/pdf/6266473.pdf (accessed on 30th October 2025).
35. Sharma, B. P., Maskay, N. M., & Panta, R. K. (2025). Foreign investment liberalization and incentives in selected Asia-Pacific developing countries: Implications for the health service sector in Nepal. https://core.ac.uk/download/pdf/7022370.pdf (accessed on 30th October 2025).

Chapter 6

Intellectual Property Rights (TRIPS Agreement)

Contents

INTRODUCTION

Intellectual property rights (IPRs) play an important role in the contemporary world economy, particularly through arrangements such as the Agreement on Trade-Related Aspects of Intellectual Property Rights (TRIPS). Formed in 1995 during the World Trade Organization (WTO) negotiations, TRIPS aims to standardize IPR protection among member states so that creators and innovators can safeguard their work from plagiarism. The importance of this accord is that it addresses important areas such as the protection of trademarks, copyrights, and patents, upon which innovation in all aspects of life, ranging from drugs to technology and agriculture, relies. As nations attempt to reconcile protecting IPRs and providing fair access to essential products, the impact of TRIPS is immense, and the only way to achieve the diversified nature of its impact is by an intensive analysis. The entwining of intellectual property rights with domestic protection necessities of traditional knowledge (TK) presents the complex situation brought about by the TRIPS Agreement. For instance, the adoption of new plant variety protection (PVP) systems in Southeast Asia illustrates the realist play of balancing compliance with international obligations and local community demands. Indonesia, Malaysia, and the Philippines have passed PVP legislation that combines mainstream IPR paradigms with specific consideration of TK driven by concerns like biotechnology development and pressure from civil society forces. However, such legal frameworks are likely to create tension between commercial agenda and just interests of the surrounding community, since the laws employed may erect barriers which impede effective recognition of TK rights (Antons et al., 2012).

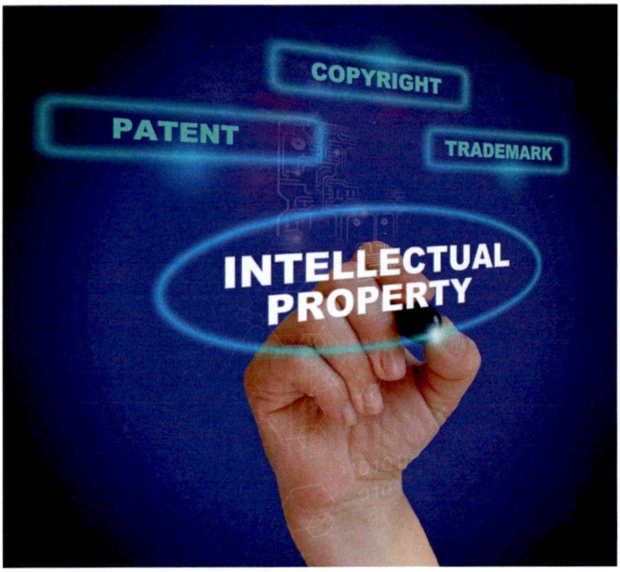

Figure 6.1. Intellectual Property Rights (TRIPS Agreement).

Source: https://external-content.duckduckgo.com/iu/?u=http%3A%2F%2Fndvlaw.com%2Fwp-content%2Fuploads%2F2013%2F04%2FIP.jpg&f=1&nofb=1&ipt=67d570e508b1b2ce189c5915ec6ccd1772d4318d07697ef959a4b80691426005.

It is therefore necessary to analyze this interface in order to assess the efficacy of available legal instruments in defending the rights of indigenous communities. In addition to managing conventional knowledge, the TRIPS Agreement inevitably raises central questions of access to vital medications, particularly in the developing world. The uniform protection term and explicit mention of pharmaceutical products as subject matter eligible for patent have significant implications for public health, especially for those users who are in low-resource settings. The probable conflict among patent holders, primarily pharmaceutical companies, and patients who need to access affordable healthcare has resulted in ongoing debate over the moral consequences of enforcing IPR. Critics of TRIPS argue that it has the potential to undermine the right to health by limiting access to drugs needed to cure diseases such as HIV/AIDS and tuberculosis, particularly in states with poor healthcare infrastructure (Khair et al., 2016). By critically examining these TRIPS Agreement dimensions, this essay aims to elucidate the competing interests and resulting societal impact, thus contributing to the debate on how best to reconcile IPR protection with the public health equity mandate (Figure 6.1).

Definition of Intellectual Property Rights (IPR)

IPR are legislative rights that provide inventors and creators sole ownership of their intellectual creations, including a variety of work like inventions, literary and artistic work, symbols, names, and images employed in trade. IPR are used to promote creativity and innovation by enabling people and entities to benefit from their inventions and artwork without fear of misappropriation. Protection under intellectual property law varies by type, generally including patents, copyrights, trademarks, and trade secrets, each serving a unique function in safeguarding intellectual works of different kinds. The significance of IPR is not only based on protection to creators but also on its role in ensuring a competitive market and economic growth through innovation and creativity. The TRIPS Agreement, or formally known as the Agreement on Trade-Related Aspects of Intellectual Property Rights, is an international code of conduct that seeks to harmonize intellectual property protection globally. The agreement sets minimum general standards for the protection and enforcement of IPR, thereby fostering international trade and investment. TRIPS addresses a large number of aspects of intellectual property, including patents, copyright, and trademarks, and attempts to resolve disputes resulting from IPR violations among member nations. By TRIPS, countries commit to putting in place and enforcing sufficient measures that are of international standards, promoting uniformity of IPR protections. Harmonization is required to promote an equitable approach that balances public interest with intellectual property rights holders' rights, responding to the need for balancing access to innovation and creative resources for the public. The discourse of intellectual property right is continued through the name for trademark anti-dilution protection, which is a core component of broader IPR debates. Anti-dilution protection of trademarks is in place to uphold the originality and goodwill of well-known marks so that their dilution or use by others in the marketplace cannot be permitted even if there is no direct competition. This IPR dimension is important for maintaining consumer trust and fair competition, which puts a high value on prestigious brands. As per literature available, anti-dilution clauses are a necessary component of forms presented by international agreements such as the TRIPS Agreement, which acknowledges that consumer interests need to be protected along with trademark rights. The controversy regarding the efficacy and advisability of such protections remains in flux, as does the transforming nature of international commerce and the challenge of reconciling domestic IPR systems with global norms (Baba, 2024; Zhu, 2024).

Overview of the Trade-Related Aspects of Intellectual Property Rights (TRIPS) Agreement

The TRIPS Agreement is a milestone development in international intellectual property law. Established in 1994 under the aegis of the WTO, TRIPS is meant to harmonize the protection of IPR among member nations, thereby having a similar foundation for the protection of patents, copyrights, and trademarks, amongst others. It was a step up from the previous, rather haphazard framework of intellectual property laws when differences did used to exist between developed and developing nations. By creating TRIPS, member states are obligated to maintain at least the required standards of protection of IPRs, innovation, and encouragement of international trade. Consistently, TRIPS aims not only to ensure creators' rights but also to encourage global economic collaboration by guaranteeing intellectual property rights are preserved worldwide. In actuality, the TRIPS Agreement has spurred significant controversy concerning its effects on developed and developing nations. While it promotes ownership and guarding of innovation, it also comes under criticism for promoting existing inequalities in technological advancement as well as market access. It is a classic example that TRIPS requires member nations to enforce robust patent laws that can render important medicines inaccessible in developing nations, which is a public health and welfare cause for concern. Moreover, the intricacy of TRIPS compliance has weighed heavily on low-income nations with limited resources, hindering them from engaging in global trade and posing hurdles to national innovation. This tension between intellectual property protection and equitable access to technology is a significant topic for debate and reform, and it calls for ongoing analysis of TRIPS impact on global economic tides. Chinas TRIPS Agreement implementation is a good case study of the challenges and opportunities of the framework. In 2001, when China joined the WTO, it committed to bringing its local law into conformity with TRIPS standards. This implementation has necessitated fundamental change in its intellectual property law to match international standards, having implications on domestic innovation as well as foreign investment. The success of the implementation by China brings into focus the issue of achieving the right balance in intellectual property protection while still being within an atmosphere of technological development. Furthermore, the historical patterns of innovation from countries like Japan and the United Kingdom bring forward the issues of achieving compliance, as each country needs to navigate its own economic realities. Concerns expressed about whether TRIPS disproportionately benefits developed nations serve to further underscore the need for ongoing discussion about the aim and efficacy of such international agreements in building a harmonious global marketplace (Dawood et al., 2001; Fojtíková et al., 2018) (Figure 6.2).

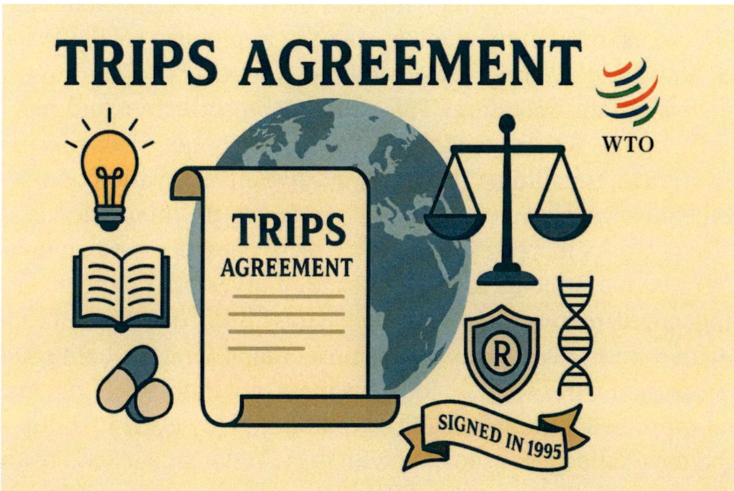

Figure 6.2. Overview of the Trade-Related Aspects of Intellectual Property Rights (TRIPS) agreement.

Source: https://kanoonpedia.com/wp-content/uploads/2025/04/TRIPS-Agreement-in-1995-Image.png.

Importance of Intellectual Property (IP) in Global Trade

The significance of IP to international trade cannot be overstated, as it lays the groundwork for building innovation and economic development. The framework established by the TRIPS Agreement is vital in harmonizing the various IP laws between various member nations of the World Trade Organization. This global synchronization allows protection of innovations, thereby promoting technological innovation as well as the creation of new goods and services vital to economic development. Furthermore, the TRIPS Agreement provides a legal framework that provides creators and inventors with the bargaining power to obtain the economic gains of their work, leading to global business competitiveness. Therefore, understanding the impact of IP is vital for nations committed to trading successfully in the contemporary world economy (Archibugi et al., 2025). Moreover, the role of IP extends beyond protection; it actually plays a role in shaping trends in trade in an increasingly interlinked global economy. Customs protection of intellectual property rights is essential in ensuring conformity with global norms and occupying violations that may arise through cross-border transactions. Trading nations must navigate various IP regimes, something that demands the understanding of national as well as international IP protection requirements. It is the TRIPS Agreement that defines these requirements, mandating member states to implement strong enforcement procedures alongside holding respect for the varied economic environments within which they are operating. This need for an effective and harmonized system of IP rights not only minimizes the likelihood of infringement but also fosters a business climate that is supportive of innovation and economic cooperation (Chernyavskaya et al., 2018). Moreover, the integration of IP rights into trade frameworks increases markets' attractiveness for foreign investment. Robust IP protection policies send a message to investors that their inventions will be safeguarded, thereby guaranteeing the possibility of inflow of capital into countries with robust IP regulations. It is most crucial for developing nations, as robust IP protection will stimulate local business and innovation and eventually bring about more equal global wealth distribution. However, it is important to comprehend the challenges associated with these benefits, such as ensuring that developing countries can maintain TRIPS compliance without compromising their economic interests. Overcoming these challenges will allow states to better leverage IP as a vehicle for long-term economic development and have a broader discussion about the importance of intellectual property in global trade (Archibugi et al., 2025).

6.1. HISTORICAL CONTEXT OF INTELLECTUAL PROPERTY RIGHTS (IPR)

The historical background of IPR explains their evolution as a system for balancing innovation and the public good. Intellectual property started in late Medieval times, with guilds beginning to advocate exclusive rights over certain crafts and trades to protect their members from unscrupulous competition. This initial form of protection provided the basis for the legal frameworks that began to emerge in the 18th century, including the Statute of Anne in England (1710), that created authors' rights. Throughout the period of the industrial revolution, societies needed more systematic protections as technology improved, driving the world towards the implementation of patent legislation intended to encourage innovation and spur economic growth. By compromising changing interests of inventors and the public, early legal systems tried to promote innovation while keeping knowledge accessible. With increased momentum for globalization in the latter part of the 20th century, there was increased pressure for intellectual property protection harmonization, with the culmination being the development of the TRIPS Agreement under the auspices of the World Trade Organization (WTO) in 1995. The TRIPS Agreement sought to harmonize intellectual property rights across member states to ensure that inventions, trademarks, and copyrights were adequately safeguarded across the world. Its development marked a paradigm shift in the thinking about intellectual property, elevating it from purely national concerns to a global phenomenon. TRIPS negotiations were marred by tension between the developed and developing countries, with the former pushing for strong IP to safeguard their economies, while the latter was concerned about the implications on access to essential goods, particularly drugs. This conflict between spurring innovation and assuring access is a core debate in the ongoing construction of IPR regimes. The intellectual property right debates always have underlying economic interests and ethical issues, most prominently with developing countries. The critical examination of the TRIPS Agreement illustrates the differing perceptions on the role of IPRs to spur economic development. On the positive side, proponents argue that intellectual property is a source of innovation and economic development, particularly in knowledge economies where ideas can be a source of huge revenue and opportunities for expansion. On the negative side, critics argue that enforcing IPR rigidly makes multinational companies wealthy at the cost of local companies and raises prices for consumers, particularly in poorer regions. This is framed in terms of arguments relating to the impact of IPR on drugs and availability of life-saving drugs, for which there is a necessity for more inclusive policies sensitive to the diverse contexts in which intellectual property operates, hence developing a more balanced framework to international intellectual property rights (Bashi et al., 2008; Rangnekar et al., 2005).

6.1.1. Evolution of Intellectual Property Laws

The process of coming up with intellectual property legislation is irrevocably connected with the increase in global trade and sophistication of technological development. As nations set forth on the path to economic development, guarding innovation and creations was at the forefront. This was the hub of many multilateral conventions that shaped today's world of intellectual property rights. Among these is the Agreement on Trade-Related Aspects of Intellectual Property Rights (TRIPS), which is significant in that it instituted international minimum standards for intellectual property protection. In TRIPS, member states are asked to commit to wide ranges of rules covering patent law and copyrights as a means of replicating the manner in which international pacts influence domestic legal frameworks. The coming into being of such legislation brings into focus not just legal protections but also the accompanying economic needs behind their creation and development. Some provisions in TRIPS can be studied, Article 27.3(b) being an important focus point in particular for developing countries. Article 27.3(b) gives countries the freedom to choose how they define biotechnological inventions keeping in mind the balance between innovation and public interest.

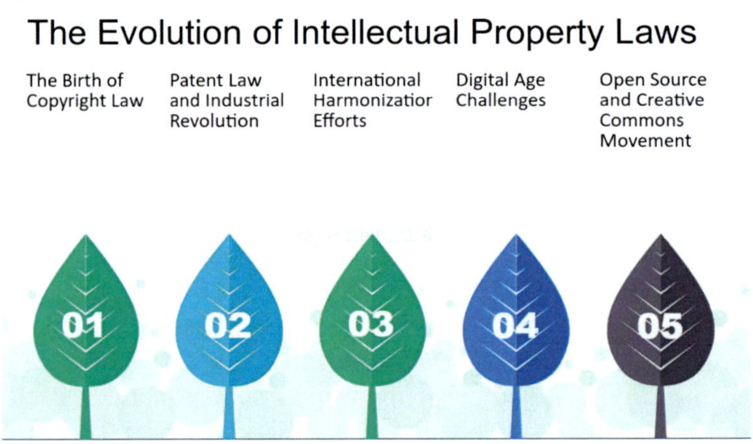

Figure 6.3. Evolution of intellectual property laws.

Source: https://fastercapital.co/i/Moral-Rights-and-Intellectual-Property--Balancing-Creator-Rights-and-Public-Interest--The-Evolution-of-Intellectual-Property-Laws.webp.

Case studies of Kenya mirror the truth of the realities and realities on the ground of adhering to such provisions. While Kenya aims at harmonizing legislation with international standards, implementation in practice falls behind, primarily due to clashes with existing laws, among them those of UPOV. The interaction dynamic between international commitments and domestic legislating priorities in itself exposes the challenges faced by developing countries as they attempt to balance intellectual property rights. The subsequent problems underscore the paradoxes in protecting innovation and reconciling access to resources and knowledge in the global economy (Rangnekar et al., 2008). The treatment of geographical indications (GIs) also mirrors the complex evolution of intellectual property law, particularly in the TRIPS system. GIs, which identify products with specified geographic source or characteristics, pose a paradox of potentiality and dispute between developing nations.

The enthusiasts are of the opinion that GIs are key tools in advancing marketability and protecting cultural heritage, hence a means to economic development. Critics, on the other hand, think that applying GIs to wines and spirits would introduce yet another barrier to trade and hamper the export capacity of nations basing their labeling practices on more traditional methods. This line of argument reflects broader concerns of international trade negotiations, particularly as nations draw a line between maintaining local identities and opening up markets. As the negotiations continue to drag on in the TRIPS Council, the divided opinions about GIs reflect the shift and ongoing challenges in the evolution of intellectual property laws to adapt to international economic trends (Grote et al., 2025) (Figure 6.3).

6.1.2. The Role of the World Trade Organization (WTO)

The WTO plays a crucial role of leading global standards in the field of trade, primarily through its Agreement on Trade-Related Aspects of Intellectual Property Rights (TRIPS). The agreement establishes minimum intellectual property protection levels among members and emphasizes the role of intellectual property in promoting technological development and economic growth. But its application has been controversial, particularly for developing nations that protest that the aggressive IP coverage can restrict access to essential commodities, especially medicines.

Policy of Brazil and South Africa regarding the TRIPS Agreement is a case in point. Through the application of national law on parallel importing and compulsory licensing of antiretroviral drugs, these countries pushed back against the purported monopolistic inclinations advocated by multinational pharmaceutical firms, forcing the WTO to reconsider its mandates in regard to public health emergencies (Rydzefski et al., 2013). The WTO function regarding the TRIPS Agreement signifies a delicate balance between promoting innovation and safeguarding public health. The Doha Declaration on the TRIPS Agreement and Public Health, adopted in 2001, is the organization's response to strong pressure from the developing world and civil society groups. The landmark decision restored the capacity of nations to prioritize public health over intellectual property rights, thereby making possible flexibility in interpreting and applying TRIPS provisions. As a result, the Doha Declaration has given a leverage to facilitate combat against diseases such as HIV/AIDS in low-capacity countries through support for more affordable sources of drugs. The resulting policy reforms indicate how the WTO has shifted in response to criticism of its impacts on health once again, reinforcing the necessity of collaborative efforts between trade and health (Rydzefski et al., 2013).

The ongoing intellectual property rights debate also reflects diverse opinions on the impact of globalization and enforcement of IP. Proponents of the knowledge economy argue that strict intellectual property protection stimulates economic growth through the encouragement of innovation, as posited by new economic growth theorists. Others highlight how these same protections can create monopolies and limit access to essential goods for the poor. This tension is dramatically brought out by apprehensions that intellectual property structures might price out small and medium-sized businesses (SMEs) in developing countries out of the possibility of growing and remaining competitive. The function of the WTO, thus, is regulatory in a more straightforward sense. It is inescapably tied up with broader socio-economic forces, calling for a continuously recurring renegotiation of the manner in which intellectual property law rings within the policy of global equity and access to essential resources.

6.1.3. Key Milestones Leading to the Trade-Related Aspects of Intellectual Property Rights (TRIPS) Agreement

There were several major turning points en route to the TRIPS Agreement that brought into sharp focus the international discourse on intellectual property. One of these milestones on this trajectory was the establishment of the World Trade Organization (WTO) in 1995, which brought together different countries under a single umbrella of trade. WTO underscored the need for coherent intellectual property rights as a means to promote fair competition and innovation. In the pre-TRIPS Agreement era, countries had very different intellectual property systems, which often caused disputes and inconsistencies that affected trade. The global economy was increasingly valuing intellectual property as an integral aspect of economic development and competitive market. It was the first such recognition that led to a fundamental shift in the way states thought about and approached intellectual property globally.

The actual coming into force of the TRIPS Agreement in 1994 was a step towards the harmonization of intellectual property laws across member states. The agreement guaranteed the enforcing of minimal standards of protection for all forms of intellectual property, ranging from patents to copyrights. Such a provision was especially relevant, since developing countries struggled with meeting the challenge of balancing innovation and public access to technology, particularly in sensitive sectors such as pharmaceuticals. The TRIPS Agreement covered the requirement for nations, especially those that were emerging, to reform their intellectual property infrastructures so as to support local as well as international economic interests. In addition, the integration of intellectual property provisions in the WTO model demonstrated intellectual property and trade interdependence as core elements of modern global economic architectures. In many countries, accession to the TRIPS Agreement has inspired far-reaching legislative overhauls to adapt to international standards. For instance, Indias 1970 Patent Act amendment was a significant national move that had brought its patent system into alignment with the demands of TRIPS, particularly in medicines and agrichemicals.

This policy measure was, however, characterized by an informal consensus among the actors, as is apparent in the findings that campaigners and critics alike had at least some sense of commonality regarding what made these reforms so vital (Rangnekar et al., 2005). The complexities of this nexus are sparking critical issues on the agenda of patent reforms, highlighting the importance of balanced voices that support global compliance and local interests. Concurrently, comprehensive strategies for intellectual property management emerged, emphasizing pragmatic plans for innovation in all sectors, observing the shifting scenario that the TRIPS Agreement had to cope with (Bennett et al., 2007) (Figure 6.4).

Figure 6.4. Key milestones leading to the Trade-Related Aspects of Intellectual Property Rights (TRIPS) agreement.

Source: https://blog.ipleaders.in/wp-content/uploads/2021/07/IPR.jpg.

6.2. OBJECTIVES OF THE TRADE-RELATED ASPECTS OF INTELLECTUAL PROPERTY RIGHTS (TRIPS) AGREEMENT

The TRIPS Agreement was created to provide a cohesive framework for the protection and enforcement of intellectual property rights (IPRs) among its constituents. The overarching objective of the TRIPS Agreement is to foster innovation through the guarantee that inventors, creators, and firms will be able to gain from their inventions and works. Through providing effective safeguards, TRIPS aims to stimulate research and development, trigger economic growth, and enhance the competitiveness of industries globally.

The system tries to balance the rights of intellectual property owners and access to low-priced products and technologies and cause issues as nations try to harmonize national laws with international obligations under the agreement. Aside from encouraging innovation, the TRIPS Agreement also explicitly addresses public health concerns, namely with respect to access to medicines. The enforcement of TRIPS has been condemned for its potential impact on international health, as greater patent protection can lead to higher drug prices and reduced access to life-saving medicine. In acknowledgment of this conflict, the Doha Declaration on the TRIPS Agreement and Public Health was passed to reaffirm the member states' rights to place public health above patent rights where necessary. This declaration is a major mandate, permitting countries to use flexibilities such as compulsory licensing in a manner that ensures public health objectives are met without infringing on their TRIPS commitments, primarily for life-saving yet costly medication that is essential to vulnerable populations (Correa et al., 2011).

Another central aim of the TRIPS Agreement is to provide an IP regime that assists with international trade by harmonizing IP law between member nations. Such harmonization should reduce barriers to trade as well as ensure an even competitive environment, which is central to the viability of the global market. Beyond compliance, though, the successful implementation of TRIPS-generated standards involves a myriad of complex interrelationships between IP rights, trade competitiveness, as well as public health issues. When countries implement national policies in harmony with TRIPS, there is a need to account for the impact of such regulations on access to goods and technology. The challenge, therefore, is striking a balance that is mindful of the economic incentives from IPRs and, in the process, ensuring that public health needs are met, hence putting forward the twin objectives of advancing health equity and stimulating innovation (Guise et al., 2006) (Figure 6.5).

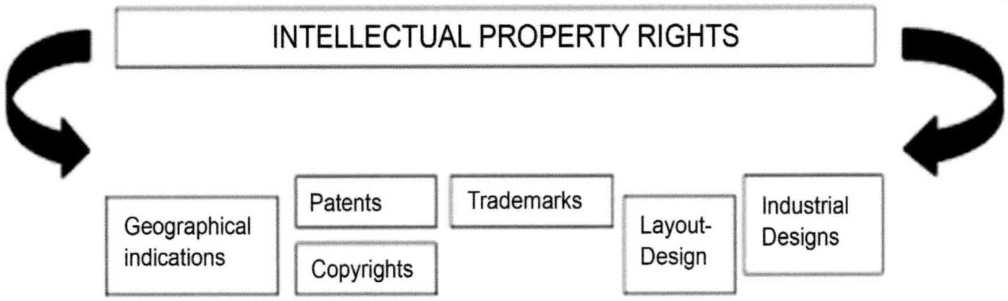

Figure 6.5. Objectives of the Trade-Related Aspects of Intellectual Property Rights (TRIPS) agreement.

Source: https://encrypted-tbn0.gstatic.com/images?q=tbn:ANd9GcTj2obMNjhau2Wz1KKiEqXTkcEKNWbT0jBwIQ&s.

6.2.1. Harmonization of Intellectual Property Standards

The harmonization of intellectual property at a standard level, particularly as contained in the TRIPS Agreement, is a significant milestone in international trade and development. In instituting minimum intellectual property protection standards and intellectual property rights enforcement, TRIPS seeks to achieve commonality among developed and developing nations. However, this harmonization of norms has caused polarizing controversy, particularly among developing nations that argue that the burdens imposed by TRIPS are biased towards developed countries. As academic writing confirms, such levels of high protection have a propensity to promote northern interests at the cost of southern welfare and regional innovation. Such tension demands critical examination of the effects of the agreement and whether it indeed balances the interests of all signatories to the global economy (Schneider et al., 2011). In addition, the intricacies of TRIPS harmonization extend beyond simple compliance with agreed-upon standards.

Current controversies surrounding TRIPS-plus agreements—such as those agreed upon in the Trans-Pacific Partnership (TPP) and the United States-Mexico-Canada Agreement (USMCA)—highlight challenges of adapting to new technology breakthroughs and disparate economic climates. Ancillary agreements have a tendency to call for higher intellectual property protection, making an already delicate balance between encouraging innovation and making goods accessible to the public, particularly in medicines and agrochemicals, increasingly more problematic. Decision-makers remain conflicted regarding whether or not these tough standards promote global economic development or stunt the welfare gains that could be achieved should developing countries have more regulatory autonomy (Yu et al., 2019). The pursuit of harmonized intellectual property standards under the TRIPS Agreement therefore ultimately boils down to bigger questions of fairness, access, and sustainable development. While the program aims to create a more secure and stable world trading system, its implementation reveals tremendous disparities in terms of economic capabilities and power relationship between states. This raises serious concerns over the adequacy of TRIPS in dealing with the unique challenges facing developing nations in the global marketplace. With the progress in global intellectual property, scrutiny not only of the achievements of the harmonization initiative but also of the limitations of a one fits all category that does not reflect on the varied realities of other regions is important (Yu et al., 2019).

6.2.2. Promotion of Technological Innovation

The encouragement of technological innovation is an inherent aim integrated in the design of the Trade-Related Aspects of Intellectual Property Rights (TRIPS) Agreement. Intellectual property rights protection must advance not only the development of innovation but also the effective transfer and diffusion of technology all around the world. By providing a consistent structure to IP rights, TRIPS provides the incentive to nations to adopt legal provisions that stimulate producers and users of technological know-how, which stimulates economic and social development. TRIPS stands out as it has integrated provisions on enforceability to facilitate compliance, which makes it a more efficient tool to drive innovation at the international level. Thus, the treaty is an impetus to harmonize national law in the area of industrial property rights, ultimately towards a more unified international market for tech progress (Sarac, 2015). Moreover, effective IP-related development cooperation is a significant parameter towards tech innovation, particularly in developing nations. A thorough study conducted on the new economies, like India and Brazil, indicates that well-focused intellectual property technical assistance (IP TA) can bring about sustainable changes in IP strategies and technology capabilities. Despite an emergent need for increased country-specific requirements and guidance to financial assistance, instances of successful training programs have been reported, such as those provided for maximizing IP administration agency effectiveness in India. Such targeted interventions not only build local capacity but also lead to increased awareness of IP rights on the part of stakeholders, fostering an atmosphere where innovation is feasible (Engel et al., 2025). For maximum dividends from innovation technology, it is necessary to acknowledge the inter-relationship between IP rights, development aid, and national creativity-supporting policies. The TRIPS Agreement underscores that there is a balance required between safeguarding the rights of inventors and the wider social goals of development and technological access. Such a balance is important in so far as it helps to make innovations reach intended recipients and drive economic growth. As nations become engaged in the pursuits presented by TRIPS, they must create policies that not only protect intellectual property but also encourage collaborative networks among governments, the private sector, and schools. The policies will better coordinate the various objectives of innovation, economic growth, and societal well-being to eventually cement the role of intellectual property rights as a foundation for sustainable development in technology around the globe (Sarac, 2015) (Figure 6.6).

Figure 6.6. Promotion of technological innovation of intellectual property standards.

Source: https://blog.ipleaders.in/wp-content/uploads/2021/10/IP.png.

6.2.3. Protection of Consumer Interests

Consumer protection is, as it were, part and parcel of the protection of intellectual property rights, particularly through mechanisms like the TRIPS Agreement. The global standard aims, as much as to advance innovation and diversity of culture, to safeguard consumers from counterfeiting and misleading practices. The growing call for authentic products, especially in the case of geographical indications (GIs), identifies the need for robust consumer protection devices. Consumers desire better-quality products native to their respective locations—like wines, spirits, and artisanal foods—so the faith that these products maintain their unique characteristics is paramount. The TRIPS Agreement facilitates this by providing legal protection and recognition of GIs, avoiding consumers being deceived by copies of original goods, thereby enhancing their overall experience and satisfaction within the global market (Creditt et al., 2009). Besides, the controversy regarding the efficacy of the TRIPS Agreement in promoting consumer interest mirrors the complexities of intellectual property law. Differences, particularly between the European Union and the United States, center on the extent to which protection must go beyond traditional goods to include a broad spectrum of goods. This argument reflects a double concern: one is the aspiration to increase economic development by virtue of innovative practices, and the other is a concern about the potential to engage in monopolistic actions that will harm consumers, most notably in developing countries.

Figure 6.7. Protection of consumer interests of intellectual property.

Source: https://external-content.duckduckgo.com/iu/?u=https%3A%2F%2Fthf.bing.com%2Fth%2Fid%2FOIP.pj9iz1Xu9cCMG2-UZv02kyQAAAA%3Fcb%3Dthfc1%26pid%3DApi&f=1&ipt=38fbd77125d54cda69d68e015e42fd63d17a812b0bdfd033b4d653258551113f.

Through understanding such opposing perspectives, it is apparent that any future changes to the TRIPS Agreement must balance the interest of the consumer with that of producers so that the market is maintained fair and competitive (Bashi et al., 2008). Navigating the complex landscape of intellectual property rights, there is an important need to examine the protection devices found within the TRIPS Agreement to address best the interests of consumers. Adherents say that expansion of protection for geographical indications and the inclusion of compulsory registration will make consumers more informed about and protected from such imitations. Such intervention would not only safeguard the authenticity of products but also preserve the cultural heritage behind such products. Moreover, this action acknowledges the contribution that local producers make to ensuring quality and keeping economies afloat. Accordingly, in policymaker deliberations on the future of the TRIPS Agreement, prioritizing consumer rights alongside intellectual property protection will be vital to ensuring equitable access to quality products in the global marketplace, thereby consolidating the trilogy of creativity, cultural diversity, and consumer welfare (Creditt et al., 2009) (Figure 6.7).

6.3. KEY PROVISIONS OF THE TRADE-RELATED ASPECTS OF INTELLECTUAL PROPERTY RIGHTS (TRIPS) AGREEMENT

The TRIPS Agreement prescribes basic guidelines for member countries, trying to institute an international intellectual property protection regime that is more harmonized. One of its significant provisions is that nations are required to grant a minimum level of protection for all intellectual property, e.g., patents, trademarks, and copyrights. This standardization is a major contributor to enhancing the predictability of intellectual property regimes globally, thus facilitating international trade and investment. By ensuring compliance by members to these minimum standards, the TRIPS Agreement seeks to balance the rights of creators and public interest, thus stimulating innovation while ensuring continued access to knowledge. As nations grapple with how to apply the implications of their national laws, the TRIPS Agreement remains a significant touchstone to the debate regarding intellectual property rights to begin its entry into the 21st century. Another significant aspect of the TRIPS Agreement is its mechanism of enforcement that has been censured on how adequate and effective it is. Critics maintain that while a framework exists for the enforcement of intellectual property rights, in reality, available mechanisms for right holders to use tend to be inadequate. The same feeling can be experienced within the realm of disputes, e.g., the high-profile U.S.-China case before the WTO Dispute Settlement Body (DSB). The findings of this case revealed the challenges of the enforcement of intellectual property rights, and proof of loopholes that many stakeholders perceive to be weak and rudimentary was unearthed. Moreover, Yu et al. (2011) emphasizes that calls for reform are now even being made by the developed world and developing nations as well, which signifies the realization of a necessity for a firmer enforcement model by all these countries. As such discussions evolve, the future of the TRIPS Agreements will be determined by whether it is able to respond more effectively to the enforcement concerns raised by a wide cross-section of member states. The intellectual property rights environment within the TRIPS Agreement is also made more complex by the technological and global factors that are challenging customary legal models. The flexibility of the Agreement allows member states to fit their law in a manner better suited to local needs, but that same flexibility risks producing inequalities in levels of protection from one jurisdiction to another. Such equalities confront stakeholders like policymakers, businesses, and right holders, particularly in the context of international cooperation and competition. Yu et al. (2011) stresses the principles learned from the existing conflicts, which manifest the importance of constant dialogue and reframing of strategies towards strengthening intellectual property protection. To this extent, the TRIPS Agreement subsists not as a code of obligations but as an agent for discourse in best practices of intellectual property protection. As the world evolves, these debates will be vital in forming a just intellectual property regime that benefits creators and society at large.

6.3.1. Copyright and Related Rights

The function of copyright and related rights has grown exponentially in international trade and intellectual property protection. Following World War II, there was a greater demand for strong protections of creator rights, and this led to many international agreements that target intellectual property protection. But many of these agreements were not backed by enforcement powers, and this gave rise to the creation of the Agreement on Trade-Related Aspects of Intellectual Property Rights (TRIPS) in 1994. The TRIPS Agreement is significant because it harmonizes copyright law among member countries, providing protection to creators across borders. It establishes a minimum standard of copyright protection and extends the duration of these rights, thereby promoting the interests of authors and enhancing their ability to control and gain benefits from their works. The corrective of historical shortcomings points to the crucial role copyrights play in promoting innovation and creative work in the global market (Fischerová et al., 2014). Moreover, evolution of copyright in the TRIPS framework recognizes the need to fit new challenges imposed by digital technology and globalization. With the advent of the internet, which facilitates easy diffusion of creative works without permission, traditional copyright remedies must be revamped to counter the challenge of infringement efficiently. The TRIPS Agreement not only sets a floor protection requirement but also calls upon member countries to establish national legislation guaranteeing a contemporary technological response. Interestingly,

TRIPS acknowledges the particular issues inherent in traditional knowledge and cultural expressions, generating controversy over the transgression of copyright and indigenous rights. As described in many analyses, such as elements of the TRIPS Agreement, legal frameworks present under existing regimes are ordinarily insufficient to meet traditional knowledge, leading to calls for change to fill gaps (Abdullin et al., 2019). The intersection of copyright and neighbouring rights within the TRIPS scheme is of greatest concern to creators and indigenous peoples alike. Whilst the agreements aim to harmonize copyright protection allows for a uniform process of enforcement, it also creates complex issues regarding proprietary rights of local and indigenous creators. The majority of indigenous people are finding that existing copyright regimes do not fully protect traditional knowledge because rights are typically based on individual concepts of ownership that are not applicable to collective cultural practice. Use of copyright, alongside other intellectual property tools, needs to be considered in order to more effectively protect traditional knowledge and to enable more equitable recognition of cultural contribution. By refining existing legal frameworks and more cooperation among nations, the global community can progress towards an inclusive intellectual property environment that respects the diverse contributions made by each creator (Abdullin et al., 2019) (Figure 6.8).

Figure 6.8. Copyright and related rights.

Source: https://bytescare.com/blog/wp-content/uploads/2023/08/Copyright-and-related-rights.svg.

6.3.2. Trademarks and Geographical Indications (GIs)

The concept of trademarks and GIs heavily overlap under the framework of the TRIPS Agreement, impacting intellectual property rights as well as global trade patterns. Trademarks are typically used by firms to distinguish and identify their goods and services, playing a crucial role in business by delivering quality and origin to consumers. On the other hand, GIs have their own niche through drawing attention to products that possess characteristics, image, or qualities as a result of their geographical origins. This variation offers a contrast to protection mechanisms where both GIs and trademarks can coexist, each addressing distinct aspects of product identity and consumer trust. The TRIPS Agreement mandates member countries to adopt some standards for the protection of both kinds, thus acknowledging the value of both in international commerce and protecting fair competition and consumers in the market. The most compelling aspect of GIs in the TRIPS regime is that they have the potential to shape the development economies. According to recent research, facilitating geographical identification through GIs can provide meaningful market opportunities to those products native to specific locations, hence aiding local economies and cultural heritage conservation (Anders et al., 2025).

However, the protection enforcement can also impose substantive costs in compliance and enforcement, and this may pose a challenge for resource-scarce developing nations. As nations navigate these nuances, the dynamic tension of capturing the benefits of GIs and overcoming the challenges involved will be determinative to the success and sustainability of such initiatives toward facilitating economic growth. The subtlety of this dynamic captures broader issues surrounding honest trade practices and intellectual property's potential to facilitate or stifle economic growth in the developing world. The connection between GIs and traditional knowledge brings an added layer of complication to intellectual property rights discussion. GIs have a tendency of appropriating indigenous communities' know-how and wisdom, entangling deeply product identity with cultural narrative and local heritage (Dagne et al., 2025). This immediate linking raises significant questions regarding ownership, identification, and equitable sharing of benefit derived from traditional knowledge. The TRIPS Agreement, though offering a regulatory framework, nonetheless needs to be significantly sharpened to effectively resolve these issues, particularly in reconciling the interests of local communities with those of international trade interests. The progressive nature of this discourse highlights the need for ongoing academic review and international collaboration, towards crafting a platform that accommodates both intellectual property rights and the cultural heritage inherent within geographical indications. With the dynamic nature of intellectual property's landscape, these discussions are still relevant in advancing just policies that cultivate innovation as well as tradition (Figure 6.9).

Figure 6.9. Trademarks and geographical indications (GIs).

*Source:*https://www.sonisvision.in/blogs/uploads/images/202401/image_750x_65b22a988a6e1.jpg.

6.3.3. Patents and Trade Secrets

There is a fine balance between patents and trade secrets-the latter being a significant component of intellectual property rights generally, but even more so under the patronage of the TRIPS Agreement. Patents provide exclusive rights to inventors, allowing them to control the production and sale of their inventions for a limited time, typically 20 years. This approach stimulates innovation since inventors have an opportunity to make back their investment in research and development. Trade secrets, on the other hand, protect confidential business information such as formulas, methods, and processes without formal registration. This two-pronged approach allows for a broader spectrum of innovation activity, covering those sectors where patenting may not be feasible, considering the extremely high price or unnecessary difficulty of securing protection through patents. Companies are thus able to resort to trade secrets to maintain their competitive edges while also being able to partake in benefits extended by patents under the TRIPS Agreement. Intellectual property aspects relating to patents and trade secrets extend beyond simple legal systems to being central to the processes of globalization as well as technological innovation. The TRIPS Agreement requires countries to establish an intellectual property system that both stimulates technological progress but, at the same time, ensures fair competition. The battle between nations in terms of the patent standards, as seen in negotiations such as the Regional Comprehensive Economic Partnership

(RCEP), has the potential to significantly influence how trade secrets and patents are handled. Nations such as India, for instance, advocate for weaker patent legislation such that medicines can be made available at affordable rates, whereas nations such as Japan and South Korea push for enhanced protection.

This negotiating environment highlights broader issues with access to innovation, especially in developing nations that might depend on affordable generics for drugs, demonstrating the intricate connection between intellectual property rights and global equity during the spread of technology (Chander et al., 2018). Further, ongoing evolution of intellectual property norms during the TRIPS Agreement has serious implications for trade secrets during an increasingly dynamic global economy.

As technological developments permeate and cross-border alliances grow more frequent, the protection of trade secrets becomes more imperative. Companies are faced with complex global legislation while being subject to varying levels of protection. The effect of globalization on the patent environment is enormous, as companies try to strategically build their portfolios by using patents and trade secrets in tandem. In the background of the recent happenings, such as allegedly stolen trade secrets disputes and emerging cyber threats, businesses are compelled to establish robust protective measures to help secure their confidential data. This realignment underscores the importance of understanding and utilizing both patents and trade secrets in the business environment today, where intellectual property is no longer a mere legal safeguard but also a competitive weapon (Lai, 2025) (Figure 6.10).

Figure 6.10. Patents and trade secrets.

Source: https://www.sonisvision.in/blogs/uploads/images/sonisvision_tradesecret_vs_patent_750x_657d8526e067b.jpg.

6.4. IMPACT OF THE TRADE-RELATED ASPECTS OF INTELLECTUAL PROPERTY RIGHTS (TRIPS) AGREEMENT ON DEVELOPING COUNTRIES

The TRIPS Agreement, which was launched in 1994, has far-reaching impacts on the developmental trajectories of emerging countries. While the regime aims to harmonize intellectual property rights globally, it puts developing countries in a disadvantageous position. The requirements of TRIPS may pressure indigenous industries, which lack the technology levels, infrastructure, and resources to comply with rigorous patent specifications. For instance, the requirement to provide patent protection to medicines may increase the cost of lifesaving drugs and limit their access to poor individuals.

This barrier to affordable healthcare undermines not just public health initiatives but also stifles innovation by increasing the interests of multinational companies over those of citizens. Hence, the TRIPS Agreement unwittingly circumscribes the potential of sustainable development in poorer countries, exemplifying the need for re-examination of its provisions to allow for equitable advancement. In recent years, the critical importance of accessible healthcare has drawn the TRIPS Agreement into the limelight, particularly during the COVID-19 pandemic. Through their proposals for temporary intellectual property rights waivers, nations like India have shown that there is a compelling need to reconcile the objectives of public health with intellectual property protection. These proposals are significant in that they point to how the pandemic has highlighted the limitations of TRIPS, showing that intellectual property legislation can be used as obstacles to timely access to vaccines and treatments, particularly for developing countries. Such situations emphasize the need to involve global stakeholders in constructive debates so that solutions are found that are neither infringing on public health nor denying the patent holders their rights.

Finally, the pandemics challenge has mobilized debate regarding how to restructure the TRIPS regime to ensure greater priority for humanitarian interests than an absolute preoccupation with intellectual property rights, calling for a balance. In addition, the intersection between international deals and national policies plays a major role in influencing innovation within developing countries. The outcomes that a greater role of advanced country multinational enterprises (AMNEs) tends to require greater compliance rigidity with TRIPS norms reflect a complex dynamic in the manner in which these nations experience institutional reforms. When AMNEs enter local markets, they introduce advanced country standards to coordinate domestic regulatory systems, yet the alignment may limit local innovation. The use of supranational institutions makes this process even more intricate, as the countries feel compelled to comply with global guidelines in order to receive trade advantages. Thus, while TRIPS generally promotes innovation in the entire world, the specifications that it lays can often get in the way of the development of local industries and technologies, putting vast emphasis on pragmatic methods that enhance development without compromising intellectual property rights (Brandl et al., 2018). In light of these issues, developing countries need to position themselves strategically in the TRIPS system in order to make the economic environment more balanced.

6.4.1. Challenges Faced by Developing Nations

Developing nations are faced with comprehensive issues of intellectual property rights, particularly in the wake of the TRIPS Agreement to establish standardized IP legislations globally. The greatest among these challenges is access to cheap medicines. The elevated patent protections TRIPS mandates can limit the availability of generics, which are essential for such countries struggling with high infection disease incidence like HIV/AIDS. Brazil and South Africa, among others, have tried to circumvent the limitations by using legislative mechanisms such as compulsory licensing to make medicines available to their people. The big pharma companies' reaction indicates the clash between the protection of IP rights and public health protection (Rydzefski et al., 2013). The settlement of such clashes indicates broader issues of fairness and sustainability in health care within the perspective of globalization and calls for the redetermination of the impact of such accords. Secondly, variable economic growth rates among countries complicate the use of the TRIPS Agreement. Whereas developed nations typically have the capacity and infrastructure to benefit from IP protections, developing countries may lack the necessary legal frameworks and institutional capability. This shortcoming restrains their competitiveness and innovation in the international market. In addition, the intellectual property climate favors multinational firms at the expense of indigenous companies and entrepreneurs, therefore tilting the balance against indigenous companies. Such actors are frequently excluded from competing with the monopolistic tendencies facilitated by robust IP frameworks, and this leads to erosion of domestic industries. The current TRIPS Agreement is not able to account adequately for the particular contexts in developing nations, and thus a conversation needs to be had regarding how IP laws can be customized to foster domestic economic development and innovation (Bashi et al., 2008). Apart from that, the impact of intellectual property enforcement is also a major contributor to the economic costs of developing nations. TRIPS conformity can lead to increased prices of primary goods and services, adding to already strained economies. In a scenario where small and medium-sized enterprises (SMEs) form the backbone of the economy, the oppressive character of these IP safeguards can constrain innovation and entrepreneurship. As the Trade-Related Aspects of Intellectual Property Rights correctly observes, any knowledge economy has a built-in contradiction in encouraging a knowledge economy and monopolistic inclinations stemming from rigorous IP protections. Such a contradiction prompts a middle way that offers an indigenous-friendly enabling environment while respecting the rights of creators. Striking down these challenges is imperative in keeping developing nations from being left behind in the competitive global economy (Bashi et al., 2008) (Figure 6.11).

Figure 6.11. TRIPS agreement challenges faced by developing nations.

Source: https://external-content.duckduckgo.com/iu/?u=https%3A%2F%2Fcdnwpedutorenews.gramedia.net%2Fwp-content%2Fuploads%2F2023%2F01%2F06075126%2Fregional-cooperation-4-1024x683.jpg&f=1&nofb=1&ipt=a6edbc3a4170d7e5b24132014f63b3cd779c2f2abe3b1b5c9abbf5304ba98264.

6.4.2. Opportunities for Economic Growth

Convergence between intellectual property rights (IPR) and economic growth presents an energetic context for developing nations, particularly in the agriculture and drug industries. The TRIPS Agreement has introduced a paradigm shift that enables countries to make intellectual property regimes that suit domestic innovation while being part of global standards. For instance, in the Philippines, the growing population underscores the need for more farm productivity. The inclusion of robust intellectual property protection can drive research and development for agricultural innovations. Through the establishment of an intellectual property culture, the country can synchronize endeavors towards food security realization, hence unlocking new economic opportunities for farmers and agents in the agricultural sector (Alfonso et al., 2013). This approach not only assists in enhancing local food production but also positions the country to venture into overseas markets, enhancing its economic status on the global stage. Besides, India's Patent Act amendment is an example of how compliance with the TRIPS Agreement can induce economic growth in the pharmaceutical sector.

Figure 6.12. The intersection of intellectual property rights (IPR) and economic growth.

Source: https://external-content.duckduckgo.com/iu/?u=https%3A%2F%2Fblog.ipleaders.in%2Fwp-content%2Fuploads%2F2020%2F02%2Fekonomi_752b4-768x432.jpg&f=1&nofb=1&ipt=c15f5fff0b57f4e883b2a6d6e5312569e6034286065cbbe8d59bca4846daa02b.

The introduction of product patents has been accompanied by a regulatory system that encourages innovation and investment into drug research and development. By protecting the inventor, the new system of patents can initiate the commercialization of new drugs that address domestic health needs and international market demands. However, the fulfillment of such transitions brings forth underlying concerns. There is a conflict that is established between encouraging innovations and offering access to affordable medicines. As observed, the limitations in completely realizing TRIPS obligations can be based on domestic resistance against intellectual property, and thus a well-balanced approach is necessary to balance economic growth with public health (Rangnekar et al., 2005). Ultimately, implementation of intellectual property rights under the TRIPS Agreement is less an exercise in adherence and more a function of aligning countries for long-term economic growth. Through a nuanced understanding of the intricacies of IPR implementation, countries can unlock the potential of innovation as a driver of economic growth. The emphasis on crop and drug research is representative of a two-fold trajectory that not only answers near-term socio-economic issues but also sets a strong foundation for long-term growth. By effective exploitation of intellectual property protections, countries can entice foreign investment, increase native innovation capabilities, and develop an entrepreneurial culture imperative to succeed in the ever-growing global economy. By so doing, nations can pursue maximum economic potential with inclusiveness as a consideration in growth and development (Figure 6.12).

6.4.3. Case Studies of Specific Countries

Brazil as a case study is specifically significant in the context of the impact of the TRIPS Agreement on developing nations, particularly concerning pharmaceutical patents. The country has been grappling to reconcile intellectual property rights with public health needs. Brazil's approach has highlighted the tension between guarding innovations and granting access to life-saving drugs. By embracing a strategic combination of compulsory licensing and local generic production, Brazil has tried to make treatment affordable for its people. This real-life response to TRIPS provisions is an indication of the ongoing debate regarding the equity of trade agreements, particularly in light of their likely enforcement, which will serve to continue existing inequalities in global health because it will accrue to the advantage of affluent nations that have robust patent regimes (Dawood et al., 2001). Kenya's experience is only another facet of the TRIPS Agreements impact, particularly in agricultural innovation and preservation of biodiversity. Under Article 27.3(b) of TRIPS, states are invited to adopt legislation to assure the protection of plant varieties. Yet Kenya's subsequent joining of the UPOV (International Union for the Protection of New Varieties of Plants) has shown inconsistency between international commitment and national law. While policymakers in Kenya attempted to guarantee just access and benefit-sharing of genetic resources, the national legal framework falls short of these ideals, thereby limiting the possibilities for just distribution of farm innovations. This case illustrates the larger predicament that many developing countries find themselves in, caught between international compacts and domestic legal systems that do not capture the essentials of distributive justice (Rangnekar et al., 2008). For India, the TRIPS Agreement has spurred extensive regulatory transformation, most notably in the pharmaceutical industry. Indias capacity to generate low-cost generic medicines has been crucial to its rising leadership of global health. But with the enforcement of tight patent protections under TRIPS requirements, drug makers have had increased incentives to innovate and maintain drug prices low. The Indian government has responded by tightening its intellectual property regime while reinforcing public health policies that favor access to medicine. The tension between the demand for robust intellectual property protections and the demand for preserving health equity underscores the persistent tension within the international trade system. The case also serves to underscore how modifications to the TRIPS system have far-reaching implications for a nation's socio-economic context, both demonstrating the potential and challenges that such international agreements present for the field of intellectual property rights (Dawood et al., 2001).

6.5. CRITICISMS OF THE TRADE-RELATED ASPECTS OF INTELLECTUAL PROPERTY RIGHTS (TRIPS) AGREEMENT

The TRIPS Agreement has been in the middle of widespread criticism, primarily due to the perceived imbalances against developing nations. The critics argue that the TRIPS model works to disproportionately benefit the developed nations, typically where huge pharmaceutical and tech firms are based, at the cost of developing economies' domestic innovation capacity. This is on the understanding that the majority of nations lack the infrastructure and funding necessary to satisfy high intellectual property standards of TRIPS. This hence results in a scenario where local businesses start to deteriorate as they are unable to compete, ultimately limiting the availability of goods that are essential, for instance, cheaper drugs. Therefore, the TRIPS Agreement has been considered perpetuating existing imbalances in world trade and economic development and hence raising fundamental questions about global justice and equality of international law (Macmillan et al., 2004). The other key argument among policymakers and scholars is the underlying governance architecture of the TRIPS Agreement. The critics call the apparent absence of democratic engagement in the negotiation and enactment of the accord, accusing the developing world of being excluded from major negotiations. This critique can further be applied to World Trade Organizations (WTO) decision-making, which is opaque and non-accountable. The absence of participatory debate means that the concerns of poorer countries, who are disproportionately affected by strict IP policy, are typically ignored. In addition, exclusion in this form questions the universality of the TRIPS system as a world standard when it cannot encompass the voices of its most impacted constituents, and making stronger cases for change that addresses various members' economic structures (Macmillan et al., 2004). In addition, criticisms directed at the TRIPS Agreement become ever more entangled with broader geopolitics, particularly with the formation of new trade arrangements as a reaction to pressures from forces induced by globalization. For instance, recent controversy in the Trans-Pacific Partnership (TPP) has stoked controversy over high-standard IP protections' consequences that would cement the inequalities condemned in the TRIPS Agreement. The TPP's negotiations have been attacked on issues of transparency and lack of participation by emerging economies and civil society organizations, and thus these new structures are reproducing the mistakes of TRIPS. The majority are concerned that these differences in power will continue to keep developing nations at the margins, stunting their technological advancement and economic progress. These fears highlight the need for reconsidering international trade agreements in order to make them inclusive and level, thus correcting the inherent failure of the TRIPS Agreement as it is currently drafted.

6.5.1. Concerns Over Access to Medicines

Access to life-saving drugs remains a core issue in the frame of the TRIPS Agreement, as the imposition of rigorous intellectual property rights (IPRs) has reconfigured the drug market globally. Particularly in developing countries, the shift away from a process patent system to a product patent regime has limited room for local manufacturers to produce low-cost generic products. The turn has been accompanied by rising drug prices, which pose an enormous obstacle for marginalized populations that are unable to afford life-saving medication. The priority of the industry on profitable treatments over needed drugs contributes to the hurdles, hampering public health advancements. Therefore, there is a need to critically evaluate how patent shields impact medication access and maintain the public health ramifications of giving precedence to corporate interests over the welfare of vulnerable groups (Singh et al., 2024). The relationship between intellectual property rights and clinical trials also makes medication access a more intricate issue. Patents grant drug firms enormous latitude in determining what to do with their products, typically to the point of leading to monopolistic pricing that can restrict access in poverty-level areas. The cost of R&D is booked by the companies as innovation-based, but such cost also creates enormous obstacles to equal access to efficacious treatments. In addition, practices such as data exclusivity are able to defer the entry of generics into the market, ultimately exacerbating public health crises. A case is the struggle for low-cost treatments for ailments such as HIV/AIDS and hepatitis C, illustrating the brutal truth faced by patients around the world. Policymakers should therefore lead the way in regulating against IPR systems undermining the healthcare priorities of population groups in need (Ahmad et al., 2024). Efforts to re-balance the innovation-access challenge are needed to foster world health equity. This involves exploring alternative models that incentivize research but safeguard public health interests. Models of patent pools, tiered pricing, and prize funds have been proposed for increasing access but not shutting out research and innovation. These strategies have the potential to create a more sustainable pharma environment in favor of corporate and humanitarian requirements. Collaborative arrangements among governments, NGOs, and the private sector are essential in creating an environment that appreciates the essential role of accessible medicines in healthcare performance. Absent these measures, the TRIPS Agreement has the potential to exacerbate imbalances in access to life-saving medicines with disastrous consequences for global public health (Ahmad et al., 2024) (Figure 6.13).

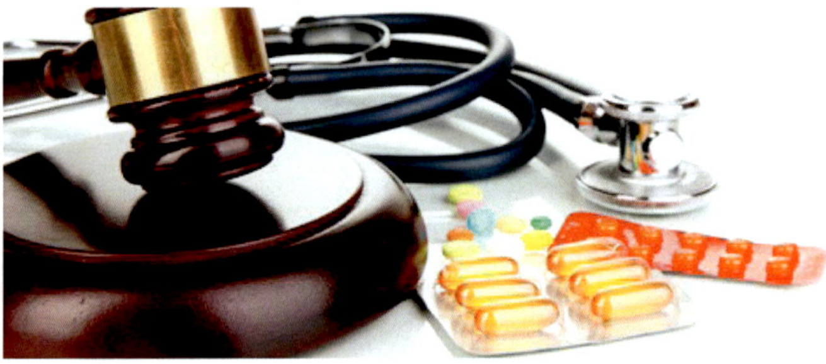

Figure 6.13. Concerns over access to medicines.

Source: https://cdn.who.int/media/images/default-source/assistive-technologies/law-medicine.tmb-479v.jpg?sfvrsn=168c7156_2%20479w.

6.5.2. Impact on Traditional Knowledge and Biodiversity

The intersection of traditional knowledge and biodiversity assumes the form of an imperative issue within the scope of the Intellectual Property Rights mandated by the TRIPS Agreement. Indigenous and local communities possess rich traditional ecological knowledge, previously held responsible for protecting and using biodiversity in a sustainable manner. However, its integration into intellectual property frameworks often causes ownership and exploitation problems. Without adequate protection, there is a risk that corporations will operate on the basis of traditional knowledge without acknowledgement or reward, disadvantage the rights of indigenous peoples and endangering local biodiversity. This exploitation not only assaults the cultural integrity of such people but also undermines the environmental intelligence that has enabled sustainable livelihood over generations. Furthermore, the implications of the TRIPS Agreement extend beyond mere questions of ownership; they cross-cut closely with international trade laws. The provisions of the Agreements on patents and protection of plant varieties can inadvertently enable privatization of genetic resources hitherto freely used by local communities. With the increasing influence of the global market on biodiversity, there is more room for biopiracy where corporations patent ancient plant species indigenous to a country and ancient knowledge that have never been in the private domain for centuries.

Figure 6.14. Impact on traditional knowledge and biodiversity criticisms of the TRIPS agreement.

Source: https://blog.ipleaders.in/wp-content/uploads/2020/05/IPR-Chart_European-Patent.png.

This situation raises issues of ethics concerning the commodification of genetic resources and countries' duty to defend their indigenous biodiversity. Furthermore, this tension is reflective of broader issues of sovereignty and the need for equitable systems to make certain that both traditional knowledge and biodiversity are protected and respected in an increasingly global economy, as discussed in many peer reviews of the Agreements impact. New European Union-Central American Association Agreement highlights the value of paying heed to such concerns in international intellectual property law. By incorporating provisions that take into account the protection of public health, genetic resources, and traditional knowledge, the agreement is a potential step towards harmonizing the interests of indigenous peoples and other broader economic interests. The terms in this framework are designed to facilitate the transfer of technology, enhancing local capacities for the management and utilization of biodiversity sustainably while respecting their traditional knowledge. These projects have the potential to act as a buffer against the negative effects typically associated with TRIPS, proving how effectively drafted intellectual property provisions can reinforce local communities' positions and improve the biodiversity conservation. Local parties and international institutions need to collaborate to devise effective strategies that safeguard the traditional knowledge holders' rights without affecting the biodiversity conservation for future generations (Bonadio et al., 2010; Tansey, 2025) (Figure 6.14).

6.5.3. The Debate on Enforcement and Compliance

The enforcement and compliance debate of the TRIPS Agreement is at the heart of understanding the international context of intellectual property rights (IPR). As governments strive to protect domestic industries with adherence to global standards, gaps emerge in the form of varying degrees of commitment and capacity on the part of member states. Most notably, however, are the developing countries that face the challenge of applying tough IP regulations since they have few resources and competing socio-economic needs. As such, this variation raises concerns regarding the fairness of the TRIPS Agreement itself, which can be advantageous to developed nations well suited to living up to these high standards while stifling the emergence of innovation and technology in lower-developing regions. Consequently, the balance required between protecting intellectual property and establishing an environment supportive of local innovation turns into a matter of first order contention in the current debate on TRIPS compliance. Furthermore, enforcement implications in the context of digitalization in sectors like manufacturing receive more emphasis in current debates. As established in the latest appraisals, nations such as China have experienced explosive industrial base growth with enormous investments that aim to bring them into compliance with TRIPS commitments. However, the transition to comprehensive IP protection has been filled with challenges. Compliance is not just upholding legal obligations but also implementing a regime of control that will secure intellectual property adequately in response to technological developments. In China, although the digital revolution reinvigorated its industries and increased foreign direct investment, it has raised issues of congruence between national law and international obligations. This example shows the sophistication involved in enforcing TRIPS provisions effectively without compromising the local industries' innovation capacity (Zou et al., 2024). Lastly, the controversy is over balancing enforcement provisions with adequate space for exceptions and limits in the public interest. The TRIPS Agreement aims to articulate the significance of a balanced intellectual property system fostering innovation and redressing global imbalances. As stated, provisions in TRIPS such as the Three-Step Test emphasize the balance required between interests of IP holders and interests in society at large. This entails aspects such as access to drugs and educational material, which may be at variance with the aims of firm enforcement policies. For the international community to realize the greatest advantage of the TRIPS Agreement, it must address these complexities while promoting an open environment that harmonizes distinctive national laws in the overall framework of international intellectual property regimes (Baba, 2024).

6.6. FUTURE OF INTELLECTUAL PROPERTY RIGHTS (IPR) IN A GLOBALIZED WORLD

The future of IPR in the globalized world is about how to walk the thin line between safeguarding innovation and making public resources available at a basic level. The TRIPS Agreement was built on establishing minimum standards for IPR to have a level of harmony in meeting the IPR interests of developed and developing nations. As countries grapple with globalization, disparities in access to knowledge and technology emerge starkly, testing the efficacy of current IPR regimes. In developing countries, the biggest issue is in handling this double burden of stimulating innovation and giving the population access to medicines and technologies that are needed. This is truly pertinent with regard to the historical context of compulsory licensing established by legislative forums under the TRIPS Agreement, demonstrated by the hallmark occurrences of the 2003 waiver for facilitating greater access to drugs among developing nations (including those that are least developed) (Arezzo et al., 2009). As globalization grows, the relationship between intellectual property rights and international trade becomes more complex. Linking IPR regimes to trade agreements has the potential to foster greater international collaboration in innovation but equally risks promoting enforcement of monopolistic forces that dampen competition. Countries prioritizing robust intellectual property rights may inadvertently stifle indigenous creativity and innovation, particularly in the context of a plural cultural and economic environment. For third-world nations, the ability to engage in technological transfer and enable knowledge sharing is necessary in their quest for economic development. The TRIPS Agreement calls for the balance between rights and access, but ongoing arguments about its enforcement underscore the necessity for ongoing reformulation to fit changing economic realities as they emerge, ultimately hoping to protect creators and consumers under an international market (Franzen et al., 1998). In the years to come, the landscape of intellectual property rights will require innovative tactics to reconcile the interests of stakeholders in developed and developing nations. Emerging technologies such as artificial intelligence and biotechnology disrupt the traditional IPR frameworks, necessitating reframing and shaping IPRs to adapt to new realities. Global cooperation is imperative, as developing countries can benefit from restructuring the IPR frameworks to drive innovation as well as ensure access to vital resources. The ability to implement measures such as compulsory licensing effectively will remain crucial in furthering public health and social justice, particularly among low-income societies. Thus, the understanding and ability to align with the evolving needs of an era of globalization will be vital in establishing a fair and sustainable intellectual property system that serves the interests of all nations during the 21st century (Arezzo et al., 2009) (Figure 6.15).

Figure 6.15. Future of intellectual property rights (IPRs) in a globalized world.

Source: https://framerusercontent.com/images/S1MqhcLbrYs6CPQpARqFB4Lxg.png?width=1024&height=1024.

6.6.1. Emerging Technologies and Intellectual Property (IP)

The intersection of emerging technologies and IP is increasingly significant in an era of globalization, particularly under the framework of the TRIPS Agreement. While nations want to make innovation easier through technology advancements, the need for good IP frameworks becomes evident. New emerging technologies such as artificial intelligence, biotechnology, and blockchain pose specific challenges and opportunities regarding the protection of intellectual property rights. Notably, these technologies often have geographical reach beyond the countries, so it is difficult to enforce IP rights, suggesting international collaboration. The TRIPS Agreement forms a pillar for the establishment of minimum standards for IP protection in member nations, observing the necessity for harmonizing legal systems to encourage innovation while controlling the risks of technological development (Engel et al., 2025). Second, the mechanism of IP protection in developing economies demonstrates the complex relationship between development aid and technology transfer. These nations are becoming well known for their technical prowess, and Brazil, India, and Thailand are excellent examples. Advanced nations' provision of intellectual property-related development aid has the tendency to aim at enhancing local capacities for the administration and enforcement of IP. However, a critical examination elicits an imbalance between the targeted countries' needs and the focus of assistance provided. For instance, development aid in India has influenced landmark legislative reforms to plant variety protection, demonstrating how foreign aid may shape IP and technological landscape. Nonetheless, the political dimension of such assistance muddles the real intentions of donor countries, such as diplomatic relations and commercial interests, complicating the narrative of technology advancement and IP growth (Engel et al., 2025). In addition, the global compliance with the TRIPS Agreement indicates the conflicting interpretations and usages of IP laws across different jurisdictions, substantially proven in China. As a world economic leader, Chinas reaction to IP rights compliance reveals balance between fostering innovation and honoring global mandates. Despite significant progress in aligning its legislation with TRIPS, ongoing issues remain in enforcing rights, demonstrating the business realities of enforced residency. Compliance is subject to as much internal force as historical precedent set by its superinnovator rivals such as Japan and the United Kingdom. This complex landscape highlights that although new technologies hold the promise of economic stimulation, they depend on a nuanced sense of intellectual property rights and the broader stakes of international agreements like TRIPS.

6.6.2. The Role of Digital Platforms

The emergence of digital platforms has revolutionized the landscape of intellectual property rights, particularly under the TRIPS Agreement. These platforms are both marketplaces and distribution channels for content, making it possible to share and create intellectual property on a large scale. As the digital economy has developed, bringing together these platforms and intellectual property is more complex. On the one hand, platforms in the digital economy will make it easier to access creative works, driving innovation and cultural exchange. On the other hand, they bring into immediate focus questions of copyright violations and abuse of intellectual property. This twofold role highlights the need for robust intellectual property systems that can adapt to the digital era, safeguarding creators sufficiently while developing a climate of innovation and collaboration. Furthermore, digital platforms play an important role in bridging the intellectual property rights divide between industrialized and developing countries. The TRIPS Agreement places great emphasis on the protection of intellectual property as a means of stimulating economic growth and development. However, the benefits of such protections have a tendency to accrue in favor of technologically advanced nations. The new media offer a unique opportunity for developing countries to exploit their cultural material and creative capital in the international marketplace. By facilitating access to foreign audiences, these platforms can support local creators and innovators and thereby ensure an improved balance of the economic rewards to intellectual property. In order to achieve this, policymakers must tackle inequalities in the intellectual property regime as they are and ensure that digital platforms are functioning within a framework that upholds the rights of all stakeholders, particularly developing country parties (Jayadev et al., 2017). Finally, as digital platforms continue to evolve, so must the legal regimes that enable them. Even while the TRIPS Agreement was a milestone in history, it may need to be revised to address completely the unique challenges of digital delivery vehicles. As piracy, data privacy, and ownership issues become highly charged topics, there must be an urgent dialogue tabled by stakeholders like governments, creators, and platform operators. This discussion must establish world standards which safeguard intellectual property without stifling imagination. By establishing an environment in which creators can thrive yet guarantee equitable use and accessibility of knowledge, the evolving face of digital platforms can contribute positively to the global economy. Lastly, revisiting intellectual property rights within the digital platform is a step towards the adoption of an equitable and efficient system that is favorable to the principles offered under the TRIPS Agreement (Zampetti et al., 2025).

6.6.3. Potential Revisions to the TRIPS Agreement

Current discussion regarding potential amendments to the TRIPS Agreement becomes increasingly vital in relation to shifting global health demands and the right to access generic medicines. As a result of the pharmaceutical industry's exponential development in the past half century, representing a tremendous growth in innovation and enhanced access to healthcare, the difficulty is reconciling intellectual property rights and public health needs. The welfare contribution of the pharmaceutical industry cannot be overstated; nevertheless, past inequalities in drug availability, on a regional and international scale, attest to the need for a re-examination of existing patent safeguards under TRIPS. The accessibility and affordability of life-saving medicines is something that must take priority, and thus requires legislative reforms that can include the inclusion of more flexibility in patent laws, especially among poorer nations, to offer more distribution of basic medications and treatments toward efforts in universal healthcare (Burakoff et al., 2002). The patenting of pharmaceuticals under India's amended Patent Act, 1970 is an interesting lens through which to examine the opportunity for changes to the TRIPS Agreement. While the amendment acts to align Indian law with its TRIPS commitments, it also marks increasing pains of playing catch-up in protecting national interests in the challenging field of intellectual property. Critically, the passing of these amendments offers a double bind between encouraging domestic pharmaceutical research and development and the assurance that drug prices are affordable to the population. The overall spirit in India with regard to patent reform, as observed, offers a limited vision that may not take into account increased implications and international cooperation within patent reform. Consequently, TRIPS updates would have to consider patent duration alteration or the inclusion of compulsory measures of licensing to establish a balanced measure of innovation and access across different economic environments in order to ensure overall public health success (Rangnekar et al., 2005). Furthermore, addressing the conflict between intellectual property rights and public health objectives, probable TRIPS Agreement revisions should also deal with the current issue of pharmaceutical access inequality on a global scale. The contemporary scenario proves that although countries like those of the European Union intend to create Single Markets to foster consumer choice and innovation, this must not come at the expense of access to healthcare on equal terms. Developing countries also find it difficult to enforce standards of TRIPS while trying to address health concerns domestically as well. As nations engage in negotiations of trade deals and consider modifications to the TRIPS agreement, it is essential that these negotiations have provisions for prioritizing the common good over profit. Through the creation of equity and access principles under the international intellectual property regime, countries can better ensure that innovations in pharmaceutical science benefit all, thus bringing into being an international environment where innovation and public health are appreciated (Burakoff et al., 2002).

SUMMARY

Review of the Intellectual Property Rights (TRIPS Agreement), it is evident that comprehension of the world's intellectual property complexities today requires a nuanced understanding of converging interests of various parties. The TRIPS Agreement, while aimed at creating a system for intellectual property protection, has often led to unequal access to resources, particularly in developing countries. For instance, Kenya's experience witnesses a broad gap between the equal access rhetoric of the TRIPS Council and national law enactment that, Ironically, can perpetuate extant inequalities. The gap points to a necessity for authoring more integrated thought that harmonizes international obligation with national legal context for facilitating actual access to innovations while maintaining the integrity of intellectual property systems (Rangnekar et al., 2008). The implications of the TRIPS Agreement are much wider than its original intent, manifesting in broader regional agreements, such as the Regional Comprehensive Economic Partnership (RCEP). The ongoing negotiations under the ambit of RCEP reflect divergences of priority among member states, with major countries such as India advocating for greater public health and access considerations against stronger protections being proposed by countries such as South Korea and Japan. This fight is a turning point moment for global intellectual property discourse, with possible repercussions that could institutionalize or destroy impediments to access for generics and innovations that developing nations rely on. The potential for TRIPS-plus provisions becoming effective is an alarming development towards one more area that is likely to be under tighter constraints on its capacity to benefit from core innovations (Chander et al., 2018). Generally, the conclusion drawn from the analysis of the TRIPS Agreement and its accompanying challenges is that there is a need to re-examine intellectual property frameworks in order to advance more fair development and access. As global dynamics shift, the balance between innovation and accessibility will increasingly have a determining impact on development patterns, particularly in low-resource environments. The TRIPS Agreement, while being a corner stone in international trade relations, must be amended to accommodate existing inequalities and establish an environment which fosters not only the protection of creators' rights but also the collective good of technological and medical advancements. It is necessary that future amendments consider the interests and needs of diverse groups so intellectual property regimes serve to be drivers of equitable growth and not constraints.

The TRIPS Agreement, as part of the intellectual property rights regime, lays a foundation for the protection of various forms of intellectual property like patents, trademarks, and copyrights. The most striking provisions of this agreement delineate its twin priorities: the IP protection harmonization in member states and encouraging innovation and creativity. By requiring member states to adhere to some standards of law, TRIPS tries to extend not only the rights of IP holders but balance these against public interests, particularly in developing nations. This balance is important because it establishes an environment of technological growth while making available the necessary goods and information. The scope of such regulation is broad, touching global trade relations and establishing an environment where intellectual property can thrive on the global platform. In examining the impact of geographic indications (GIs) in the TRIPS framework, it is evident that such legal designations are both an economic boon and a source of trouble, particularly for developing countries. GIs are able to safeguard products linked with a given region, enhancing marketability and encouraging traditional cultural practice. However, the inherent intricacies of GIs have the tendency to bring about a complex combination of legal, social, and economic factors. The benefits that they can provide, e.g., economic growth and cultural resilience, must be carefully weighed against potential drawbacks, e.g., restrictions on market access and heightened competition. To nations that intend to capitalize on the advantages of GIs, careful understanding of these variables is critical. As explained in the explanation of GIs, caution must be exercised when pursuing such protection in a global marketplace setting, pointing to the significance of rigorous evaluation in policy formulation (Giovannucci et al., 2025). The TRIPS Agreement's enforcement mechanisms present opportunities and challenges for actors engaged in intellectual property protection and development. By providing a platform for conflict resolution and enforcement, TRIPS aims to protect intellectual property rights of holders against infringement and promote compliance among member nations. The effectiveness of these measures, however, may vary significantly across jurisdictions, and the problem of equitable treatment and enforcement of IP rights becomes an issue of concern. Policies of aggressive enforcement are needed to deter infringement; but aggressive methods would prejudice innovation and access to essential goods, particularly in the fields of health and education. While the intellectual controversy over how IP rights should be balanced continues, the TRIPS Agreement is an essential source material to understand the complexities of doing so, particularly in the context of international trade and access to knowledge (Cardwell et al., 2025).

REFERENCES

1. Abdullin, A. I., & Gazizova, A. S. (2019). Traditional knowledge and intellectual property rights. https://core.ac.uk/download/666531260.pdf (accessed on 30th October 2025).
2. Ahmad, H., Shabbir, I., Iqbal, I., & Akhtar, M. M. (2024). The crossroad between intellectual property and clinical trials: Balancing incentives for innovation with access to healthcare. *Trends in Intellectual Property Research*. https://www.semanticscholar.org/paper/4dd091f937c16bbd430984fed0b6f846a6386cf2 (accessed on 30th October 2025).
3. Alfonso, A., Estigoy, R., Grimes, H., Jones, M., et al. (2013). Intellectual property and opportunities for food security in the Philippines. https://core.ac.uk/download/72052053.pdf (accessed on 30th October 2025).
4. Anders, S., & Caswell, J. A. (2025). The benefits and costs of proliferation of geographical labeling for developing countries. https://core.ac.uk/download/pdf/7035297.pdf (accessed on 30th October 2025).
5. Antons, C., & Kanniah, R. (2012). Plant variety protection and traditional agricultural knowledge in Southeast Asia. http://hdl.handle.net/10536/DRO/DU:30048975 (accessed on 30th October 2025).
6. Archibugi, D., & Filippetti, A. (2025). The globalization of intellectual property rights: Four learned lessons and four theses. https://core.ac.uk/download/pdf/6483381.pdf (accessed on 30th October 2025).
7. Arezzo, C., Danzon, P., Debrulle, J., Drahos, P., Drexl, J., et al. (2009). Compulsory licensing of patented pharmaceutical inventions: Evaluating the options. https://core.ac.uk/download/62564103.pdf (accessed on 30th October 2025).
8. Baba, A. (2024). The Agreement on Trade-Related Aspects of Intellectual Property Rights (TRIPS). *The Annals of the University of Oradea. Economic Sciences*. https://www.semanticscholar.org/paper/70bcf2981da59550c5290f0bc65a71a7315350d2 (accessed on 30th October 2025).
9. Bennett, A. B., Fernandez, C., Graff, G. D., Kowalski, S., et al. (2007). *Intellectual Property Management in Health and Agricultural Innovation: A Handbook of Best Practices, Vol. 1*. https://core.ac.uk/download/72056337.pdf (accessed on 30th October 2025).
10. Bonadio, E. (2010). IP provisions of the EU-Central America Association Agreement and development issues. https://core.ac.uk/download/228176803.pdf (accessed on 30th October 2025).
11. Brandl, K., Darendeli, I. S., & Mudambi, R. (2018). Foreign actors and intellectual property protection regulations in developing countries.

Journal of International Business Studies, 50, 826–846. https://doi.org/10.1057/s41267-018-0172-6 (accessed on 30th October 2025).

12. Burakoff, A., & Costa-Font, J. (2002). An overview of progress in the international regulation of the pharmaceutical industry. https://core.ac.uk/download/72053014.pdf (accessed on 30th October 2025).
13. Cardwell, R. T., & Ghazalian, P. L. (2025). The effects of the TRIPS Agreement on international protection of intellectual property rights. https://core.ac.uk/download/pdf/6671288.pdf (accessed on 30th October 2025).
14. Chander, A., & Sunder, M. (2018). The battle to define Asia's intellectual property law: From TPP to RCEP. https://core.ac.uk/download/213035745.pdf (accessed on 30th October 2025).
15. Chattu, V. K., Singh, B., Kaur, J., & Jakovljević, M. (2021). COVID-19 vaccine, TRIPS, and global health diplomacy: India's role at the WTO platform. *BioMed Research International, 2021*, 1–8. https://doi.org/10.1155/2021/6658070 (accessed on 30th October 2025).
16. Chernyavskaya, E., Gayko, E., & Shishkina, O. (2018). Customs protection of the rights for intellectual property items–Improvement in the Eurasian Economic Union. https://core.ac.uk/download/647822514.pdf (accessed on 30th October 2025).
17. Correa, C., & Matthews, D. N. (2011). The Doha Declaration ten years on and its impact on access to medicines and the right to health. https://core.ac.uk/download/30696283.pdf (accessed on 30th October 2025).
18. Creditt, E. C. (2009). Terroir vs. trademarks: The debate over geographical indications and expansions to the TRIPS Agreement. https://core.ac.uk/download/479061863.pdf (accessed on 30th October 2025).
19. Dagne, T. (2025). Law and policy on intellectual property, traditional knowledge and development: Legally protecting creativity and collective rights in traditional knowledge-based agricultural products through geographical indications. https://core.ac.uk/download/pdf/6447857.pdf (accessed on 30th October 2025).
20. Dawood, M. (2001). Is TRIPS suffering from Big Giant's Syndrome: Good economics versus self-interest? https://core.ac.uk/download/12013227.pdf (accessed on 30th October 2025).
21. Engel, J., & Ghafele, R. (2025). Intellectual property related development aid: Is supply aligned with demand? https://core.ac.uk/download/pdf/6832324.pdf (accessed on 30th October 2025).
22. Fischerová, N. (2014). Protection of industrial property rights and

copyright in international trade. https://core.ac.uk/download/94756022.pdf (accessed on 30th October 2025).

23. Fojtíková, L. (2018). China's intellectual property rights commitments in the WTO: Legal and economic implications. https://core.ac.uk/download/161960388.pdf (accessed on 30th October 2025).
24. Franzen, M., Jonason, D., & Ranius, T. (1998). Bargaining around the TRIPS Agreement: The case for ongoing public-private initiatives to facilitate worldwide intellectual property transactions. A comment on the paper presented by David Lange and J. H. Reichman. https://core.ac.uk/download/62547649.pdf (accessed on 30th October 2025).
25. Ghafele Bashi, R. (2008). Perceptions of intellectual property: A review. https://core.ac.uk/download/28970391.pdf (accessed on 30th October 2025).
26. Giovannucci, D., Josling, T., Kerr, W., O'Connor, B., et al. (2025). *Guide to Geographical Indications: Linking Products and Their Origins (Summary).* https://core.ac.uk/download/pdf/6668248.pdf (accessed on 30th October 2025).
27. Grote, U. (2025). Environmental labeling, protected geographical indications and the interests of developing countries. https://core.ac.uk/download/pdf/6449325.pdf (accessed on 30th October 2025).
28. Guise, M. S. (2006). Comércio international, patents e saúde publica. https://core.ac.uk/download/30369682.pdf (accessed on 30th October 2025).
29. Jayadev, A., Baker, D., & Stiglitz, J. (2017). Innovation, intellectual property, and development: A better set of approaches for the 21st century. https://core.ac.uk/download/86445449.pdf (accessed on 30th October 2025).
30. Khair, H. (2016). Is the right to health undermined by the agreement of Trade-Related Aspects of Intellectual Property Rights? https://core.ac.uk/download/294760318.pdf (accessed on 30th October 2025).
31. Lai, E. (2025). Intellectual property protection in a globalizing era. https://core.ac.uk/download/pdf/6266419.pdf (accessed on 30th October 2025).
32. Macmillan, F. (2004). If not this World Trade Organization, then what? https://core.ac.uk/download/15005.pdf (accessed on 30th October 2025).
33. Rangnekar, D. (2005). No pills for poor people? Understanding the disembowelment of India's patent regime. https://core.ac.uk/download/47665.pdf (accessed on 30th October 2025).
34. Rangnekar, D. (2008). Geneva rhetoric, national reality: Implementing

TRIPS obligations in Kenya. https://core.ac.uk/download/105927.pdf (accessed on 30th October 2025).

35. Rydzefski, J. (2013). A developing says against AIDS. https://core.ac.uk/download/56325378.pdf (accessed on 30th October 2025).

36. Sarac, J. (2015). The role of the agreement on Trade-Related Aspects of Intellectual Property Rights (TRIPS) in the system of intellectual property protection. https://core.ac.uk/download/33294650.pdf (accessed on 30th October 2025).

37. Schneider, M. T., & Schäfer, A. (2011). Endogenous intellectual property rights and North-South trade. https://www.econstor.eu/dspace/bitstream/10419/48689/1/VfS_2011_pid_393.pdf (accessed on 30th October 2025).

38. Singh, A., & Singh, A. (2024). Product patent regime and public access to essential medicines: A concern for the Indian pharmaceutical industry. *International Journal of Pharmaceutics and Drug Analysis*. https://www.semanticscholar.org/paper/141f4ebd3beb3fa3974ab8ad6ab3dccef835ff27 (accessed on 30th October 2025).

39. Tansey, G. (2025). Global rules, patent power and our food future: Controlling the food system in the 21st century. https://core.ac.uk/download/pdf/7032870.pdf (accessed on 30th October 2025).

40. Yu, P. K. (2011). The TRIPS enforcement dispute. https://core.ac.uk/download/217217670.pdf (accessed on 30th October 2025).

41. Yu, P. K. (2014). TPP and Trans-Pacific perplexities. https://core.ac.uk/download/144230028.pdf (accessed on 30th October 2025).

42. Yu, P. K. (2019). Data exclusivities and the limits to TRIPS harmonization. https://core.ac.uk/download/232854749.pdf (accessed on 30th October 2025).

43. Zampetti, A. B. (2025). WTO rules in the audio-visual sector. https://core.ac.uk/download/pdf/7035121.pdf (accessed on 30th October 2025).

44. Zhu, X. (2024). The importance of maintaining trademark anti-dilution protection. *Advances in Economics, Management and Political Sciences*. https://www.semanticscholar.org/paper/0b3dcc3c0c8f475395cebe66a2f6f4a0e3165884 (accessed on 30th October 2025).

45. Zou, X., Mohd Ali, K. A., & Wan Hussain, W. M. H. (2024). Assessing the compliance and competitive prospects of China's manufacturing industry's digital transformation under the WTO Agreement on Trade-Related Aspects of Intellectual Property Rights. *China and WTO Review*. https://www.semanticscholar.org/paper/03f1ebd092c5aae8b30dfd872bbf9de5cfd427d3 (accessed on 30th October 2025).

Chapter 7

Trade Remedies and Safeguards

Contents

INTRODUCTION

The advanced dance of world trade necessitates instruments that assist countries in protecting their domestic industries while engaging in international commerce. Trade remedies and safeguards are important instruments that allow countries to respond to surprise imports or unfair trade. These instruments—antidumping duties, countervailing duties, and safeguards—are supposed to remove distortions from the market as well as enhance fair competition. The core objective of this introduction is to highlight the significant role played by trade remedies within the World Trade Organization (WTO) framework, under which international trade rules are governed. As countries rely on such policies as a buffer against the adverse effects of their economies, their formation, use, and implications become essential knowledge for understanding contemporary trade relations. Despite appearing to be the need of the hour, trade remedies often accompany contentious arguments and litigations in the WTO. Critics state that such policies open the door to protectionism, curtailing the benefits of free trade while threatening retaliatory measures from affected countries.

Figure 7.1. Trade remedies and safeguards.

Source: https://external-content.duckduckgo.com/iu/?u=https%3A%2F%2Ftse2.mm.bing.net%2Fth%2Fid%2FOIP.v-_Mn5y72feiCAcrDWIDJgHaDf-%3Fpid%3DApi&f=1&ipt=93f5a1b5ea99796290cfdaeb9db55c12b09e9ca429940be6e99b1755b40b5e81.

The WTOs system of dispute settlement has the important function of settling disputes regarding the imposition of such measures in order to make globalization commitments. An insightful observation in this context is that while trade remedies tend to be challenged, they do not necessarily result in litigation. Research has established that whether a government will challenge trade remedies may be decided by the threat of retaliation or whether domestic industries can carry out their own antidumping actions. This development captures the strategic behavior of countries when acting in the domain of international trade (Bown et al., 2025). Such effectiveness is further guaranteed through policy flexibility to address unforeseen economic circumstances. Safeguards, as provided by Article XIX of the General Agreement on Tariffs and Trade (GATT), are an example of this type of flexibility. These instruments allow states to temporarily withdraw from trade liberalization undertakings to address sudden and steep increases in imports. The structure of such arrangements is the key subject of research, given that the equilibrium between unilateral opt-outs and bilateral renegotiations can serve as a strong determinant for countries' willingness to comply with trade agreements. Empirical data suggest that sound design of trade policy flexibility can minimize anticipated regrets over incomplete contracts and unanticipated contingencies, which in turn will promote nations to embrace liberalization ex ante and provide them with proper means of protection ex post (Schropp et al., 2025). Based on a close examination of these characteristics, the essay will address the implications of trade remedies and safeguards in terms of advancing a balanced approach to international trade (Figure 7.1).

Definition of Trade Remedies

Trade remedies are specific measures used by countries to protect their domestic industries against unfair trade practices and to ensure a balanced trade environment. At the focal point of these remedies is the concept of fair trade practices, with major tools being anti-dumping duties, countervailing duties, and safeguards. Anti-dumping duties are levied when a foreign exporter sells items below market price, whereas countervailing duties are levied to counter subsidies provided by foreign governments that give an unfair advantage. Safeguarding, as used in international agreements, is a temporary mechanism which allows countries to restrict imports if a surge would hurt local industries. Practice in trade remedies explains commitment to guaranteeing equitable trade relationships, encompassing both political and economic dimensions underlying international trade mechanisms. Trade remedies can be studied structurally by the institution of agreements under the World Trade Organization (WTO). In this case, trade remedies, as structured for protection as they are, have been condemned for their potentiality to increase trade tensions. As elaborated by Finger and Dhar, the application of GATT regulations has, in certain instances, given precedence to national processes over the principles of free trade and hence expanded the gap in the system (Dhar et al., 2025). Thus, the challenge for nations is how to stringently negotiate between protection of local industries and the broader interest of international cooperation. Remedies to trade, used wisely, may be a valuable tool in the hands of countries hit by unforeseen economic hardship, but their misuse can cause more robust conflicts by undermining the norms of global trade. Further, the elasticity incorporated in the trade policy tools such as the Art. XIX safeguards clause facilitates the ability of countries to react to unforeseen circumstances. This architecture is particularly relevant in the context of partial trade agreements, where protectionism is unavoidable recourse as a signatory regrets having made liberalization pledges while it is compelled (Schropp et al., 2025). Partial withdrawal from making these commitments by way of trade remedies provides an availed avenue for countries to protect their economic interests without total resort to isolationist policies. But their success also hinges on their proper application and adherence to international norms, in such a manner that they benefit world trade patterns rather than eliciting retaliatory measures. Thus, the theory and application of trade remedies are multifaceted and necessitate a balanced understanding of both their protectionist motives and broader implications for global politics.

Importance of Safeguards in International Trade

The utilization of safeguards in international trade is crucial in terms of fostering economic stability across nations, especially in the case of unforeseen market shocks. Safeguards are available as mechanisms whereby states can regulate sudden surges in imports that could disrupt local industries. This degree of regulatory adaptability, as incorporated in trade deals such as the "safeguards clause" under GATT Article XIX, allows nations to withdraw temporarily from trade concessions already made. These actions are indispensable not just in the maintenance of balance in markets at the national level but also in the guarantee that countries can cope with unexpected crises without resorting to blanket protectionism, which could lead to international trade disputes. In this way, safeguards are indispensable in the reconciliation between free trade and the need for the protection of economic interests on a national level and facilitating adaptive policy frameworks (Schropp et al., 2025). Moreover, the connection between safeguards and the general architecture of trade agreements cannot be overstated. Safeguards offer a degree of contractual flexibility that accounts for the incompleteness of trade agreements, under which long-term interactions are often subject to unexpected variables. Understanding the frailty of such contracts allows for the best architecture of policy instruments that have the ability to trigger better renegotiations in the event of a protectionist shock. By providing a way to diverge in the short term from established-down agreements, safeguards encourage judicious trading practices and protect against remorse resulting from unfavorable market changes. The situation is particularly pertinent considering the context of dynamic economic conditions, where the ability to act rapidly towards responses to fluctuations in international trends of trade can be a determining factor in the economic resilience of a country (Schropp et al., 2025). In addition to economic stabilization, protections also have extensive implications for ensuring equitable access to vital goods, for example, in healthcare. The operation of patent policy, as discussed in the case of institutions such as the WTO, illustrates how international trade institutions affect access to vital medicines and technologies. For instance, while strong patent protection can promote innovation, it equally discourages access to medicines that can save lives, particularly in the developing world. This imbalance supports the call for protective measures that enable countries to exert a certain level of control over their markets and protect public health above mindless adherence to IP commitments. In this context, safeguards become not only an instrument of international trade flow management but also a fundamental instrument to maintain human rights and health equity on the international platform (Figure 7.2).

Figure 7.2. Safeguards in international trade.

Source: https://external-content.duckduckgo.com/iu/?u=https%3A%2F%2Fwww.dfat.gov.au%2Fsites%2Fdefault%2Ffiles%2FAustralian-safeguards-support-program-agreement-signing-2.jpg&f=1&nofb=1&ipt=7a72bfa8e7030e423ec3dc44548ea023614852f8588132e862c993660087795b.

7.1. HISTORICAL CONTEXT OF TRADE REMEDIES

Historical context of trade remedies is required to know the present situation of international trade practices. Trade remedies emerged in response to various protectionist practices by nations in the period of economic hardship, particularly following the Great Depression. The subsequent protectionism caused nations to learn that such practices hindered international economic recovery and escalated tensions in global relations. As a result of these problems, a system to control trade practice was developed, reviving doctrines of free trade while leaving space for protection. This balancing act emphasized the difficulty of protecting domestic industries without resorting to overly protective policies that could induce retaliatory actions by trading partners, representing a critical development in global economic policy. The establishment of the World Trade Organization (WTO) in 1995 significantly shaped the historical reality of trade remedies with the adoption of formal rules and procedures intended to reconcile the interests of member states and ensure free trade. This new multilateral structure was designed to provide a formal platform for the resolution of trade disputes, including recourse to trade remedies such as antidumping and countervailing duty actions. Even though these instruments were initially created to protect domestic industries against unfair trade and harm, their use has caused concerns over potential abuses that would erode the ideals of fair trade. Critics argue that the WTO has institutionalized an unequal trade system of advantages to multinationals, which has raised controversy on trade remedies reform in the application of such in the world trade system (Lovett et al., 2000). The increasing protectionist reflex in times of economic downturn, as during the 2008 financial crisis, has again brought trade remedies back into the spotlight. While nations grapple with the consequences of global economic instability, an increasing awareness exists that the proliferation of trade remedies in the guise of antidumping and safeguards may destroy the good of liberalized trade. The WTOs' challenge is to weigh enabling such remedies as a true protection against curtailing their application to enable free worldwide trade. Regionals may offer an answer to reducing reliance on such remedies in the future—perhaps aligning closer to stricter WTO rules to preserve international trade (Voon et al., 2010). Ultimately, the historical evolution of trade remedies is an ongoing clash between protectionism and free trade in pursuit of equitable global market practice (Figure 7.3).

Figure 7.3. Historical context of trade remedies.

Source: https://irp.cdn-website.com/66c1fa8b/dms3rep/multi/web+images+600x400.png.

7.1.1. Evolution of Trade Laws and Regulations

Creation of trade regulations and laws is the dynamic process of interaction between political influence, economic principles, and global interests. Originally established to promote balanced trade practices and combat protectionism, for example, the General Agreement on Tariffs and Trade (GATT), designed to create stability in world trade. But in expanding global trade, the imposition of these regulations had a tendency to reveal inconsistencies, causing questions of equality between member countries. The GATT system, according to critics such as Finger and Dhar, has become an instrument of authority rather than an instrument of regulation, wherein state practice dictates GATT norms rather than vice versa. Thus, this evolution is a deviation from the founding principles of equality and balance, indicating the need for constant updating of trade law to meet the changing situation of the international trading environment (Dhar et al., 2025). As trade regimes keep evolving, the function of trade remedies and safeguards has also appeared more prominently.

These mechanisms attempt to protect home industries from the unfair competitive acts of foreign nations, particularly in instances of dumping or subsidization by foreign nations. With the establishment of the World Trade Organization (WTO) and following trade negotiations, attempts have been made to achieve more certainty as to the rules governing such trade remedies, providing a formal process for the settlement of disputes. However, the implementation process has a tendency to replicate the intricate game of member states' interests, occasionally resulting in loopholes and exceptions. These create tensions because the definition of acceptable practice in trade varies from one state to another, thereby making enforcement and cooperation more complicated. With shifting trade remedies, they must be scrutinized to ensure that they fulfill their intended roles as protectors without infringing fair competition principles (Said et al., 2012). In recent years, the discourse on trade laws has broadened to include important debate on how global regulation overlaps with issues of public health, particularly in the area of intellectual property (IP) rights.

The function of patent policies has far-reaching consequences for drug and medical technology access, especially in the developing world. More stringent patent protection, even as it is intended to stimulate innovation, can have the side effect of limiting access to life-saving treatments, as witnessed in the extreme case of HIV/AIDS drugs that were priced so high as to be out of reach for the majority. The consequences of such an event demonstrate the conflict between protecting public health and stimulating innovation. Therefore, while trade laws and regulations keep changing, they owe it to themselves to balance the interests of IP holders against the pressing need for access to affordable health resources to ensure that safeguards do not violate fundamental human rights (Said et al., 2012) (Figure 7.4).

Figure 7.4. Evolution of trade laws and regulations.

Source: https://fastercapital.co/i/International-trade-regulations--International-Trade-Regulations--Boosting-Business-Growth-and-Market-Expansion--The-Evolution-of-International-Trade-Laws.webp.

7.1.2. Key International Agreements Influencing Trade Remedies

The structure of world trade is extensively penetrated by milestone accords for ensuring uniform guidelines for trade remedies as well as safeguards. A pillar among those accords is the General Agreement on Tariffs and Trade (GATT), which articulates principles that shape international trade practices. The GATT was created to reduce trade barriers and provide a stable trading platform, but others argue that it has worked to reinforce the economic and political power of strong nations over fair trade ideals. Specifically, Finger and Dhar contend that the application of GATT rules will reflect existing national practices and not effective restraints on these practices, hence making it difficult to make fair trade remedy requests in the international arena. This situation stresses the need for a more balanced and robust international trading system where rules actually govern the power dynamics among trade relationships, making the need for reform in trade agreements timely and urgent (Dhar et al., 2025). Another crucial agreement that governs trade remedies is the Agreement on Safeguards, established under the Uruguay Round of negotiations. This agreement allows member countries to implement temporary protection measures to protect domestic industries from overwhelming imports that would cause enormous harm to domestic producers. In establishing a legal framework for such measures, the Safeguards Agreement aims to balance the need for free trade with the imperative to protect vulnerable industries. However, effectiveness in the safeguards depends on member states' understandings and uses, leaning towards sparking controversies that are likely to destabilize trade relations. With countries turning to such provisions, there is a risk of abuse, supporting the proposition that adherence to international treaties must be monitored on an ongoing basis in order to avoid destabilizing their roles of protection and upholding integrity of the international trading system (Dhar et al., 2025). In addition to facilitating trade in a straightforward manner, the effect of international agreements transcends simple facilitation of commerce; they carry gigantic public health and access to basic goods implications, too. To illustrate, the intersection of intellectual property rights and access to drugs is the epitome of complexity in trade agreements. Robust patent rights have the ability to deter competition, which results in exorbitant prices of vital medications, for instance, HIV drugs. When developing nations are prevented from obtaining such drugs due to restrictive patent policies, it raises ethical issues regarding the right to health. The interaction of intellectual property and trade remedies, thus, addresses the critical necessity of developing policies that enhance access while still encouraging innovation. The ongoing controversy regarding these issues highlights the necessity for a re-examination of how international agreements impact public health, showing how their impact goes far beyond financial interests.

7.1.3. Case Studies of Historical Trade Remedy Applications

An examination of historical trade remedy applications provides immense benefit into how international trade regulation operates. Trade remedies such as anti-dumping, countervailing duties, and safeguard measures have been sought by countries to protect their industries against unfair trade practices. A case in point is the United States imposing anti-dumping duties on Chinese steel goods in the early 2000s for predatory price practices. This intervention also shielded American steel manufacturers and exemplified the contentious character of trade remedies, which, while often warranted, can lead to retaliation by the targeted countries. These instances thereby demonstrate the complexity of balancing national economic interests with the principles of free trade, which the World Trade Organization (WTO) seeks to facilitate through its rules and agreements (Voon et al., 2010). On the other hand, the use and abuse of trade remedies are illustrated by other examples in history. The European Union's imposition of safeguard measures on low-cost textiles from developing countries in the early 2000s, for instance, was criticized for being disguised protectionism. The example illustrates the adverse criticism of the selective application of trade remedies having a tendency to breed nationalist sentiments and destroy the notion of free trade. These measures not only portray economic necessities but also wider socio-political settings, wherein economic downturns can create a rise in protectionist politics amongst policymakers. To investigate such instances, it is apparent that trade remedies, even though meant to aid domestic industries, can mislead market forces, with subsequent long-term effects on international trade relations (anonymous, 2025). Besides, the trade remedy climate is continuously impacted by changing economic times and political will. From past case studies, it is noted that while trade remedies might play a stabilizing role at times of economic crisis, they too tend to escalate trade tensions. The ongoing WTO member debate on trade remedy reform highlights the importance of speedy formulation of guidelines that limit abuse while allowing effective protection. Regional trade agreements have even proposed models for limiting trade remedy applications, suggesting that trade practices harmonization can result in a more equitable global trading system. The lessons learned from previous practice are insightful for policymakers of the present, who aim to balance protecting domestic industries from the forces of multilateral trade liberalization (Voon et al., 2010).

7.2. TYPES OF TRADE REMEDIES

The international trade regime is generally regulated by a number of trade remedies that are aimed at protecting domestic industries from undue competition and unforeseen market distortions. Of the most importance among the remedies are antidumping measures, which are designed to stem the situation in which foreign producers export products at prices below their normal value, much harm being thereby inflicted on domestic industries. Antidumping duties serve to increase import prices to a level that is competitive and fair in the market, hence defending local producers from the adverse effect of price undercutting. This remedy not only preserves local jobs but also encourages even competition in the market. Their implementation is, however, contentious in the sense that it involves a reconciliation of free trade and protectionism, with resulting controversies among policymakers and economists on the most suitable mechanism of regulation of international markets. Countervailing duties constitute another essential component of the trade remedy toolbox, with which subsidized imports competing unfairly to receive favorable treatment are effectively countered. When governments provide subsidies to local industry that leads to artificially lower prices in foreign markets, it is able to kill local competition. Charging of countervailing duties allows affected countries to level the playing field by imposing a tariff on imported goods equal to the subsidy itself. While advocates maintain that such obligations are essential in assisting in the facilitation of competitive balance, critics believe their inception can trigger trade tensions and potentially provoke counter-measures from trading partners. Ultimately, the correct implementation of countervailing duties is a product of the complexities present in attempting to balance domestic interests against the principles of international trade and hindering continued evaluation of their broader implications throughout global economic relationships. Safeguard measures constitute a critical element of trade remedy regimes allowing countries to respond to unforeseen and sudden increases in imports likely to cause material injury to the domestic producers of the country. Unlike antidumping and countervailing duty actions, which are directed against unfair behavior, safeguard measures can be applied more broadly regardless of the trading partners' behavior. They constitute a short-term protection policy, allowing home industries to adjust to increased competition. The urgency and efficiency of imposing safeguard measures were especially emphasized when, in the United States, in the steel crisis of 1999–2001, a number of steel companies were on the brink of bankruptcy due to the flooding of cheap imports (Goodrich et al., 2025). Critics argue, however, that the application of such measures should be cautious so as not to trigger unnecessary protectionism and stifle innovation, hence detracting ultimately from the benefits of an open trading system (Dhar et al., 2025) (Figure 7.5).

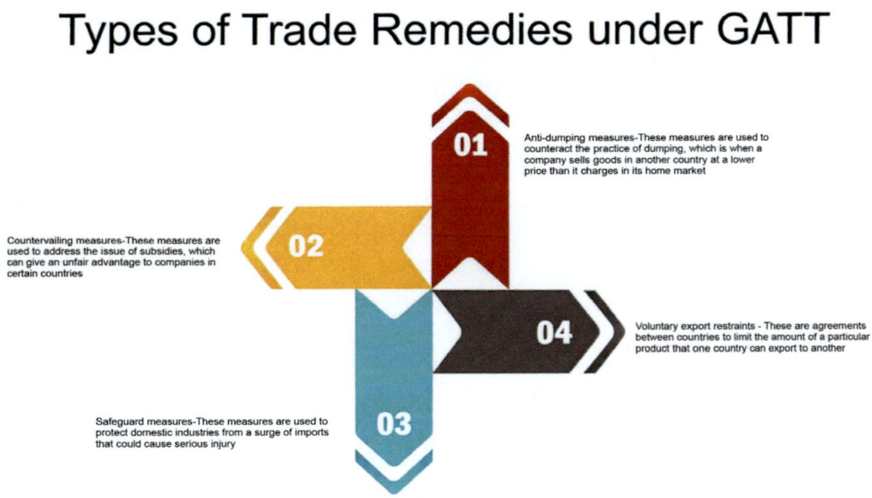

Figure 7.5. Types of trade remedies.

Source: https://fastercapital.co/i/Trade-remedies--GATT-s-Trade-Remedies--Protecting-Domestic-Industries--Types-of-Trade-Remedies-under-GATT.webp.

7.2.1. Anti-Dumping Measures

Anti-dumping measures are a significant aspect of international trade that seeks to protect domestic industries against foreign competitors involved in unfair price practices. Such practices under Article VI of the General Agreement on Tariffs and Trade (GATT) are for marketing goods in a market at less than their normal value, which can displace domestic producers and distort trade in a market. Imposing anti-dumping duties provides countries with the ability to equalize the playing field by compensating for such effects, hence enhancing fair trade practices. Despite this, the use of these measures is not controversy-free because they may also be used as protectionist tools and cause trade tensions among countries.

The problem, therefore, is to balance protection needs with the WTO requirements for liberalization of trade and an avoidance of unnecessary barriers to market access (Voon et al., 2010). In the WTO era, anti-dumping actions are not only an instrument of protection against unfair competition but also raise complex issues about their application. Countries have to establish a direct cause-and-effect link between dumped imports and material injury to their domestic industries before imposing such actions. This requires serious investigations, typically needing enormous resources and expertise. In addition, new realities of global trade, as characterized by regional trade agreements, call into question the effectiveness and efficiency of these practices. While some of the agreements offer templates of low utilization of anti-dumping practices, steps toward their elimination are still missing in the current agenda of WTO negotiators (Voon et al., 2010). With changing global economic fortunes, the threat of higher protectionism casts further complicities on the conversation regarding the use of anti-dumping actions, forcing a mindful re-examination of their intent and effect. For nations such as Zimbabwe, the success of anti-dumping actions demonstrates the difficulty of its enforcement within domestic trade. Although Zimbabwe is a member of the GATT since 1948 and the WTO since 1995, the sufficiency of its anti-dumping strategy has come into doubt, particularly its enforcement of its Competition (Anti-Dumping and Countervailing Duty) (Investigation) Regulations. Although players have agitated for stronger anti-dumping legislation to protect native industries, the Competition and Tariff Commission has failed to conduct any effective dumping investigations. As a result, domestic industries continue to face threats from unfairly priced imports. This situation underscores a broader need for an overhaul of Zimbabwe's anti-dumping framework, drawing lessons from more established systems in regions such as the European Union and South Africa, to better safeguard its economic interests in an increasingly competitive global market (Dari et al., 2018).

7.2.2. Countervailing Duties (CVDs)

CVDs are a key tool in the general architecture of trade remedies, intended to offset the adverse effect on their domestic industry of subsidies provided by foreign governments. By imposing additional tariffs upon subsidized foreign imports, CVDs aim to level the competitive playing field for domestic producers who otherwise would be prejudiced by artificially low prices. This policy tool is especially significant for international trade, where an imbalance in state support can lead to distortions in the market. The application of CVDs is far from controversy-free, however, with overseas exporters often challenging their validity and their appeal to the dispute settlement facilities of the World Trade Organization (WTO).

Figure 7.6. Countervailing duties (CVDs).

Source: https://i0.wp.com/gokulamseekias.com/wp-content/uploads/2023/12/image-38.png.

Application for countervailing duties is grounded in WTO agreements, which prescribe conditions for initiating investigations and determining the existence of subsidies. The initiation of a CVD investigation is typically by way of petition by the domestic industry injured by the complained-of subsidies, prompting an inquiry into whether the complained-of subsidies are actually causing material injury. The strict process highlights the primacy of empirical evidence and economics to trade remedy determinations. However, despite their utility, academic debate still rages about the effectiveness and economic rationale of CVDs, particularly in the light of the risk of trade war generated by retaliations against these actions. Recent accounts have noted that the incidence of CVD cases brought to international tribunals is still quite limited, perhaps due to the preference to seek reciprocal antidumping countermeasures instead, as harbingers of a pattern of vigilante justice in international trade relations (Bown et al., 2025). With shifting global economic fortunes, particularly in the wake of crisis events such as the recent financial crisis, concerns over heightened protectionism drive the agenda. Remedies in trade, e.g., countervailing duties, are matters of controversy as nations try to shield their industries from aggressive competition. The absence of sanity in going for these protectionist policies is a matter of doubt regarding long-term economic policy and trade relations. While elimination of CVDs is not currently on the WTO negotiating table, some regional trade agreements provide channels for reducing reliance on such trade remedies among members, which is in line with WTO standards and general international public law (Voon et al., 2010). This evolution highlights the intricacies of reconciling domestic interests with the goal of ensuring a more harmonious world trading system, and therefore ongoing dialogue and reform between trading partners (Figure 7.6).

7.2.3. Safeguard Measures

Safeguard measures in international trade are the tools required for countries to protect domestic industries from unexpected imports that can harm the local markets. These measures enable nations to impose interim import restrictions, such as tariffs or quotas, on particular goods. These measures are essential, not only for developing nations but also for all nations, so that they receive the proper breathing room to cope with international market competition. Through the use of safeguard action, governments aim to maintain economies at a stable level and preserve jobs in open sectors that would otherwise suffer from invasions of cheaper imported foreign goods. Therefore, these mechanisms are included in trade agreements and are highly regulated by international institutions in order to ensure they are compliant and implemented in a fair manner within the trade framework (Gallagher et al., 2012). The use of safeguard measures is subject to some procedural mandates under trade agreements like those under the World Trade Organization (WTO). These regulations mandate that countries invoking protection should conduct thorough investigations to justify complaints of harm due to increasing imports. The investigation process must be transparent and grounded on solid evidence, such that the measures are indeed necessary and proportionate. Additionally, the duration of such measures is usually short-term, compelling countries to devise long-term solutions for the local industry. This system of regulation enhances predictability and stability in international trade while avoiding the abuse of safeguards as protectionist tools (Cooney et al., 2008). While safeguard measures provide an essential source of relief to domestic industries hit by surges in imports, they also generate hot battles over their impact on international trade flows. Critics of the trade protection argue that, when abused, the tools can lead to distortions in trade and retaliatory measures by trading partners, thereby heightening tensions in international economic matters. A precise balance must be struck so that the application of safeguards indeed serves its intended purpose without undermining the principles of free trade. As the global trading environment continues to evolve, the effectiveness and fairness of safeguard measures will remain key issues to policymakers for facilitating economic growth on a sound footing while securing national interests (Gallagher et al., 2012).

7.3. LEGAL FRAMEWORK GOVERNING TRADE REMEDIES

The trade remedy law operates in the dynamic interplay of national laws and international agreements, largely supported by the mandate of the World Trade Organization (WTO). Trade remedies such as antidumping duties and countervailing measures are essential for nations determined to protect their domestic industries against harmful trade action that could undermine their economic integrity. The WTO's Antidumping Agreement and Agreement on Subsidies and Countervailing Measures establish the general principles that must be adhered to by the member countries, so that the imposition of such measures becomes rational and the result of objective investigations. Most notably, these agreements establish precise steps for determining dumping or subsidization, designed to provide transparency and equity in foreign trade. However, their application has been controversial, with countries referring each other's trade remedy to the WTO dispute settlement mechanism. The efficacy of the WTO dispute settlement mechanism in resolving trade remedy cases is evidenced by numerous rulings that have brought countries into line on inconsistency in observance of obligations already set. As evidenced by relevant research, trade remedies tend to be disputed, showing the issues that arise when nations use them to advance their own interests. Some cases, particularly those involving the United States, have created a lot of controversy regarding the issue of balance of power within the WTO regime. Empirical data indicate that factors such as market size of the impacted market and potential for mutual action can dictate whether or not nations engage in responding to perceived imbalances via the WTO. This creates an impression that the legal framework is to sanction trade remedies but, in reality, political and economic logic plays a crucial role in resolving the issue of trade disputes internationally (Bown et al., 2025). Besides the legal framework offered by the WTO, there is growing concern regarding the asymmetry of the global trading system, which is said to favor multinational corporations at the expense of smaller businesses and workers. The entrenched voting systems and structural imbalances in the

WTO may render reform impossible, leading many to speculate that other bilateral and regional trade agreements will be the preferred method of trade negotiation and enforcement in the future. This new phenomenon is indicative of nations possibly circumventing the WTO mechanism as inflexible and ineffective in addressing contemporary challenges of trade. This trend, in turn, calls into question the future of equity in international trade as well as calls for a reconsideration of legal frameworks governing trade remedies so that they become more congruent with the needs of diverse economic actors (Lovett et al., 2000) (Figure 7.7).

Figure 7.7. Legal framework governing trade remedies.

Source: https://external-content.duckduckgo.com/iu/?u=https%3A%2F%2Fwww.shutterstock.com%2Fimage-photo%2Fshipping-cargo-containers-hammer-judge-600nw-2466319653.jpg&f=1&nofb=1&ipt=9b9640a75da024658d2bb4234e590e4b3866fd88b3c97c43520f361ab03b0c37.

7.3.1. World Trade Organization (WTO) Regulations

The WTO has established a multi-dimensional regulatory framework that supports the practice of fair trade among its member countries. The main obligation of the organization revolves around the facilitation of trade liberalization through curbing tariffs and eliminating non-tariff obstacles, thereby encouraging increased market access. Under such a framework, there are rules that are intended to ensure that everyone follows established principles of trade, and these are important in creating a predictable trading environment. A good example is agreements that direct antidumping actions as an important mechanism for addressing unfair trade practices that undercut domestic industries. These regulations also reflect the commitment of countries like Indonesia towards upholding international trade levels, as well as reveal the burden to harmonize national policies with WTO provisions as reflected in the need to alleviate the detrimental import impacts on home markets, thus the existence of safeguards guarding sensitive industries from sudden spikes in imports (Febriza et al., 2023). Under trade remedies, WTO has specific provisions for applying safeguards and countervailing measures.

Figure 7.8. World Trade Organization (WTO) regulations.

Source: https://cdn.educba.com/academy/wp-content/uploads/2024/06/WTO-World-Trade-Organization-1-1.png.

These are crucial for countries facing serious injury due to increased imports from abroad that could be dumped at prices lower than the fair market value, and domestic industries concerned must recover and adjust. Use of such actions must be justified through comprehensive investigations that establish the occurrence of dumping or subsidization, as laid down under the WTO's Anti-Dumping Agreement and Agreement on Subsidies and Countervailing Measures. Furthermore, such legislation demands member states to use reasonable diligence before invoking protectionism, maintaining the principle of equity and finding a balance between the interests of local producers and foreign producers. It is important that nations, particularly nations like Indonesia, navigate these policies carefully to protect their local industries while remaining compliant with the WTO's trade liberalization principles (Febriza et al., 2023). The complexities of augmenting trade policies are also highlighted in discussions concerning capital account regulations (CARs) and whether they comply with WTO provisions. After the global financial crisis, all countries tried to restrict capital flows in an attempt to stabilize their economies. This is, however, contrary to provisions under trade and investment agreements aimed at free capital flows. It hinders countries from having proper fiscal policies without risking the violation of international obligations. Therefore, it is imperative to conduct a critical evaluation of the compatibility between CARs and international trade system regulations in order to provide developing countries with the autonomy to make use of these instruments while still being actively engaged in foreign trade. The call for greater compatibility is a reflection that it's realized trade and economic stability are not opposing factors but rather combined by concerted regulation and policy implementation (Figure 7.8).

7.3.2. National Laws and Their Implications

The intersection point of national law and international trade significantly affects safeguard instruments and remedies for trade. Countries have a tendency towards creating national law that implements antidumping as well as countervailing duties as safeguarding measures against unfair foreign competition. These legal regimes play the critical function of regulating the conduct of trade, and this is very pertinent when dealing with the World Trade Organization (WTO). National legislations are usually disputed at the WTO, as it must be harmonized with international trade obligations. The discrepancy is brought about by varying views on what constitutes equitable trade, and this leads to a considerable number of disputes. This environment provokes some nations to walk on eggshells in challenging trade remedies imposed by powerful players, such as the U.S., primarily for retaliatory measures rather than utilizing formal dispute settlement mechanisms, as noted by Bown et al. (2025). Domestic legislation impacts more deeply in that they can shape the parameters within which trade remedies can operate. For instance, while national legislation is supposed to give protection against harmful imports, it works to distort market forces if extended too comprehensively or discriminatory. Finger and Dhar emphasize that GATT rules, though directed towards limiting national trade barriers, themselves tend to be an image of the existing national practices and not actually a restraint on them. Such a dynamic suggests that countries can use legal loopholes to perpetuate protectionist practices, thereby defeating the intent of international agreements. Such occurrences serve to verify how local legislations tend to take precedence over the regulatory framework crafted by international protocols, opposing the idea of a stable and fair trading system as advanced in Dhar et al. (2025). Moreover, the effectiveness of trade remedies crafted according to national legislations is often avoided due to the geopolitical backdrop. States apply these laws not only for economic benefits but as political tools of leverage, determining their policies of commerce in line with strategic national interests. Where there are significant economic implications, the exchange of national law and international law tends to result in strategic decisions likely to cause trade wars. The unwillingness to challenge a foreign nation's trade policy at the WTO indicates a preference for alternative avenues, i.e., retaliatory antidumping measures. This attitude is a situational prioritization of short-term economic remedy in preference to longer-term compliance with global standards. This kind of situation distorts the landscape for effective global trade governance, and meticulous scrutiny of the relevant national legislation and broader implications for cross-border trade relationships is therefore essential.

7.3.3. Dispute Resolution Mechanisms

The design of the mechanism for the resolution of disputes in trade agreements is central to the facilitation of compliance and conflict resolution arising from the application of trade remedies and safeguards. At the heart of the mechanisms is the World Trade Organization (WTO), which provides a platform for member states to resolve disputes resulting from trade behavior that is in violation of rules that have been established. The WTO dispute settlement mechanism's architecture is aimed not only to encourage observance of agreed rules but also to provide a means of rebalancing trade relations whenever one of the parties believes its rights have been undermined. The recent debate in WTO literature regarding compliance versus rebalancing is meant to underscore the complex character of this system, which demands a structure capable of responding to the dynamics of international trade interactions. Significantly, the dispute settlement frameworks must incorporate trade policy flexibility in a way that allows states to address unforeseen circumstances that may trigger temporary deviations from trade commitments. This is particularly relevant with respect to safeguard measures, which extend a vehicle for nations to respond to import surges that are threats to domestic industries. A good system reconciles the need for states to keep their commercial commitments with giving them the discretion to change such commitments in light of sound economic reasons. As referred to in the WTO optimal design literature, tools like the safeguards clause of Article XIX of GATT are an indication of the importance of utilizing a structured, reliable mechanism for resolving disputes arising out of such policy shifts (Schropp et al., 2025). The interconnection of compliance and remedial mechanisms introduces yet another dimensional complexity to the dispute settlement debate. Theorists pursue a debate regarding the effectiveness of different methods of enforcement, focusing in particular on the issue of whether or not compliance or rebalancing should be the primary goal of dispute settlement. The two positions depict a helpful insight: rather than being mutually exclusive, they perhaps in fact do embody complementary aspects of the WTO agreement, addressing different facets of the multi-layered nature of trade relations. By understanding this complexity, policymakers and scholars can assist in working towards one cohesive research agenda that seeks to balance these views and thereby build the WTO's system of dispute settlement so that it includes the best solutions along with appropriate mechanisms for flexibility (Schropp, 2025) (Figure 7.9).

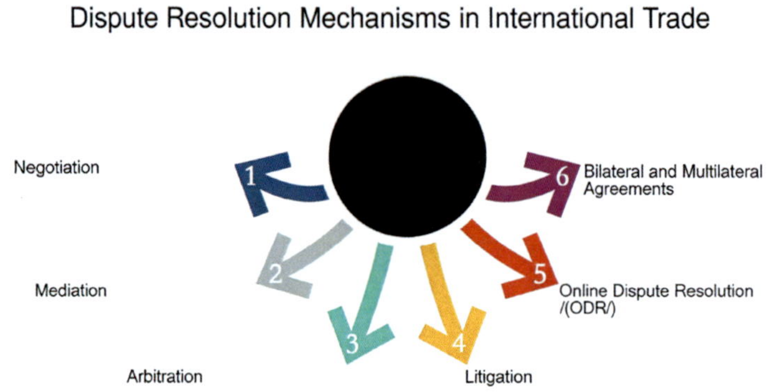

Figure 7.9. Dispute resolution mechanisms in international trade.

Source: https://fastercapital.co/i/International-trade-law--What-You-Need-to-Know-About-International-Trade-Law-and-Regulations--Dispute-Resolution-Mechanisms-in-International-Trade.webp.

7.4. ECONOMIC IMPACTS OF TRADE REMEDIES

Economic consequences of trade remedies, particularly tariffs and safeguards, run very deep and far-reaching. By design, these efforts aim to protect domestic industries against unfair competition and deteriorating market conditions due to foreign imports. Importantly, remedial actions have a tendency to produce unintended consequences when implemented. For instance, increasing tariffs can raise the price of production for domestic manufacturers that rely on foreign materials, which will, in turn, inflate consumer prices. Besides, while trade remedies may bring relief to the worst-performing industries in the short term, they may also induce inefficiency by shielding industries from the competitive pressures that spur innovation and improvement. This paradox reflects a broader fear that in an effort to protect domestic employment and production, trade remedies are actually capable of retarding economic growth and competitiveness in the longer run. Additionally, employment of trade remedies can create tensions in the world trading system, particularly as countries navigate the perils of retaliation. Tariffs imposed by a country can prompt the responding partners to retaliate through the imposition of their own barriers, precipitating a tit-for-tat situation hurting world supply chains and trade relations. The World Trade Organization (WTO), designed to mediate such disputes, is usually criticized as being inadequate to handle such complexities. Its critics argue that the current system makes asymmetries more permanent in the direction of multinational firms and developed economies to the detriment of weaker economies, as identified in recent studies (Lovett et al., 2000). It is an occurrence that triggers important questions on trade remedy equity and its consequences in the economic context, calling for reform to ensure global trade practices are equitable and sustainable.

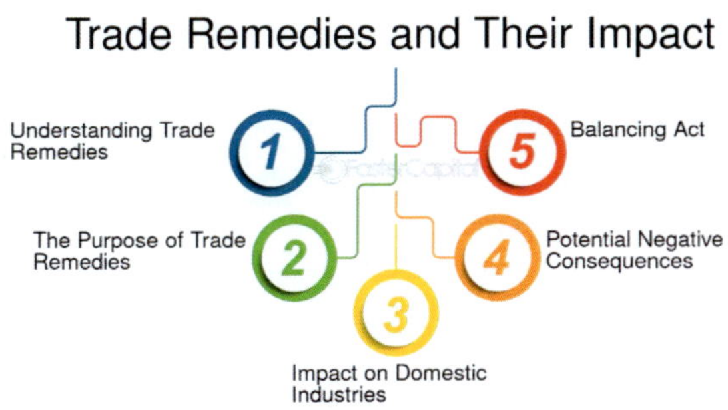

Figure 7.10. Trade remedies and their impact.

Source: https://fastercapital.co/i/Market-distortion--Dumping-and-Market-Distortion--Balancing-Global-Trade-update--Trade-Remedies-and-Their-Impact.webp.

In addition, the economic impacts of trade remedies are most strongly experienced in nations that have fragile agricultural sectors. Economic Partnership Agreements (EPAs) have been faulted for the probable negative impact they may have on the food security of their signatory nations. While the agreements were meant to deepen and make trade relations more predictable, they incorporate obligations that extend beyond World Trade Organization (WTO) requirements, as revealed in controversies surrounding ACP states (Matthews, 2025). Most ACP countries are faced with challenges in reconciling their EPAs commitments with their duty to guarantee that the domestic agriculture economies are protected. Such measures, such as the ban on export taxes and safeguards, undermine the ability of governments to implement policies that ensure food security as well as help farmers in the home environment. Thus, the tension between protectionist measures and trade liberalization suggests that a balance of finesse is called for to facilitate economic resilience without sacrificing vital domestic industries to the vagaries of international market forces (Figure 7.10).

7.4.1. Effects On Domestic Industries

The impact of trade remedies and safeguards on domestic industries is significant, typically governed by the changing rate of global competition. In such instances where domestic industries are confronted with rising foreign competition, U.S. trade protection tools such as antidumping duties and countervailing duties are employed to safeguard such industries against unfair trade practices. The actions, however, have the side effect of holding back necessary changes in industries, resulting in inefficiencies. As observed in the analysis of U.S. trade policy, trade policies that postpone industry adjustment can contribute to new entry in the home market, which may aggravate troubles for established producers. Lastly, while designed to rescue home industries, these remedies can have the paradoxical effect of sustaining outdated structures that do not contest fiercely in an open economy (Bown et al., 2025).

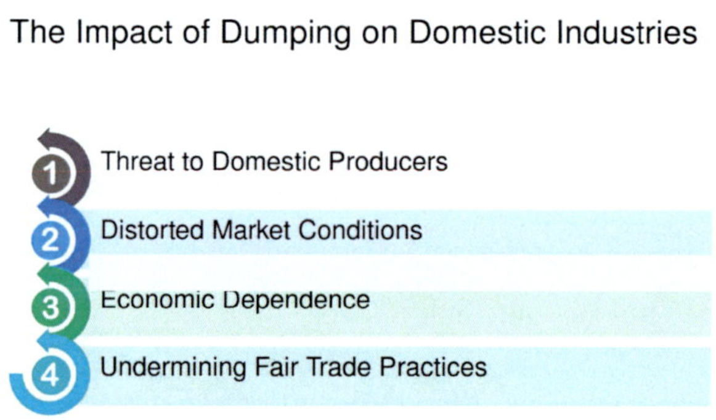

Figure 7.11. The impact of protectionism on domestic industries.

Source: https://fastercapital.co/i/Leveling-the-Playing-Field--Anti-Dumping-Duties-and-Import-Competition-update--The-Impact-of-Dumping-on-Domestic-Industries.webp.

Local industries also bear unintended effects stemming from the utilization of trade protection, especially innovation and competitiveness. When businesses realize the existence of safeguards, they tend to relax, allocating fewer funds to research and development. The trend discourages innovation and murders competitiveness in the long run. Additionally, those industries that are protected from competition may not become more efficient or implement the best practices, and foreign competitors would dominate them. The trade rules capture the power of national practices rather than suppressing them, as suggested by Finger and Dhar. Therefore, while safeguard measures can provide short-term relief, their eventual impact defeats the progressive adjustment that will allow industries to thrive in an international competitive economy (Dhar et al., 2025). Furthermore, the trade remedy experience is also a self-reinforcing cycle for indigenous industries. Companies that gain advantage from these measures will cause policy-makers to continue enforcing them, even as things get better. This kind of dependence can create an environment where firms stand to gain more from government action than from engaging in necessary restructuring or efficiency improvements. This can generally inhibit the overall economic responsiveness of the sector, as sectors trapped into protection mechanisms will ultimately have more to overcome when reacting to changing market forces. Thus, there is a significant assessment of the utility and implications of trade remedies necessary in promoting an adaptive and competitive industrial climate to ensure that local businesses can face external pressures while fostering innovation and growth (Bown et al., 2025) (Figure 7.11).

7.4.2. Implications for International Trade Relations

The structure of trade remedies and safeguards lies at the core of international trade relations design, especially in the context of rising protectionist pressures. The balance between free trade and safeguard measures generally occupies the foreground of international debate among nations. Unilateral action by states in the form of tariffs or quotas can work to significantly disrupt global value chains and induce retaliatory action. And as the economic-political dance unfolds, countries intermittently employ shield measures to protect domestic industries, interpreting global regulations to permit this. Under close scrutiny, GATT provisions that claimed to limit national trade restrictions are utilized by powerful nations to advance their own causes (Dhar et al., 2025). This discord raises a doubt on the justice of international trade regulations and highlights the importance of reformation of the structure of international trade, encouraging justice and stability. In addition, the growing dependence upon trade remedy indicates a new growing divergence in the execution and interpretation of trade regulations between countries. Economic power generally induces nations to cater to their national interests, usually at the expense of multilateral agreements. This is also exacerbated by recent shocks globally, including economic crises and geo-economic tensions, as countries go in pursuit of their trade policies due to perceived threat. The unstable global nature of capital flows and trade channels has made more policy flexibility necessary, particularly for developing economies. A comparative analysis shows that existing trade agreements have a tendency to limit the capacity of nations to put regulations on capital accounts, thereby interweaving their trade relations (Gallagher et al., 2012). Such limitation calls for timely domestic policy-friendly treaties to enhance the stability and robustness of international trade relations. Moreover, implications of trade remedies stretch beyond short-run economic interests to the extent of influencing diplomatic relations and strategic partnerships. Nation-states deploying safeguards run the risk of unintentionally alienating trading partners and increasing tensions and conflict within the world trading system. In this context, international institutions and trading forums are asked to mediate disputes and promote dialogue. The requirement that multilateral regimes be observed can be a stabilizing factor by encouraging balanced compliance with trade rules. But as the GATT controversy indicates, the potential for discrimination in the application of rules undermines the legitimacy and effectiveness of such institutions. Ultimately, making trade relations open and equitable requires rethinking the rules governing trade remedies so that such instruments promote more cooperation than fuel conflict on the world trade stage (Dhar et al., 2025).

7.4.3. Analysis of Consumer Prices and Choices

In trade remedies and safeguards, consumer price and decision dynamics are crucial to be understood. Tariff-based trade policies as well as antidumping directly affect market conditions, which in turn affect the supply and cost of goods. The costs of importation rise for consumers, exacting hugely higher prices as a consequence, thus limiting their buying power. Where trade relationships are unstable, e.g., in wars, the cost of commodities could increase even more. This is the best way to describe markets of low transparency and macroeconomic instability high where firms could accept cheaper products of poor quality. Such choices not only impact consumer satisfaction but also destabilize the overall competitive pattern, creating superficial trading relationships that can heighten price volatility and market inefficiency, thereby threatening the stability of consumer choices and preferences (Chisik, 2025). Moreover, the link between consumer well-being and trade policy is heightened when researching historic case examples. Those countries like Argentina, Chile, and Colombia have experienced trade reforms amidst their economic crises that reveal the subtleties of consumer price adjustments in a liberalizing environment. Although these countries attempted to modernize their trade practices through adherence to GATT rules, resort to antidumping and reference pricing as relief measures reflects a deceptively complicated interplay between consumer protection and assistance in trade. Households in these countries usually face sheltered industries, such as automobiles and textiles, which can limit their choices and raise prices due to less competition. Therefore, the implications drawn from such nations lean toward the necessity of constant assessment and readjustment of trade policy to ensure that consumer needs are met while guarding markets from undue protectionism (Rajapatirana et al., 2025). Lastly, the evolution of trade remedies is all about increased transparency and stakeholders' participation in trade policy-making. Trade policies intended to deal with import surges are not just supposed to consider the opinions of domestic producers but also the opinions of consumers who actually pay for protection. A system for open communication and effective resolution of public problems is vital in the achievement of a balance favoring consumer choice and equitable competition. Governments can readily address the effects of price volatility and interruptions in trade by building advisory institutions independent from daily policymaking regarding trade. This approach ensures the long-term national interest requirements for imposing safeguards and prevents protectionism entrenchment of protectionist trade policies and encourages a more consumer-focused and equitable trade platform (Rajapatirana et al., 2025).

7.5. POLITICAL CONSIDERATIONS IN TRADE REMEDIES

The intersection of political elements and trade remedies experiences complex dynamics, which have a strong influence on the way nations tackle trade policy. Drastic measures, such as the imposition of safeguards, often owe their genesis not so much to economic imperative as to political considerations. Political interests will demand protection measures in the interests of national interest, mobilizing the people against perceived external threats. This politicization of trade remedy issues suggests that trade remedies can be instruments of domestic political policy, rather than merely economic remedies against market disruption. For example, trade remedy laws like antidumping and countervailing duties can benefit specific industries at the expense of consumer choice, which shows how political interests can take precedence over broader economic concerns. Such an environment can lead to inefficient allocation of resources, as protected industries can slack off and become less competitive under the umbrella of government interference (Bown et al., 2025). Compounding the problem is the presence of international trade agreements, some of which include provisions for trade flexibility. The World Trade Organizations safeguards clause is an excellent case in point of the conflict between trade liberalization promises and the protection of domestic industries. As countries navigate through the political dynamics of building such safeguards, there can be a reaction from trading partners and domestic constituents both. Political parties against protectionist policies can counter that using trade policy creates a vicious cycle of retaliation, which harms world relations and economic stability. In analyzing these tensions, it is critical to acknowledge that the political structure of trade remedies can either permit positive adjustments for shifting comparative advantages or lock countries into a pattern of protectionism that hinders sustained growth (Schropp et al., 2025). The political ramifications extend even further into the field of policy design and restructuring. Policymakers must weigh carefully domestic pressures against the imperative of sustainable trade relations. The design of trade remedies must thus be underpinned by a sensitive understanding of the economic reality as well as the political environment. Political cycles and popular opinion, for instance, can be factored in by policymakers in the design of trade adjustments. Ensuring that trade policy architecture is sensitive not just to economic shocks but also to political reality is crucial in building robust economic frameworks. Designing policies that react to such twin pressures enables nations to better handle the complexities of international trade and ensure that there is a competitive and equitable marketplace (Bown et al., 2025) (Figure 7.12).

Figure 7.12. Political considerations in trade remedies.

Source: https://external-content.duckduckgo.com/iu/?u=https%3A%2F%2Freidellawfirm.com%2Fwp-content%2Fuploads%2F2024%2F04%2Fe4cc3989-1758-413d-8da4-be7a01bcb3c8.png&f=1&nofb=1&ipt=e3d9b5358c0fa07797d9ef2cd367f652a609c36e9c72fa148952d24b999dd85c.

7.5.1. Influence of Lobbying and Interest Groups

The function of lobbying and interest groups is at the heart of trade remedy and safeguard making, usually shaping government policy to benefit specific sectoral interests. Policymakers are argued by interest groups using the different mechanisms, such as antidumping measures and tariffs, on high-stakes events. For instance, in the instance of Latin American countries that have in the recent past undergone broad trade reform, it is evident that though such nations are part of international trading systems like the General Agreement on Tariffs and Trade (GATT), lobbying remains a basic way through which specific industries strive to gain protection from import surges. Lobbying behavior of this type highlights the tension between open trade policy ideals and national economic interests, in turn affecting the efficiency as well as reputation of trade policy reforms (Rajapatirana et al., 2025). In addition, the strategic use of lobbying is typically reflective of firms' size and capability, which further affects their engagement with administrative agencies managing trade policy. Larger firms possess the means to address the complexities involved in lobbying because they can harmonize their interests more effectively with regulatory bodies. This pattern illustrates the principles of transaction cost theory, where larger firms organize their lobbying activities effectively to prevent issues like free riding among trade associations. Small firms, however, do not have the ability to utilize the same measure of power as their large counterparts, and this emphasizes a disparity in their lobbying effectiveness because they possess fewer resources and are poorly organized in the lobby system (Tiller et al., 2025). The lobby climate, thus, emphasizes the significance of economic power in determining trade protection and solutions. Ultimately, the dynamic between lobbying, interest groups, and trade policy holds profound consequences for the future of global trade. With policymakers facing pressures from across the board, the benefits of transparency and inclusiveness in trade policymaking rise as fundamental issues. The requirement of an appropriate balance in reacting to industry lobbying demands instruments that speak to the general public interest without overlooking sectoral concerns. As the experience of countries using GATT provisions illustrates, the integration of diversified perspectives can minimize the prospect of becoming too reliant on protectionist mechanisms that favor particular sectors. Therefore, establishing an open platform for debating the costs and benefits of trading policies—coupled with good analysis and public scrutiny—becomes paramount in shaping a viable trade remedies and safeguard regime in an inherently conflict-ridden environment (Rajapatirana et al., 2025).

7.5.2. Role of Government Policy in Trade Decisions

Government policy is a key player in trade determinations, employed frequently as a mechanism to protect home industries from unfair trade. Antidumping measures and countervailing duties are employed most frequently by governments as measures in cases involving trade remedy and safeguard actions, being responses to perceived breaches of fair trade practices. These interventions are not just defensive but also aim to achieve competitive balance in home markets in a manner that ensures local businesses thrive without foreign businesses pricing them out. Such policies have far-reaching effects, as they have the ability to alter the character of international trade, provoke reactions from trading nations, and impact the overall efficiency in the functioning of markets. This environment highlights the need for government policy in dealing with intricate trade matters while respecting global commitments. The World Trade Organization (WTO) offers a system in which these trade remedies find their order, but the system is generally faulted for its imbalances. Based on recent evaluations, the WTOs structure can inadvertently benefit multinational firms to the detriment of smaller players, therefore distorting the level playing field of global trade. The governments apply their trade policies to correct these imbalances and resort to bilateral or regional level talks, which are more rewarding than the existing formats. It makes global commerce dynamics even more complex as governments move more towards these other forms of trade arrangements. In addition, the challenge is one of balancing domestic protection with compliance with international trade arrangements, and of marking out how government policy is required in resolving these competing imperatives and defending national interest in attempting to come together in international trade. While the application of trade remedies is prevalent, their effectiveness and the grounds for their application must be critically assessed. Studies have shown that the choices of governments to pursue settlement of disputes regarding trade remedies are usually subject to various issues, such as the market size involved and retaliation capabilities. Surprisingly, research indicates that governments may avoid official complaints through the WTO when foreign industries have the potential to apply reciprocal antidumping measures. This trend demonstrates a desire for what can be called vigilante justice, in which nations resort to open retaliation instead of going through costly and time-consuming dispute resolutions. This type of behavior indicates the nuance of government policy in trade decisions and emphasizes the need for a policy response that is adaptive to the evolving realities of international trade relationships, e.g., the necessity for cooperation and fair competition within the global economy (Bown et al., 2025; Lovett et al., 2000) (Figure 7.13).

Figure 7.13. Role of government policy in trade decisions.

Source: https://fastercapital.co/i/Trade-policy--Net-Exports-and-Trade-Policy--Shaping-Economic-Strategies--The-Role-of-Government-in-Trade-Policy.webp.

7.5.3. Case Studies of Political Motivations Behind Trade Remedies

Political motivations behind trade remedies typically emerge in the case studies that demonstrate the relationship between government action and domestic industry interests. The 1999–2001 U.S. steel crisis, for instance, demonstrates how political pledges influence trade policy. The steel sector went through extreme hardship during the years 1999–2001, with over 30 steel-making companies going bankrupt. The crisis worsened with the accession of George W. Bush to power, for whom he had made the Steelworkers a bailout promise during the election campaign. With increasing pressure at home both from the steel sector and the United Steel Workers of America, political pressures forced the Bush administration to put on trade remedies. This example points out that trade policy is frequently determined not only on economic grounds but also on election imperatives and the government's responsibility to fulfill campaign promises, illustrating the complex character of political forces guiding trade remedies (Goodrich et al., 2025).

The agricultural trade remedies challenge also illustrates a new dimension of political motivation where the concentration of market power becomes significant in shaping policymakers' behavior. Agriculture has increasingly consolidated over the years, but political motivations for such an industry structure are a matter of suspicion. The economic theories employed traditionally examine the competitive firm conduct in concentrated markets but fail to consider ulterior motives for integration horizontal and vertical. The result may be the creation of powerful lobbies that mystify the government into invoking trade remedies. Policymakers, recognizing such motivations, will become susceptible to the pressure of well-organized industry groups rather than act on behalf of consumer welfare or broad economic grounds. This demonstrates how domestic political forces and industry pressures successfully leverage trade policy to the specific benefit of concentrated markets (Martin et al., 2025). Moreover, the Obama administration's steel import restriction case illustrates how economic downturn can even increase political incentives for trade remedies. Following a surge of imported steel having been viewed as threatening to domestic employment, the administration was subjected to intense pressure to implement protective measures. Political calculation came into play, with members of Congress from states that are major producers of steel calling for tariffs and other protections. Thus, trade remedies were utilized not only as an economic tool but also as a strategic tactic to maintain voters' allegiance in significant electoral constituencies. The entanglement of domestic economic interests and international trade policy underscores the intricate relationship between political accountability and trade remedial measures.

These case histories illustrate the complexity and rationale for government action to address trade issues, frequently bending to political agenda to satisfy constituents and industry lobbies (Goodrich et al., 2025).

7.6. CRITICISMS AND CHALLENGES OF TRADE REMEDIES

Trade remedies like antidumping duties and safeguard action are designed to protect domestic industries from unfair foreign competition. Nevertheless, they come under criticism for generating distortions in global trade flows. For instance, their application can lead to increased prices for consumers and can inadvertently shield inefficient domestic producers from necessary market pressures. Critics fear that these measures will be employed more as protectionist tools than as genuine responses to objectionable trade practices. Such worry is particularly realized in the case of ongoing debates surrounding Economic Partnership Agreements (EPAs), where countries' commitments as signatories end up exacerbating food security issues by lessening their ability to exert effective trade remedy measures. Overreaching in terms of country commitments also initiates controversy over the applicability and legitimacy of such protection, particularly when applied to situations outside the original context of safeguarding vulnerable industries from the effects of international competition (Matthews, 2025). Furthermore, the issues of trade remedies similarly extend to their enforcement and implementation. National governments are highly pressured by domestic country constituents advocating for policies beneficial to specific industries. Such political interests complicate the regulation of trade remedies, most times resulting in conflicting with global trade obligations. In the World Trade Organization (WTO) framework, divergent national interests have witnessed protracted negotiations relating to antidumping duties. Member states' variable positions, whereby they are keen on limiting the use of such practices while others want to keep them intact, simply portray a built-in contradiction in the governance of global trade. This diversity in priorities can work to preclude cohesiveness and practicality of trade policies in the end, which, in turn, influence the stability and predictability of global trade (Wainio et al., 2025). Implementation of the trade remedies in a transparent and effective way is also hindered by transparency and access issues. In most instances, the processes of conducting antidumping investigations and safeguard actions are opaque, and this discourages the meaningful engagement of affected parties in decision-making. The absence of transparency can discourage small and medium-sized enterprises from being able to fully protect their interests, thereby remaining vulnerable to the arbitrary application of trade remedies. Moreover, the complexities involved in the cases of antidumping can cause prolonged investigations, deterring companies from embracing genuine trading practices. According to critics, the focus should be shifted towards making the procedures more transparent in a manner that all parties involved have an opportunity to participate, thus ensuring a more balanced trading platform. Addressing these critiques is key to enhancing trade remedies and ensuring they function their intended protecting role without incurring unnecessary impediments to international commerce (Matthews, 2025) (Figure 7.14).

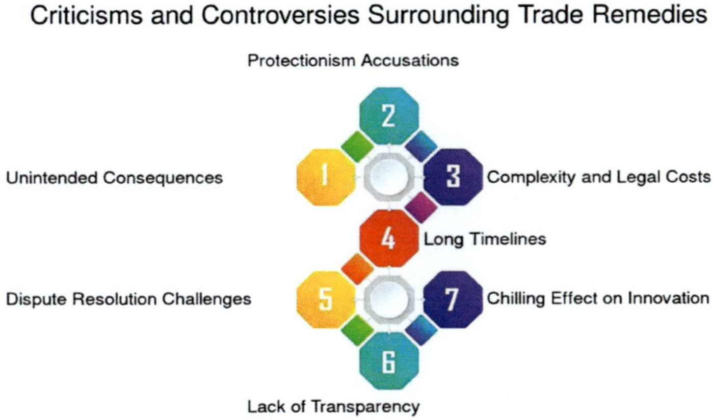

Figure 7.14. Criticisms and challenges of trade remedies.

Source: https://fastercapital.co/i/Trade-remedy-investigations--Unveiling-the-Truth-Behind-Dumping-update--Criticisms-and-Controversies-Surrounding-Trade-Remedies.webp.

7.6.1. Arguments Against the Effectiveness of Trade Remedies

Trade remedy success, in the form of anti-dumping measures and countervailing duties, is often in doubt due to their probable inclination to misshape, rather than right, markets. They are said to have the tendency of creating inefficiencies by protecting domestic industries from overseas competition at consumer detriment. For instance, while such remedies are intended to safeguard domestic businesses against unfair trade, they can also cause higher prices for consumers and fewer choices in the market. Far from supplementing competition, trade remedies might actually serve to enshrine monopoly tendencies in domestic industries. This preferential trend for mature industries, while theoretically legitimate, would forget the dynamic and competitive character of global markets and make innovation stagnate and domestic companies have fewer incentives to improve their product and services. In addition, the use of trade remedies also lacks transparency and can be politically motivated rather than based on true economic needs. As countries bargain for trade agreements like the Trans-Pacific Partnership (TPP) and the Trans-Atlantic Trade and Investment Partnership (TTIP), the enforcement provisions are contentious. These treaties could accord disproportionate emphasis to specific sectors, outrunning smaller industry actors and reinforcing the entrenched market structures in the economy. The biased application of trade remedies has the tendency to give rise to suspicion among trading partners, which may take away from the shared interest of free trade as espoused in international law. These interactions are indicative of the over-enforcement risk discussed in the case of world norms, where focus on compliance creates unproductive impacts in international trade (Pauwelyn et al., 2006). Finally, the skepticism of the effectiveness of trade remedies can also be held for their administrative burden. The actions involved in undertaking investigations into dumping or subsidies can be incredibly complex and man-power-intensive for governments. This regulatory overhang tends to cause inefficiencies and delays that undermine the mechanisms to protect domestic industries. The economic costs of maintaining such remedies may outweigh their purposes, especially for small companies that cannot afford prolonged legal actions. In addition, such remedies' additional layer of regulation can deter foreign investment, ultimately leading to a net decrease in economic growth. The complexities involved highlight that, while trade remedies are intended to serve a protective function, they can destabilize the overall efficiency and dynamism of the economy, and raise serious doubts about their effectiveness (Gallagher et al., 2015).

7.6.2. Potential for Abuse and Protectionism

The potential for abuse of trade remedies and safeguards is a significant concern in global trade dynamics. Governments have a habit of implementing protective policies that are purportedly aimed at safeguarding domestic industries against foreign competition, only for such tools to become protectionism tools. As the 2008–2009 economic crisis proved, even though WTO rules effectively contained a rise in industrialized economies' import tariffs, still, there were huge distortions in the market. Governments turned to aggressive interventionist strategies, e.g., in the car manufacturing sector, where companies leveraged their global presence to draw concessionary state subsidization from different governments. This subsidy race environment exemplifies a subtle facet of protectionism that holds back the original intent of trade agreements, revealing how multinationals can exploit government dependence to achieve gains over equitable trading practices (Francois et al., 2009). The design of trade agreements is often full of loopholes that expose them to exploitation by national governments, which complicates the landscape of trade remedies further. The WTO is subject to incomplete contract circumstances where unforeseen contingencies can create a backlash against liberalization of trade. Flexibility devices such as the safeguards clause allow nations to provisionally withdraw from the trade concessions they had previously undertaken due to protectionist shocks. Although conceived to protect national interests, they can become a cycle of retaliation and additional protectionism that undermines confidence and cooperation among traders if abused. The presence of these safeguards accentuates a significant trade policy tension: the need for flexibility versus the risk of commoditizing protections, which eventually makes international trade institutions less effective (Schropp et al., 2025). Governments, in a bid to navigate such subtleties, must walk on eggshells such that they do not encourage abuse but maintain genuine free trade. Protectionism taking precedence over collaborative economic policy is a risk that necessitates robust watch mechanisms within the WTO framework. Stiffer rule enforcement in state aid and subsidies, with transparent-reporting practice, would also help mitigate risks of exploitation. Moreover, initiative to develop enhanced opt-out provisions or renegotiation clauses will enhance member states' accountability, ensuring an environment where trade flexibility generates no conflict or unintended economic isolationism. International trade's long-term sustainability relies on the ability to maintain equal practices discouraging excessive protectionism while ensuring necessary safeguarding mechanisms (Francois et al., 2009; Schropp et al., 2025).

7.6.3. Challenges in Enforcement and Compliance

The enforcement and compliance regimes of trade remedies and safeguards are usually faced with fundamental hindrances that can be harmful to their intended effectiveness. Inconsistency in legal systems and institutional capacity between developed and developing countries is one of the issues. There are few developing countries that have the robust legal structure to bring about effective enforcement and application of trade laws. This loophole is most commonly responsible for the trouble of tracking compliance, with goods imported and evading tariffs or anti-dumping charges ending up in the market unhindered. Consequently, trade remedies to protect domestic industries fail in their purpose, as domestic producers are left open to unfair competition. The impact of such deficiencies is all the more significant in sectors wherein price undercutting could threaten the very survival of newly arising industries, highlighting the need for tighter compliance mechanisms that consider these imbalances in capacity and resource allocation. Over imbalances in legal frameworks, political calculation also complicates enforcement and compliance on the trade remedy side. National governments may have the inclination to prefer political allegiances or economic strategies to doctrinal adherence to trading regulations. Such a tendency may lead to differential application of remedies, where certain industries or sectors get special treatment based on national interest or political lobbying, rather than neutral criteria. For example, during times of economic duress, governments may relax anti-dumping measures to facilitate cheaper imports, which might be at the expense of local industry. Such unequal application not only undermines public trust but also fosters an environment in which compliance is inconsistent, thus making the marketplace unstable. Such inconsistency may even complicate negotiation within global trade agreements, where countries attempt to protect their interests within the bounds of previously agreed-on commitments, highlighting the need for having more specific guidelines and more dynamic governance mechanisms. Lastly, the complexity of global trade agreements is yet another degree of complexity in effective compliance and enforcement. Trade agreements, particularly those arranged by organizations like the World Trade Organization, often have loopholes that nations looking for loopholes to circumvent their obligations exploit. The incomplete nature of such agreements puts countries in most instances to grapple with ambiguous provisions and uncertain terms, which lead to misinterpretations that could escalate into trade disputes. The safeguards clause in Article XIX of GATT is intended to provide mechanisms for countries to withdraw trade liberalization concessions temporarily due to unforeseen circumstances. However, the realizability of invoking such a clause most frequently results in contentious negotiations where the targeted actors sense they have been ill remunerated for the recapture behavior of their trading partners, which exacerbates tensions in a trading relation (Schropp et al., 2025). In the absence of enforceable regimes and reliable compliance patterns, the effectiveness of trade remedies and protection is largely lost.

SUMMARY

The disagreement over trade remedies and safeguards thus also directs attention to the thin line between protecting industries locally and obeying global trade commitments. As countries navigate the intricacies of trade policy, the deployment of tools such as antidumping actions and countervailing duties can strain the multilateral trading system. While such remedies shield vulnerable sectors from foreign competition, their routine exposure to the WTO dispute settlement process reveals a regular inconsistency with agreed commitments. This suggests that while trade remedies are created to be protectionist tools, they tend to spiral into trade disputes that ultimately end up undermining the very liberalization measures that are meant to guarantee trading efficiency on the global front (Bown et al., 2025). Furthermore, the efficacy of protective measures is contingent upon their design and implementation, which is of top priority for states seeking more policy autonomy. The concept of ex post regret in trade agreements underscores the significance of procedures for countries to respond to unanticipated economic occurrences. In such situations, the safeguards clause provides an orderly procedure for the temporary withdrawal of concessions made in trade liberalization. By offering countries the option to apply protective interventions in the event of unexpected adversity, the WTO model would be endeavoring to encourage a pragmatic strategy towards trade policy that acknowledges the inherently dynamic character of international markets. The never-ending debate regarding how to best conceive of these mechanisms nevertheless remains crucial to enhancing compliance and building accountability in trade relations (Schropp et al., 2025). The ongoing exploration of trade remedies and safeguards reflects a broader debate concerning the future of global trade policy. As nations are finding it increasingly difficult to reconcile the twin aims of protecting domestic interests with a focus on free trade, calls for an integrated framework to deal with protectionist measures become more evident. The relationship between domestic pressure and international commitments has the tendency to come up with complex situations that challenge policymakers. As the world economy evolves, the WTO might need to refine existing trade remedy tools so that they become effective without descending into protectionism that ultimately retards economic growth. It is necessary to understand the rationale for instituting such remedies and their consequences, which could be a starting point for more discussion on how to make the world of international trade more harmonious (Bown et al., 2025; Schropp et al., 2025).

With the existing situation of global trade, safeguards and trade remedies have emerged as the major steps taken by countries to address the effect of unfair competition. Of these, antidumping actions are particularly prevalent, with some of the world's largest importing nations in the World Trade Organization (WTO) system utilizing them to restrict the flow of goods that are regarded as being valued below market. Interestingly, although such remedies are frequently in the spotlight and contested under the WTO, why more cases are not brought to formal proceedings is unclear. There is evidence that the economic interests at stake, combined with the potential for reciprocal retaliation, play a significant role in influencing WTO members' decisions to challenge or not challenge the application of American trade remedies, and that this is the result of a sophisticated interaction between economic and legal incentives (Bown et al., 2025). Trade agreements lean toward aligning with the imposition of trade remedies, as seen in the case of the U.S.-South Korean Free Trade Agreement (KORUS FTA), where one finds the delicate balance of promoting trade and enforcing safeguards. In 2007, the KORUS FTA was signed with the vision to eliminate tariffs for a variety of manufactured products while addressing sensitive sectors such as agriculture and automobiles where trade remedies are rampant. The agreements' negotiations underscored the trade-offs of liberalization against the interests of affected domestic industry. Indeed, various groups, including automaker and steel producer groups, had expressed concerns regarding the potential for unfair trade practice. Discontent from such groups therefore best describes the balance between the benefits of free trade and protection of domestic industry, revealing the complex dynamics of global trade policy (Cooney et al., 2008). The implications of trade remedy measures are even broader than the provisions of individual agreements and responses to unfair trade. They are a more widespread policy instrument that nations use in an effort to protect domestic industry as globalization happens. Such instruments not only shelter home-grown firms but influence diplomatic relations and alliances, as with the relationship between the U.S. and South Korea. The KORUS FTA debate, including concessions and leverage, describes how policy and economic interaction can be informed by trade remedies. Moreover, as players in the global market move in and about such efforts, their decisions bear not just implications for trade flows but for the overall functionality and stability of global relations, emphasizing the complex nature of trade remedies and safeguards in economic systems (Bown et al., 2025; Cooney et al., 2008).

REFERENCES

1. Anonymous. (2025). Abstracts: Policy Research Working Papers Series - Numbers 3540–3650. https://core.ac.uk/download/pdf/6522054.pdf (accessed on 30th October 2025).
2. Bown, C. P. (2025). Trade remedies and World Trade Organization dispute settlement: Why are so few challenged? https://core.ac.uk/download/pdf/6719600.pdf (accessed on 30th October 2025).
3. Bown, C. P., & McCulloch, R. (2025). U.S. trade policy and the adjustment process. https://core.ac.uk/download/pdf/7177625.pdf (accessed on 30th October 2025).
4. Chisik, R. (2025). Trade disputes, quality choice, and economic integration. https://core.ac.uk/download/pdf/6698758.pdf (accessed on 30th October 2025).
5. Cooney, S., Cooper, W. H., Jones, V. C., Jurenas, R., et al. (2008). The proposed U.S.-South Korea Free Trade Agreement (KORUS FTA): Provisions and implications. https://core.ac.uk/download/5129465.pdf (accessed on 30th October 2025).
6. Dari, T. T. (2018). A critical assessment of Zimbabwe's anti-dumping laws. https://core.ac.uk/download/200282905.pdf (accessed on 30th October 2025).
7. Dhar, S., & Finger, M. J. (2025). Do rules control power? GATT articles and arrangements in the Uruguay Round. https://core.ac.uk/download/pdf/6521558.pdf (accessed on 30th October 2025).
8. El Said, M., & Kapczynski, A. (2012). Access to medicines: The role of intellectual property law and policy. https://core.ac.uk/download/42137810.pdf (accessed on 30th October 2025).
9. Febriza, S. (2023). Langkah WTO menyelesaikan sengketa pembatasan impor daging sapi dan hortikultura antara Indonesia terhadap Amerika Serikat. https://core.ac.uk/download/620927384.pdf (accessed on 30th October 2025).
10. Francois, J., & Stöllinger, R. (2009). New shades of protectionism and the role of multinationals. https://www.econstor.eu/bitstream/10419/121873/1/FIW_PolicyBrief_02en.pdf (accessed on 30th October 2025).
11. Gallagher, K. P., Porterfield, M. C., & Van Harten, G. (2015). Investment provisions in trade and investment treaties: The need for reform. https://open.bu.edu/bitstream/2144/23387/1/Investor-State-Disputes-Policy-Brief.pdf (accessed on 30th October 2025).
12. Gallagher, K., & Stanley, L. (2012). Global financial reform and trade rules:

The need for reconciliation. https://open.bu.edu/bitstream/2144/22732/1/Pardee-IIB-024-Sept-2012.pdf (accessed on 30th October 2025).

13. Goodrich, B., & Hufbauer, G. C. (2025). Steel policy: The good, the bad, and the ugly. https://core.ac.uk/download/pdf/6454285.pdf (accessed on 30th October 2025).
14. Lovett, W. A. (2000). The WTO: A train wreck in progress? https://core.ac.uk/download/144229623.pdf (accessed on 30th October 2025).
15. Martin, L. J., & Mussell, A. (2025). Firm-level forces underlying concentration in agriculture. https://core.ac.uk/download/pdf/6407350.pdf (accessed on 30th October 2025).
16. Matthews, A. (2025). Economic partnership agreements and food security. https://core.ac.uk/download/pdf/6297974.pdf (accessed on 30th October 2025).
17. Pauwelyn, J. H. B. (2006). How strongly should we protect and enforce international law? *University of Chicago Law School Workshop, March 2006*. https://core.ac.uk/download/62562448.pdf (accessed on 30th October 2025).
18. Rajapatirana, S. (2025). Post trade liberalization policy and institutional challenges in Latin America and the Caribbean. https://core.ac.uk/download/pdf/6644619.pdf (accessed on 30th October 2025).
19. Schropp, S. (2025). Revisiting the "compliance-vs.-rebalancing" debate in WTO scholarship: A unified research agenda. https://core.ac.uk/download/pdf/6513505.pdf (accessed on 30th October 2025).
20. Schropp, S., & Mahlstein, K. (2025). The optimal design of trade policy flexibility in the WTO. https://core.ac.uk/download/pdf/6513480.pdf (accessed on 30th October 2025).
21. Tiller, E. H., & de Figueiredo, J. M. (2025). The structure and conduct of corporate lobbying: How firms lobby the Federal Communications Commission. https://core.ac.uk/download/pdf/6586665.pdf (accessed on 30th October 2025).
22. Voon, T. (2010). Eliminating trade remedies from the WTO: Lessons from regional trade agreements. https://core.ac.uk/download/70373369.pdf (accessed on 30th October 2025).
23. Wainio, J., & Young, L. M. (2025). The antidumping negotiations: Proposals, positions and antidumping profiles. https://core.ac.uk/download/pdf/7035249.pdf (accessed on 30th October 2025).

Chapter 8

Dispute Settlement Mechanism

Contents

INTRODUCTION

International dispute settlement mechanisms have developed to become the core aspect of contemporary global governance. Historically, such institutions were confined to such limited definitions of inter-governmentalism and formal legalism, which explicitly dealt with relations between states. A revolutionary process is underway, as international institutions move towards wider frameworks which emphasize accountability, transparency, and popular participation. This broader constitutional emphasis stimulates the establishment of new grievance and complaint procedures that extend beyond traditional legal mechanisms, indicating a healthily assertive reaction to the complexities of modern international relations. Such transparent measures enhance legitimacy while enabling meaningful governance of international institutions, such that the need for flexible mechanisms in dispute settlement is greater than ever before (French et al., 2009).

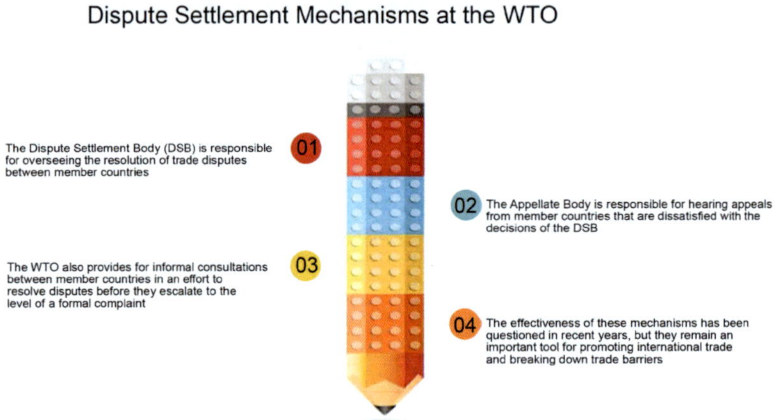

Figure 8.1. Dispute settlement mechanism (DSM).

Source: https://fastercapital.co/i/Breaking-Down-Trade-Barriers--Understanding-the-WTO-s-Efforts--Dispute-Settlement-Mechanisms-at-the-WTO.webp.

In addition, the emergence of second-generation international tribunals is a break from normative models of adjudication. While conventional bodies like the International Court of Justice are seen as helpless to deliver binding decisions, these newer tribunals have managed to capitalize on viable jurisdictions with the capacity to render enforceable judgments. Characterized by their capacity to confer compulsory jurisdiction, they have disseminated at light speed, particularly in fields of international commercial law and investment arbitration. Their evolution demonstrates their importance, not only in facilitating cross-border transactions, but also in solidifying a more advanced appreciation of the international laws functional capacity. Through their greater utilization, second-generation tribunals debunk the traditional narrative of international adjudication as powerless and suggest a paradigm change in states' reaction to international law (Born et al., 2012). With greater progression of globalization, the need for efficient and resolute mechanisms of settling conflicts increases. The dialogue between the international courts and tribunals and domestic legal regimes reveals a complex scenario of overlapping jurisdictions often challenging new methodologies in conflict resolution. New mechanisms are not ex post facto developments of existing patterns but, rather, expressions of responsive governance adapting to transformed international relations patterns. These developments reflect the need for an effective system of dispute resolution commensurate with the aspirations of an interdependent global order. Through both established and emerging structures under this framework, the debate on mechanisms for dispute settlement has the potential to provide us with highly pertinent information about how they can promote peace, stability, and cooperation among states, ultimately shaping the future of international jurisprudence (French et al., 2009) (Figure 8.1).

Definition of Dispute Settlement Mechanism (DSM)

The concept of a DSM is at the core of the successful functioning of international trade agreements, particularly because it helps maintain an order of resolving trade practice disputes, tariffs, and other economic activity-related conflicts in an orderly way and judicially, promoting fairness and cooperation between nations. Institutions like the World Trade Organization (WTO) have had DSMs that have formal arbitration and adjudication processes, and a legal framework for dispute settlement. If disputes are not resolved properly, states may resort to unilateral actions, which can escalate tensions and destroy the norms of free trade. Hence, an efficient DSM needs to inculcate a culture of predictability and stability in foreign trade relationships. The DSM is also employed to protect the rights of foreign investors under other agreements on trade. A case in point is the North American Free Trade Agreement (NAFTA), whose provisions allow investors to dispute government behavior deemed to be against their interests. As highlighted, business interests have employed these mechanisms to seek billions in damages, underlining the extensive implications of such dispute clauses on public health initiatives and local policies. Balancing investor right protection and government regulatory freedom is no simple task, as is illustrated by the growing backlash against investor-state dispute settlements. Such mechanisms are argued to undermine local legal frameworks and favor the interests of foreign businesses at the expense of the public good. Therefore, the differentiation and application of DSM assume a vital role in navigating such complex legal interfaces without compromising fair solutions. Furthermore, the evolving nature of international trade dynamics requires a re-examination of current DSM architectures. The standstill in the Doha Round negotiations is a symbol of the challenges facing the WTO to adapt to new global economic realities, such as the rise of international production networks and increasing non-tariff barriers. With the value of maintaining an evenhanded regime of investments and of pursuing trade facilitation comes also an increasing need for DSMs capable of solving these contemporary issues. New disciplines that account for these complexities can enhance the effectiveness of processes of resolving disputes so that more diverse and dynamic outcomes of international trade conflicts are possible. As explained in some academic controversy, enhanced DSMs can better respond to a progressively developing global market, ultimately enhancing the role of institutions engaged in facilitating international economic cooperation (Dhar et al., 2013).

Importance in International Relations

The importance of international mechanisms for the settlement of disputes cannot be overstressed, as they form essential frameworks for the resolution of inter-state disputes. Such mechanisms, particularly those under institutions such as the WTO, not only facilitate enforcement of trade agreements but also promote predictability and stability of global economic relations. As nations become more interdependent, so is there a greater chance of disputes arising; thus, a structured process of settlement is vital. However, there are patterns that can be seen indicating that there are certain regions, namely the Arab world, which are not taking full part in such systems. Volume of trade, poor technical know-how, and fiscal constraints are barriers to their full participation, thus their failure to benefit from these systems (Malkawi et al., 2012). Facilitating participation can empower such countries so that their voices will be heard on the global front. Moreover, the evolution of international trade agreements further underscores the significance of international dispute settlement in international affairs. Recent negotiations, such as the proposed China-GCC Free Trade Agreement, serve as testament to the complicated nature involved within regional trade unions. A robust mechanism for dispute settlement can be a powerful tool for conflict resolution, through which the parties can resolve disputes in a constructive manner. Opportunities and challenges of such arrangements underscore the significance of a smooth mechanism of dispute resolution to settle potential disputes arising under it (Puig et al., 2017). By fostering cooperative relations, such mechanisms provide for the de-escalation of tensions among partners in trade so that regional stability as a whole is fostered and additional economic cooperation promoted. With these considerations in mind, the role of dispute settlement mechanisms extends beyond mere conflict resolution; it plays an important role in determining diplomatic relations among nations. As nations become more reliant on advanced mechanism of trade, an efficient dispute resolution process can be a stimulus towards the building of trust and long-term relationships. Enhanced participation by hitherto underrepresented states, such as those of the Arab world, through recognized mechanisms could lead to a more balanced international environment of trade.

These states' active involvement in dispute settlement processes can not only make their voice more audible in international negotiations but also balance the international system by encouraging cooperation, rather than confrontation. The emphasis on strengthening such institutions is thus still of central importance as the international community confronts the challenges of today's interdependent political economy (Figure 8.2).

Figure 8.2. Importance in international relations.

Source: https://encrypted-tbn0.gstatic.com/images?q=tbn:ANd9GcT0FXbsktGhJhAZwCYjKwBjHqA7E8dGJdrIlQ&s.

8.1. HISTORICAL CONTEXT

The historical background of mechanisms of dispute resolution is shaped by both the classic and contemporary legal systems, which have evolved over time in response to the complexity of international relations and inter-state conflict. Since the earliest days of diplomacy, states have employed a variety of methods of settlement of disputes ranging from bargaining and mediation to more formalized processes of arbitration. These mechanisms have evolved from great events in history, such as the institution of the United Nations and the codification of international law following World War II. Greater development of world institutions towards peace promotion revealed the need to have organized resolution of conflicts, leading to the creation of mechanisms that would ensure impartiality and fairness in conflict resolution. As governments progress through the intricacies of global diplomacy, their own historical experience of resolving conflict continues to inform and guide contemporary practice, presenting us with a rich source of information on how successful contemporary frameworks are. The history of the Universal Water Tribunal (UWT) reflects the traditional trend toward more participatory methods of conflict resolution, beyond the traditional state-sponsored models. Emerging in the early part of the 21st century, the UWT seeks to address environmental disputes, the majority of which are related to water resources, by bringing state and non-state actors into the legal establishment.

Figure 8.3. The historical context of dispute settlement mechanisms.

Source: https://i.ytimg.com/vi/aMUqVTs6_O4/hq720.jpg?sqp=-oaymwE7CK-4FEIIDSFryq4qpAy0IARUAAAAAGAElAADIQj0AgKJD8AEB-AHUBoAC4A-OKAgwIABABGGUgVihKMA8=&rs=AOn4CLCwCLtLK1rUyKdVQvwjRRkVKgO8OA.

This is in recognition that the traditional interstate conflict resolution mechanism has, in most cases, left behind the voices of local communities and persons adversely affected by environmental degradation. In facilitating the participation of these state-less actors to present their arguments in a formalized court setting, the UWT represents a massive diversion from how conflicts are resolved in the larger arena of social justice and environmental law. With states being confronted by increasingly sophisticated environmental challenges, the historical evolution of such mechanisms to date further testifies to the need for innovative frameworks that can absorb different stakeholder interests in the resolution process (Majzoub et al., 2018). Also, the development of mechanisms for dispute resolution has been influenced by technological advancement and societal norms. For instance, information technology has transformed the way disputes are resolved and dealt with, through real-time access to information and remote access to adjudicative procedures. At the same time, the changing attitudes of cultures toward justice and responsibility have shaped the expectations of individuals and states to be increasingly transparent and inclusive in settling disputes. The introduction of new techniques, such as the algorithmic techniques discussed in more current research, captures the growing concern with efficiency and precision in legal processes, especially relevant to environmental conflicts (Abbott et al., 1999). With these technological and social advancements on the go, they form integral parts in constructing the backdrop of dispute settlement mechanisms, hence enabling better and more equitable settlements in the future (Figure 8.3).

8.1.1. Evolution of Dispute Settlement Mechanisms

The evolution of dispute settlement mechanisms has largely been influenced by the dynamics of evolving international trade and diplomacy. The establishment of the General Agreement on Tariffs and Trade (GATT) in the post-World War II period was a milestone in international economic relations. It aimed at reducing the barriers to trade while providing a forum for resolution of trade disputes by consultation and negotiation. But as global interdependence grows, the failings of GATT in managing disputes became apparent, and the World Trade Organization (WTO) was formed in 1995. The WTO introduced a more structured and formal mechanism for resolving disputes, an indication of the growing realization of the need for robust mechanisms in ensuring effective management of escalating trade tensions, as experienced through the challenges in the global trading system (Jackson et al., 2000). The features of design inherent in the WTO's system of dispute settlement have contributed both to its strengthening and to complicating its operation. Underlying its success are precepts such as obligatory compliance and the right of appeal, which have seemingly boosted the process of resolution into greater efficiency and reliability. But trade tensions are mounting, and a record number of disputes are being filed with the WTO, evidencing continuing institutional flaws. Such factors such as unequal power dynamics between member countries and procedural complexities may discourage fair treatment of all parties involved. This necessitates careful examination of how institutions of dispute settlement may be enhanced and made readily accessible, particularly for developing countries that may lack the ability and means to navigate the complex regulations of international trade (Nelson et al., 2025). As globalization speeds up, the efficiency of institutions for resolving disputes must keep up with the dynamic nature of global relations. New challenges such as electronic commerce, environmental protection standards, and public health issues call for adaptive mechanisms that can face contemporary challenges. The attempts of the WTO to modernize have raised controversy over the reform of its dispute settlement bodies, particularly in the face of the impact of recent geopolitical tensions. The organization is being pressured to better represent the interests of developing countries and to make certain that member states can contribute constructively to the process of dispute settlement. This follows larger trends in global governance, in which inclusiveness and equity are key to maintaining stability in the international trading system. The debate of these reforms presents an opportunity to formulate mechanisms that resolve not just conflicts but also foster cooperative relationships among all stakeholders (Jackson et al., 2000).

8.1.2. Key Historical Treaties and Agreements

International law has been influenced significantly by significant historical treaties and agreements, which established frameworks for mechanisms of dispute settlement. An example of this is the Treaty of Westphalia, which in 1648 was agreed to and brought an end to the 30 Years War. It initiated a new international relation era and set the precedent for the sovereignty of states and territorial integrity as the basis for modern diplomacy and methods of resolving differences. Through the establishment of sovereign equality between states, the Westphalian system provided for the formation of a range of different international treaties for resolving conflict. Through the course of history, the system has developed, with later treaties creating more formalized and binding mechanisms through arbitration and adjudication, thereby redefining states' approaches to resolving conflict and ensuring the rule of law around the world. In the 20th century, the formation of different international tribunals was a turning point in the epoch of dispute settlement. Herding the anarchic consequences of international conflicts, agreements like the United Nations Charter facilitated the establishment of organizations like the International Court of Justice (ICJ). Although the ICJ is often faulted for lacking jurisdiction and strong enforcement powers, it constitutes a milestone towards internationalizing international law and resolving disputes. The post-World War II era also witnessed a proliferation of multilateral treaties to govern a variety of matters from trade to human rights. This second-generation spread of international tribunals, as criticized in Born et al. (2012), has drawn immense attention for their ability to provide enforceable awards and enforce state compliance, thereby enhancing the effectiveness of international legal institutions. The contemporary challenges of international mechanisms of dispute settlement reveal ongoing complexities that are worth studying in a constitutional perspective. As Helfer et al. (2003) defined, decentralization and compliance problems point to the intricate relationship between treaties and the evolving needs of international governance. Various treaties such as those for international trade and the environment bear witness to the dependency on strong compliance and accountability mechanisms among states. However, these arrangements primarily lack innate flaws in enforcement, raising substantial concerns regarding their legitimacy and effectiveness. The setbacks and successes of past agreements hint at the necessity of ongoing evolution and adaptation in international legal systems, prompting scholars to reconsider the role of constitutional analogies in understanding the new international legal world and the ongoing quest for equitable conflict resolution (Figure 8.4).

Figure 8.4. Key historical treaties and agreements.

Source: https://bestedlessons.org/wp-content/uploads/2023/12/Treaty-of-Brussels-1948-Signing.jpg.

8.1.3. Impact of Historical Conflicts on Current Mechanisms

The shadows of previous conflicts can be strongly felt in contemporary mechanisms of dispute resolution, often shaping their form and efficacy. Past grievances are part of a heritage of suspicion and enmity, potentially contributing to inefficacious negotiating and resolution processes. In conflict-prone areas, outcomes of previous disputes will shape the frameworks in which current conflicts are addressed, limiting the potential for resolution. This can manifest itself as a reliance upon tried and tested rules of thumb—easy heuristics involving past experience rather than rigid scientific dogma. Designers, for example, will reach to the old models in order to tackle challenging issues, a mismatch between demands for technology and the knowledge pool. As explained in the critique of technological practices, the application of such variable yet simple mechanisms would provide temporary solutions but are incapable of confronting the intricacies of evolving wars and emphasize the need for a more complex appreciation of historical accounts within contemporary paradigms (Chang et al., 2004). With ongoing resource and territory disputes still defining modern governance issues, it becomes clear that a historical perspective plays a pivotal role in the comprehension of the present mechanisms. The dynamics between persistent land conflicts and past grievances highlight an overarching governance challenge. Present interventions focus mainly on conflict management rather than seeking deep conflict resolution. This. This strategy is not sufficiently, since it does not address well the underlying power dynamics and history context underpinning these conflicts. Also, with no integrative political measures that recognize the depth of conflict such as identity narratives and aspirations for territory, mechanisms for resolving disputes might lack the relative depth to achieve long-lasting peace. Here, the integration of historical knowledge requires consideration, guiding more holistic governance interventions and constructing a more sustainable path of resolution (Mathys et al., 2016). The complexities of historical conflicts necessitate the development of mechanisms of dispute settlement that use lessons from the past. As societies try to rebuild and heal, memory of past conflict finds expression in institutional structures that predispose them to favor traditional styles of negotiation or mediation. These styles can perpetuate patterns of violence unintentionally if they do not adapt to address the specifics of the present moment. Through observing how past conflicts have shaped current mechanisms, stakeholders can identify the limitations of practices that exist and implement new approaches that are inclusive and equitable. Also, understanding how past narratives shape identities makes possible a more complex resolution to conflict that recognizes the needs of differing groups. By doing so, modern systems can overcome the limitations of their ancestors, eventually creating a milieu conducive to resolution and durable peace (Chang et al., 2004; Mathys et al., 2016).

8.2. TYPES OF DISPUTE SETTLEMENT MECHANISMS

The range of mechanisms for resolving disputes in the international order enhances the ability of states to resolve differences effectively and bring stability. Among the mechanisms, diplomatic negotiation ranks first and is most desired because it enables the parties to negotiate settlements peacefully without passing through formal adjudication. Negotiated settlements foster cooperation and common understanding and allow states to design solutions sensitive to their respective interests. But if parties cannot reach consensus by negotiation, then other processes such as conciliation and mediation step in. These entail third-party intermediaries who serve as middlemen between opposing parties to oversee a better structured dialogue that can be probable to yield acceptable results. Though diplomatic negotiation and mediation succeed in the beginning, their reliance on the benevolence of states at times leads to recurring conflicts, necessitating more structured processes of resolution. Besides diplomacy, there are established formal legal mechanisms in which states are obligated to resolve conflicts using structured processes. Arbitration is perhaps the best-known form of formal conflict resolution, in which an impartial panel delivers a binding decision based on evidence and arguments presented by each party. Arbitration's drawback is speed and enforceability of resulting awards, typically kept by international agreements such as the New York Convention. Yet, arbitration hinges on the collaboration of states in maintaining its outcomes.

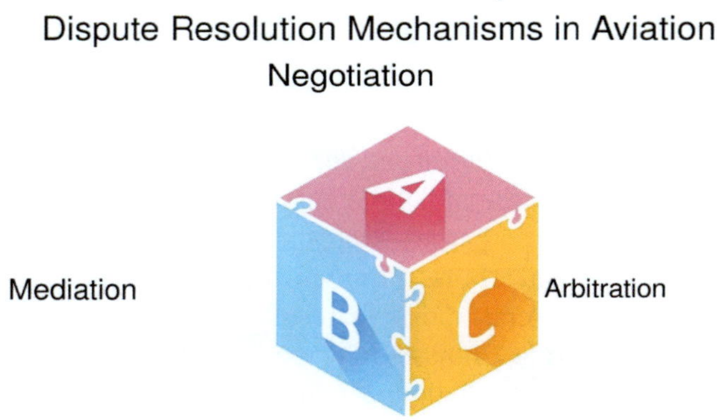

Figure 8.5. Types of dispute settlement mechanisms.

Source: https://fastercapital.co/i/Aviation-Legal-Training-Services--How-to-Navigate-the-Legal-Aspects-and-Issues-in-Aviation--Dispute-Resolution-Mechanisms-in-Aviation.webp.

This sort of wholeness occurs, for instance, in international business, where expert arbitration institutions settle particular disputes arising out of intricate legal and regulatory frameworks. Thus, while arbitration offers a viable alternative to simple negotiation, its application may still be vulnerable to greater geopolitical forces, as evidenced by the nuances that exist in international business disputes. Judicial processes, particularly in the case of international law, exemplify a more advanced process of conflict settlement outside the confines of bilateral relations. The International Court of Justice (ICJ) and the

World Trade Organization (WTO) dispute settlement mechanism are instances of institutionalized processes of conflict resolution. These courts create a forum for adjudication, providing authoritative definitions of international law and an avenue for grievance redressal that may not be possible otherwise. Yet, as the debate around judicial independence indicates, the efficacy of these institutions can be undermined by political pressures and states' resistance to complying with judicial decisions. For example, the recent setbacks for the WTO in its efforts to ensure its legitimacy have reawakened discussions regarding the necessity for institutional reforms. Particularly, the advocates of limited independence contend that while designs of judiciary have the potential to consolidate commitments and enhance predictability in international transactions, structural changes may be necessary to enhance their effectiveness and legitimacy in the situation of evolving world order dynamics, such as emphasized by recent studies Basedow et al. (2018) and Helfer et al. (2005) (Figure 8.5).

8.2.1. Diplomatic Negotiation

Diplomatic negotiation is of supreme relevance in the institutional frameworks established for mechanisms to settle disputes. Diplomatic negotiation is all about dialogue and accommodation and seeks to bridge ideological differences between fighting parties. Successful diplomatic negotiations are predicated upon a deep understanding of each parties interests and the power dynamics at play. In modern-day international affairs, activities like trade agreements demonstrate how negotiations can generate positive results for all involved parties. The current negotiations for the China-GCC Free Trade Agreement are evidence of the possible gains that negotiations could produce when customized to suit the needs of the involved parties, including improving economic relationships and mutual interests. The complexity involved in negotiating such exchanges highlights the necessity of diplomacy being carried out with tact and crystallized strategy, reflecting how capable negotiators are able to negotiate solutions that would otherwise seem unattainable (Puig et al., 2017). Further, the strategies for resolving conflicts typically involve consensus-building strategies based on cooperative negotiation processes. In intra-regional conflicts, institutions like ASEAN bear witness to the success of diplomatic negotiation towards conflict resolution. The Thailand-Cambodia border dispute is a classic example where diplomacy, with the support of ASEAN, came out with a peaceful settlement through negotiation and mediation. These initiatives bear witness to the value of institutionally designed dialogue processes that encourage parties to sit down at the negotiating table with the promise of consensus within sight. This particular case points out that diplomatic negotiation is not so much about wielding power, but creating atmospheres of cooperation and understanding. By employing diverse tactics such as shuttle diplomacy and informal meetings between foreign ministers, regional blocs can effectively resolve differences while maintaining stability and peace in the region (Farida et al., 2014). Lastly, the success of diplomatic negotiation in settlement mechanisms is highly contingent on how willing the participants are to engage in constructive dialogue and find middle ground. Negotiation skill not only involves effective communication but also empathetic approaches toward understanding conflicting opinions. Each dispute's complexities, including historical grievances or cultural sensitivities, have to be skillfully managed for constructive solutions to prevail. Furthermore, establishing a foundation of rapport and trust among negotiating parties is important, as it fosters a more co-operative setting. Amidst conflicts still propagating across geopolitical realms, the role of diplomatic negotiation in forming peaceful resolution continues to remain unequivocally essential. More awareness of negotiation styles and forms can empower states to resolve their conflicts without violence, ultimately fostering global co-operation and stability (Figure 8.6).

Figure 8.6. Diplomatic negotiation.

Source: https://www.shutterstock.com/image-photo/international-relations-diplomats-talking-during-600nw-2501774411.jpg.

8.2.2. Mediation and Conciliation

Mediation and conciliation are central processes in the realm of mechanisms for managing disputes that transcend conventional channels of litigation. Through them, collaborative problem-solving is encouraged, which allows disputing parties to engage freely in discussion as a third party serves as a facilitator.

Unlike adversarial systems that have the tendency to escalate tensions, mediation provides a platform in which parties can articulate their interests and concerns, thus foster better mutual understanding of one another. As other authors have suggested, including those who have written on whistleblowing disputes, such new ways of managing disputes can be able to efficiently resolve complaints likely to linger through formal legal processes, and ultimately benefit a more peaceful workplace environment (Lewis et al., 2013). Conciliation also improves mediation in the sense that, besides facilitating discussion, it provides advice on how to resolve issues.

Figure 8.7. Mediation and conciliation.

Source: https://i0.wp.com/lawtimesjournal.in/wp-content/uploads/2019/01/conciliation-Mediation.jpg?fit=696%2C341&ssl=1.

The process is particularly helpful in complex conflicts where parties may struggle to identify points of agreement or are experiencing a massive emotional trauma. That way, through the use of a conciliator, parties can be convinced to revisit their positions and devise innovative solutions that will accommodate all. The success of conciliation is reflected in various labor-management relations cases, where legal frameworks such as the National Labor Relations Act allow for the application of such procedures. Especially in cases of labor disputes, promoting conciliation can prevent lengthy and costly disputes while fostering better employer-employee relations (Hegji et al., 2012). Not only are mediation and conciliation efficient substitutes for litigation, but they also promote a culture of resolution by following dialogue over conflict. The adoption of these methods into formal processes of dispute resolution tends to result in more enduring settlements because the working environment allows for trust and ownership of solutions to develop. As the current body of research on whistleblower policies implies, the incorporation of mediation and conciliation into organizational channels for resolving conflict can improve compliance with workplace transparency while minimizing adverse effects of retaliation against whistleblowers (Lewis et al., 2013). Therefore, the encouragement of such alternative dispute resolution tools is important not only in resolving pressing complaints but also in promoting an effective setting that promotes ethical conduct and open communication in various industries (Figure 8.7).

8.2.3. Arbitration and Adjudication

The escalating complexity and expense of construction disputes highlight the imperative of effective processes for settling disputes like adjudication and arbitration. The conventional processes tend to result in lengthy litigation that can heighten tensions between parties, slow down business relations, and raise overall expenses. In a sector where high-value projects coexist with a high prevalence of disputes, the inefficiencies of the customary procedure can prove very damaging. More and more stakeholders now realize the weaknesses of such traditional channels, triggering the move towards alternative means, particularly ADR processes such as arbitration. As suggested in contemporary literature, the urgency for rapid and low-cost solutions has become imperative in mitigating the negative impacts of conflicts on reputations and business relationships within the construction sector, further justifying the value of arbitration in resolving conflict promptly and effectively (Agapiou et al., 2012). Adjudication has also proven to be a vital mechanism within the sphere of dispute resolution, particularly in international law and commerce. As opposed to the conventional litigation, with its concomitant certainty of jurisdiction and enforceability, adjudication by international tribunals is more accommodative in character. Recently, there has been identification of a new generation of international adjudicative institutions, which poses great alternatives to the conventional tribunals. Second-generation tribunals, such as investment and commercial tribunals, have been of very great effectiveness in settling disputes. Their increasing application suggests a widespread shift towards binding awards and obligatory jurisdiction, reshaping the way in which states and entities interact within international law. Their use can facilitate cooperative outcomes that favor international trade and investment, highlighting their part in the broader dispute settlement environment (Born et al., 2012). Despite the clear advantage of arbitration and adjudication in dispute resolution, challenges remain to their uptake and function. Parties can resist relinquishing conventional approaches, frequently because they are not familiar with or do not perceive risks in new procedures. Additionally, the cultural and legislative environments within which these instruments apply can contribute to their adoption and use. In sectors like construction, where the use of personal contacts and established practices endures, a cultural transformation may be required to move toward arbitration or adjudication. To implement specific measures to raise awareness and insight into these mechanisms could bridge such impediments, paving the way for wider acceptance. With mediation and other forms of alternative approaches gaining prominence in different zones, including the construction industry in Scotland, their promulgation could strengthen the effective application of arbitration and adjudication in different contexts towards more streamlined resolution of disputes (Agapiou et al., 2012) (Figure 8.8).

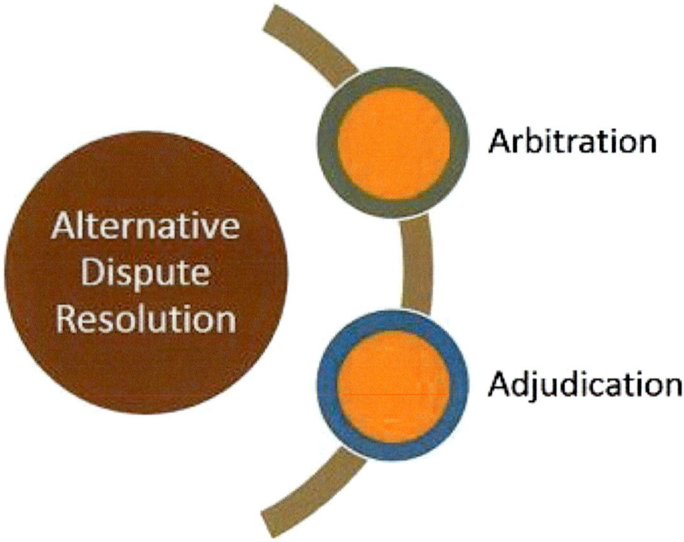

Figure 8.8. Arbitration and adjudication.

Source: https://keydifferences.com/wp-content/uploads/2021/05/arbitration-vs-adjudication.jpg.

8.3. ROLE OF INTERNATIONAL ORGANIZATIONS

International organizations play a crucial role in the effective management and resolution of conflict between states and other agents of the international system. They provide frameworks that facilitate negotiation and dialogue, allowing parties to conflict to resolve their conflicts without fighting or resorting to unilateral actions. Through institutions like the United Nations, World Trade Organization, and regional bodies, states can bargain multilaterally in a manner conducive to cooperative solutions. This not only serves to sustain world order but also fosters trust and security among states. Their ability to solve disputes may lead to more long-lasting solutions since groups are more likely to agree to those that come out of an agreed process than the application of violence or coercion. Aside from facilitating negotiations, international organizations now have the aspects of redress for injustice and accountability as part of their functions, with their actions aligned with aspects of good governance and more legitimacy. The evolution of such mechanisms marks a shift away from strict inter-governmentalism towards more flexible alignments that consider the interests of various stakeholders such as non-governmental organizations and civil society. As French et al. (2009) portray, concepts like transparency and public involvement have become key in the functioning of such institutions. This shift not only empowers individuals and groups affected by decisions of international governance but also enhances the legitimacy of the organizations themselves. By providing channels of complaint and grievance, international organizations are actively engaging with the power dynamics normally inherent in disputes, and thereby enhancing the wider dispute resolution landscape. Furthermore, the role of international organizations in the resolution of disputes is illustrated in how they influence in specific fields, i.e., intellectual property rights. The World Trade Organization's Agreement on Trade-Related Intellectual Property Rights (TRIPS) is a good example, particularly for countries such as China that have been evaluated for conformity to international standards. As Fojtíková et al. (2018) describe, observance of national legislation in terms of such agreements is relevant in that it ensures there exists an environment conducive to international business. Enforceable intellectual property rights minimize conflicts resulting from infringements and stimulate innovation, resulting in international economic stability. Therefore, international institutions not only serve as mediators in disputes but also help establish norms and standards influencing the actions of states to ensure that a collective method is in place to deal with conflicts at the international level.

8.3.1. United Nations (UN) and Its Agencies

The UN plays a critical role in international relations through its agencies, which address a spectrum of issues at the global level, including peace, security, and humanitarian aid. Of all its agencies, UNs involvement in conflict settlement mechanisms is significant as it seeks to forge dialogue and cooperation among member states for conflict resolution on peaceful terms. The UN provides a platform of negotiation and mediation, thereby enabling states to resolve their grievances without resorting to unilateral actions or armed interventions. Through understanding and dialogue, the UN and its agencies prevent conflicts and maintain international peace, which eventually contributes to increased global stability and security. Particularly, the functioning of the World Trade Organization (WTO), as a specialized UN agency, illustrates the complexity of international conflict resolution. The WTOs dispute settlement procedures are most often complimented on their formalistic approach, which provides a legal framework to the member countries that they can rely upon. The WTO Appellate Body, for example, has used its authority to perform judicial lawmaking, hence reducing trade barriers that otherwise would be difficult to address through normal negotiations. Such capacity, as much as it is unintended in the sense that it arose by setting an underspecified rulebook, highlights the importance of having a robust system to address disputes in a way that will ensure compliance by member states.

Figure 8.9. Specialized agencies of the United Nations (UN).

Source: https://www.99notes.in/wp-content/uploads/2025/04/specialized-agencies-of-UN.webp.

These tensions between political necessity and legal stringency are the grounds of WTO success within the UN's wider system of dispute settlement (Goldstein et al., 2008). Furthermore, the need for increased investigatory authority within the WTO's system of dispute settlement has been requested as a necessary sophistication in the response to evidentiary deficits. There exist significant differences in the ability of member states, particularly developing countries, to organize thorough records of disputes. Such an agency with a permanent mandate to conduct fact-finding would improve the quality of evidence submitted to resolve hearing disputes and thus the validity of the decision-making process. This would enable panels to seek necessary information, again accommodating the different capacities of member states while remaining impartial in the settlement of disputes. Ultimately, resolving these matters in the UNs agencies will be vital for improving the overall effectiveness of international mechanisms of dispute settlement and preserving the integrity of justice and fairness in foreign trade (Collins et al., 2006) (Figure 8.9).

8.3.2. World Trade Organization (WTO)'s Dispute Resolution

The WTO Dispute Settlement Mechanism (DRM) is a pillar of global regulation of trade, keeping member states under agreed trade rules. It begins with consultations, whereby parties are encouraged to resolve their issues amicably. This initial step is crucial, as informal communication of problems may be made prior to the case proceeding to formal hearing. According to the statistics on specific trade concerns (STCs), most of the trade issues could be addressed through communication, thus emphasizing the significance of communication towards avoiding conflicts. Between the years 1995 and the early stages of 2019, only a small percentage of notifications led to formal disputes, implying that the informal channels provided by the DRM significantly reduce the likelihood of conflict escalation (Wolfe et al., 2020).

Not only do these mechanisms foster cooperation but also guarantee the credibility of the WTO in overseeing fair international trade practices. In the event consultations fail, the case can proceed to a panel stage, where a panel of officials renders a decision on the basis of WTO agreements. The panels' report is important, as it considers both the legal aspects at stake and the facts that had informed their decision. Interestingly, the DRM has an appellate stage, which plays an important check against preliminary decisions by panels. These measures indicate the institutionalized process of the solving procedure, which aims for equilibrium between enforcing trade rules and variations in member states' contexts. Efficiency of this mechanism also creates issues of compliance and enforcement, the third challenge of international law. Lack of compliance by one party may erode the legitimacy of the system as a whole and trigger calls for stronger frameworks of governance to offer assurance of compliance with decisions (Helfer et al., 2003).

Moreover, the geopolitical context influences the effectiveness of the DRM within the WTO, as relations of power dictate the willingness of member states to seek resolution of disputes. The existence of uneven economic power can cause dynamics in which the poorer nations may not bring claims against the more powerful members because of fear of retaliation or inability. Such uneven balance of power raises legitimate concerns about democracy and legitimacy in the international legal system. As the trade disputes increasingly mirror underlying political tensions, it is imperative to redirect the dispute settlement structure to facilitate more justice and reinvigorate the confidence of all countries involved. Ultimately, the reforms can be invoked to address the structural challenges facing the credibility and efficacy of the DRM and establish a more equitable international trading framework (Helfer et al., 2003; Wolfe et al., 2020).

8.3.3. Regional Organizations and Their Mechanisms

In regional organizations, the mechanisms used by them for conflict resolution have transformed significantly, with a shift towards more holistic and answerable systems. Earlier models, which were primarily inter-governmental and legalistic, have gradually embraced broader constitutional values such as legitimacy and governance. This transformation has led to the acceptance of complaint and grievance mechanisms that enable individuals and groups to complain beyond the classical legal avenues. These trends are noteworthy in that they enhance the transparency and responsiveness of regional bodies, and as such, maximize their legitimacy among member states and the global community. The ongoing challenge is to harmonize these mechanisms with the established legal norms such that the disputes are resolved in an efficient manner without compromising the pillars of good governance and public participation as highlighted in current international relations discourses (French et al., 2009). Regional trade agreements (RTAs) provide a unique set of challenges to dispute settlement, particularly in combination with the World Trade Organization (WTO). As the number of RTAs grows, so does the complexity of their own respective dispute settlement mechanisms, which oftentimes coincide with those of the WTOs Dispute Settlement Understanding.

The most obvious example is the case of Brazil's import restrictions on retreaded tires, wherein the Appellate Body had to examine the interface between regional undertakings under MERCOSUR and WTO obligations. This case is illustrative of the potential contradictions that may arise due to differing legal interpretations under regional and international frameworks. Scholars have debated extensively on the implications of such overlaps, calling for more nuanced guidelines to govern the intricate relationship between RTAs and WTO rules so that trade policy remains equitable and legally defensible (Hillman et al., 2009). The efficacy of mechanisms of dispute settlement largely revolves around whether member states willing to react and accept such institutions as being legitimate. Mechanisms in regional institutions must be designed not merely to settle disputes but also encourage cooperation among member states by negotiations and dialogue. With greater emphasis on participation and accountability being placed by regional institutions, the adopted mechanisms have to remain faithful to these principles if they are to win the confidence of members. Success of the mechanisms depends partly on open processes which they encourage and how capable they are of adapting according to the changing global environment. Repeated re-evaluation and refinement of such frameworks will be necessary to address emerging conflicts and challenges, eventually enhancing the general stability and legitimacy of regional organizations within the international trading system (French et al., 2009) (Figure 8.10).

Figure 8.10. Regional organizations and their mechanisms.

Source: https://fastercapital.co/i/Countering-Protectionist-Policies--The-Role-of-Most-Favored-Nation--The-Role-of-International-Organizations-in-Promoting-MFN-Status.webp.

8.4. LEGAL FRAMEWORK

Legal framework underpinning mechanisms of dispute settlement is essential in ensuring justice and order in international relations. It is a heterogeneous collection of rules, principles, and practices governing the way in which disputes are administered and resolved among states and other international trade and diplomatic actors. There has been a dramatic change in recent years away from a formalistic inter-governmental and strict legalistic approach towards a wider interpretation embracing good governance, transparency, and accountability values. This new direction reflects greater sensitivity towards the need for systems that not only settle disputes but also enhance legitimacy in international governance. These developments raise the imperative of developing mechanisms handling complaints in a universal manner so that the scope of legal frameworks being used in dispute resolution is broadened to cover diverse interests and perspectives within the global community (French et al., 2009). The focus of contemporary international law is the World Trade Organization (WTO) as a focal point of conflict resolution among member states. Despite the WTO's initial purpose of establishing a stable culture of trade, recent years have witnessed increasingly rising questions about whether or not it is resilient and effective enough to address new upcoming challenges. The perception of the WTO being in crisis also stems from a broader concern regarding its ability to solve disagreements and maintain multilateral relationships. Indeed, peaks and troughs of its operational capacity reveal significant issues in its legal framework, namely as increasing external pressures are being exerted by competing trade agreements. This situation calls for strategic reconsideration of how the WTO can make its system of dispute settlement more fine-tuned in order to enhance legitimacy while fostering a culture of cooperation among members in meeting the challenges of modern international trade (Bäumler et al., 2020). Besides, the evolving paradigm of legal approaches to dispute resolution highlights the need for incorporating innovative approaches that are capable of addressing contemporary challenges. As the international reality evolves, the traditional approaches grounded in hard-line legalism become inadequate. The operation of complaint and grievance mechanisms outside the confines of traditional law has become an integral component of this responsive strategy. These new mechanisms are more accessible to the public and more transparent, making the process of dispute resolution more legitimate. By balancing traditional formal legal systems with these new avenues of redress, the international community is able to establish a society where disputes are resolved equitably and sustainably. Therefore, by tapping on many legal systems, not only is the current issue addressed, but also the general goal of building cooperative international relations (French et al., 2009).

8.4.1. International Law Principles Governing Disputes

The rules of international law controlling disputes have evolved markedly, particularly with the emergence of various adjudicating bodies and forums. Perhaps one of the most striking developments in this area is the evolution of the second-generation international tribunals, which have been noted for their ability to render binding judgments and exercise what is tantamount to compulsory jurisdiction. This stands in comparison to classical first-generation tribunals like the International Court of Justice, which are typically not invested with these powers. The institution of such tribunals is held to be significant in international law, as this adds to the number of ways through which states can effectively resolve disputes. This change marks a crucial transformation of international law practice, as it shows the significance of more refined appreciation of contemporary adjudication processes. As these new mechanisms gain hold, they also give support to a more robust system of resolving disputes in the international legal system, thus changing its foundations entirely (Born et al., 2012). Dispute resolution norms also reflect the multidimensional interaction between state sovereignty and the imperative of collective action within the international realm. For example, arbitration has become an increasingly popular method, particularly in nations like Saudi Arabia, whose arbitrations are governed by local lex arbitri as well as international norms. The policy of the Kingdom demands ratification of arbitration clauses and compromise by a valid authority, thereby imposing certain procedural requirements on them. This blending of national and international law signifies not only the requirement for convergence but also reflects some level of adjustment, as evidenced by interpretive techniques borrowed from Hanbali jurisprudence, which can impact arbitral proceedings. This thus indicates an adaptive legal system that is reconciling traditional ideas about the law with contemporary expectations of efficiency and equity in dispute resolution (Baamir et al., 2009). Furthermore, the evolution of international mechanisms of dispute settlement transcends mere procedural reforms; it constitutes an even deeper thematic shift towards enforceability and accessibility in international law. The success and efficacy of second-generation tribunals reflect how states are progressively realizing that they require mechanisms capable of ending disputes speedily and decisively. These courts have been on the rise in environments that range from commerce to investment, underscoring their indispensable role towards facilitating international cooperation and economic exchanges. This development not only reconsiders traditional presuppositions regarding the obsolescence of international adjudication to contemporary times but also demystifies the pragmatic utility of such mechanisms. As states continue to embrace these new paradigms, international law's map will likely keep evolving, as a response to continuous developments in the principles and practice governing disputes (Born et al., 2012) (Figure 8.11).

Figure 8.11. International law principles governing disputes.

Source: https://fastercapital.co/i/International-Law--International-Law-and-Its-Implications-for-International-Business--International-Law-and-Dispute-Resolution.webp.

8.4.2. Treaties and Conventions Related to Dispute Settlement

The evolution of treaties and conventions on dispute settlement has played a major role in international relations in the modern world. Governments in the past have relied upon a limited group of formal adjudicative organizations, such as the International Court of Justice, to resolve disputes. The increasing complexity of international relations has led to the development of a new generation of international tribunals, reflecting the need for adaptive mechanisms able to address issues of complex international law. These second-generation tribunals, such as international commercial and investment tribunals, have been the new innovative solutions to traditional constraints, offering enforceable awards that are far removed from the last generation. These advancements imply that international law is dynamic and not fixed, but rather a system that can evolve in order to cater to the needs of modern times under globalization and interdependence among states, something that refutes previous assumptions regarding the efficacy of international adjudication (Born et al., 2012). Besides, the rule of law instituted in the various treaties and conventions has permitted states to engage in active practice of treaty-making that results in more accessible entry into dispute settlement processes.

For instance, the rising number of second-generation tribunals accepting jurisdiction, with states entering approximately 50 relevant treaties per year, which reflects a clear shift towards accepting enforceable international arbitration. This active engagement not only indicates confidence in such new mechanisms but also highlights their potential to advance international cooperation, trade, and investment. These frameworks are thus essential in ensuring that conflicts are able to be addressed effectively and equitably, thereby promoting an orderly international society. The potential of these mechanisms to yield timely and binding outcomes places them at the focus of the language of dispute settlement, going beyond what is traditionally known about international law (Born et al., 2012). In addition, the circumstances underpinning counterclaims in investor-state disputes emphasize the level of sophistication in comprehension required when handling these treaties and conventions. As the law on such counterclaims unfolds, it is observed that substantive duties imposed on foreign investors can exceed the confines of investment treaties, thus extending the scope of responsibility and liability. So much has been maintained by commentators to the point that investor obligations may be discerned from various sources of international law, which in turn complicates the process of adjudication. This is also evident in tensions between states in terms of human rights, the environment, and corporate responsibility in international investment. The ability of tribunals to make claims that may pierce the veil of the corporation in counterclaims is a key area of debate regarding the intersection of international norms and the behavior of investors, and as such, how treaties and conventions on dispute settlement remain at the forefront of legal debate as well as regulatory practice.

8.4.3. Case Law and Precedents

The role of precedents and case law in conflict resolution mechanisms is inherently central, as such legal frameworks provide both a model and guidance on conflict resolution. Case law, developed from court rulings, creates legal rules to be followed in future cases by courts and thereby ensures consistency and predictability in the enforcement of law. This reliance on precedents guarantees that similar disputes are dealt with similarly, which is instrumental in guaranteeing public confidence in legal institutions. Of specific relevance is the creation of international mechanisms, like the Universal Water Tribunal, to emphasize the inclusion of customary and conventional laws in the regime of settlements, offering a forum for non-state actors to express grievances and seek redress. The existence of such a mechanism illustrates a broader trend towards environmental justice, emphasizing the dialectical interaction between established legal precedents and emerging jurisprudence in contemporary dispute resolutions (Majzoub et al., 2018).

While case law solidifies legal knowledge, the disputing process also illustrates profound shifts in social and professional values, particularly in the context of settlements. Perhaps the most recognizable feature of modern litigation is the rise of settlements at the expense of trial, with far-reaching consequences for how case law is read and applied. The Federal Rules of Civil Procedure were historically aimed at terminating cases by trial, but the prevailing trend towards settlement has revealed systemic deficits in the rules. As the majority of civil cases end in settlements, the integrity of the underlying principles of the law gets compromised as non-merits considerations become the deciding factors in settlements. This evolution necessitates an urgent requirement to revisit existing procedures so that there is closer alignment with substantive law to ensure that settlements are reflective of the merits in a dispute and not mere transactional solutions based on extraneous considerations (Glover et al., 2012). Evolution of precedents and case law is ever required to clear inconsistencies in dispute settlements, particularly as the parties navigate sophisticated legal climates. As the Federal Rules are reconsidered from time to time in light of modern-day practices in litigation, it should be the aim to build a procedural framework that not only facilitates settlements but also causes settlements to align with the substantive value of claims. This alignment is important in maintaining the rule of law since it places priority on the instruction that legal answers must be grounded on established rights and obligations and not concluded from the nitty-gritty of negotiation. A fresh vision for dispute settlement mechanisms thus must incorporate entrenched reforms that guarantee the precedence of precedents, which would guarantee that the solution mechanisms further promote conformity in legal standards and justice. Through this, legal systems can achieve a more equitable approach towards conflict resolution that is sensitive to both the letter and spirit of law (Glover et al., 2012) (Figure 8.12).

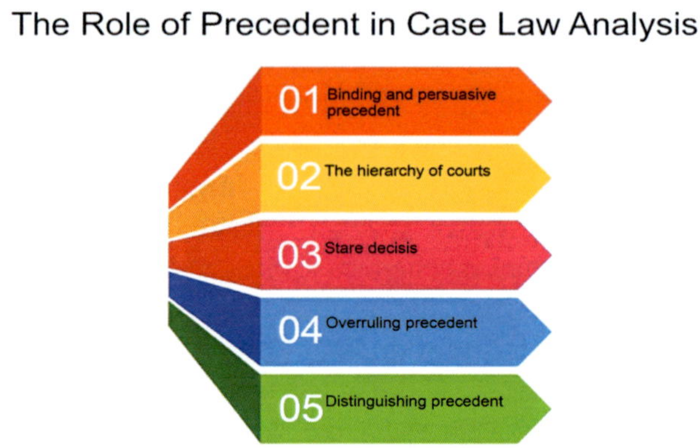

Figure 8.12. Case law and precedents.

Source: https://fastercapital.co/i/Case-law--Analyzing-Case-Law--A-Must-Know-Skill-for-Legallists--The-Role-of-Precedent-in-Case-Law-Analysis.webp.

8.5. CHALLENGES IN DISPUTE SETTLEMENT

The landscape of dispute settlement mechanisms is usually dominated by intricate barriers that could complicate processes of conflict resolution. One of the significant challenges is because of legal diversity and varying perceptions of justice among conflicting parties. For instance, businesses with international trade may be significantly troubled with reconciling their conflicts under various frameworks of law with its precedent and procedure. Such a variation leads to miscommunication and slow negotiation as the parties are not able to arrive at a common denominator. Further, these issues are compounded when intellectual property rights, whose protection and enforcement varies extensively across jurisdictions, are involved. As international conformity, such as with the WTO Agreement on Trade-Related Intellectual Property Rights (TRIPS), relies on national legislation like in China, the complexity of handling such legal frameworks takes on an even higher intensity (Fojtíková et al., 2018). Secondly, the political actors in dispute settlement are usually to blame for significant hindrances. National interests may thwart fair settlement because states would prefer their own economic and political interests over fair dispute settlement. Political pressures can assume numerous varied forms, such as noncompliance in enforcing arbitration awards or biased interpretations of international agreements. Consequently, this can hinder the effectiveness of available mechanisms of dispute, with resulting long delays and waning trust in the institutions that are meant to settle them. Additionally, with no enforcing body in common, parties are often left with few alternatives should a ruling be ignored or ineffectively implemented. This lack of responsibility helps contribute to declining trust in the dispute settlement process, also complicating the resolution landscape (Carolyn, 2025). Lastly, increasing the complexity of international trade relationships has escalated the challenge of settlements of disputes. As economic interdependencies increase, disputes increasingly constitute parties and jurisdictions, rendering multi-sided disputes difficult to manage. The intricacy of negotiating settlements in such cases may require professional skills and facilities beyond the reach of all parties involved. Furthermore, such complexity is even increased by the rapid evolution of technology and market procedures, which are capable of overspending existing legal frameworks. As this occurs, they provide an impetus towards ongoing changes in means of settling disputes, which may not be capable of keeping up with the pace of international trade. Thus, the mechanisms can fail to correct problems at the moment, ultimately weakening the legitimacy of the dispute settlement process itself (Fojtíková et al., 2018) (Figure 8.13).

Figure 8.13. Challenges in dispute settlement.

Source: https://fastercapital.co/i/Entrepreneurship-policies-and-regulations-Navigating-the-Legal-Landscape--Entrepreneurship-Policies-and-Regulations--Legal-Challenges-and-Dispute-Resolution.webp.

8.5.1. Political Influences and Bias

Political influences and bias are essential to the effectiveness and legitimacy of dispute settlement mechanisms. The intricate relationship between states, political ideologies, and international institutions leads to variations in perceptions and interpretations of fairness. For instance, the majority of authors assert that independent international tribunals have the potential to undermine the credibility of judges due to potential ideological biases introduced by appointed judges. As contended by Helfer et al. (2005), such biases can contribute towards decisions based on the moralities of particular states at the expense of an objective judgment based on standards of law. Further, the use by tribunals of pressures from states, as much as it may bring about efficiency, is undesirable for the moral fiber of decisions in that it suggests political pressures have a corrupting influence on the basic aim of impartial conflict resolution. Besides, the nationality of mediators can also bring powerful prejudices into mediation procedures and thereby reinforce disputing parties' perceptions of neutrality. Politically renowned mediators, as in Katsoris et al. (2016), can have their cultural identity and nationality potentially affect their ability to serve as neutral arbiters.

The specific ethical needs of mediation differ across cultures, and failure of attunement by a mediator to such differences has the potential to generate misunderstandings as well as mistrust. For example, renowned mediators such as George Mitchell and Lakhdar Brahimi have faced challenges where there was incompatibility between their cultural expectations and those of the parties they were hired to assist. Such disparity not only complicates mediation dynamics but also emphasizes the need to pay attention to cultural milieus and political loyalties when choosing mediators in conflict resolution. Ultimately, the identification and correction of political influences and prejudice are essential to the quality of conflict resolution mechanisms. Ideologies that underpin judicial bodies can determine decisions, weighing the scales of justice in favor of powerful states. The findings of Helfer et al. (2005) on bounded independence indicate that states form international tribunals but without in fact granting them complete autonomy so that judicial excesses are prevented where these are desired or feared. The balance between independence and political dependence radically impacts perceptions of the parties involved about judicial legitimacy. Emphasis on transparency and accountability in such mechanisms can enhance public trust and result in more balanced outcomes, ultimately solidifying the effectiveness of dispute resolution across the world. These are most essential to ensure that political agendas do not harm the overarching requirement of impartiality in resolving international disputes.

8.5.2. Enforcement Issues and Compliance

Problems of enforcement and compliance are most essential within the framework of mechanisms of dispute settlement, particularly within the framework of international regimes of trade. Any system of settlement of disputes relies on its ability to bind member states to abide by decisions of adjudicative organs. The main challenge arises when the enforcing of judgments is based on the political goodwill of states, and therefore states may be reluctant to enforce judgments that they consider as unfavorable. As in the instance of China's compliance with the WTO's Agreement on Trade-Related Intellectual Property Rights (TRIPS), for instance, an examination is discovered to have complexities arising from both local laws and global obligations. It was observed that while there has been improvement in having China bring its intellectual property legislation into line with TRIPS standards, de facto enforcement remains uneven due to socio-political factors influencing degrees of compliance. Therefore, the intricate interdependence between enforcement and compliance is a significant domain of investigation in international trade regulation (Fojtíková et al., 2018).

In addition to problems of state compliance, the character of international tribunals significantly impacts the enforcement of their judgments. Traditional international adjudicative institutions, such as the International Court of Justice, are generally lacking in the ability for compulsory jurisdiction or direct enforcement of their judgments. Instead, compliance is typically a function of the good faith of the participating states, which translates into different degrees of implementation and compliance. In comparison, a new generation of international tribunals, including those handling commercial and investment arbitrations, has emerged as a robust alternative with a reputation for enhanced enforcement powers. Such tribunals are in a position to render decisions that are more enforceable, thereby guaranteeing a higher level of compliance by states.

Their rapid spread and application point to a shift in the way international law operates in practice, emphasizing the indispensable role that effective enforcement must play to optimize the effectiveness of settlement of disputes mechanisms (Born et al., 2012). The interaction between enforcement challenges and compliance also affects the strategic priorities of the states involved in international trade. In balancing whether or not to engage in trade agreements that have mechanisms of dispute settlement, states must weigh the potential effects of non-compliance against the benefits of economic engagement. As an example, the philosophy behind the TRIPS agreement offers incentive for countries to strengthen intellectual property systems to avoid legal action and trade sanctions. In addition, the success of the second generation of tribunals also shows that states value the benefit of enforceable awards that can enable free trade and investment. By supplying a system in which compliance is not so much a desire but structurally encouraged through enforceable awards, the general effectiveness of systems for dispute settlement is improved. This complex dynamic highlights the necessity for effective tools of enforcement that can guarantee compliance, thus inducing stability and predictability in international trade (Born et al., 2012; Fojtíková et al., 2018) (Figure 8.14).

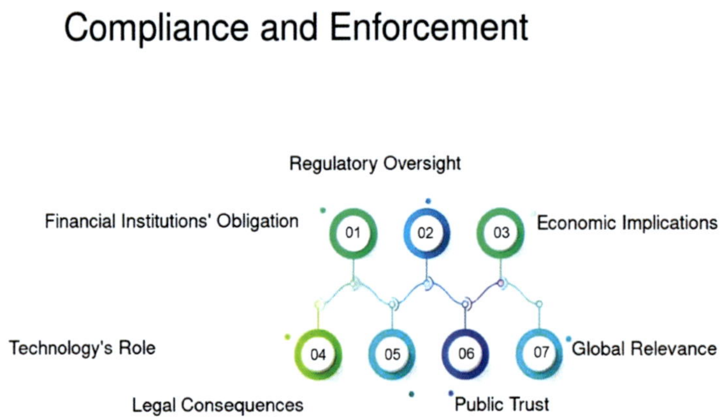

Figure 8.14. Enforcement issues and compliance.

Source: https://fastercapital.co/i/Regulation-J--Understanding-its-Influence-on-Reserve-Requirements-update--Compliance-and-Enforcement.webp.

8.5.3. Cultural Differences and Misunderstandings

Cultural differences significantly impact the dynamics of conflict resolution with varying perceptions of neutrality and ethical standards playing a critical role. In cross-cultural mediation cases, mediators must navigate the intricacies of competing cultural norms that can have a tremendous impact on their effectiveness and negotiating outcomes. For instance, expectations of ethical standards may differ dramatically across cultures, leading to misunderstandings that complicate the process of mediation. As can be observed in mediators such as George Mitchell and Lakhdar Brahimi, cultural dissonance results in frustration and public outcry when mediators venturously move out of the known ethical norms of their respective societies. This serves to underscore the importance of an appreciation of cultural nuances and the working towards a shared set of principles that can guide the process of mediation, ultimately to bring about an improved harmonious resolution of disputes. The role of neutrality, per se, must be understood as a culture-specific phenomenon and not as something that serves as a universal norm (Katsoris et al., 2016). Culture-based conflict is likely to arise in conflicts over communally-held resources, validating the necessity for effective mechanisms of dispute settlement. In the Middle East, where water itself is often a source of conflict between nations, cultural perceptions regarding resource management and entitlement can be a source of increased tension. The historic division of water resources in the Middle East illustrates how cultural narratives frame notions of justice and fairness, making it more difficult for individuals to collaborate in resource management. As nations fight for limited supplies of fresh water, as cited in recent studies, the problem is worsened by cultural beliefs of scarcity and ownership. Parties in such situations must be addressed by mediators not just to the tangible barriers of resource distribution but also to the cultural and historical narratives that underpin parties' positions. Therefore, these dimensions of culture need to be addressed in creating sustainable conflict resolution methods (Wolf et al., 2025). Effective resolution of conflicts depends on the building of a high degree of cultural competence, which is both knowledge of one's own cultural biases and sensitivity to the cultural origins of all parties. This involves not just the determination of how cultural differences can lead to miscommunication but also the tailoring of mediation methods to bridge these gaps in a successful manner. Mediator training and preparation often involve the study of case studies, like the mediators experience in Ireland or Israel-Palestine, so that lessons can be learnt from them how cultural dynamics can inform mediation practices. The ability to understand and value multiple cultural values has the potential to transform conflict into avenues of communication. By establishing an environment that fosters cultural sensitivity, mediators can gain more credibility and the possibility of a desirable outcome, thus resulting in a more evolved and efficient system of settlement of disputes (Katsoris et al., 2016).

8.6. CASE STUDIES

Case study analysis provides useful information regarding the functioning of the Dispute Settlement Mechanism (DSM) and how it affects international trade relations. Investigating specific instances of disputes lodged with the World Trade Organization (WTO) assists scholars in determining trends regarding the participation of members and dispute settlement. For instance, specific nations may have heightened participation as complainants or respondents depending on underlying political or economic interests. The thick legal context governing such conflicts allows gradations of enforcement and compliance, ultimately shaping member states' expectations in trade negotiations. This empirical examination highlights the importance of understanding not just the legal text but strategic country behavior as well when turning to the complexity of the DSM, as Horn et al. (2025) contends. In addition, case studies emphasize the determinants of states' choice between dispute settlement mechanisms. In instances involving grievances by companies, the resolution process's choice may be pivotal not just to financial compensation in the short run but also to the long-term sustainability of inter-company relationships. Economic studies demonstrate that spatial proximity and membership in business associations strongly influence the path that conflicts take. Firms are generally faced with options that weigh potential outcomes against business costs of operating within their settings, proving that behavioral responses are significantly related to the business environment of firms in concern. This finding sparks additional studies into conflict resolution dynamics and their influence on market expansion, as proven through Pyle et al. (2005). In tandem with these considerations, case study results have broader policy implications in the area of dispute settlement. Trends from past disputes can inform the creation of improved mechanisms under the DSM so that it may be more successful at encouraging international trade cooperation and stability. The policymakers must draw upon the findings produced by studies of history's case studies to formulate new frameworks which not only mirror legal doctrine but also address the economic realities which are challenges to the member states. Efficient resolution of conflicts may diminish costly legal wars and create a more harmonious international trading system. This full understanding of case studies is an essential element for the reconsideration and enhancement of the current DSM, making it more effective in resolving trade disputes and enforcing compliance among member states.

8.6.1. Successful Dispute Resolutions

Successful mechanisms for dispute resolution are essential to the effectiveness of various conflict situations, particularly for organizational and international contexts. The choice of different alternative dispute resolution (ADR) techniques, such as mediation and arbitration, largely relies on the strategic interests behind the parties' interests. Those organizations with the ability to synergize their ADR strategies with higher-order purposes fare better in resolving disputes, enhancing relationships and outcomes. Research indicates that companies commitment to mediation or arbitration can make the selected approach effective, proving strategic alignment necessary for successful resolution (Avgar et al., 2017). This higher-order knowledge of a company reveals how various practices of ADR can resolve specific conflict situations so that tailored solutions can be attained while preserving relationships and facilitating constructive dialogue, which are attributes valued in today's complex conflict situations. The creation of international tribunals has reshaped the landscape of international dispute settlement, bringing in radical innovations challenging traditional understanding of international law. These new-born institutions of international commercial and investment arbitral tribunals have emerged as viable tools for resolution of transnational disputes as well as state-private party conflicts. As opposed to the less effective first-generation traditional international courts that were older and less enforceable, these tribunals can issue binding rulings that must be enforced by states. The efficacy and extensive application of these second-generation tribunals attest to their effectiveness in promoting international trade and investment and in being instrumental in promoting peace and stability in international relations. These new adjudicatory frameworks offer compelling illustrations of how effective dispute resolution can foster cooperation and moderate conflict in a more interdependent world (Born et al., 2012). Most notably, the organization and design of dispute settlement mechanisms are determinative for their success. Second-generation international tribunals also have a combination of characteristics that transcend the narrow dichotomies so commonly assumed in academia, for instance, independence and dependence. Rather than rigidly adhering to a single model, effective tribunals employ tailored designs which are responsive to the specific contexts of the cases they are adjudicating. This adaptability allows them to handle the complexities of international law, making them more effective as well as more compliant with judgments. Success in these tribunals also speaks not just to their capacity to ensure effective conflict resolution but to their capacity to influence the evolution of international law itself, confirming the very real need for constant scholarly attention to mechanisms which ensure successful resolutions of disputes (Born et al., 2012).

8.6.2. Notable Failures in Dispute Settlement

There have been remarkable failures of dispute settlement mechanisms in international trade history, which have pointed to the inadequacies in existing structures. The mechanisms for resolving conflict are weak in relation to the enforceability required to force member states into compliance. For instance, there are numerous regional trade agreements whose dispute resolution mechanisms are not defined, and hence have uneven application and interpretation. This is particularly true within the agreements with BRICSAM countries, where the unrivaled level of obligation clarity and commitment hinders appropriate resolution approaches. As acknowledged, the different levels of specificity and clarity between such agreements make enforcement difficult and suggest a potential drift from the norms within the World Trade Organization (WTO) towards increased fragmentation in dispute settlement, thereby destabilizing efforts at collective global trade (Antkiewicz et al., 2025). Moreover, the convergence of these regional agreements challenges their inclusion within the WTOs regime of dispute resolution. While these newer buildings may have important diplomatic functions, their ability to handle material conflicts is questionable. The vagueness present in the majority of agreements renders the determination of duties and rights challenging, with protracted negotiations often becoming a necessity that ultimately prevents settlements. Where nations prefer bilateral or multilateral talks outside the WTO, utilization of less official mechanisms will likely slow down the settling of trade grievances, thus discouraging overall economic cooperation. The lack of coordinated monitoring provided by the WTO can result in a patchwork of principles and remedies that are not sensitive to the complexity of global commerce, further handicapping smaller economies (Pauwelyn et al., 2004). In general, the serious setbacks in the dispute settlement mechanisms point towards a widespread systemic deficiency in international trade regulation. As countries work on a more complex set of agreements, the effectiveness of these mechanisms is undermined by both vague language and prioritization of national over collective interests. These breakdowns not only burden the parties but also threaten the legitimacy of the international trading system, underscoring the need for firmer and more unified dispute resolution mechanisms. In order to overcome such challenges, it is imperative to be committed to upgrading current mechanisms so that they are equipped with the appropriate structures required for expediting equitable resolution of disputes, therefore supporting a healthier environment of international trade.

8.6.3. Lessons Learned from Case Studies

Examining case studies in the area of dispute settlement mechanisms provides critical information that can support a greater awareness of conflict resolution mechanisms. One of the strongest lessons drawn from several case studies is that contextualization is key to it, emphasizing that different situations necessitate unique response rather than a blanket solution. Both practitioners and scholars are recognizing that mere application of broad theories may not adequately deal with the complexities involved in individual conflicts. This is consistent with ongoing controversies in the field, as reflected through questioning if such relevant theory is capable of addressing large sectors of conflict or if it must be in the form of accurate, context-specific descriptions. The reflective examination raised in these publications not only questions the viability of generalization but also warrants further inquiry into shared propositions that will lead to improved resolution outcomes in controversies (Menkel-Meadow et al., 2003). Again, another valuable lesson from case studies is learning about the importance of understanding the relation between compliance and enforcement in resolving disputes. The compliance versus rebalancing in the World Trade Organization (WTO) is a harsh reality of what various interpretations can do to the effectiveness of dispute resolution. The advocates of compliance advocate for the imposition of rulings as a means of discouraging future contraventions, while rebalancing patrons note the repercussions of "pay-or-perform" strategies.

Both models, even as they are seemingly incompatible, give insights into the natural nature of contractual arrangements and the optimum remedies needed in ensuring enforcement efficacy. Acknowledging these multi-dimensional perceptions heralds the reality that a more integrated understanding can render the WTOs system of dispute settlement much more comprehensive and realistic (Schropp, 2025). Lastly, case studies illustrate the significance of empirical studies in refining mechanisms for dispute settlement. Through a review of specific instances of dispute and resolution, stakeholders can identify what works in practice and methodology, and what doesn't. This cycle of learning generates a framework whereby lessons can be transferred and thus build on better successive attempts at resolving conflict. Moreover, the combination of anecdotal evidence and theoretical models adds support to the argument that experience-based practical wisdom or lived insight underlies the acquisition of conflict resolution strategies. Lastly, what is being learned from these empirical investigations not only informs policy, but also establishes a better appreciation for the many-sided dynamics at play in effective dispute settlement (Menkel-Meadow et al., 2003).

SUMMARY

The success of the DSM in the WTO is directly tied to its evolving dynamic with regional trade agreements (RTAs). As RTA proliferation continues across the globe, the threat to the DSM becomes more significant. These international treaties tend to have their own mechanisms of dispute resolution, which can complicate issues when there are overlapping problems. The Appellate Body's decision in the Brazil Tyres case is a good example of such conflicts and the kind of complications that can arise when different legal systems interact. While academics debate the implications of these overlaps, the reality is clear that there must be a soundly coherent approach to respond to the interdependencies and conflicts occasioned by the overlap of RTA measures and WTO dispute settlement principles, occasioning the need for clarification in the frontline trade negotiations (Hillman et al., 2009). It is not merely an academic concern that the divergences are resolved; it is a condition for international trade law to be legitimate and efficient. Bringing the DSM to operate at its best together with RTAs entails having a thorough understanding of the nexus of law between different mechanisms. Having systems simultaneously operating may lead to having different perceptions of obligations, hence creating ambiguity for member states. As is seen from a number of scholarly controversies, such management may involve reconsideration of the current DSM structure and potential reforms in accordance with the Doha Round mandate. Note in such analysis of the systemic character of the interaction between intersecting mechanisms emphasizes the necessity for WTO members to actively ensure the legal contours framing the trade-related disputes conduct in an evolving global environment (Abbott et al., 1999). The future involves initiating a dialogue process between WTO member states with a view to making the working of the DSM and RTA settlement mechanisms more harmonious. Further integrated action will not only make measures towards settlement of disputes stronger but also build confidence among trading partners, thus making international trade more smooth. Further, learning from those landmark cases such as Brazil Tyres can help determine areas that require immediate legal clarification. With rising competition in the global economy, it is the job of policymakers and trade negotiators to give an effective, regular, and fair process for dispute resolution. The long-term sustainability of the WTOs DSM depends on whether the DSM can keep pace with rising complexity in global trade agreements, which calls for cooperation in order to sustain the rules-based trading system (Hillman et al., 2009).

The DSM is a cornerstone of international trade agreements, ensuring that its member nations abide by mutually decided rules and duties. Fundamental to it is the ability to resolve disputes arising from alleged breaches, thus creating economic stability as well as confidence among trading nations. For instance, the inclusion of labor provisions in Free Trade Agreements (FTAs) indicates the position of the DSMs in upholding pledges to respect workers' rights alongside trade interests. As seen in the case of the North American Agreement on Labor Cooperation (NAALC) and subsequent NAALC agreements, these labor provisions have been broadened to encompass core ILO principles and are subject to the same dispute settlement procedures as other obligations, reflecting the increasing interdependence of labor rights and commercial interests (Cimino-Isaacs et al., 2018). Moreover, the design of the DSMs is not a post-factum response but is a constructive one to prevent confrontation through a framework for compliance and negotiation. Such an anticipatory nature is evident in the operation of the Agreement on the Application of Sanitary and Phytosanitary (SPS) Measures. In this case, countries have opted to delegate regulation to an international organization so as to streamline processes and mitigate local political costs associated with policymaking. Although domestic interests weighed heavily in this decision-making process, it is also an example of a strategic approach to coping with regulatory sovereignty against the backdrop of international norms. The politics of such interaction will show that DSM is multifaceted and finds itself balancing national sovereignty and the demands of international cooperation on trade and environmental protection (Buthe et al., 2008). Moreover, the creation of mechanisms for conflict resolution indicates the evolving nature of international trade and mounting demands for accountability and transparency. The intersection of labor standards with trade regimes illustrates an overall trend towards ethically responsible economic practice in addressing concerns raised by various actors. This shift has deep implications for future trade agreements, as the integration of complete labor standards and environmental safeguards is bound to become the standard. The DSM is essentially pivotal to enabling compliance and cooperation between nations so that trade can function in an atmosphere conducive to sustainable and fair economic growth for all interested parties. This development contributes to the plausibility of global institutions formed to settle disputes so that there is a context conducive to long-term coalition and general well-being.

REFERENCES

1. Abbott, A., Albou, A., Anache-Ménier, A., Bakun, A., Bakun, B., Bath, A., et al. (1999). The friendly settlement of human rights abuses in the Americas. https://core.ac.uk/download/62547645.pdf (accessed on 30th October 2025).
2. Agapiou, A., & Clark, B. (2012). Construction clients and mediation: A follow-up study of attitudes and experience. https://core.ac.uk/download/9559025.pdf (accessed on 30th October 2025).
3. Antkiewicz, A., & Whalley, J. (2025). *BRICSAM and the non-WTO.* https://core.ac.uk/download/pdf/6562980.pdf (accessed on 30th October 2025).
4. Avgar, A. C., Lamare, J. R., & Lipsky, D. B. (2017). Organizational conflict resolution and strategic choice: Evidence from a survey of Fortune 1000 companies. https://core.ac.uk/download/127600102.pdf (accessed on 30th October 2025).
5. Baamir, A., & Bantekas, I. (2009). Saudi law as *lex arbitri*: Evaluation of Saudi arbitration law and judicial practice. https://core.ac.uk/download/19784834.pdf (accessed on 30th October 2025).
6. Basedow, R. (2018). Strengthening the World Trade Organization–Critical demands for imperative success: Identifying politically viable options for incremental reform. https://core.ac.uk/download/322823605.pdf (accessed on 30th October 2025).
7. Bäumler, J. (2020). *Between a Rock and A Hard Place.* https://core.ac.uk/download/322846649.pdf (accessed on 30th October 2025).
8. Born, G. (2012). A new generation of international adjudication. https://core.ac.uk/download/62560047.pdf (accessed on 30th October 2025).
9. Buthe, T. (2008). The globalization of health and safety standards: Delegation of regulatory authority in the SPS Agreement of the 1994 Agreement Establishing the World Trade Organization. https://core.ac.uk/download/62553315.pdf (accessed on 30th October 2025).
10. Chang, S. W. (2004). Interaction between trade and competition: Why a multilateral approach for the United States? https://core.ac.uk/download/62547461.pdf (accessed on 30th October 2025).
11. Cimino-Isaacs, C. D. (2018). Labor enforcement issues in U.S. FTAs. https://core.ac.uk/download/219377158.pdf (accessed on 30th October 2025).
12. Collins, D. A. (2006). Institutionalized fact finding at the WTO. https://core.ac.uk/download/2707916.pdf (accessed on 30th October 2025).

13. Deere, C. (2025). *International Trade Technical Assistance and Capacity Building*. https://core.ac.uk/download/pdf/6248816.pdf (accessed on 30th October 2025).
14. Dhar, B. (2013). The future of the World Trade Organization. https://core.ac.uk/download/18615812.pdf (accessed on 30th October 2025).
15. Farida, E. (2014). Penyelesaian sengketa perbatasan antara Thailand dan Kamboja melalui mekanisme ASEAN. https://core.ac.uk/download/201346439.pdf (accessed on 30th October 2025).
16. Fojtíková, L. (2018). China's intellectual property rights commitments in the WTO: Legal and economic implications. https://core.ac.uk/download/161960388.pdf (accessed on 30th October 2025).
17. French, D., & Kirkham, R. (2009). Complaint and grievance mechanisms in international law: One piece of the accountability jigsaw? https://core.ac.uk/download/5223577.pdf (accessed on 30th October 2025).
18. Glover, J. M. (2012). The Federal Rules of Civil Settlement. https://core.ac.uk/download/74539279.pdf (accessed on 30th October 2025).
19. Goldstein, J. L., & Steinberg, R. H. (2008). Negotiate or litigate? Effects of WTO judicial delegation on U.S. trade politics. https://core.ac.uk/download/62553324.pdf (accessed on 30th October 2025).
20. Hegji, A. (2012). Federal labor relations statutes: An overview. https://core.ac.uk/download/9347071.pdf (accessed on 30th October 2025).
21. Helfer, L. R., & Slaughter, A. M. (2005). Why states create international tribunals: A response to Professors Posner and Yoo. https://core.ac.uk/download/62563361.pdf (accessed on 30th October 2025).
22. Helfer, L. R., Hathaway, O. A., Goldstein, J., Lutz, E., Chayes, A., Raustiala, K., et al. (2003). Constitutional analogies in the international legal system. https://core.ac.uk/download/62563345.pdf (accessed on 30th October 2025).
23. Hillman, J. A. (2009). Conflicts between dispute settlement mechanisms in regional trade agreements and the WTO–What should WTO do? https://core.ac.uk/download/213034966.pdf (accessed on 30th October 2025).
24. Horn, H., & Mavroidis, P. C. (2025). A survey of the literature on the WTO dispute settlement system. https://core.ac.uk/download/pdf/6656937.pdf (accessed on 30th October 2025).
25. Jackson, J. H. (2000). The perils of globalization and the world trading system. https://core.ac.uk/download/70373967.pdf (accessed on 30th October 2025).
26. Katsoris, M. (2016). Does nationality influence neutrality? The ethical

standards and expectations of international mediators. https://core.ac.uk/download/144231257.pdf (accessed on 30th October 2025).

27. Kryvoi, Y. (2011). Counterclaims in investor-state arbitration. https://core.ac.uk/download/220906.pdf (accessed on 30th October 2025).
28. Lewis, D. B. (2013). Resolving whistleblowing disputes in the public interest: Is tribunal adjudication the best that can be offered? https://core.ac.uk/download/15236747.pdf (accessed on 30th October 2025).
29. Majzoub, T., & Quilleré-Majzoub, F. (2018). The time has come for a universal water tribunal. https://core.ac.uk/download/212892726.pdf (accessed on 30th October 2025).
30. Malkawi, B. H. (2012). Arab countries' (under) participation in the WTO dispute settlement mechanism. https://core.ac.uk/download/186331592.pdf (accessed on 30th October 2025).
31. Mathys, G., & Vlassenroot, K. (2016). 'It's not all about the land': Land disputes and conflict in the eastern Congo. https://core.ac.uk/download/55857770.pdf (accessed on 30th October 2025).
32. Menkel-Meadow, C. (2003). Correspondences and contradictions in international and domestic conflict resolution: Lessons from general theory and varied contexts. https://core.ac.uk/download/70373725.pdf (accessed on 30th October 2025).
33. Nelson, M. B. (2025). International rules, food safety and the poor developing country livestock producer. https://core.ac.uk/download/pdf/7055418.pdf (accessed on 30th October 2025).
34. Pauwelyn, J. H. B. (2004). Non-traditional patterns of global regulation: Is the WTO 'missing the boat'? https://core.ac.uk/download/62562456.pdf (accessed on 30th October 2025).
35. Pyle, W. (2005). Resolution, recovery and survival: The evolution of payment disputes in post-socialist Europe. http://www.wdi.umich.edu/files/Publications/WorkingPapers/wp761.pdf (accessed on 30th October 2025).
36. Schropp, S. (2025). Revisiting the "compliance-vs.-rebalancing" debate in WTO scholarship: A unified research agenda. https://core.ac.uk/download/pdf/6513505.pdf (accessed on 30th October 2025).
37. Villalta Puig, G., & Yee, A. T. H. (2017). Challenges and opportunities of the China–Gulf Cooperation Council Free Trade Agreement. https://core.ac.uk/download/151161890.pdf (accessed on 30th October 2025).
38. Wallach, L., & Bottari, M. (2005). NAFTA Chapter 11 investor-state

cases: Lessons for the Central America Free Trade Agreement. https://core.ac.uk/download/71339037.pdf (accessed on 30th October 2025).

39. Wolf, A. T. (2025). Middle East water conflicts and directions for conflict resolution. https://core.ac.uk/download/pdf/6345319.pdf (accessed on 30th October 2025).

40. Wolfe, R. (2020). Reforming WTO conflict management: Why and how to improve the use of "specific trade concerns." *Bertelsmann Working Paper*, 24/02/2020. https://core.ac.uk/download/287647976.pdf (accessed on 30th October 2025).

Chapter 9

WTO and Developing Countries

Contents

INTRODUCTION

World Trade Organization (WTO) is one of the prominent organizations on the global map of trade, especially concerning developing country dynamics. Established to increase trade liberalization and economic cooperation across the world, the WTO also recognizes the particular issues of developing countries. The issues include limited access to markets, weak infrastructure, and lower bargaining power in the negotiating process. Therefore, the WTOs function extends beyond the sphere of economical exchanges, as it now enters an arena of ethical thinking and equitable development. The entry of fairness issues, particularly in the field of trade relations and benefits, makes the WTO an important forum where developing countries' aspirations can be heard and translated. Understanding this context is important to studying the complexity and implications of trade for these nations. The ethical dimensions of trade are further emphasized through contrasting opinions among developed and developing nations. Developed nations often demand several conditionalities for trade preferences that have something to do with environmental and labor conditions.

Figure 9.1. World Trade Organization (WTO) and developing countries.

Source: https://static.pib.gov.in/WriteReadData/userfiles/image/image0017S84.jpg.

For example, the Generalized System of Preferences (GSP) offers non-reciprocal tariff preference to developing nations with the aim of triggering their industrialization and economic development (Switzer et al., 2008). However, negotiations regarding such conditionalities are tense because developing nations feel like they are being coerced into adhering to standards that may not be precisely what they need at a given point in time. Secondly, such policies also stand the risk of increasing inequalities if poor countries fail to reach the threshold specified. Hence, the convergence of trade policy and moral responsibility demands a precise examination of how the WTO interacts with developing countries. An ethical examination of global trade by way of academic research sheds light on the means by which the WTO can evolve to be more beneficial to poor countries. In other academic contexts, the importance of an interdisciplinary appreciation of fairness in business has been a common thread, particularly in relation to Africa's unique economic climate (Moore et al., 2010). Addressing issues of prosperity building and well-being can enhance the viability of trade deals and promote sustainable development in such territories. The consideration of such factors not only highlights the imbalances in trade relations but also emphasizes the necessity of inclusive and participative mechanisms of trade policy-making. In the best scenario, facilitation of a discussion with the participation of developing nations can lead to more balanced trade practices, thus stimulating their economic growth and integration into the world economy (Figure 9.1).

Definition of the World Trade Organization (WTO)

WTO is one of the central organizations involved in global trade governance, which offers an institutional and legal framework that facilitates negotiating trade and resolving disputes between member countries. Since 1995, WTO has been an outgrowth of the General Agreement on Tariffs and Trade (GATT) and is tasked with making trade run as smoothly and as reliably as possible. Its most important functions are overseeing trade deals, acting as a platform for trade negotiations, and providing technical assistance to developing countries. The agency has 164 member states, each of which is seeking its individual economic interest and thereby forming a complicated matrix of negotiations in an attempt to achieve an equitable global trading environment. Additionally, the adherence of WTO to transparency and principle of non-discrimination sounds all the more true when considering its impact on developing countries, who have a tendency to face specialized challenges in this international trading system. In the context of developing countries, both opportunities and challenges are presented by the WTO. The institution is committed to being inclusive through a number of agreements which ostensibly allow developing countries to engage more effectively in international markets. But these nations are prone to deal with issues of capacity and resources that can derail their ability to maximally utilize the WTO provisions. Those nations falling under this category have worries about the adverse effects of trade liberalization on domestic economies and domestic industries. The negotiations under way, particularly the negotiations regarding financial services in the WTO, exhibit the disparity between developed and developing countries' market access. For instance, while financial services are geared towards promoting economic development, the majority of developing nations fear their susceptibility to destabilizing capital flows, an issue that has been highlighted by various submissions that have been tabled in trade negotiations (CORNFORD, 2025). The topic of the WTOs facilitation of developing countries' trade is further complicated by the demand for regulatory transparency and their inclusion in decision-making. The majority of developing nations require an integrated approach under which they are actively involved in establishing international standards, especially how these relate to national treatment and market access. Attitudes of developed versus developing nations towards financial services regulations tend to result in a stalemate, particularly issues surrounding enforcement of international protocols and the prudential carve-out in financial transactions (CORNFORD, 2025). This binary suggests the acute need for the WTO to re-invent and change its paradigms in a way that they are in consonance with the diverse economic profiles of its member nations. Predominantly, instilling an impression of justice in these negotiations can significantly enhance the role of the WTO as a catalyst for empowerment of developing countries amidst adversity in the international trade landscape.

Importance of Trade for Developing Countries

Trade plays a prime role in the economic development of poor countries, as a pulling force towards poverty reduction and sustainable development. By integrating with the global economy, developing nations can strengthen their export base, create jobs, and increase national income. The WTO ensures this by establishing a rules-based trading system benefitting member countries, particularly those which are striving to raise economic vulnerabilities. Specifically, countries can export their farm products in overseas markets, a key sector for the majority of developing nations. However, to fully reap these benefits, such countries have to supplement these with internal reforms that displace market distortions and develop their agricultural sectors. For developed countries to achieve the full potential of trade liberalization, developing nations also need to unlock their potential and avail themselves of new market opportunities, as it seems to be emphasized by the call for domestic reform as specified in Anderson (2025). The delicacy of agricultural trade reform offers the crux of the bigger picture of global trade implications on developing nations. Agricultural markets of low-income nations are highly distorted according to current research, which makes them unable to compete internationally. The Doha Development Agenda, initiated by the WTO, aims to address these disparities, with emphasis on agricultural trade liberalization as a method of alleviating rural poverty. In a twist, countries that adapt to changing market forces and increase their agricultural productivity are likely to gain a lot from trade reform. With the intricacies of trade negotiations that developing countries are faced with, it is necessary that they examine their internal policies in conjunction with foreign treaties. Through enhancing the harmony between their internal markets and the world scenario, countries can efficiently utilize their agricultural sectors and make trade a potent tool of economic development, as argued in Wilson et al. (2025). Moreover, trade has spillover impacts that extend beyond mere economic benefits and produces broader social progress in developing nations. Increased trade has the potential to lead to enhanced food security, enhanced access to essential commodities, and improved infrastructure, all of which are determinants of overall well-being. Developing countries, when they enter world trade in a productive manner, also generate investments in education and technology, which are the supports in the formation of human capital. Meanwhile, these nations can count on knowledge transfer from advanced countries since they are part of global supply chains. While there are challenges, such as the volatility of foreign markets and the attendant risks of depending on a sole export, the prospect of trade to elevate entire communities remains significant. Hence, knowing and addressing the various sides of trade is paramount to making sure that developing countries can effectively harness its power to drive growth as well as alleviate poverty, as suggested in both Anderson (2025) and Wilson et al. (2025) (Figure 9.2).

Figure 9.2. Importance of trade for developing countries.

Source: https://fastercapital.co/i/International-trade--Boosting-International-Trade-with-Currency-Pegs--The-Importance-of-International-Trade.webp.

9.1. HISTORICAL CONTEXT OF THE WORLD TRADE ORGANIZATION (WTO)

The establishment of the WTO in 1995 was a milestone in regulating international trade, superseding the General Agreement on Tariffs and Trade (GATT) established in 1947. While GATT primarily centered on the reduction of trade barriers, the WTO introduced a more comprehensive approach with services, intellectual property rights, and agricultural accords. This expansion was pivotal in bringing developing countries into the fold, which were seeking more role and dividends from global trading systems. However from a historical angle, the processes of the WTOs were controlled by developed nations, inclining to marginalize the interests of less economically developed countries. Thus, the developing world, even within the WTO arrangement, has lagged behind in deriving the best out of the scope presented before it, accompanied by the additional complications of different capacities to bargain about intricate agreements and negotiations. Besides, WTO agricultural agreements have shown how the developing countries have been disadvantaged. For instance, as outlined in the SPS Agreement, developed countries have tended to dominate the formulation of food safety requirements through practices like the CODEX. As developing countries themselves are industriously involved in an effort to sustain their export efforts of agriculture, they may lack institutional strength to effectively be part of the technical negotiations required in order to apply meaningful influence. These imbalances induce a structural weakness hindering the ability of such countries to enforce strict standards, ultimately affecting their export potential. Thus, it is evident that while the WTO is to promote international trade, the history shows a constant struggle for the developing nations, as their inputs and needs are not well addressed in the grand scheme. The complexities of the World Trade Organizations history also include environmental aspects of trade policies, particularly with the Generalized System of Preferences (GSP). The GSP, on behalf of WTO, authorizes developed countries to offer non-reciprocal tariff concessions to developing nations, whose intention is ostensibly to benefit economic growth and industrialization. Environmental conditionality can, however, be attached to such preferences by imposing certain standards on developing countries before they can avail themselves of lower tariffs. While these moves are framed as a step in the right direction, they serve to inappropriately complicate trade for poorer countries, whose capacity to maintain stringent environmental standards will likely be less. This tension recognizes the ultimate balancing act that the WTO must do between equitable trade practices and the imposition of standards that are beneficial within the world community but can suppress the very economic development they set out to promote.

9.1.1. Formation of the World Trade Organization (WTO) in 1995

The establishment of the WTO in 1995 was a significant advance in the global trading order, triggered by the inadequacies of its predecessor, the General Agreement on Tariffs and Trade (GATT). The GATT regime, which started operating in 1948, principally addressed the issue of tariff and border trade barrier regulation between the industrialized economies. With increasing complications in international trade dynamics, particularly the rise of developing economies, there arose a necessity for an augmented institutional framework. The WTO was not only established to advance trade liberalization and cooperation between members but also to address issues of trade imbalances overwhelmingly affecting developing countries. Given that these nations often face colossal challenges in accessing foreign markets, the WTO was created to promote a more equitable trading system, thus promoting economic growth and development in the international South.

Figure 9.3. Formation of the World Trade Organization (WTO) in 1995.

Source: https://www.wto.org/images/img_10anniv/ph2_500.jpg.

The inclusion of a comprehensive dispute settlement mechanism in the WTO framework guarantees a fundamental development aimed at promoting good trade practices. As a difference from the GATTs consultative process, the WTOs Dispute Settlement Understanding (DSU) provides a binding dispute resolution process, thereby enhancing international trade predictability and stability. This is particularly worth much to developing countries, whose negotiating strength tends to be weaker than that of other big economies. The DSU plays a crucial role in leveling the playing field, allowing the smaller nations to bring to book what they perceive to be unfairness and violations of trade commitments credibly. Since its founding, more than 330 cases have been initiated, with significant involvement of principal trade players such as the USA and the EU, thereby giving evidence of the systems effectiveness and applicability in resolving trade disputes across different economic structures (Breuss, 2025). Furthermore, the founding of the WTO witnessed several agreements being instituted with the objective of enhancing the participation of developing countries in global trade mechanisms. Initiatives such as the

Trade-Related Aspects of Intellectual Property Rights (TRIPS) and Special and Differential Treatment (SDT) provisions aim at addressing the unique needs of these nations. These agreements also provide developing countries with the ability to apply trade rules according to their unique economic realities. Furthermore, the WTO actively promotes capacity-building programs that enhance the technical expertise of these nations so they can play a greater role in international trade. According to studies, the presence of international institutions like the WTO can actually stem protectionist behavior during recessions, thereby creating a more stable trading system (Baccini et al., 2011). The effectiveness of such mechanisms suggests that aside from the pledge of free trade, there is also a pledge to equity in economic growth, a significant concern for developing countries which are faced with the ills of globalization (Figure 9.3).

9.1.2. Evolution of Trade Agreements and Policies

Evolution of trade agreements and policies has been greatly influenced by the emerging dynamics of world economies and the requirement for world cooperation. Trade deals at the WTO have shifted from tariff-reduction only models to increasingly intricate deals addressing a list of matters that range from the standards of labor to environmental safeguards. This reflects the perception that trade cannot be detached from its socio-economic implications. Developing countries experience both threats and opportunities in adapting to these new benchmarks in their effort to be competitive on the global stage and yet react to local needs. The European Union's policy on labor standards is symptomatic of this subtle dynamic, revealing how consensus is consistently found in the member state bargains' lowest common denominator that can choke firm implementation of policies in different contexts (Adriaensen et al., 2011). At the same time, the negotiation that has occurred on agriculture within the WTOs Doha Development Agenda highlights the challenge of securing equitable agreements that are sensitive to developing countries' interests. Historically, agricultural trade has been heavily protectionist, particularly in the developed world, and distorting market forces. The EU's own internal agriculture policy reform, the Common Agricultural Policy (CAP), illustrates the tension. While these reforms attempt to reduce distorting market effects, the pace and timing of change have a significant impact on the EUs negotiating position within the WTO framework. As developing countries seek more equal access to farm markets, the shifting regional free-trade agreements' context heavily influences these talks and offers new possibilities of forming potentially beneficial partnerships (Anania et al., 2025). In addition, the integration of domestic policy reforms with international trade talks is critical in understanding the ongoing evolution of free-trade agreements and their implications for developing countries. As nations like the EU reorient their agricultural policy towards more of a market solution, the effects reach beyond borders. Such positioning allows the EU to not only become a more viable negotiating partner during WTO negotiations but to prepare itself as well for more positive relations with developing nations. Since the tilt of preferences in the direction of more liberalized trade arrangements by way of regional pacts, developing countries have to ride such trends, securing opportunities while confronting structural vulnerabilities in their economies. The formation of trade policy is thus a relentlessly evolving process, intertwined with broader trends in socio-economy and the pursuit of equitable trade in an open world (Figure 9.4).

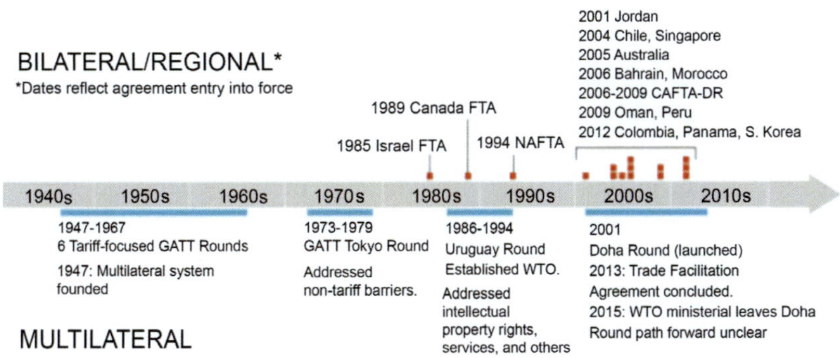

Figure 9.4. Evolution of trade agreements and policies.

Source: https://www.everycrsreport.com/files/20180517_R45198_images_1002687b24ad73848ed88635800d60db48c33e88.png.

9.1.3. Impact of Globalization on Developing Nations

The process of globalization has profoundly affected the developing world, in some cases bringing along opportunities as well as challenges. At the center stage, increased access to global markets has enabled them to accelerate economic growth through exportation. The role played by the World Trade Organization (WTO) in this respect is fundamental in establishing rules that regulate international trade practice. Benefits brought about by globalization do not trickle down evenly. While some developing nations have managed to become integrated into the global economy, there are those that are characterized by structural imbalances and dilapidated infrastructure, lessening the capacity to compete effectively. The increasing inequality within and between countries therefore raises basic questions regarding the fairness of trade agreements since it is drawn into broader discussions on the need for reform in the WTO's rule-making regime (Higgott et al., 2009). Resolving such problems is essential to ensure that globalization contributes its share to the socioeconomic development of all the nations. Moreover, the impact of globalization in developing countries can also be perceived within the periphery of cultural interaction and social transformation that typically accompanies increased trade. Foreign products, services, and ideas going into a local economy can lead to large-scale changes in habits and customs. In other nations, this results in greater cultural diversity and creativity. But widespread global brands and Western cultural patterns are threatening to devalue the native cultures and cause fear about homogenization of culture. The problem raises important questions regarding maintenance of cultural identity in the face of relentless globalization. Besides, the accompanying economic change can exacerbate disparities in society because the majority of the gains accrued from globalization find their way into the elitist echelons of society, thus increasing marginalization. The intersectionality of the challenge requires rethinking policy strategies in coming up with a more comprehensive approach to globalization (Gheyle et al., 2016). Interestingly, the relationship between globalization and the environment is being understood more and more, particularly for developing nations which suffer from environmental degradation. While these nations compete with each other for foreign investment and conformity to rules of international trade, they may be forced to prioritize economic growth more than environmental sustainability. This can give rise to overexploitation of natural resources, which exacerbates a cycle of environmental degradation. In addition, the effects of climate change have a tendency of disproportionately impacting developing nations, compounding factors such as poverty and famine. It is therefore important that the WTO and other international organizations incorporate environmental sustainability as part of trade deals. Proactively dealing with the environmental component of globalization not only boosts the future well-being of developing nations but also guarantees that international trade produces a sustainable world (Higgott et al., 2009). By doing this, the WTO can harmonize economic objectives with environmental requirements and establish a complete model of sustainable development.

9.2. BENEFITS OF WORLD TRADE ORGANIZATION (WTO) MEMBERSHIP FOR DEVELOPING COUNTRIES

WTO membership for developing countries is full of benefits, the main one being access to a rules-based and regulated world trade system. Through WTO membership, the developing countries are able to participate in an international market place where there exist stable and predictable rules under which they can trade with the advanced countries and other developing countries too. The Most-Favored-Nation principle of treatment by the organizations ensures that member states receive equal trade concessions, hence an equal playing field. This equal access can enhance region-specific industry competitiveness as well as contribute to developing countries' ability to diversify exports, thereby reducing economic vulnerability in times of financial crises. In addition, as nations struggle with the complexities of globalization, WTO membership serves as a tool for diplomacy whereby nations negotiate trade agreements that will garner precious economic benefits and allow for increased economic integration into the global economy, necessitated by the need to keep at bay globalizations pressures (Hoekman et al., 2017).

In addition, the WTO allows for more technical assistance and capacity-building programs, which are particularly useful for developing nations. These initiatives play a critical role in helping countries enhance their knowledge in trade regulation, implement international standards, and develop national policies that are in line with international practices. Through taking advantage of such projects, countries can enhance their trade infrastructure and enhance export capacity. Proof of the emphasis on developmental concerns is the new Trade Facilitation Agreement, which recognizes the particular challenges these nations are facing and aims to streamline customs procedures in order to facilitate their participation in global trade. This capacity building is essential to economic development that is sustainable because it empowers local firms with the capacity they need in order to compete globally, thereby driving economic development and overall well-being (Hoekman et al., 2017). Last but not least, WTO membership equips developing countries with an effective dispute-settlement mechanism that enables these countries to settle trade disputes fairly and constructively.

The presence of a formal system for dispute settlement minimizes the threat of falling prey to one-sided trade action by stronger nations, therefore creating a sense of security in trading relationships. Such an arrangement takes on a pivotal role in a time when regional preferential arrangements are becoming more common, with a tendency to undermine multilateral trading systems. By reinforcing multilateralism, the WTO enhances the legitimacy of trade governance and promotes equitable treatment of all members regardless of size or economic clout. Through this, the ability to negotiate and settle disputes in this framework not only sustains the interests of developing nations but also raises an enduring international trading system, imperative to long-term economic stability (Figure 9.5).

Figure 9.5. Benefits of World Trade Organization (WTO) membership for developing countries.

Source: https://c8.alamy.com/comp/2AEAMH9/benefits-of-wto-2AEAMH9.jpg.

9.2.1. Access to Larger Markets

Increased access to markets is one of the key areas where the World Trade Organizations (WTO) influence develops countries. Through access liberalization and dismantling access obstacles, the WTO provides entry points for these countries to enlarge their exports and reach global consumer markets. This ability is especially significant for those countries that rely heavily on agricultural or textile goods, which in the past were under significant trade barriers. As with the criticisms of free trade, such as the negative consequences of phased removal of textile quotas, liberalization into unrestricted markets usually injures weak industries within those economies (Bas et al., 2003). Nonetheless, exposure to greater markets is essential in order to spur economic growth, foster innovation, and enhance the prospects for employment. In the end, the WTOs role in integrating markets more globally can allow developing countries to escape economic stagnation. Nonetheless, exposure to greater markets is no unmixed blessing. Developing countries are often subject to structural barriers that put limits on their competitiveness in these greater marketplaces. Inadequate infrastructure, inadequate technology level, and limited financial resources can become hurdles for these nations to access high-value markets. Furthermore, underling imbalances in trade deals can place them at a disadvantage compared to the more industrialized nations, who can utilize their economic muscle to push their agenda. With the WTO attempting to deal with such structural issues, it is absolutely imperative to address issues of justice and fairness in its governance model. The increasing demand for equitable treatment in trade negotiations is an expression of this need, and the need for reforms that allow developing countries to become an influential part of global trade (Higgott et al., 2009). Second, the ability of developing countries to access more extensive markets directly correlates with the stability of the international trade regime as a whole. Since the WTO is confronted with a number of challenges, including the waning of free trade support in the developed world, the resilience of the trading system will directly impact developing countries' chances of development. Regional preferentialism is increasingly eroding the multilateral rules that the WTO stands for and may impede the flow of trade and investment to poor countries. Without a policy that is consistent and satisfies both the urgency of the economic crises of the day and the needs of the less-developed nations, the WTO risks being a failure as an advocate for global commerce. It is therefore essential that developing countries access the greater markets on a fair basis for their economic health as much as for the WTO to survive as an institution in the 21st century (Higgott et al., 2009).

9.2.2. Enhanced Foreign Investment Opportunities

World Trade Organization (WTO) is one of the most notable promoters of the field for enhanced foreign investment opportunities in developing countries. By creating an environment for trade liberalization, WTO assists these nations in accessing larger markets and thereby attracting multinational enterprises (MNEs) seeking to expand their business and capitalize on growing markets. When emerging economies open up their markets, they become more appealing to MNEs, who are looking for new means of expanding globally. Further, this foreign investment has a tendency to spill over into technology transfers and best practices adoption, both of which are crucial to the economic growth of these economies. It is required, though, that governments collectively ensure that they create favorable regulatory regimes in order to effectively harness these benefits because market forces are insufficient to balance out systemic distortions that such economies continually suffer (Benito et al., 2025). Although the prospect of enhanced foreign investment is very promising, opportunities as well as challenges are presented to developing countries. The economic environment is altered as FDI will result in the creation of employment, the improvement of infrastructure, and productivity. This inflow should be dealt with appropriately to prevent dependency or distorting the local industries. MNEs might focus on profit maximization, which might exclude indigenous businesses and result in a race to the bottom in the case of labor practices and environmental protection. Therefore, it is imperative that host countries formulate robust industrial policies that ensure sustainable development and also reap the benefits of the expertise brought in by foreign investors. By establishing a link between the attraction of foreign investment and the nurturing of domestic capabilities, these countries can position themselves favorably in the global economy (Dymond et al., 2025). The new trends of global value chains also underscore the need for strategic foreign investment in the developing countries. As nations grow more interdependent with one another through trade relations, the right investment decisions can spur economic development and raise competitiveness at the global level. The experience of nations which pursue trade agreements aggressively reveals that a friendly environment for investment can yield explosive benefits. Recognizing the role of commercial and regulatory integration, particularly with big economies, developing countries can modify their policies to derive the greatest gains from globalization. Hence, developing cooperation and partnerships with MNEs enables these countries to better integrate into global economies, creating a strong basis for long-term economic resilience and foreign investment potential (Dymond et al., 2025) (Figure 9.6).

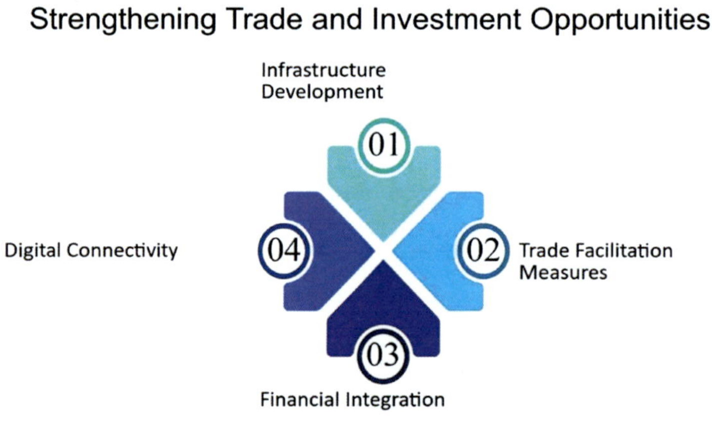

Figure 9.6. Trade and investment opportunities.

Source: https://fastercapital.co/i/Economic-Integration--Fostering-Prosperity-along-the-One-Belt-One-Road--Strengthening-Trade-and-Investment-Opportunities.webp.

9.2.3. Technical Assistance and Capacity Building

The capacity building and technical assistance function in the context of the World Trade Organization (WTO) is crucial in ensuring developing countries are able to play a significant role in the global trading community. By providing assistance in negotiating the complexity of trade as well as adherence to rules, disparity between advanced economies and emerging markets is minimized. Strategies meant to bolster institutional capacities, such as training efforts and resource sharing, assist in empowering developing countries. They enable them not only to uphold trade obligations but to also avail themselves of growth opportunities. The emphasis on capacity development is most appropriate in the framework of WTOs special and differential treatment principles, which require supportive measures sensitive to the specific circumstances and needs of developing member states (Misovicova, 2025). Additionally, the outcomes of WTO negotiations, particularly in the General Agreement on Trade in Services (GATS), underscore the function of robust technical assistance for developing countries. While nations like India are confronted with new regulatory hurdles that arise from these negotiations, technical support is essential to assist them in navigating the shifting trade landscape. The interdependence between trading rules, capacity building, and specific industries, including the maritime industry, highlights the need for focused support strategies that conform to member states' distinctive economic conditions. The unfavorable condition of marine exports in developing economies is a classic example of the possible consequences of international trade agreements, highlighting the reason for proactive initiatives in capacity building (Kamat et al., 2025). In the development of a balanced global trading system, the WTO emphasis on technical assistance and capacity building can ensure sustainable growth in less-developed countries. By boosting local competence and institutional competitiveness, these measures not only improve compliance with international trade rules but also increase economic diversification and resistance to external shocks. These measures mirror the broader objectives of the WTO to build an inclusive system enabling developing nations to participate positively in international trade. Customizing assistance to reflect regional and sectoral needs has the potential to counteract the adverse consequences of globalization, ensuring that the benefits of trade benefit a wider populace. Ultimately, good quality capacity building and technical assistance can serve as agents of transformative change, aligning the WTO agenda with the development aspirations of its member states (Misovicova, 2025).

9.3. CHALLENGES FACED BY DEVELOPING COUNTRIES IN THE WORLD TRADE ORGANIZATION (WTO)

Developing countries face a set of challenges in the context of the WTO, which significantly discourage them from benefiting from all facets of international trade. One of the key obstacles is the tendency for the rules and agreements of the WTO to be highly complex, disproportionately disadvantaging countries with lower administrative capacity and resources. For instance, such nations lack the specialist staff to negotiate sophisticated legal systems and effectively represent themselves in the course of negotiations. Secondly, the different economic conditions that exist in third-world nations render it difficult for them to compete on an equal level, particularly with advanced countries that possess greater access to high-tech tools and greater market access. Therefore, these imbalances create an uneven playing field that truncates economic growth and exacerbates poverty levels in the majority of developing regions in the world. Moreover, developing nations, particularly Sub-Saharan Africa, have their agricultural exports frequently impaired by excessive external market access barriers.

Figure 9.7. Challenges faced by developing countries in the World Trade Organization (WTO).

Source: https://fastercapital.co/i/URDG-Dispute-Resolution--Navigating-Challenges-in-International-Trade--Common-Challenges-in-International-Trade-Disputes.webp.

The WTO agreements, the Agreement on Agriculture (AoA) in specific, impose terms that repeatedly favor the developed nations and subsidized agricultural products from the developed world. As attested by a number of studies, Sub-Saharan African countries have their market access restricted by tariff peaks and escalation, particularly in the case of agro-processed products, which inhibits them from agricultural export diversification. The issues become more compounded when non-tariff barriers such as sanitary and phytosanitary (SPS) and technical barriers to trade (TBT) are accounted for, which hinders them from exporting and reducing the competitiveness of these nations' products. Therefore, short of ironing out these bottlenecks, the DDA negotiations remain important to level the playing ground and expand export possibilities. Last but not least, the issue of enforcing trade reform remains another barrier confronting developing nations engaged in the WTO. As is demonstrated by the Vietnamese experience of becoming a market economy, rapid liberalization has the potential to result in conflicting forces and incomplete reforms in other essential spheres, i.e., state enterprises and public administration. Though Vietnams initial efforts at trade reform hold promise for expansion, they also exhibit the inherent flaws that these reforms carry, i.e., a sluggish rate of complementary changes required to sustain long-term growth. This is a common situation for the majority of developing countries; the simultaneous need for paired reforms and trade liberalization can result in systemic instability and regression. Hence, effective implementation of policy of trade accompanied by paired reforms is critical for developing countries to maximize the benefits of WTO membership and achieve sustainable economic development, as reflected by their continuous failure to balance market access and the quality of infrastructure (Figure 9.7).

9.3.1. Limited Negotiating Power

In the context of global trade negotiations, developing countries are generally faced with a number of challenges by virtue of their limited negotiating capacity under the umbrella of the World Trade Organization (WTO). Asymmetry of economic powers between developed and developing countries leads to a divergence that affects the latter's potential to influence trade agreements and policies. Because these kinds of negotiations benefit stronger economies, developing countries are usually inclined to accept terms that are not necessarily aligned with their development needs. Apart from denying them the capability to advance equitable trade practices, this limitation also exacerbates already existing inequalities in the global economic system, thereby sustaining the cycle of dependency and underdevelopment. Furthermore, the issue is also aggravated by the nature of high-stakes trade agreements such as the Trans-Pacific Partnership (TPP). While these agreements have long been promoted as a way of boosting trade and economic integration, they have been criticized as being secretive and elitist in their approach. For developing countries, the implication of being locked out or relegated to second-tier positions is massive-scale. The lack of transparency undermines their ability to successfully lobby for provisions that could protect their interests and stimulate sustainable development. Of specific concern is the charge in relation to the TPP negotiations, which identified exclusion from decision-making processes propelling main trade rules by leading players such as emerging economies and civil society players (Yu et al., 2014). This omission calls into question the universality and legitimacy of agreements which have profound effects on the developing nations. International trade competitive forces even reinforce weak bargaining abilities of the developing nations. For instance, competitive interdependence in the US-EU relationship illustrates how leading nations utilize regional trade pacts to augment economic power. While they expand their scope with strategic alliances, developing nations are disadvantaged, possessing weak bargaining leverage to counter unfavorable terms or adapt to the rapidly evolving global trade trend. Such a competitive landscape is made all the more complex when developing countries attempt to ally themselves with experienced economic powers that can manipulate and maximize the WTO provisions for their benefit. Consequently, as the EU and US increase their spheres of influence through varying agreements, developing nations are faced with a negotiating culture that is not only unequal but also antagonistic to their development and economic opportunities (Sbragia et al., 2009).

9.3.2. Trade Barriers and Tariffs

Tariffs and trade barriers have been a contentious issue in global trade negotiations, having an enormous impact on developing countries. These restrictions, in turn, have the opposite effect of slowing economic growth and restricting access to markets for exports. WTO expects elimination of such restrictive policy measures will lead to a more balanced playing field in trade. Notably, in the Doha Round of talks, the persistent challenge of subsidies on agricultural products in developed economies has proven to be enormous challenges for developing nations. The extremely high level of protectionism in agriculture, especially among the United States and Europe, inhibits the ability of these countries to compete, hence shortchanging their future growth and development in the international market (Bouet et al., 2025). This is an illustration of the complex interaction between domestic policy decisions and foreign trade pressures. The potential for liberalization of trade in the developing world depends on reducing tariffs and other trade barriers, which would be potentially beneficial for turning around economic fortunes. Evidence based on application of the MIRAGE computable general equilibrium model has indicated that a huge shift towards free trade would imply very large benefits for developing economies, particularly agriculture that is a major source of livelihood for the majority of individuals (Bouet et al., 2025). The benefits of such reform can extend beyond facile economic growth; they can contribute to alleviating rural poverty as well as food security in those regions where farmers compete fiercely with subsidized farm produce from wealthier nations. In this instance, the Doha Development Agenda seeks to establish a more balanced trade agreement that addresses the needs of developing countries so that they can enjoy fully their participation in the new world order of the global market. Moreover, the trade barrier effects do not differ proportionally across developing regions. For instance, the estimates from the GTAP database and the World Banks LINKAGE model suggest that multilateral trade reform can yield significant income gains to Sub-Saharan Africa, even at the expense of some potential short-term trade losses. In circumstances where tariffs are lowered, farm incomes in this region, and others, will rise, reducing rural poverty. Further, some degree of liberalization of trade by the Doha Round could be an important step towards such goals, provided there is cooperative effort on the part of developing countries to reduce their own applied tariffs, in particular on major farm imports. Such a strategy emphasizes the necessity of all-encompassing knowledge about trade policy and its impact on the international economy, specifically on developing countries in the context of the WTO (Figure 9.8).

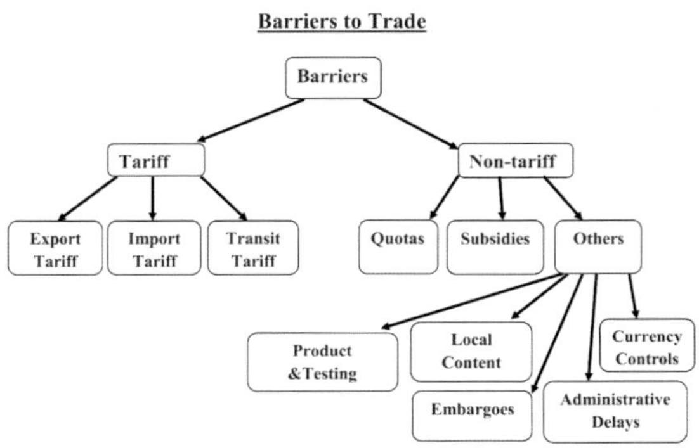

Figure 9.8. Trade barriers and tariffs.

Source: https://www.simplynotes.in/wp-content/uploads/2016/03/Barriers_to_Trade-final.jpg.

9.3.3. Compliance with World Trade Organization (WTO) Regulations

Compliance with WTO rules by developing countries is a multifaceted phenomenon driven by economic, political, and social factors. For most developing countries, the compliance with WTO norms tends to require major adaptations of national laws and practices. Such compliance tends to burden industries at the national level, especially those that are heavily dependent on protective tariffs and subsidies, requiring a delicate balancing act between international commitments and national interests. Furthermore, capacity to comply is frequently unevenly distributed, with some suffering more entrenched structural issues. As recognized through a number of studies, Chinas intellectual property rights experience under the WTOs Agreement on Trade-Related Intellectual Property Rights (TRIPS) illustrates these complexities, illustrating how different domestic variables can affect compliance outcomes and inform more general economic strategies nations employ to encourage international competitiveness (Fojtíková et al., 2018). The compatibility of WTO rules with national law constantly challenges sovereignty and the autonomy of developing countries in making their own domestic policy. Compliant governments within these countries usually consider compliance as a loss of policymaking autonomy, an argument that can trigger resistance from domestic players. For instance, the decision to bestow regulatory authority under such as the Agreement on the Application of Sanitary and Phytosanitary Measures is one of strategic intent by states, whereby regulatory coherence is more desirable than the compromises inherent in international agreements (Buthe et al., 2008).

This situation is pointing out that each time there is compliance, each encouraging global collaboration and trade relations but with the potential side effect of undesirable consequences such that national interests do not align with the global market expectations. In the end, successful compliance of WTO norms by developing countries relies on strategic interaction and capacity building. The countries must take an integrative understanding of their global obligations as well as each establishing an environment that facilitates economic development. Moreover, technical and financial support from developed countries can play a significant role in alleviating compliance obligations of developing nations so that they are able to establish systems that are not just compliant with WTO standards but also responsive to national developmental needs. This calls for a mature view that strikes a balance between compliance and national interests, lest the differential gap between the international trade requirements and domestic economic realities widens and the long-term sustainable development efforts are compromised.

9.4. CASE STUDIES OF DEVELOPING COUNTRIES IN THE WORLD TRADE ORGANIZATION (WTO)

The dynamics of the WTO have a tendency to impact developing countries in sophisticated manners that are visible through the various policies that members like Brazil and Mexico undertake. Developing countries that are subject to the same legal obligations of the WTO have disparate trade and litigation policy strategies that reflect their own economic aims and development environments. According to Santos et al. (2012), Brazil utilized an activist strategy, utilizing litigation and legal means to advance its interests and expand its regulative space. Mexico, on the other hand, has a more tempered approach, operating within compliance parameters in response to the intricate dynamics of international economic law. Through these case studies, it comes to be understood that developing countries do possess the strategic ability to utilize the WTO in order to not just gain access to new markets but even protect their domestic policies, highlighting the flexibility that exists within the seemingly rigid systems of WTO norms. The broader implications of the Doha Development Agenda highlight ongoing challenges in striking a balance between trade liberalization and developmental objectives for such countries. To begin with, the agenda aimed at rectifying past imbalances in market access and acknowledged the difficulties of developing countries. As found in Chabe-Ferret et al. (2007), evaluations demonstrate that trade liberalization is capable of delivering economic benefits but with differing development outcomes based on specific country contexts.

For instance, differences in economic frameworks, industrialization rates, and ability to implement policies can influence the success of a country in benefiting from these liberalization measures. Thus, the failure to find an uniform outcome from trade liberalization illustrates the complexity of bringing development into world trade negotiations, reflecting the need for differentiated approaches addressing individual country situations. Lastly, reading the case studies of Mexico and Brazil in the context of the WTO is a rich source of information regarding how global trade laws intersect with development agendas. These countries are exemplary of how policy making and strategic litigation can help developing nations be able to direct the intricacies of global trade towards their benefits. Apart from that, they enlighten us on the significant fact that while WTO commitments can impose some limitations, they can also be avenues through which states can articulate their economic interests and advance development objectives. This complex understanding calls for rethinking the assumed WTO regulation inflexibility, a narrative that embraces the reality of growth and expansion in an interdependent world economy, as evident in Santos et al. (2012).

9.4.1. Success Stories: Brazil and India

Brazil and India are traditional case studies that highlight the ability of developing nations to succeed in managing the complexities of global trade under the patronage of the World Trade Organization (WTO). The two nations have adopted different strategies which are in line with their diverse economic status while attempting to integrate into the international economy. Brazil's policy interventions to support agribusiness have turned it into one of the world's leading agricultural exporters, leveraging its massive natural assets and favorable climate. Similarly, India has focused on developing its information technology and services sectors, with large-skilled human labor base to enhance its economic profile. All of these successes demonstrate the path that strategic use of WTO principles can lead to effective national policy efforts toward economic growth, ultimately transforming these countries into global players in their respective market segments. But the Indian and Brazilian experiences also mirror the issues that arise in the context of global trade and the WTOs regulatory regime. Both nations have had to contend with the restrictive forces of global trade regulations, which have the effect of stifling local entrepreneurship and innovation. For instance, even as Brazil has benefited from its agriculture exports, the need to conform to export requirements and subsidies from more advanced nations has complicated the life of its policy.

Figure 9.9. Brazil and India developing countries in the World Trade Organization (WTO).

Source: https://miro.medium.com/v2/resize:fit:1400/1*AwtxORHqUoj9BG_e9z-v4DA.jpeg.

Concurrently, India too is struggling with the dilemma of positioning small-scale industries within supply chains globally, where strict WTO regulations can hinder new enterprises to enter the market. The dilemma between protecting home-industries and observing external trade norms reflects the intricate trade-offs developing countries must embark upon in an attempt to find balance in sustainable growth within the international economy. Interestingly, the Brazilian and Indian experiences suggest that industrial policy remains essential to leading economic growth, even despite the new setting presented by globalization. Sound industrial policy can reverse market failures that inhibit development, particularly in lagging industries on the global landscape. As discussed in contemporary discourses on the objectives of industrial policy, emerging economies must reform their approach in an attempt to overcome the hurdles brought by the WTO framework and global market dynamics (Irfan ul Haque,

2025). Brazil's focus on farming productivity and India's on technology and services exemplify this precept, with both countries having experimented with tailor-made solutions that reflect their specific realities. These success stories buttress the critical appreciation that while globalization presents difficulties, it also offers opportunity for developing nations to establish differentiated trajectories towards economic development (Figure 9.9).

9.4.2. Struggles Faced by Least Developed Countries (LDCs)

The LDCs are characterized by a specific set of challenges that discourage their economic development and integration into world markets. Such nations typically are burdened with high levels of poverty, limited access to education and health, and inadequate infrastructure. Their human capital development is thus stalled, further exacerbating their socio-economic situation. In the realm of international trade, LDCs also face significant challenges such as weak export capacities and trade facilitation issues that aggravate their capacity for global value chain participation. Therefore, they are vulnerable to external shocks, driven by factors of climate change and political instability. Tackling the latter is imperative for LDCs' capacity-building in making meaningful contributions to the World Trade Organization (WTO) policies, which would maximize their economic potential in the global economy. Secondly, the role of foreign aid and aid mechanisms cannot be discounted in mitigation of the set of problems with LDCs.

Assistance from the industrialized countries and foreign institutions can go a long way in complementing infrastructure development, health improvement, and educational initiatives. Trade policies supported by the WTO are likely to open doors to economic growth but will be most effective when supplemented by targeted aid focused on LDCs' varied needs. For instance, proposals to raise agricultural productivity can directly influence food security and income levels. However, the sustainability of such efforts requires a participatory strategy where knowledge transfer and capacity-building are prioritized. This facilitates that LDCs are not just aid recipients but are active participants in their own development, which ultimately results in stronger economic results in the long term. Regardless of the promise of world trade, LDCs tend to be trapped in a paradox where more trade doesn't automatically equate to effective development. The internal inequalities in international trade systems present daunting challenges to LDCs. Tariffs and quotas by industrial nations, for example, can limit the exposure of LDCs to major markets, thus stifling their economies. Further, relying on a narrow range of exports exposes nations to market risks, leading to poverty traps. Towards this end, better communication between WTO member states is key to correcting the structural imbalances that serve LDCs ill.

Engaging in negotiations that prioritize their particular development interests can unlock the avenue to more equitable trade agreements, which ultimately translate into a more inclusive world economy. This is essential in ensuring that the interests of LDCs are recognized and integrated into the overall framework of international trade.

9.4.3. Comparative Analysis of Different Regions

The World Trade Organization (WTO) plays a pivotal role in shaping trade policies that affect developing countries in various regions. Comparative analysis seeks out vast inequalities in how these nations deal with WTO frameworks based on specialized economic, social, and political considerations. For instance, regions that possess stronger systems of governance and higher education levels, like parts of East Asia, are in a better position to utilize WTO regulations to their advantage for economic growth. Sub-Saharan Africa, however, is in a very bad place in terms of access to technology and less strong institutional systems. The regional disparities underscore the need for tailored trade policies cognizant of local context and ability, rather than a uniform one-size-fits-all approach, to foster sustainable development in these nations. The regions differ in technological advancement and diffusion levels and, in turn, impact their performance within the global trade system. A case study of such regions as the Russian Federation reveals substantial heterogeneity of technological use among business organizations. Advanced countries with developed urban centers and built-up scientific bases will likely be innovation leaders, as local technological surveys have established. The study brings to the forefront the importance of identifying local characteristics in applying new technologies in business in order to attain innovative development. Accordingly, the deployment of technological rejuvenation models must be informed by local contexts, promoting effective public-private partnerships and ecosystems that respond to the particular demands of industries within these emerging economies, as highlighted in the findings of Garina et al. (2025). In addition to technological determinants, demographic and socioeconomic determinants also play an important role in shaping the experiences of emerging economies under the WTOs regime. For instance, variations in pregnant women's health outcomes at risk of gestational diabetes across nations buttress the importance of cultural and environmental contexts in shaping policies for health. When comparing different sites, there is significant heterogeneity in risk factors that affect maternal health, so trade policy must account for these differences among populations. Taking a contextual approach, policymakers will then be able to develop targeted interventions that address the specific issues of every region. This underscores the importance of the WTO engaging member states in meaningful discussion that considers local circumstances, ensuring that trade benefits are redistributed equitably and align with the diverse needs of developing countries, as hinted at by the variations set by O'Reilly et al. (2025) (Figure 9.10).

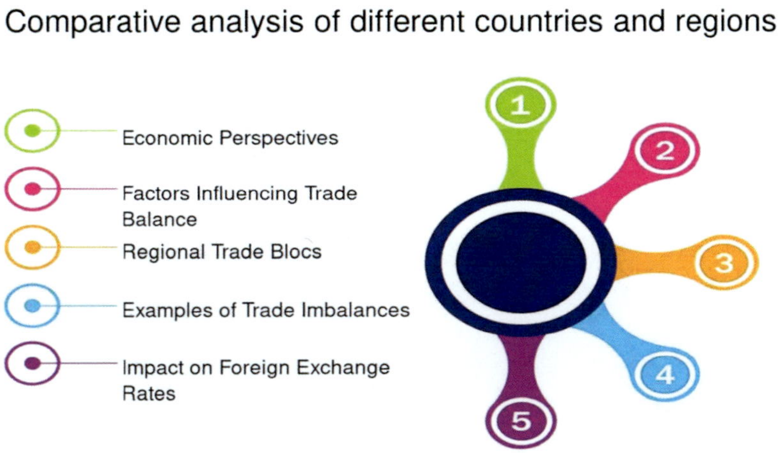

Figure 9.10. Comparative analysis of different regions.

Source: https://fastercapital.co/i/Trade-Balance-and-Volume-of-Trade--A-Comparative-Analysis--A-comparative-analysis-of-different-countries-and-regions.webp.

9.5. THE ROLE OF AGRICULTURE IN WORLD TRADE ORGANIZATION (WTO) NEGOTIATIONS

The role of agriculture is central to the WTO negotiations, especially with the economic dependence of most developing countries on this sector. The agriculture market is the most closed market with elevated barriers such as tariffs and subsidies that significantly favor developed countries. Reshaping farm policies is therefore central to increasing market access and ensuring equitable trade practices. The US-European impasse over the Doha Round is a pointer to differences regarding farming negotiations, illustrating the extent of entrenched protectionist policies that hamper talks. The Doha Development Agenda was intended to cut down these protections, but there is serious contention regarding the extent of commitments developed countries should make. This standstill has extensive implications for developing nations, wherein agriculture remains a rural economy lifeline and a poverty reduction mechanism (Bouet et al., 2025). Besides, the complexity of agricultural negotiations at the WTO is more than mere market access; it entails food security, rural development, and sustainability of the environment. The agricultural sector provides employment for a considerable percentage of laborers in developing countries, contributing food to national stocks and economic stability. Consequently, the outcome of WTO negotiations within the sector directly impacts the lives of millions of citizens. The disparity in bargaining capacities between developing nations and developed nations traditionally results in outcomes unfavorable to the former. This imbalance of power calls into question whether poorer countries are in a position to adequately articulate their priorities and needs in the negotiating process.

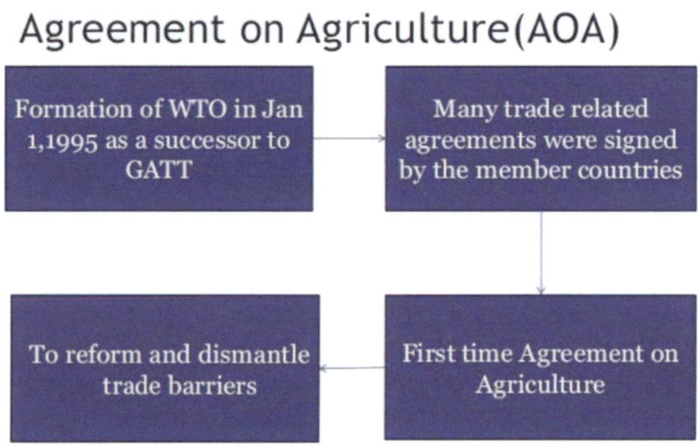

Figure 9.11. World Trade Organization (WTO) agreement on agriculture.

Source: https://external-content.duckduckgo.com/iu/?u=https%3A%2F%2Fimage.slidesharecdn.com%2Fwto-agreementonagriculture-150103020257-conversion-gate02%2F95%2Fwto-agreement-on-agriculture-2-638.jpg%3Fcb%3D1420250836&f=1&nofb=1&ipt=5aafd524de9cf952e12e04c6abf7ec41c0ff9cdd7ed251c4376e4d32d3dca1a3.

Adequate representation and support are called for to ensure that agricultural trade reforms contribute constructively to rural development and do not exacerbate existing imbalances (Dominique van der Mensbrugghe et al., 2025). As negotiations continue, it is crucial that all parties realize the multi-faceted benefits of agricultural trade liberalization to developing countries. Economic analysis has shown that multilateral trade reform can yield large gains, particularly for agricultural sectors that have high protection currently in place. Removing subsidies and tariffs can lead to higher real incomes and reduced rural poverty in developing regions such as Sub-Saharan Africa. But these gains will be realized only through a common effort by all members of the

WTO to implement their obligations equally. Moreover, developing countries must take an active role in negotiations, advocating policies that consider their particular needs and capacities. By treating agriculture as the highest priority in the WTO negotiations, there is the potential not only to enhance the equity of trade but also to support sustainable development consistent with international food security goals (Bouet et al., 2025; Dominique van der Mensbrugghe et al., 2025) (Figure 9.11).

9.5.1. Importance of Agriculture for Developing Economies

Agriculture is a central industry in the economies of developing nations, with the primary source of work, income, and food security. Despite developments in industrial and technology sectors, the majority of developing nations remain reliant on agriculture to sustain their economic pillars. The reliance comes with particular issues regarding how agricultural productivity and market access can be affected by global trade policies, such as those promoted by the WTO. The potential impact of agreements such as Trade-Related Aspects of Intellectual Property Rights (TRIPS) identifies the intricacies of these nations. Though stronger intellectual property rights have the potential to enhance technological advancement, they also have the potential to disconnect farmers from the resources they require in farming, paving the way for highly balanced policy measures that genuinely encourage agricultural activities without precisely instituting burdens that can stifle growth (Lall and Albaladejo, 2025). Trade liberalization under the WTO framework has the potential both to benefit and challenge the agricultural sectors of the developing economies. Market entry could enhance the volume of agricultural exports, but the benefits are found to be unevenly distributed among countries, as recent studies attest (Bureau et al., 2025). To the majority of developing nations, the immediate gains of trade liberalization can be trumped by the adverse effect of forfeited preferential treatment and increased competition from highly subsidized agricultural products from wealthier countries. Accordingly, while tariff cuts are crucial gains, they cannot necessarily compensate for the non-tariff barriers that hinder the poorer nations' ability to penetrate the market. These barriers, typically established on rigorous sanitary and phytosanitary standards, require tailored solutions recognizing the particular barriers built-up agricultural producers encounter. Agriculture in developing nations also encompasses more than basic economic data, but social and environmental factors too. Agriculture not only contributes to the living of millions but to national identity and social cohesion as well. While developing nations enter the global trade system, ensuring priority is given to sustainable agriculture capable of resisting the pressures of globalizations is urgent. Placing food sovereignty and ecological resilience at the forefront is critical in formulating trade policies that respond to local aspirations and requirements. For this purpose, differentiated treatment in WTO negotiations is required, which supplies remedies that bolster the agricultural sectors of developing countries while enabling them to compete globally. This multi-dimensional comprehension of agriculture's role can better direct trade negotiations so that they are representative and inclusive of the different realities of developing economies (Bureau et al., 2025).

9.5.2. Subsidies and Their Impact on Trade

The role of subsidies in global trade, as it is under the WTO and their implication on the developing world, is a critical field of study. Subsidies distort market competition by creating a level playing field for some domestic producers, by default, at the expense of developing-world producers whose agriculture might be export-oriented. Such as the systems of tariff and non-tariff barriers layer these problems with complexity. For instance, the negotiation outcome of the Doha Round of trade talks has been pivotal in finding solutions to the agricultural subsidy problem, but loopholes are still present. Developed country nations, such as members of the European Union and the United States, still maintain high levels of agricultural subsidies that hinder more even competition. This discrepancy calls into question the efficiency of the WTO in ensuring that the playing ground is leveled for the emerging nations, as observed in research on the Indian Marine Trade and Service industry in relation to subsidies and trade policies (Kamat et al., 2025). Subsidies are not monetary instruments only; they are blocks upon which the global agricultural market is structured and have a significant contribution towards establishing the dynamics of trade. Indeed, the heavily subsidized farm economies of the West are a great challenge for developing countries to gain market access. The Doha Round talks were supposed to deliver significant reforms in this sector, but after two years from Cancún, there is little progress. The United States-European Union agriculture conflict shows the character of fair solutions elusive. Subsidies in such sectors result in an unbalanced competitive landscape that diminishes the ability of developing countries to compete effectively on the international market. Hence, the highly protected nature of such sectors permits ongoing protectionism, suppressing trade expansion as well as economic growth in the developing world (Bouet et al., 2025). Subsidy impacts go beyond direct effects on trade, such as overall systemic issues within the agricultural sector. For developing countries, reliance on agricultural exports can contribute to their vulnerabilities, particularly when facing subsidized competition from industrial nations. The interaction between subsidies and trade policy generally generates a vicious cycle of dependence where developing countries cannot develop autonomous agricultural systems. In this context, the implications of Special and Differential

Treatment provisions then become vital issues for policymakers. They are able to provide some advantage to developing nations but the effectiveness of such provisions remains hampered by the vested interests of the developed world. Ultimately, elimination of the damages caused by subsidies must occur through a multi-faceted process consisting of both targeted negotiations and institutional changes in the WTO framework so that developing countries can improve their ability to fend for themselves in the midst of global trade complexities (Kamat et al., 2025) (Figure 9.12).

Figure 9.12. Subsidies and their impact on trade.

Source: https://fastercapital.co/i/Subsidies--The-Role-of-Government-Support-in-Protectionist-Policies--The-Impact-of-Subsidies-on-International-Trade.webp.

9.5.3. Ongoing Debates on Agricultural Trade Policies

Ongoing debates regarding agricultural trade policy are directly linked with the World Trade Organization (WTO) contributions towards advocating fair trade practices. Multifunctionality is the theme of such debates, as it seeks to recognize agricultures various social functions beyond economic assessment. These developing country negotiators argue that this template can be utilized to justify more protections and subsidies, such as those granted developed nations. This strategy also focuses on defending local food industries, promoting food security and sustainable development. These negotiations are complicated because history involves the use of protectionist policies to bring about industrialization in developing countries, with all the benefits for society. Thus, the discussion of multifunctionality identifies the necessity of a holistic analysis of current agricultural policies in terms of synchronization with economic development and social welfare in the context of developing nations (Diaz-Bonilla et al., 2025). Globalization poses a paradox to developing nations in the context of agricultural trade. On the one hand, it promises economic development, but on the other hand, it tends to aggravate inequalities that negatively affect the poorest sections of society. High tariffs, protectionism among richer nations, and several non-tariff barriers strongly restrict developing-country access to world markets for their goods. Such obstacles identify a structural imbalance in the practice of trade under which playing field conditions in which developing economies can thrive are unfairly weighted against them. Constraints like impenetrable regulation also restrict smallholder farmer ability to compete in global markets. As such, it is important that the debate in the WTO recognizes such disparities and demands both prudent trade practices and removal of harmful protectionist measures which exacerbate the differential between developing and developed countries (Diaz-Bonilla et al., 2025). Moreover, domestic policies in developing countries as well as international trade agreements also play an important role in shaping agricultural outcomes. For small farmers to compete, governments in developing nations need to tackle underlying issues like access to education, health care, land, and capital. Without proper support systems, even the best trade deals would not benefit poor farm communities. Public policy needs to place a high value on programs that strengthen infrastructure, market access, and research capacity to allow small farmers to compete more vigorously in the global market. The ongoing debates regarding agricultural trade policies, thus, need a two-pronged approach: reforming domestic situations and concurrently advocating for equitable international trade rules. These collective efforts are crucial in reconfiguring the agricultural sector and ensuring that globalization can minimize poverty and enhance sustainable livelihoods among rural poor (Diaz-Bonilla et al., 2025).

9.6. FUTURE PROSPECTS FOR DEVELOPING COUNTRIES IN THE WORLD TRADE ORGANIZATION (WTO)

Future prospects for developing countries within the WTO system in the future heavily depend on the world trade policy dynamics as well as prevailing trends in geopolitics. As these nations seek to enhance economic growth through integration into the international trade system, they face critical challenges in the form of rising protectionism as well as regional trade agreements that have a tendency to by-pass multilateral bargaining. These situations underscore the necessity of a robust WTO as a platform for balanced trade processes. The developing countries have been using the WTO to drive negotiations for good terms of trade; however, the recent shift of global sentiments towards open markets, particularly among the major OECD countries, threatens to undermine those advantages. Addressing these concerns is not merely a question of completing current negotiations, such as those of the Doha Round, but of re-conceiving the WTO's role in facilitating systems of equitable and equitable world trade relations (Higgott et al., 2009). Another crucial determinant of the future of developing countries in the WTO is the change in global economic governance in the context of a rapid evolution towards a digital economy. As the production pattern changes with a focus on technology and services, fresh policy challenges arise that come very hard on the developing nations.

Figure 9.13. Future prospects for developing countries in the World Trade Organization (WTO).

Source: https://www.cato.org/sites/cato.org/files/styles/optimized/public/2023-05/world-flags-cropped.jpg?itok=nUVz893b.

The WTO must adapt itself to these developments by making it possible for the developing nations to articulate their interest and concern. That means there has to be some removal of agriculture subsidies and non-tariff barriers. The discovery of such differences in perspective among member states highlights the need for rigorous debate of ongoing and upcoming trade policies. Moreover, in the absence of consensus and receptiveness to reform on the WTO platform, the developing world holds a chance of getting pushed further towards the periphery in global trade discourse (Hoekman et al., 2017). Despite the pressing problems, there remains space for the developing world to unlock the cooperative potential of the WTO. Recent developments, for instance, the Trade Facilitation Agreement, demonstrate commitment to addressing development problems while consolidating basic trade regulations. These initiatives demonstrate that the WTO is able to evolve in harmony with member states' demands by stimulating new means of managing trade. For developing countries, engagement in such agreements offers a possibility of enhancing their trade capabilities, hence driving economic progress. As stakeholders consider cooperative structures that account for social preferences and diverse national circumstances, the potential for reinvigorating multilateral cooperation becomes increasingly viable. By constructing an inclusive discussion within the WTO, developing nations may be well positioned to benefit from a rules-based trading system fostering equity and resilience in a global interdependent economy (Higgott et al., 2009; Hoekman et al., 2017) (Figure 9.13).

9.6.1. Potential Reforms within the World Trade Organization (WTO)

The WTO is at a crossroads and requires reforms that can more effectively address the interests of developing nations. Developing countries are generally disadvantaged in the multilateral trading system due to structural imbalances and insufficient negotiating capacity. Introducing reforms that aim at expanding participatory mechanisms in trade negotiations could provide such countries with the strength they require to better champion their interests. Importantly, developing countries must endure industry-specific pressures, and thus the need for industry-specific trade facilitation and adjustment measures. By establishing a system through which these nations can participate in setting trade policy, the WTO can make the trading system more equitable worldwide and promote sustainable development and address the specific needs of its member nations. Trade facilitation on the WTO agenda is just one such area of reform. Trade facilitation measures may increase the efficiency of trade flows and reduce costs, particularly of countries that do not have quality infrastructure and administrative ability, particularly in least developed countries (LDCs). For instance, as seen, sustained customs reform in Bangladesh is a model of the benefits derivable from using trade facilitation programs. But these countries also have to be able to manage the related challenges of these reforms, such as the capability and willingness to comply with new standards. Thus, the WTOs focus on capacity building and technical assistance is triggered, ensuring that developing countries not only become part of the game but also participating players of trade facilitation programs (Bhattacharya et al., 2025). Moreover, development of industry adjustment policies to offset agricultural trade reform is most important in reducing the negative impact on sensitive industries of developing nations. Industry-based strategies are required for the intricateness of trade reforms owing to varying challenges that developing nations undergo as opposed to those encountered by the developed economies. It is crucial that the WTO reacts to such imbalances through adjustment of assistance and funding to suit the specific conditions of different economies. Successful adjustment policies can help bridge the transitions developing countries have to undergo to fulfill their international trade obligations while shielding domestic industries from undue disruption. This focus on differential treatment and support will enable a more equitable implementation of WTO reforms that really works to the benefit of all members (Harris et al., 2025).

9.6.2. The Role of Emerging Economies

The role of the emerging economies in shaping the trends of international trade has increased prominence, particularly through their involvement in the World Trade Organization (WTO). Other nations such as China, India, Brazil, and South Africa, or CIBS as they are termed together, have transitioned from the margins of the global economy to being significant players in the global economic scene. Their growing economic influence not only makes them more potent negotiators in multilateral negotiations but also upends the underlying structure determining global trade. As these economies insist on more equitable rules of trade, the consequences for the WTO multilateral trading system are profound. The engagement of emerging economies calls up essential questions regarding the adequacy of current agreements and their ability to serve the special needs and ambitions of the developing nations in the global market (Nenci et al., 2025). Inclusion of emerging economies into the WTO framework is a two-edged sword that presents prospects and challenges. Despite the fact that the accession of these nations has enriched the discussion on trade policy, it has also exposed the disadvantages experienced by developing economies, particularly in the domain of marine trade. For example, Indias marine export industry is facing new regulatory barriers posed by WTO negotiations as well as changing European Union regulations, which have the potential to form additional barriers to trade (Kamat et al., 2025). These issues are meant to highlight the necessity for emerging economies, not only to negotiate but to build endogenous capacities that will be able to withstand external pressures. In order to accomplish this in this very complicated landscape, developing countries need to cultivate resilience through selective policy intervention and cooperation with international institutions. In addition, emerging economies' growing power highlights the necessity to bring into account special and differential treatment provisions within the WTO regime. As these nations get increasingly engaged in world trade, they get increasingly confronted with idiosyncratic issues demanding specific solutions, especially in subsidy-related negotiations, tariff related, and non-tariff barrier related. For instance, the terms imposed by the General Agreement on Trade in Services (GATS) could disproportionately affect sea exports of such developing economies as India (Kamat et al., 2025). By encouraging fair trade practices and increased technical assistance, emerging economies are able to actively influence the rules of international trade. Their development towards more representative engagement in the WTO not only enhances their domestic industries but is also to the benefit of the welfare of the global trading system, hopefully establishing a more balanced approach to development.

9.6.3. Strategies for Enhancing Participation and Benefits

Under the World Trade Organization's world trading system and developing nations, enhanced participation and benefits necessitate strategic action that can capacitate developing countries to participate more assertively in WTO negotiations and dispute settlement. The building of legal and institutional capacities is among the strategies that can capacitate developing countries to become capable of participating more aggressively in WTO negotiations and dispute settlement. Through the creation of a robust "developmental legal capacity," states can utilize international economic law to protect their developmental interests when advancing market opportunities. Brazil and Mexico are excellent cases in point regarding how adaptable legal strategies allow them to manage the complexity of WTO obligations effectively. They have successfully interpreted and employed legal provision to create policy space in accordance with their respective economic conditions, showing that judicious legal engagement can be utilized as an intermediary for advancing country interests in the face of the constraints of international trade law (Santos et al., 2012). Moreover, addressing the problem of least-developed countries (LDCs) in accession to the WTO process is crucial for enhancing their membership. These nations frequently encounter long and complex formalities that can deter them from acceding to the multilateral trade regime. To counter such difficulties, it is required that country-specific capacity-building programs be formulated that educate LDCs about the benefits and implications of acceding to the WTO. Permitting these nations greater awareness and preparation will enable them to negotiate their accession terms in a manner that will permit their developmental aspirations to be safeguarded in the process. By encouraging a more extensive accession strategy with more focus on addressing the specific needs of LDCs, the world at large can be able to attain increased membership and wider gain from the global trading system (Delelegn et al., 2025). Lastly, creating strategic partnerships among developing countries within the WTO framework can be able to enhance group bargaining leverage and result in better negotiation terms. Collaboration, such as the formation of coalitions to further collective interest, may enable smaller developing nations to speak more forcefully in negotiations controlled by more powerful economies. Coalitions then represent a vehicle through which collective knowledge and best practice can be shared, and countries equipped with more effective capability to negotiate successfully complicated trade agreements. Additionally, these alignments can prove to be crucial in promoting reforms within the WTO that consider the unique challenges faced by developing and least-developed countries. Through rallying around common objectives, developing nations can restructure the rules of international trade in a way that membership is no longer merely a matter of size, but first and foremost, an opening into actual benefits (Delelegn et al., 2025).

SUMMARY

In attempting to simplify the complexities surrounding the World Trade Organization (WTO) and how it affects developing countries, it is critical to recognize that the way toward evening the playing field in the context of world trade is far from straight. The WTO has implemented systems aimed at simplifying trade and promoting economic growth within member countries. However, the use and success of these systems within developing contexts often encounter significant hindrances. This framework requires tailored approaches as far as the unique problems these nations face are concerned, such as inadequate infrastructure, government issues, and varying economic capacities. Thus, existing trade policies in the WTO need to be redone so as to ensure that they promote actual development, not merely free trade as a goal. A core component of this controversy is the concept of Special and Differential Treatment (SDT) that is designed to offer greater flexibility in protecting domestic industries for developing countries. The move has been highly controversial in terms of its utility and relevance to existing trade practices. While their advocates highlight SDTs role in allowing developing countries to develop their economies, critics maintain that these provisions may have the unintended consequence of maintaining dependency on protectionist measures, and therefore hampering further integration into world markets. Recent literature reopened debates over whether SDT is needed and how it should be designed, pointing to the need for a major reconsideration of its implications. Addressing the problems in SDT would redefine its application, stimulating the objectives of development cooperation to recipient countries as well as the integrity of the international trading system in general (Hoekman et al., 2025). Additionally, integrating effective competition policies tailored to the specific needs of developing countries is required in responding to challenges posed by giant multinational corporations. The examination of competition policy shows that the majority of developing nations are not well-positioned to respond to the challenges of a more globalized economy. Acknowledging that mere emulation of the regulatory frameworks employed in industrialized economies may not suffice, the establishment of a development-oriented international competition authority now becomes a necessity. Such an authority would not only ensure competition in the developing markets but also promote economic growth at the cost of the domestic industries that form the backbone of the developing economies (SINGH, 2025). Last but not least, the conclusion of this argument emphasizes the necessity for harmonized action bringing together trade liberalization, SDT, and competition policy with a view to create a more balanced playing field that ensures genuine development in the world economy.

The WTO's role in the development of developing countries' trade policies is significant, namely by virtue of United States Congress trade preference programs. Since 1974, several programs have been instituted to foster economic growth, reform, and development in the less developed countries. By providing temporary, non-reciprocal, duty-free access to the U.S. market for qualifying countries' selected exports, such programs serve as a focal point for trade relationship enhancement. Nevertheless, this trend has its own pitfalls, as exemplified by looming deadline threats to these preference programs and therefore calls for continued monitoring and potential legislative overhaul. With Congress reconsidering these policies, developing countries' implications remain of the highest significance, emphasizing these countries' need to embrace and take advantage of existing opportunities for economic growth under legislative ambiguity (Hornbeck et al., 2010). Developing countries face unique challenges in taking advantage of their agricultural resources, particularly under international standards that relate to livestock production and food safety. The speed at which international phytosanitary and sanitary standards are being developed has presented hurdles that hinder the ability of poorer nations to gain the greatest benefit from their livestock sectors. The necessity for increased international rule-making inclusiveness is therefore critical, prioritizing those policies guaranteeing these producers are heard in international fora. Developing country governments also have an international role, asserting themselves in global forums responsible for developing such standards. By making their participation stronger, they can express their own interests even more and design policies that would provide support to their agricultural sectors and, ultimately, their broader economies (Nelson et al., 2025). Coordination among agencies in developing countries is vital in resolving these colossal issues. Increased interministerial collaboration between agriculture, health, and international trade ministries will ensure that a concerted effort is made to shape international rule-making effectively. In addition, international cooperation among other developing countries can also ensure that the bargaining power of such countries during negotiations is harnessed. Technical assistance in conformity with international standards is also crucial, as it enables countries to effectively deal with the complexity of international trade. By taking these steps, the developing world can maximize their presence in the world market, advance the well-being of their agricultural producers, and make significant contributions to their own sustainable economic growth in the world trade context (Nelson et al., 2025).

REFERENCES

1. Adriaensen, J., & Garibay, M. G. (2011). The illusion of choice: The European Union and the trade-labor linkage. https://core.ac.uk/download/286053999.pdf (accessed on 30th October 2025).
2. Anania, G. (2025). Multilateral negotiations, regional integration processes and the CAP. What's ahead? https://core.ac.uk/download/pdf/7011034.pdf (accessed on 30th October 2025).
3. Anderson, K. (2025). Agricultural trade reform and poverty reduction in developing countries. https://core.ac.uk/download/pdf/7032885.pdf (accessed on 30th October 2025).
4. Auffret, P. (2025). Trade reform in Vietnam: Opportunities with emerging challenges. https://core.ac.uk/download/pdf/6372913.pdf (accessed on 30th October 2025).
5. Baccini, L., & Kim, S. Y. (2011). Institutions, information, and trade policy in times of crisis. https://core.ac.uk/download/12096060.pdf (accessed on 30th October 2025).
6. Bas, N. F., & Foo, L. J. (2003). Free trade's looming threat to the world's garment workers. https://core.ac.uk/download/5120108.pdf (accessed on 30th October 2025).
7. Benito, G., & Narula, R. (2025). States and firms on the periphery: The challenges of a globalizing world. https://core.ac.uk/download/pdf/6941356.pdf (accessed on 30th October 2025).
8. Bhattacharya, D., & Hossain, S. S. (2025). An evaluation of the need and cost of selected trade facilitation measures in Bangladesh: Implications for the WTO negotiations on trade facilitation. https://core.ac.uk/download/pdf/7022396.pdf (accessed on 30th October 2025).
9. Bouet, A., Mevel, S., & Orden, D. (2025). More or less ambition? Modeling the development impact of U.S.–EU agricultural proposals in the Doha Round. https://core.ac.uk/download/pdf/6289067.pdf (accessed on 30th October 2025).
10. Breuss, F. (2025). Economic integration, EU-US trade conflicts and WTO dispute settlement. https://core.ac.uk/download/pdf/6224019.pdf (accessed on 30th October 2025).
11. Bureau, J. C., Jean, S., & Matthews, A. (2025). Agricultural trade liberalization: Assessing the consequences for developing countries. https://core.ac.uk/download/pdf/7034589.pdf (accessed on 30th October 2025).
12. Buthe, T. (2008). The globalization of health and safety standards:

Delegation of regulatory authority in the SPS Agreement of the 1994 Agreement Establishing the World Trade Organization. https://core.ac.uk/download/62553315.pdf (accessed on 30th October 2025).

13. Chabe-Ferret, S., Gourdon, J., Marouani, M. A., & Voituriez, T., et al. (2007). Trade-induced changes in economic inequality. Assessment issues and policy implications for developing countries: Document de travail. http://agritrop.cirad.fr/549144/1/document_549144.pdf (accessed on 30th October 2025).
14. Chowdhury, N., & Kumar, S. (2008). Technical capacity, policymaking and food standards: An overview of Indian experience. https://core.ac.uk/download/pdf/11481870.pdf (accessed on 30th October 2025).
15. Cornford, A. (2025). The WTO negotiations on financial services: Current issues and future directions. https://core.ac.uk/download/pdf/7043289.pdf (accessed on 30th October 2025).
16. Delelegn, M. (2025). Accession to the World Trade Organization: Challenges and prospects for the least-developed countries (LDCs). https://core.ac.uk/download/pdf/7035265.pdf (accessed on 30th October 2025).
17. Delpeuch, C., & Messerlin, P. (2025). Aid for trade effectiveness: What do evaluations say? https://core.ac.uk/download/pdf/6277874.pdf (accessed on 30th October 2025).
18. Diaz-Bonilla, E., & Tin, J. (2025). That was then but this is now. https://core.ac.uk/download/pdf/6388618.pdf (accessed on 30th October 2025).
19. Diaz-Bonilla, E., Gulati, A., von Braun, J., Watkins, K., et al. (2025). Trade policies and food security: Essays from IFPRI's 2002-2003 Annual Report. https://core.ac.uk/download/pdf/6289091.pdf (accessed on 30th October 2025).
20. Dymond, B., & Hart, M. (2025). Navigating new trade routes: The rise of value chains, and the challenges for Canadian trade policy. https://core.ac.uk/download/pdf/6844521.pdf (accessed on 30th October 2025).
21. Fojtíková, L. (2018). China's intellectual property rights commitments in the WTO: Legal and economic implications. https://core.ac.uk/download/161960388.pdf (accessed on 30th October 2025).
22. Garina, E., Kozlova, E. P., & Garin, A. P. (2025). Modern approaches to application of newest technologies and their role in the innovative development of enterprises in the regions of Russia. *Economics and Management*. https://www.semanticscholar.org/paper/66d5271db3f80ec08dace3c379b5d302cc552f43 (accessed on 30th October 2025).

23. Gheyle, N., & Martens, D. (2016). Understanding the debate about policy space: From the WTO to EU FTAs. https://core.ac.uk/download/74665673.pdf (accessed on 30th October 2025).
24. Haque, I. U. (2025). Rethinking industrial policy. https://core.ac.uk/download/pdf/7043273.pdf (accessed on 30th October 2025).
25. Harris, D. N. (2025). Agricultural trade reform and industry adjustment in Indonesia. https://core.ac.uk/download/pdf/6253596.pdf (accessed on 30th October 2025).
26. Higgott, R. A. (2009). Not just a "second order" problem in a wider economic crisis: Systemic challenges for the global trading system. https://core.ac.uk/download/47382.pdf (accessed on 30th October 2025).
27. Hoekman, B., & Özden, Ç. (2025). Trade preferences and differential treatment of developing countries: A selective survey. https://core.ac.uk/download/pdf/6615921.pdf (accessed on 30th October 2025).
28. Hoekman, B., & Schuman, R. (2017). Bolstering global trade: Governance—A work program for the WTO presented by the High-Level Board of Experts on the Future of Global Trade Governance. https://core.ac.uk/download/322823606.pdf (accessed on 30th October 2025).
29. Hornbeck, J. F., Jones, V. C., & Villareal, M. A. (2010). Trade preferences: Economic issues and policy options. https://core.ac.uk/download/5132231.pdf (accessed on 30th October 2025).
30. Jensen, M. F. (2025). Capacity building for pro-poor trade: Learning from the limitations in current models. https://core.ac.uk/download/pdf/6248655.pdf (accessed on 30th October 2025).
31. Kamat, M., & Kamat, M. (2025). Implications of the WTO on Indian marine industry: Issues and policy perspectives. https://core.ac.uk/download/pdf/7301996.pdf (accessed on 30th October 2025).
32. Lall, S., & Albaladejo, M. (2025). Indicators of the relative importance of IPRs in developing countries. https://core.ac.uk/download/pdf/6759466.pdf (accessed on 30th October 2025).
33. Matthews, D. N. (2012). Counterfeiting and public health. https://core.ac.uk/download/30696282.pdf (accessed on 30th October 2025).
34. Misovicova, M. (2025). WTO negotiations on trade facilitation: Update. https://core.ac.uk/download/pdf/6402341.pdf (accessed on 30th October 2025).
35. Moore, G. (2010). Fairness in international trade: The case of economic partnership agreements. https://core.ac.uk/download/65138.pdf (accessed on 30th October 2025).

36. Nelson, M. B. (2025). International rules, food safety and the poor developing country livestock producer. https://core.ac.uk/download/pdf/7055418.pdf (accessed on 30th October 2025).
37. Nenci, S. (2025). The rise of the southern economies: Implications for the WTO-multilateral trading system. https://core.ac.uk/download/pdf/6484307.pdf (accessed on 30th October 2025).
38. Nyangito, H. O. (2025). Performance of African agricultural exports and external market access conditions under international trade reforms. https://core.ac.uk/download/pdf/7075776.pdf (accessed on 30th October 2025).
39. O'Reilly, S., Greene, E., McAuliffe, F., Teede, H., Campoy, C., Burden, C., Geraghty, A., et al. (2025). Clinical and behavioral heterogeneity among women at increased risk for gestational diabetes: A four-country analysis. *International Journal of Environmental Research and Public Health, 22*. https://www.semanticscholar.org/paper/7b33be01eb26e2beb09b1941a78e519269491102 (accessed on 30th October 2025).
40. Popov, V. (2025). Development theories and development experience: Half a century journey. https://core.ac.uk/download/pdf/6726621.pdf (accessed on 30th October 2025).
41. Santos, A. (2012). Carving out policy autonomy for developing countries in the World Trade Organization: The experience of Brazil and Mexico. https://core.ac.uk/download/70374668.pdf (accessed on 30th October 2025).
42. Sbragia, A. (2009). The EU, the US, and trade policy: Competitive interdependence in the management of globalization. https://core.ac.uk/download/7434528.pdf (accessed on 30th October 2025).
43. Singh, A. (2025). Competition and competition policy in emerging markets: International and developmental dimensions. https://core.ac.uk/download/pdf/7043203.pdf (accessed on 30th October 2025).
44. Switzer, S. (2008). Environmental protection and the generalized system of preferences: A legal and appropriate linkage? https://core.ac.uk/download/9053220.pdf (accessed on 30th October 2025).
45. van der Mensbrugghe, D., Anderson, K., & Martin, W. (2025). Doha merchandise trade reform: What's at stake for developing countries? https://core.ac.uk/download/pdf/6764252.pdf (accessed on 30th October 2025).
46. Wilson, J. S. (2025). Liberalizing trade in agriculture: Developing countries in Asia and the post-Doha agenda. https://core.ac.uk/download/pdf/6372903.pdf (accessed on 30th October 2025).

Chapter 10

Contemporary Issues and Future of the WTO

Contents

INTRODUCTION

The World Trade Organization (WTO) has ever been regarded as an epicenter of forces in the global trade world, carrying out negotiations and building a model for trade globally. However, with the trends changing in global trade, the institution is faced with various contemporary challenges that weaken its usefulness and effectiveness. Challenges such as rising protectionism, shifting geopolitics, and the complexities of trade in services and digital products necessitate a reconsideration of the role of the WTO in the world economy.

Additionally, as nations are attempting to manage environment-related issues and the necessity of climate change, the policies of the organization must adapt to incorporate environmentally friendly trade practices. The convergence of these factors identifies the need for a more advanced comprehension of the issues of the day by the WTO and sets the organization up for debates regarding its future course. The WTO is confronted more and more with the issues of climate change and international cooperation, which complicate its historical agenda of trade. Since recent debates have highlighted, global climate cooperation mechanisms, such as the Paris Agreement, pose the question of how to address concerns like carbon leakage, which is a risk to threaten environmental aims and fair trade practices. Border carbon adjustments are an excellent example of the intersection of trade law and environmental policy, demonstrating the WTO's inability to address these pressing issues appropriately (Mehling et al., 2019). Moreover, the shift towards a low-carbon global economy also poses questions regarding the role of international institutions of global governance in bridging the gaps between environmental sustainability and economic growth. Examining such contemporary challenges unfolds that it is imperative to address climate imperatives for the WTO to remain relevant in an increasingly changing global order (Newell, 2018). In the future, the fate of the WTO is not only a function of how it successfully tackles present challenges but how it can change in response to address emerging global needs. As nations attempt to balance economic growth with environmental preservation, the WTO must reorient its policies to oversee trade activity that supports sustainability and therefore restore confidence among member states. The ongoing negotiations and dispute underscore the need for institutions to be reformed in such a way that they promote inclusiveness and guarantee that trade dividends cross the board. The importance of having a robust and resilient WTO framework cannot be overstated, as its reinvention will have significant implications for international trade relations in an era marked by opportunity and uncertainty. Addressing these intricate issues provides the WTO with an opportunity to reaffirm its position on the international stage through the promotion of equitable and sustainable trading practices in accordance with contemporary global desires.

Overview of the World Trade Organization (WTO)

WTO is a central institution in the global system of trade regulation, responsible for regulating and promoting free trade among nations. Established in 1995, the WTO was a consequence of the General Agreement on Tariffs and Trade (GATT), which had been in operation since 1948. This was a deliberate transition towards addressing the increasing sophistication of international trade, reflecting increasing interdependence among economies. The epicenter of the WTOs agenda is to establish a rules-based trading system that minimizes tariffs and trade barriers and maximizes fair trade relations. Nonetheless, as the global economy has changed in the last decades, WTO has come under increased scrutiny for its effectiveness, especially with the protectionist upsurge and questioning of multilateralism as the main paradigm of global trade. The issues that affect the WTO today represent the flexibility of the organizations but also the hurdles that the organization will have to overcome in the future.

Figure 10.1. Overview of the World Trade Organization (WTO).

Source: https://ebnw.net/wp-content/uploads/2024/03/A-200-696x522.png.webp.

Among these problems, the widespread discontent with free trade in several OECD countries is a killing threat to the multilateral trading system. There is clear declining public support for open markets due to sentiments of inequality and injustice in the trade outcome. Furthermore, the collapse of the Doha Round negotiations evidences the challenge of achieving a consensus among the diverse member countries. The agenda of the WTO is accused of being opaque and unable to properly address modern trade dynamics. Agreeing to these issues is not only a question of concurrence; it is vital in a bid to revive the organizations legitimacy and functionality as a balancer of global trade rules (Higgott et al., 2009). The growing tendency towards regional preferentialism also poses a severe threat to the WTOs overall goals and its effectiveness in regulating trade. Regional trade agreements have a tendency to induce trade diversion rather than trade creation, which is in conflict with the underlying principles of multilateralism expressed by the WTO. As nations move towards bilateral or regional regimes, the vision of a single integrated global trading system may unravel, exacerbating native inequalities and inducing competitive distortions. Moreover, as empirical research into individual trade relationships, say the Ugandan exporter-European importer relationship, notes, poor soft competitiveness weakens good participation in Global Value Chains (GVCs). These challenges underscore the necessity of the WTO to promote fair trading practices based on increased cooperation and stronger ethical standards to make international trade governance more effective in a globally more fragmented environment (Wiegratz et al., 2008) (Figure 10.1).

Importance of the World Trade Organization (WTO) in Global Trade

The WTO plays a central role in the global trade architecture by acting as a framework that encourages stability and predictability in the economic interactions of nations. When countries sign trading agreements with each other, the WTO sets rules which guide the practices of trade, eventually creating an environment that supports economic growth. This regulatory system not only reduces trade dispute risk but also enhances countries' confidence to trade. The current world trade landscape, however, offers system issues confronting the WTO. These are declining support for free trade in major OECD countries and emerging regional trade agreements that challenge the WTOs effectiveness as a multilateral trading system. The implications of all these challenges underscore the need for successful reforms, not only for making advances in talks such as the Doha Round, but also for addressing deeper issues regarding the relevance and effectiveness of the institution in the modern world (Higgott et al., 2009). In addition to its regulatory roles, the WTO is increasingly regarded as a central institution for addressing global concerns beyond traditional economic norms, particularly regarding climate change and agricultural sustainability. The intersection between trade regimes and environmental concerns presents a pressing challenge to the WTO that remains embroiled in 20th-century agricultural issues while remaining unresponsive to emerging challenges such as hunger, poverty, and climate vulnerability. The pressing need for sustainable agricultural trade reflects a severe lacuna in the current decision-making process of the WTO. Such concerns are further deepened by a projected food supply gap by the year 2050 that necessitates anticipatory actions beyond traditional trade negotiations. With advocates worldwide demanding a more adaptable organization, the WTO must be willing to change in order to weather such multifaceted realities and further establish itself as a lead facilitator to ushering in sustainable development and equitable trade practices (Kim et al., 2025). In addition, public legitimacy and opinion form the core of the importance of the WTO in global trade. The legitimacy of the institutions is brought into question even more as it struggles with the issue of internal conflict and the protectionist tide swelling in its member nations. It is important to make sure that developing nations and silent communities are very audible in trade negotiations in a bid to maintain the legitimacy of the WTO. Balancing all the different stakeholders' interests is important for instilling a sense of responsibility and ownership in global trade governance. In addition, public narratives of trade need to shift from a zero-sum game vision of trade to a more inclusive form of vision that recognizes the long-term benefits of globalization. Ignoring these legitimacy concerns risks delegitimating the WTO as the prime pillar of global trade agreements and leads to further fragmentation of the global trading system (Higgott et al., 2009) (Figure 10.2).

Figure 10.2. Importance of the World Trade Organization (WTO) in global trade.

Source: https://external-content.duckduckgo.com/iu/?u=https%3A%2F%2Fwww.wallstreetmojo.com%2Fwp-content%2Fuploads%2F2023%2F06%2FWorld-trade-organization.png&f=1&nofb=1&ipt=fb017c709fde57b2d2209c17b9433aa199522946130e4ffdbcd94985c97380ab.

10.1. HISTORICAL CONTEXT OF THE WORLD TRADE ORGANIZATION (WTO)

The establishment of the World Trade Organization (WTO) in 1995 marked a fundamental shift in the international trading system, superseding the General Agreement on Tariffs and Trade (GATT) that had been in force since 1948. The WTO was established against the context of post-Cold War global order in need of a better system of international trade amid the complexities of globalization. As trade agreements increased and interdependence between nations grew, the WTO was born to provide a more structured and official means of trade management. This was not merely an administrative shift; it was a shift in philosophy directed towards multilateral liberalization of trade and reduction of trade barriers. But with the birth of the WTO came the beginning of contentious arguments regarding free trade, equality, and developing nations' interests, which would echo for years to come regarding how it would grow. With the

WTO now poised to address urgent concerns on international trade, it was faced with institutional problems that challenged its legitimacy and competence. The most significant factor has been growing disillusionment with liberal trade ideals among most OECD countries, as majority views supporting open markets have plummeted. The ability of the WTO to ride out these sentiments is important because it is at the center of world economic management. Moreover, compared to its predecessor GATT, the WTO also brought into existence a more strict mechanism for settlement of disputes, which although enhanced accountability, also faced charges of bias and inefficiency in processes. It is imperative to address such issues not only for organizational survival but also for the role of the organization in maintaining the normative institutions governing international trade, especially within the backdrop of rising regionalism and preferential trade arrangements, the advocates of which challenge its jurisdiction and scope (Higgott et al., 2009). Furthermore, the background of the WTO incites a critical review of the philosophical underpinnings of its trade policies, especially concerning the interplay between liberal capitalism and democratic interests. The organization is caught between a precarious balance where the power dynamics which support the neo-liberal agenda have a tendency to overwhelm inclusive dialogue as well as other economic ideologies. The critics suggest that the WTOs decision-making is similar to a closed epistemic community in which necessary normative deliberations are stunted that can potentially head towards more equitable trade practices. It has resulted in stifling different voices, particularly those calling for ethical reasoning in trade, such as the interests of farm workers in developing countries. Such imperatives create ethical questions regarding the leadership of the WTO, compelling stakeholders to consider the implications of sustaining a process that may be more economically efficient than just and fair (Gruin et al., 2011).

10.1.1. Formation and Objectives of the World Trade Organization (WTO)

The WTO was established on January 1, 1995, as a result of the need for an organized and disciplined framework of global trade. The WTO substituted for the General Agreement on Tariffs and Trade (GATT), which had negotiated trade since 1948 but lacked an institutional structure. The primary goal of the WTO is to promote free trade by means of an atmosphere that is stable and predictable. This market openness is complemented by the process of lowering tariffs and other trade barriers. Through its agreements, the WTO aims to create economic cooperation between its member states on a global basis, working towards the final goal of economic progress and poverty reduction. However, the ability of the WTO to achieve these has been challenged, especially against the backdrop of altering trends in economic flows on the global scene. At the core of creating the WTO was the goal of making more representative the forum for discussion among its members so that negotiations would be representative of a broader cross-section of member interests. This goal has, however, faced severe setbacks, particularly diminishing support in the large OECD countries for open markets.

Figure 10.3. Objectives of World Trade Organization (WTO).

Source: https://external-content.duckduckgo.com/iu/?u=https%3A%2F%2Fcdn-images.prepp.in%2Fpublic%2Fimage%2Faabf2196767337c9c1f264127ea6ede7.png%3Ftr%3Dw-480%2Ch-368%2Cc-force&f=1&nofb=1&ipt=be8ce39b54b8e148468d11511dd24707beffec07bcde6fa2de4318c86f4d4b61.

The socio-economic consequences of globalization have brought with them calls for re-examination of trade priorities with focus on justice and equity in international governance, referred to as the legitimacy question. As the literature discusses, such systemic issues pose basic questions for the WTO, showing that mere completion of ongoing rounds of negotiations, e.g., those emerging from the Doha Round, will no longer be sufficient enough to address deep issues surrounding global trade policies (Higgott et al., 2009). Thus, the objectives of the WTO must be altered with regard to these new issues. Additionally, the WTOs commitment to multilateralism is further being questioned by increasing regional trade agreements that have become a dominant feature of the new economic environment. While these agreements can potentially boost trade between member nations, they are likely to disintegrate the global trading regime and give more importance to the bilateral talks under regional agreements compared to the multilateral talks under the WTO. This adjustment presents an issue for the organization—to remain relevant while adapting to the growing sophistication of international trade relationships. Enabling these new challenges is a consolidated approach that harmonizes regional agendas and the inherent principles of multilateralism. As international trade is increasingly researched, there must be a discussion between paradigms to observe how to proceed with these challenges as well as reinterpret the WTO goals for future generations (Kerremans et al., 2013) (Figure 10.3).

10.1.2. Key Agreements and Trade Rounds

The World Trade Organization (WTO) has funded numerous landmark agreements and rounds of trade that have had a profound effect on international trade patterns. Of these, the Uruguay Round (1986–1994) was a turning point because it brought in root changes, wherein the WTO itself was established. The round extended the trade negotiations agenda to services and intellectual property, previously untouched areas of prior agreements. The successful completion of the Uruguay Round confirmed the feasibility of multilateral cooperation in tackling complex issues in trade and thus opened the door to further negotiations. The ratification of the General Agreement on Trade in Services (GATS) throughout the period is reflective of the transition towards the recognition of the role of services in the global economy as it stresses the dynamic nature of trade agreements and their implications on member countries. Further, the Doha Development Agenda (2001) was formulated to address the needs of the developing world, a growing recognition of the inherent inequalities in world trade systems. This round tried to strengthen the pledge to phase out subsidies on agriculture and market access for developing countries, thereby placing their concerns in the world trading order. But the Doha Round deadlock is a symptom of the complexities and challenges of reconciling plural national agendas and economic interests within the multilateral trading system. Negotiations between development goals and free trade principles underscore a necessary tension in the WTOs mandate. Moreover, it also reminds us that although free trade agreements have the potential to activate economic growth, they can also ensure that those on the margin continue to be disenfranchised unless accurately measured to the advantage of all member states. The contribution of legal mechanisms under the WTO, especially the Appellate Body, was a determining variable in ensuring the enforcement of trade agreements and shaping the composites of compliance across member states. As Goldstein and Steinberg argue, the Appellate Body's judicial lawmaking authority plays a significant role in facilitating trade barrier reduction, often enabling countries to achieve more preferred liberalized trade policies than their initial negotiation offers. This has led to increased emphasis placed on compliance with Appellate

Body decisions, though not mandated by circumventing formal delegation, provoking domestic lobbying for trade liberalization. Here, it is important to understand the ways in which states deal with the complexity of compliance and domestic interests—especially in the governed field like the Agreement on the Application of Sanitary and Phytosanitary (SPS) measures—because it makes it important to see how the WTO's future direction will be and whether it can effectively govern international trade disputes (Buthe et al., 2008; Goldstein et al., 2008) (Figure 10.4).

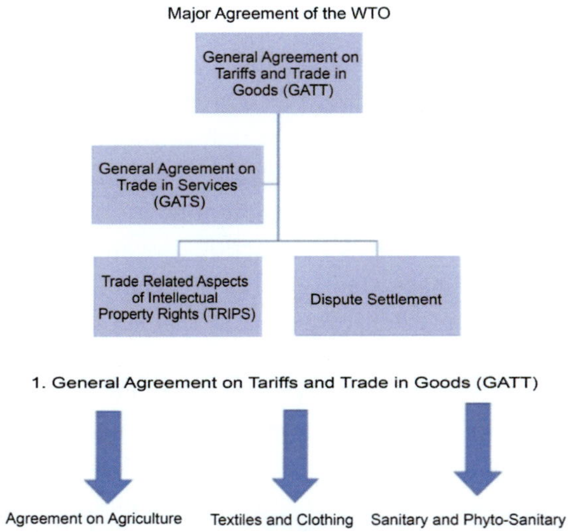

Figure 10.4. Key agreements and trade rounds of the World Trade Organization (WTO).

Source: https://external-content.duckduckgo.com/iu/?u=https%3A%2F%2Fd18x2uyjeekruj.cloudfront.net%2Fwp-content%2Fuploads%2F2017%2F09%2Fword-image56.jpeg&f=1&nofb=1&ipt=2e2e748ca80e4b4397f06eb6fe5db869fb1a7d4c5f6da49b5003f709f4330ad5.

10.1.3. Evolution of the World Trade Organization (WTO)'s Role in International Trade

The World Trade Organization (WTO) has evolved significantly since its inception, evolving with the fluidity of international trade. Initially created to facilitate trade liberalization and resolve conflicts, the WTO's purpose has expanded to cover even broader economic matters like sustainability and social justice. As the practice of global trade has become increasingly complex, the WTO has adjusted its structures to accommodate more contemporary concerns like electronic trade, investment flows, and the global economic imbalances' impact. This adaptability is essential, for the WTO strives to remain effective within a setting in perpetual change wherein developed models of trade are incessantly challenged. The evolution of the WTO is a testament to its efforts at dealing with the needs of a perpetually changing global economy, having its arsenal for the facilitation of trade also comprise newer challenges. A breakthrough in the WTOs evolution is its evolving role in dealing with gender inequalities in global trade. The institution has previously been condemned for its conventional failure to prioritize gender issues, yet there have been recent developments towards mainstreaming gender analysis within trade policy and agreements. One of those major moves was the 2017 signing by over 100 member countries of the Buenos Aires Declaration on Women and Trade, aimed at promoting women's economic participation in global trade. This initiative, among others, is the WTOs declaration of the importance of inclusivity in the trade development process. As gender equality becomes increasingly important to international governance, the WTOs action towards reinforcing women's economic rights is a necessary step towards an equitable trading atmosphere and a demonstration of greater respect for the social elements that form economic progress (Hattunen et al., 2021). Aside from this, the evolution of the WTO role has seen it expand to address challenges in the form of regional trade agreements and protectionism that counter the multilateral trading system. At a period in time when countries have a predisposition towards pursuing bilateral or regional trade agreements, the WTO is faced with maintaining its jurisdiction as an international trade organization. This has provoked controversy regarding the reform of the WTO to make it more efficient in the face of increasing trade fragmentation. Reform may entail simplifying the negotiation process and updating rules to fit contemporary trade practices such as e-commerce and digital products. While the organization is faced with such daunting issues, its ability to adapt and reform will be critical in shaping the world trade of the future, enabling it to not just respond to issues of today but also foresee the future of trends in the trade industry (Boulin et al., 2025).

10.2. CURRENT CHALLENGES FACING THE WORLD TRADE ORGANIZATION (WTO)

The WTO is faced with numerous challenges that jeopardize its effectiveness in managing international trade relations. One of the most significant challenges facing it is declining public confidence in free markets, particularly in bigger OECD economies. As protectionist schools of thought gain grounds, citizens increasingly doubt the dividends of globalization, leading to calls for stricter trade regimes. Such a backlash raises questions regarding the WTO's appropriateness to play the role of a mediator and a free trade advocate. Furthermore, the hindered progress in the Doha Round negotiations has contributed to such doubts since it indicates a lack of member nations' agreement on addressing key trade issues at stake. These threats call for a redefinition of the WTOs mission and objective in the light of an evolving world economic order, more so with regional trade arrangements as a formidable alternative to multilateralism (Higgott et al., 2009). In addition to declining popular approval, the WTO must confront the complexities of moving towards a new global economic equilibrium. As nations are yet to grasp the meaning of the implications of the rapidly changing digital economy, there is uncertainty regarding what type of governance architecture will be needed for effective regulation of trade. The digital revolution has itself reorganized the matrix of goods, services, and information across borders, placing pressure on the WTO to make its frameworks more adaptive to accommodate new technologies and business models. Thus, the organization is not only pressured to conclude existing negotiations but also to establish explicit priorities and goals for its future trade governance. The necessity for effective trade governance framework addresses more specifically the issues of smaller economies that rely significantly on international trade for their advancement and that are faced with mounting challenges with regard to economic governance and policy effectiveness (Anderson, 2025). Lastly, legitimacy and equity in WTO governance continue to be paramount in managing the issues of the times. Member states call more urgently for fairness and openness in the institution, driven by beliefs that existing arrangements favored developed nations at the detriment of developing nations. These perceptions pose a serious threat to the WTO's legitimacy and relevance. These legitimacy concerns must be resolved not only for the intragovernmental coherence of the organizations but also in order to maintain the faith of its heterogenous membership. In addition, with regional trade agreements proliferating, they undermine the WTO multilateral system by threatening to undermine the foundations of openness and non-discrimination that support international trade. Thus, creating a sense of ownership and responsibility among the member states is vital in revitalizing WTO's role in governing international trade (Higgott et al., 2009).

10.2.1. Trade Tensions and Protectionism

International business environment in the recent past has been highly influenced by trade tensions and protectionism in significant ways, critically weakening the founding principles served by the World Trade Organization (WTO). Where nations pursue self-interest under an unstable political backdrop, they implement tariffs and quotas that harm the ideal of free trade, long the cornerstone of international economic collaboration. Apart from those impacts on the economy, these measures have spillover implications in diplomatic ties as nations respond to perceived unfair practices. Herein, WTO is forced to act in a complex scenario where its core objectives of encouraging trade and resolving conflict are challenged, and the need for change and adaptation in its institutions to address contemporary realities in trade is one that cannot be ignored. Protectionism lies in a prevailing narrative which encourages global cooperation against national sovereignty.

Figure 10.5. The impact of protectionism on global trade.

Source: https://fastercapital.co/i/Global-trade--Trade-Wars-and-Price-Changes--Navigating-the-Global-Market--The-Role-of-Tariffs-and-Protectionism-in-Global-Trade.webp.

When the attention to domestic industries in the presence of foreign competition is invoked by leaders, a huge backlash against current multilateral trade agreements follows. Not only does this form of economic nationalism contribute to rendering the WTO ineffective, but it also suspends collective action to fight global challenges such as climate change and public health crises, which require multilateral action. The challenge for the WTO, then, is not simply one of facilitating conflict resolution but one of keeping pace with changes in the dynamics of global relations which compete with the interests of member countries and yet continue to advance an open and balanced system of global trade, as noted in recent literature on international trade policy (Bochniarz et al., 2025). Thus, to foster a more constructive debate on trade relationships, the WTO would have to adopt newer models of global governance and incorporate references pertaining to protectionism that are deemed pertinent to contemporary realities. Policymakers and scholars alike agree that the institution must examine its strategy of conflict resolution and negotiation to more accurately represent the evolving incentives of member states, particularly those within the

European Union that are under certain pressures both internally and externally (Kerremans et al., 2013). It entails a prolonged inter-paradigmatic debate that acknowledges the complexity of modern trade politics and seeks innovative strategies towards cooperation. The WTO's future, therefore, hinges on how it can balance rival interests while promoting a robust trade atmosphere that benefits all member states, charting the way for more stable and collaborative world order (Figure 10.5).

10.2.2. Dispute Resolution Mechanisms and Their Effectiveness

Dispute settlement structures are essential to the functioning of the World Trade Organization (WTO) because they constitute the foundation of stability and predictability of international trade relationships. The WTOs Dispute Settlement Understanding (DSU) provides a proven framework for member states to resolve trade disputes, promoting compliance with international trade norms. The effectiveness of such mechanisms, particularly through panels and appellate bodies, hinges on their ability to provide binding decisions that are enforceable. The second-generation tribunals, as reflected in the contemporary discourses on international law, have the potential to provide enforceable orders that influence state action, thereby revolutionizing the manner in which disputes are resolved at the international level once and for all (Born et al., 2012). Thus, the efficiency of the WTO dispute settlement can be observed in its significant effect on member countries compliance with trade commitments, an outstanding enhancement of international governing frameworks. Despite the success by the WTO dispute settlement process, there are issues that compromise its perceived legitimacy and operational effectiveness. One of these issues is the issue of compliance and enforcement, which is significantly parallel to the asymmetries within international law. A majority of the commentators contend that horizontal character of global governance results in inconsistency of states' approach towards decisions by WTO. While there are some states that will adhere to unfavorable rulings, others adopt non-compliance strategies, indicating an essential dearth of horizontal enforcement devices (Helfer et al., 2003). This observation reflects the necessity for WTO to enhance its institutional mechanisms and the system of governance to create more equity and efficiency in dispute settlement. These developments may involve establishing more open channels for compliance, settling imbalance of powers, and reasserting the centrality of multilateralism to resolve disputes within the international trading order. Furthermore, the existing landscape of dispute settlement mechanisms must be innovated and made more flexible in order to respond to the evolving realities of globalization and interdependence. While the WTO is still being criticized for its responsiveness and efficacy, it is time to explore the intersection of international and constitutional law in order to establish better frameworks based on what is needed today. Structural problems such as decentralization and normative pyramids require a full review of current legal structures (Helfer et al., 2003). The incorporation of modified, unobtrusive institutional structures has the ability to bring about an environment in which dispute settlement processes not only resolve differences but foster cooperation and trust among member states. Ultimately, the future of the WTO rests in its ability to manage these nuances while reaffirming its original functions in guaranteeing fair trade practices and clearing conflicts on the global stage.

10.2.3. Criticism of the World Trade Organization (WTO)'s Decision-Making Processes

The WTO has come under significant criticism for its decision-making style, which is considered to be non-inclusive and non-open. The technocratic nature of decision-making blocks a substantial number of civil society and member states from accessing and shaping the decisions. This disconnect has generated a sense of disenfranchisement among the actors that feel their interests are not being taken into consideration. Furthermore, the WTO's legitimacy crisis is also a reflection of broader societal problems where global governance is being viewed as unjust. With CSOs mobilizing to force alternative agendas and narratives within global governance, the WTO's decision-making structures are increasingly under fire, pushing forward a perceived need to reform and respond to these legitimacy concerns (Rauh et al., 2019). Secondly, the WTO has been wanting for its top-heavy management style that usually disregards the interests of the general public or fails to involve various stakeholders in its decision-making. The institutions of the WTO can wield powers that sometimes result in decisions making economic efficiency the benchmark and not fair outcomes, thus perpetuating socio-economic imbalances at home and among member states. These institutional characteristics elicit opposition and test the readiness to receive the WTO's rulings, heightening calls for increased democratization of the policymaking process. By foreclosing legitimate avenues of opposition and popular debate, the WTO is poised to invite even greater opposition to the liberal international order as a whole. This political backlash symptomizes a more fundamental institutional crisis in which the loss of legitimacy feeds deeper societal unhappiness (Kreuder-Sonnen et al., 2020). The failure to adapt its decision-making procedures not only undermines the legitimacy of the WTO but also poses significant challenges to future performance in global trade governance. While international institutions grapple with mounting distrust, it is critical that the WTO consider reforms to make it more representative and open. Involvement of stakeholders outside government can be a mechanism through which legitimacy is regained and public trust in the institution restored. Such reforms may include the integration of stakeholder input mechanisms and channels for greater civic engagement. By responding to these critics and streamlining its decision-making framework, the WTO can better confront contemporary challenges, enabling its operations to be relevant and defensible within the world's trade landscape. Through this, it may be able to eschew future legitimacy crises and encourage its role in cooperative economic relations (Rauh et al., 2019) (Figure 10.6).

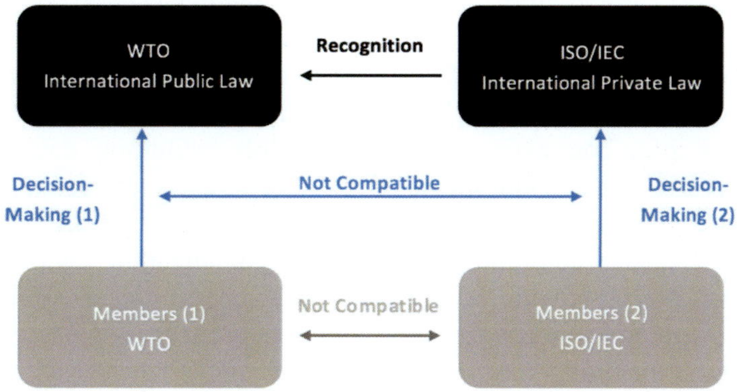

Figure 10.6. Criticism of the World Trade Organization (WTO)'s decision-making processes.

Source: https://media.springernature.com/lw685/springer-static/image/chp%3A10.1007%2F978-3-030-03263-0_9/MediaObjects/978-3-030-03263-0_9_Fig1_HTML.png.

10.3. IMPACT OF GLOBALIZATION ON THE WORLD TRADE ORGANIZATION (WTO)

The impact of globalization on the WTO has been profound, reshaping the governance and negotiation of international trade among member nations. As global markets have grown, the WTO has faced pressure to adapt to the new trend of trade led by emerging economies as well as the proliferation of regional trade agreements. This shift has caused many member states to question whether the WTO is capable of addressing the challenges of contemporary trade imbalances, protectionism, and the complexity of electronic commerce. The increasing dominance of multinational corporations and demands for more economic integration complicate the mandate of the WTO further, which creates controversy among member states challenging the mandate and capabilities of the organization to be able to successfully regulate global flows of trade as seen in the controversy in international trade politics strategic framework (Kerremans et al., 2013). In addition, the concept of multifunctional agriculture, an outcome of the Uruguay Round trade negotiations, suggests another aspect of the WTOs function in the age of globalization. The broad array of interpretations across different member countries of the concept reflects the complex interlinkage between international trade arrangements and domestic farm policies. As seen, the economics approach to multifunctional agriculture is threatened by contradictory interpretations in nations such as the U.S., EU, and developing countries. These differences arise from the unique cultural, environmental, and economic factors affecting each nation's agricultural setting (Moon et al., 2025). The WTO subsequently then faces the challenge of reconciling these contrasting perspectives while facilitating equitable trade practices that take into account members' exigencies and realities. In the future, the WTO must re-examine its policies to remain relevant in a globalizing world. As economic relations continue to be driven by globalization, the organization can transform by embracing openness, inclusiveness, and flexibility in its dealings and agreements. The member countries are increasingly recognizing the value of multilateralism in responding to global challenges such as climate change, pandemics, and technological shifts. This recognition would pave the way for new trade agreements that reflect this era's priorities and foster sustainable development. In addressing these pressing issues in its purview, the WTO can reassert itself as the center of world trade, making it sensitive to the evolving needs of its constituents in a highly integrated and interconnected global economy (Figure 10.7).

The Impact of Globalization on International Trade

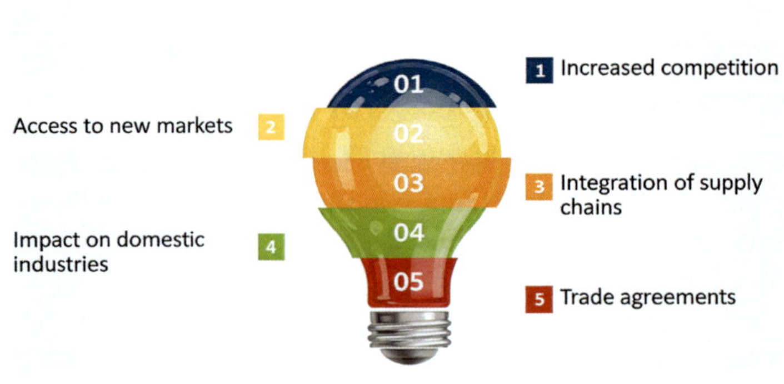

Figure 10.7. The impact of globalization on international trade.

Source: https://fastercapital.co/i/Globalization--The-Influence-of-Globalization-on-Pest-Analysis--The-Impact-of-Globalization-on-International-Trade.webp.

10.3.1. Changes in Trade Patterns and Economic Interdependence

There has been a deep transformation in global patterns of trade and economic interdependence over the last three decades, which demands re-evaluation of the World Trade Organizations (WTO) role in emerging market dynamics. With the rise in regional trade agreements and the increasing visibility of non-traditional trading partners, the traditional lines between national economies have been diminished. So profound has the impact of this global trend towards globalization been that economic interdependence has increased, with countries now relying on one another for commodities, services, and capital. With countries embracing more integrated trade relations, the impact of this on the WTOs negotiating capacity and enforcement has become more apparent. The changing environment necessitates the WTO to adapt in a manner that it remains valid and functional in controlling international trade, particularly solving the complexities arising from newly formed alliances and varying standards of trade etiquette between participant nations. Besides, the challenge to the prevailing liberal global order underscores the challenges of institutions like the WTO in proving their legitimacy in the midst of mounting populist sentiments and internal pressures.

The indignation against globalization and economic dependence has most typically expressed itself in the public's growing suspicion of international institutions as remote from the affairs of local communities. These trends suggest that the WTO, and similar institutions, are being ever more critically examined in terms of legitimacy, with civil society organizations mobilizing to challenge prevailing trade conventions. The current situation is a fluid one where the authority of the WTO is questioned but also allows for other stories to emerge that have the ability to reconfigure global governance arrangements. Political discourse and economic relations engage with each other in such a way that reform of global institutions has to emerge through an exercise of considering the vast array of voices and interests that shape contemporary international relations (Rauh et al., 2019). With patterns of trade shifting, the pressure on the WTO to stay abreast with such changes is even higher, resulting in a complex system of global economic management. Economic interdependence has opened new horizons for development and cooperation, yet has fueled tensions among members as countries pursue self-centered economic agendas. The rise of e-commerce and cyber trade has only served to compound such complexities, as traditional frameworks of trade fall behind the trajectory of technology. To counter these new realities, the WTO has to make strenuous efforts at re-legitimation that supplement today's realities of trade. Addressing issues such as inequality, sustainable environments, and labor rights in the context of trade can enhance the WTO's legitimacy and ensure that it remains an essential global facilitator of economic cooperation. Not only does the new global trade represent a challenge to the WTO paradigms of today but also calls for an innovative approach to redesigning its future role (Lamy, 2025) (Figure 10.8).

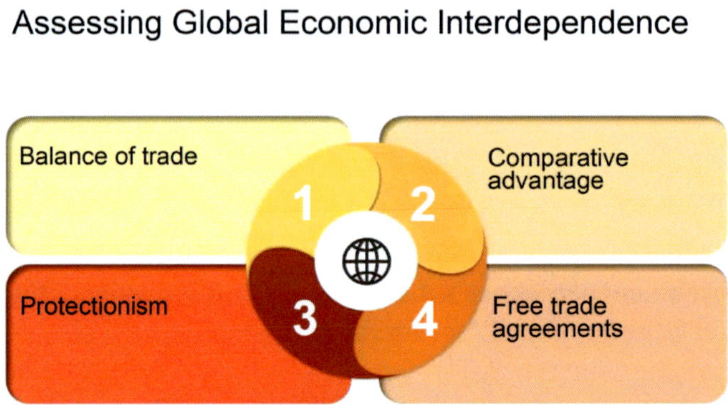

Figure 10.8. Globalization and economic interdependence.

Source: https://fastercapital.co/i/Economic-indicators--Speculating-on-the-Economy--Analyzing-Key-Indicators--Assessing-Global-Economic-Interdependence.webp.

10.3.2. Influence of Multinational Corporations (MNCs)

MNCs' role on the global economic landscape is an issue of universal discourse in the debate surrounding the World Trade Organization (WTO). MNCs exert great power and might be more powerful than the economic production of other nations, thus shifting the trade equation for the world. Their ability to cut through complex global regulations allows them to effectively leverage market opportunities, which raises concern about the effects on host economies and national sovereignty. This phenomenon is likely to lead to public policies favorable to the interests of corporations at the expense of essential public sector investment, particularly in developing countries. As has been noted, investment in innovation is often neglected, resulting in below-par growth performance for these sectors, which ultimately sets the trajectory for economic development across the world (Singh et al., 2025). MNCs also expand their dominance by influencing intellectual property law, which affects access to essential goods, especially in the pharmaceutical sector. This situation is even brought alive by the Indian experience, as the restrictive patent regimes created by MNCs have elicited a response from domestic activists. The activists are against corporate control of the patent regime and assert their entitlement to access life-saving drugs and healthcare products. By leveraging indigenous knowledge systems such as Ayurveda, indigenous healers effectively pushed back against MNC plans, creating a countermovement to the corporate-led mainstream agenda. As explained in research, the engagement between local stakeholders and MNCs is to blame for unstable drug prices within poor nations, focusing on the complex interaction between local agency and corporate power within the WTO setup (Halliburton et al., 2017).

In the future, the engagement between MNCs and the WTO presents opportunities and challenges for promoting fair global trade practices. The increasing MNC domination demands a reconsideration of trade agreements and regulatory mechanisms to align them with sustainable development. This may include creative initiative by national governments and international institutions for placing public interests first, particularly in the health and innovation fronts. The future WTO will rely on its ability to balance these competing interests so that the power of MNCs does not strangle competition or continue inequality. While the trend of globalization continues to evolve, the fate of multinational companies will inevitably shape the everyday dynamics of trade policy operation, and therefore their influence is an important area of concern for the future agenda of the WTO.

10.3.3. The Role of Technology in Shaping Trade Dynamics

The intricate relationship between trade patterns and technology has restructured economic activity globally at its foundation level. Technological advancements such as blockchain and e-commerce platforms have transformed traditional supply chains, making them efficient and transparent. These advancements enable business organizations to access markets around the world with ease, encouraging competition and minimizing new entrant barriers. This transformation is best observed in the European Union, where there are ongoing debates regarding trade politics that are being increasingly subjected to the influence of technological innovations.

Through its ability to facilitate data exchange and provide connectivity between firms, technology does not only enhance existing trade mechanisms but also necessitates new structures of regulation capable of addressing new challenges and ensuring equitable access to the international market (Kerremans et al., 2013). Moreover, the spread of digital means has provided governments and institutions with new means of overseeing and applying trade treaties. Due to the growth in international trade and its sophistication, applying and reporting technology is crucial. Machine learning algorithms and data analytics offer policymakers the tools to examine market trends and evaluate the impacts of trade policies in an effective manner. The WTO is at the forefront in gearing up to respond to these developments, realizing that effective governance mechanisms matter in order to safeguard fair trade practice in the wake of exponentially rising technological advancement. As the digital economy expands, the sheer volume of transactions demands that existing standards and institutions be re-examined to factor in new technology and determine its effect on traditional trading procedures (Bigg et al., 2011). Lastly, the relationship between trade and technology underscores the importance of cooperation at the international level in setting the standards that shape digital trade. As countries grapple with differing regulations and technology policy reactions, there is a need for harmonized frameworks. The WTO has the responsibility of convening member states to close the gaps and harmonize policies that support the application of technology responsibly in trade. This collaborative approach can help in avoiding risks associated with technology disruptions while capitalizing on their benefits. In this case, the shifting environment of trade trends requires an imaginative and visionary approach in embracing technology advancements while safeguarding the interests of all the respective parties in the global economy (Kerremans et al., 2013) (Figure 10.9).

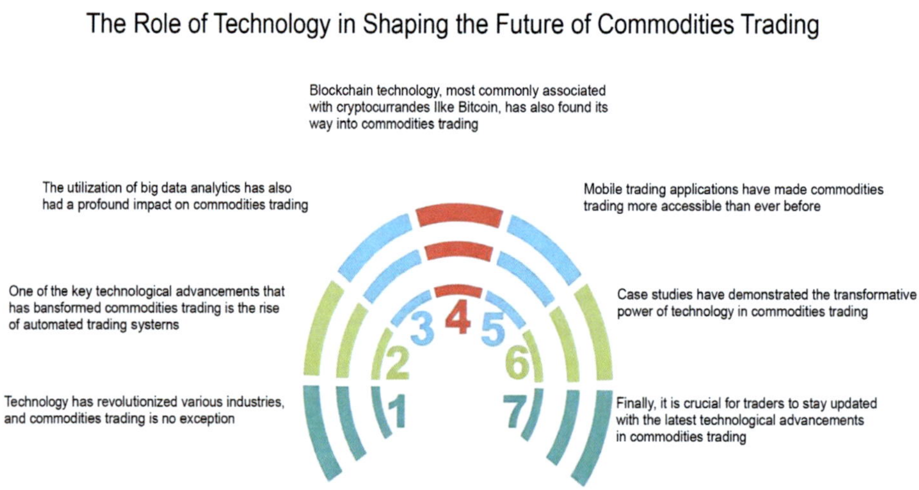

Figure 10.9. The role of technology in shaping trade dynamics.

Source: https://fastercapital.co/i/Commodities--Tapping-into-Resources--Commodities-and-Capital-Growth--The-Role-of-Technology-in-Shaping-the-Future-of-Commodities-Trading.webp.

10.4. ENVIRONMENTAL CONCERNS AND THE WORLD TRADE ORGANIZATION (WTO)

The Point of Intersection between Environmental Concerns and World Trade Organization (WTO) law is a complex argumentation between ecologic sustainability and economic liberalization. WTOs foundational postulates concern free trade, yet the realities of today have revealed the need to integrate environmental regulation within these structures. With nations fighting against challenges like global warming and biodiversity loss, the role of WTO in coordinating trade policy and environmental policy becomes increasingly important. Arguments at forums like the 2012 United Nations Conference on Sustainable Development highlighted the necessity for institutions to address sustainable development in international trade mechanisms more urgently. Experts convening in the Pardee Center stated that prudent management of these twin mandates is essential towards the attainment of a green economy, underlining the necessity for innovative and creative governance structures in aligning trade practice with protection of the environment (Bigg et al., 2011). Moreover, environmental matters are informing the policy debate in the WTO, particularly regarding how trade rules ring with national environmental policies. Critics of free trade agreements argue that those most often undermine local efforts at establishing environmental standards, creating the potential conflict between international expansion of trade and protection of the environment. The challenge lies in getting a measure of balance that upholds nations' rights to manage their environments while within WTO undertakings. Recent literature, such as that in specialist trade periodicals, encourages an inter-paradigmatic strategy, arguing that multinational plans can help balance the differences. By studying other models and frameworks, the discourse of trade policy can be reoriented to develop pathways emphasizing sustainable development without sacrificing the pace of economic growth (Kerremans et al., 2013). In the future, the WTO must align its mechanisms more attuned to the increasingly pressing environmental concerns. More dialogue between trade and environmental policies would be a superior strategy in order to create mutually preferred outcomes. The adoption of stricter regulations towards environmentally sustainable practice in trade can be among the first steps that will allow green action. Also, encouraging cooperation between member states can facilitate broader participation in environmental rule-making, ultimately synchronizing trade practice with principles of sustainable development. As emphasized by specialists in various forums, the developments will not only benefit the well-being of the global environment but also significantly contribute to ensuring that the WTO remains relevant in a world where there is increased concern for sustainability and ecological presence (Bigg et al., 2011).

10.4.1. Trade Policies and Climate Change

The intersection between climate change and trade policy is a complicated situation which significantly impacts the functioning and future of the World Trade Organization (WTO). As nations grapple with the repercussions of global warming, increasing awareness exists that trade policies can either aggravate or mitigate environmental devastation.

For instance, the policy of imposing a tariff on products that cause pollution can be both an economic deterrent to pollution as well as a motive to innovate clean technologies. However, instituting such barriers must be done with caution in order not to be at odds with existing trade agreements. The challenge lies in bridging international trade commitments and domestic environmental goals, one that calls for concerted cooperation and reconsideration of the principles behind the architecture of the WTO to accommodate sustainable practices without hampering global business. Moreover, the character of international cooperation is most forcefully highlighted in the context of debate over developing economies and their role in trade policies addressing climate change. Emerging markets often identify trade barriers as obstacles to their economic growth, potentially conflicting with ambitious climate action. This juxtaposition creates a critical tension as countries seek to balance economic aspirations with environmental responsibilities. Others have posited that encouraging South-South cooperation would be a possible avenue for developing nations to attain sustainable development through the sharing of green technology and best practices in energy efficiency, which can reorient the world trading system (Gray et al., 2016).

This is based on the premise that climate change is a shared problem, whose solution lies with regional cooperation that will not only make economies more resilient but also the environment. Finally, the future of the WTO rests on it being able to incorporate climate change concerns in its trade policy successfully. As the institution faces mounting pressures from member states as well as international civil society to become environmentally conscious, it has to adapt in order to survive. The recent turn to appreciating the vulnerability of liberal internationalism indicates that the WTO has a potential leadership role to play in securing a more sustainable and equitable global order (Ikenberry, 2018). By incorporating climate goals into trade agreements and ensuring transparency and accountability, the WTO has the ability to spur the larger commitments necessary for environmental stewardship. Such a transformation can also restore public trust in international institutions, offering a platform to a more sustainable and equitable economic future that is consistent with the imperative of climate change (Figure 10.10).

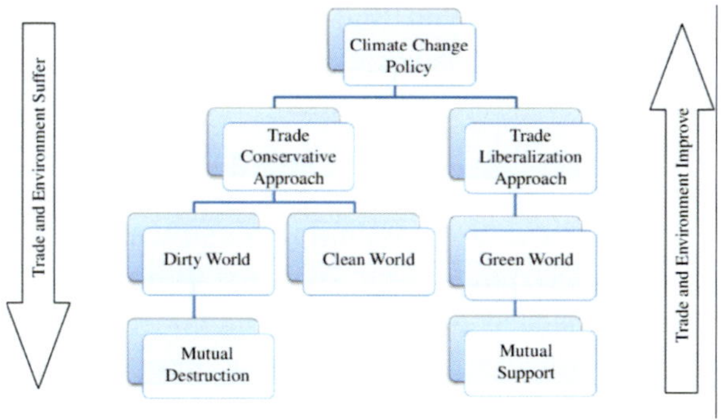

Figure 10.10. Climate change policy implications in trade perspective.

Source: https://www.researchgate.net/profile/Khalid-Ahmed-60/publication/260943104/figure/fig1/AS:613944108527644@1523387090519/Climate-change-policy-implications-in-trade-perspective.png.

10.4.2. Sustainable Development Goals (SDGs) and Trade

SDGs are a holistic strategy towards ensuring economic development but in social equity and environmental sustainability. In international trade, these aspirations require a revisit of practices and policies in trade. The World Trade Organization (WTO) is at the center of enabling trade that promotes sustainable development, but its integration with SDGs is a challenge. Emphasizing green practices can help countries bring their trade agreements into alignment with SDGs to enable a trade mechanism to support the transition towards green practices and technologies. Policymakers and negotiators, thus, must put sustainability on the first priority list to enable economic growth without compromising ecological health, thereby creating a viable path towards the achievement of SDGs under an open economy. The link of trade to the SDGs is then further multiplied by inequalities and poverty. Certain trade policies can increase inequalities within and between countries and offset the action for achieving Goal 10, which is the eradication of all forms of poverty. The inclusion of fair and equitable fair trade might enhance the positive effects of trade on the reduction of poverty and promote overall social goals. Through efforts for balanced trade agreements that advance the agenda for developing nations, the WTO would ensure a more equitable kind of globalization. This is consistent with the SDGs, ensuring mutually beneficial systems that gain by sharing resources and helping the poor. Eventually, this reform would work towards a more balanced world economy and strengthen the role of trade in contributing to sustainable development. There are vast opportunities for innovation and technology to bring trade practices in sync with the SDGs. New digital platforms and digital supply chain management options can make trade processes more efficient and transparent, reducing waste and promoting better use of resources. In addition, the integration of zakat management into economic frameworks has been suggested as a step to augment efforts toward sustainability through enhanced community investment and development, as per studies citing that zakat may have a vital role to play in assisting with the achievement of SDGs focused on poverty reduction and equality (Fazial et al., 2025). WTO can facilitate collaboration and best-practice sharing among member nations in order for technology and innovative solutions to be utilized. This collaborative approach would not only spur economic development but also make sure that trade serves to meaningfully contribute toward the overall goals of sustainable development so that societies can flourish with regard to environmental and social limits.

10.4.3. The World Trade Organization (WTO)'s Role in Promoting Environmental Standards

The WTO has a key role to play in addressing environmental standards in the context of international trade. Through the formulation of policies that provide for sustainable development, the WTO encourages its member states to consider environmental impacts in trade policy. This role becomes increasingly significant as international trade is now directly linked with environmental issues such as climate change, loss of biodiversity, and consumption of resources. The WTOs Trade and Environment Committee conducts discussions that promote the integration of environmental concerns within trade agreements, hence fostering a cooperative forum through which nations can harmonize their economic practices to achieve sustainable development goals. This endeavor attempts to minimize the tension between trade liberalization and the protection of the environment, ultimately giving rise to a more robust global system that values the integrity of the environment over economic development. The intersection of trade and environmental policy is fast becoming a crucial issue in current discourse regarding the WTO's future. In addition, the WTO's focus on advancing environmental standards fits into the larger context of the global movement toward appreciation of the limitations of conventional economic globalization. With a liberal international order being threatened and a shift away from multilateralism, the WTO has room to pivot its mission towards more inclusivity in environmental stewardship. The new multipolar world, Mearsheimer argues (2019), is a sign that the time has come for greater global cooperation transcending nation-state interest. This can be enabling for a more substantial focus on shared environmental concerns with respect for sovereignty. By creating a climate in which countries can work well together on sustainability and climate problems, the WTO can assist in reducing the backlash against hyperglobalization. As countries are struggling to contend with growing nationalistic feelings, the WTO's ability to encourage standards on the environment will be more crucial in reaching agreement and cooperative action on critical global problems. In terms of environmental sustainability, the WTO can have an impact and respond to changes in local practices and global ecological concerns. For example, medicinally important plant research in areas like Northern Peru points towards the intersection of indigenous practice and modern regulatory policies (Bussmann et al., 2018). The inclusion of local knowledge into broader sustainable practices not only identifies indigenous contribution but also expands biodiversity conservation efforts. The WTO has the potential to make such programs possible by encouraging cooperation between member nations and local stakeholders. Drawing from local experience and expertise, the institution can initiate frameworks that ensure sustainable resource management while ensuring economic development. Implementing this two-way approach would make the WTO a strong advocate for sustainable practice in trade and adhere to the world's call for responsible environmental guardianship. As the company moves forward into the future, maintaining environmental standards should remain at the forefront of its agenda, ensuring that trade enhances and does not compromise ecological integrity (Figure 10.11).

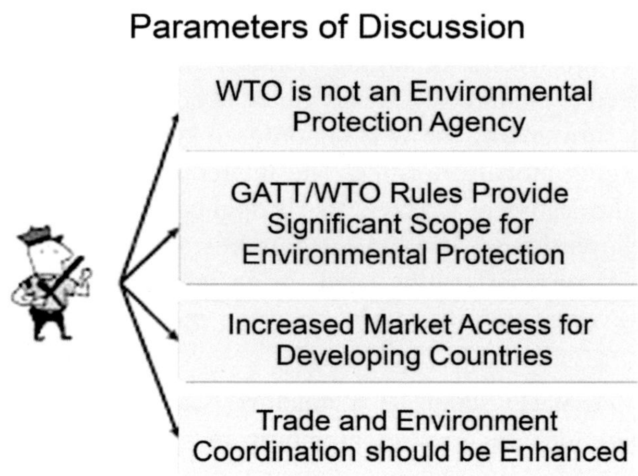

Figure 10.11. The World Trade Organization (WTO)'s role in promoting environmental standards.

Source: https://encrypted-tbn0.gstatic.com/images?q=tbn:ANd9GcRmlifWXiqd2dWhVHIUCvBO94ZEcJaIq59BrQ&s.

10.5. THE ROLE OF EMERGING ECONOMIES

Rise of the new economies has fundamentally changed the geography of world trade, and this has necessitated the reevaluation of the role of World Trade Organizations (WTO) in encouraging global economic collaboration. Brazil, India, and China are now leading nations that have transformed from being peripheral actors in the world trading system to critical players, depicting the shifting dynamics of economic power. This new paradigm necessitates that the WTO create new frameworks and policies that are able to cater to the specific needs and desires of these emerging markets.

Their incorporation is not merely a matter of economic weight; it also reflects a broader call for representation and fairness in global governance. With the greater complexities of trade management in a more multipolar world, the WTO will have to take new approaches to incorporate the voice of these economies into its considerations. Against this background of rising power of such emerging economies, the WTO is faced with systemic issues that transcend negotiating multilateral trade agreements. As suggested by recent research, there has been a sharp falling off in the popularity of open market policies among leading OECD nations, which has contributed to an ethos of skepticism regarding globalization (Higgott et al., 2009). This skepticism is manifested in the form of rising protectionism and the tendency toward regional as opposed to multilateral free trade accords, producing disintegration of the international trade regime. Here, the need to sustain a healthy multilateral trading system cannot be overemphasized. Emerging nations, in cooperation with current superpowers, need to champion reforms aimed at correcting the legitimacy and equity concerns surrounding the WTO in order to keep it relevant and effective in light of changing global priorities. The interconnection between emerging economies and the destiny of WTOs is also brought out by the evolving narrative of trade politics, particularly within the European Union. The complexity of EU trade policies summarizes the need for an inter-paradigmatic framework to address the diverse interests within emerging economies (Kerremans et al., 2013).

Therefore, the WTO stands at a juncture, where it will be essential to construct cooperation amongst its members in order to deal with today's challenges effectively. By placing inclusive dialogue at center stage that incorporates the voices of new economies, the WTO is not only able to stabilize the global trading system but also promote the legitimacy of its governance structures. Ultimately, empowering and actualizing these economies is a turning point towards reviving multilateralism and making the global trading regime viable for the next few decades.

10.5.1. Influence of BRICS Nations on World Trade Organization (WTO) Policies

The BRICS nations, including Brazil, Russia, India, China, and South Africa, have emerged as key players at the WTO, with strong influence over its policies and functioning. Over the last couple of years, these countries have together pushed for greater representation and reform within the WTO to reflect the changing trade dynamics in the world. Together, their efforts have challenged established power dynamics long controlled by developed nations, demanding more even-handed trade rules that account for the development ambitions of emerging economies.

By their positioning as big markets and developing economies, BRICS have initiated debates that address agricultural subsidy issues, market access, and the elimination of trade barriers that disproportionately impact developing countries, thus reforming the agenda of the WTO and advocating for a better multilateral trade system. Apart from the BRICS' collective voice, their core role within the establishment of some policy areas at the WTO is also notable. Their participation in negotiations on trade facilitation, sustainable development, and e-commerce is proof of a move to include the realities of contemporary economics into the agenda of the organization. As these economies improve, their interests tend to orient towards technology transfer and intellectual property rights matters, particularly with regard to farm markets that are central to food security in developing nations. The initiatives that are undertaken through the umbrella of the BRICS alliance, such as cooperation in sharing best practices for evolving agricultural policy (Chadha et al., 2025), demonstrate their interest in developing a system through which trade will be able to generate economic growth that will be inclusive in character while engaging actively in reforms necessary in global governance mechanisms through which trade is facilitated. Moreover, the influence of BRICS on WTO policies is also seen through their resolution of trade conflicts. These countries have traditionally been more aggressive in utilizing the WTOs dispute settlement mechanisms, reflecting their determination in upholding global trade conventions. This assertive policy not only aids in protecting their economic interests but also aids in asserting their role as multilateralists' champions against increasing nationalism and protectionism. For instance, the cooperative strategies observed in massive trade negotiations have exposed the extent to which BRICS nations are willing to demand rules more reflective of a wider range of economic realities. As the world evolves, the BRICS nations will most likely continue shaping WTO policies and calling for reforms that enhance their power and advocate a balanced and inclusive trading system that addresses the issues of developing economies (Steinbock et al., 2011) (Figure 10.12).

Figure 10.12. Influence of BRICS nations on World Trade Organization (WTO) policies.

Source: https://img.republicworld.com/all_images/brics-nations-slam-us-tariffs-as-wto-rule-violations-1751830569600-16_9.webp.

10.5.2. Challenges Posed by Developing Countries

The problems that developing countries pose to the World Trade Organization (WTO) are multilateral and contribute to the organization's ongoing crisis. As these nations increasingly grapple with the effects of globalization, they increasingly become marginalized in the WTO framework. The power dynamics that govern tend to tilt developed countries towards unequal negotiations and outcomes. For instance, the majority of developing nations are poorly represented and have limited resources, which hampers their ability to meaningfully participate in trade negotiations. Consequently, while the WTO was designed for equitable and fair trade for all, the persistent economic imbalances are evidence of structural weaknesses in its operational structure, limiting the efficacy of the organizations and jeopardizing its usefulness in a dynamic international landscape (Bäumler et al., 2020). Coupling with this issue, developing countries have unprecedented issues confronting their agricultural sector which usually forms a bedrock of their economies. The WTO, tuned historically to trade challenges of the 20th century, struggles to adapt to global challenges like climate change, food security, and sustainability that are particularly of interest to these nations. As developing countries require support to innovate and adapt to climate effects on agriculture, the existing governance structure of the WTOs fails to address these emerging challenges. This inadequacy can exacerbate existing inequalities with poor policy efforts from agriculture likely leading to increased hunger and poverty among these countries. Thus, the inability of WTOs to evolve and address 21st-century issues makes it challenging to ensure equitable solutions for all member countries (Kim et al., 2025). Also, this entrenchment is giving rise to a very fundamental question regarding the future of WTO. The emergence of bi- and plurilateral trade arrangements indicates a preference among member states, particularly the developed ones, to move away from the WTO framework in toto to more flexible arrangements. This is not only against the multilateral trading system the WTO represents but also risks further marginalization of developing nations, which might not possess the negotiating clout to bargain effectively in these alternative arrangements. As a result, the legitimacy and credibility of WTO are challenged, particularly when it appears to be unable to provide equitable solutions or reforms to the shifting international trade environment. In the coming years, the WTO will have to reexamine its purpose and effectiveness to ensure it adequately deals with the concerns of developing countries in order to establish an authentic inclusive international trading system (Bäumler et al., 2020).

10.5.3. The Future of Trade Negotiations with Emerging Economies

With the global balance of economic power shifting, emerging economies have become central players in trade negotiations, affecting WTO and global decision-making. The ascendance of countries like India, Brazil, and members of the Association of Southeast Asian Nations (ASEAN) is indicative of a revolutionary era in global trade relationships. These economies generally adopt different objectives from their developed counterparts, prioritizing sustainable development, equity, and stronger social protections. Negotiations thus have to face this additional complexity, balancing the conflicting interests of the established and developing economies. The outcomes of such negotiations will not only influence trade policy but also re-orient the WTO as a force for dialogue among various economic actors, highlighting the need for flexibility in multilateral negotiations as they grapple with path-breaking challenges (Yu et al., 2014). The recent debate around trade treaties like the Trans-Pacific Partnership (TPP) points to the critical necessity of inclusiveness and transparency in trade negotiations with emerging economies. Detractors of such treaties invariably point to a shortfall of stakeholders' engagement and secretive nature of negotiations as causes of unfortunate disenfranchised local economies and voices excluded from the decision-making process. Furthermore, the effects of exclusion of key players—such as China and other BRICS nations—from vital trade agreements have to be considered. The effects of exclusions are enormous in that they tend to create layers of complexity and defiance within global trade negotiations, even to extend to confrontation and trade imbalances whose consequences further make global disparities increasingly entrenched (Yu et al., 2014). Thus, developing a spirit of openness and collaboration will be crucial to establishing equitable and sustainable trade talks. As the WTO is striving to keep up with the dynamics of international trade, adapting its framework to suit the needs of new economies is imperative. The described difficulties are the slowing of encouragement for open markets and the halting of more universal economic change, which necessitates a reconsideration of the organizations priorities. Responding to the issues of legitimacy and governance around trade agreements has to be an urgent task for the WTO, as inaction threatens to alienate emerging economies from the world trading system and weaken the multilateral trading system. Emerging economies, therefore, not only enrich conventional trade systems but also act as drivers of reform for the current global order. Effective interaction with these nations will be pivotal for the WTO's future, making sure that it maintains the required nature of a balanced and impartial trade facilitation forum in an ever more complex world (Higgott et al., 2009) (Figure 10.13).

Figure 10.13. The future of trade negotiations with emerging economies.

Source: https://media.licdn.com/dms/image/v2/D4D12AQHgCmxi026Nig/article-cover_image-shrink_720_1280/article-cover_image-shrink_720_1280/0/1731649473995?e=2147483647&v=beta&t=pXZtWj9qXSSJOV6-n8wHOYTZlmNASt-K7a2nmcvEHT_o.

10.6. REFORM PROPOSALS FOR THE WORLD TRADE ORGANIZATION (WTO)

The WTO has faced increasingly intense scrutiny amidst ongoing economic troubles and changing geopolitical tensions. Reform demands center on enhancing the organizations legitimacy and effectiveness, appeasing criticism from developed and developing nations alike. One of the most prominent routes toward reform is that of the Appellate Body, which has experienced operational gridlock due to disagreement on member appointments. The body's ability to engage in judicial lawmaking has been faulted for being outside its terms of reference and causing uncertainties among trade rules. The critics argue that it is essential to restore the Appellate Body's functional capacity as it not only induces compliance with trade rules but also towards a more rational and stable global international trade regime, which has become imperative in the ever-changing global environment. Therefore, the re-establishment of this body can be a driving force for broader reforms within the WTO system. Together with emphasis on the function of the Appellate Body's role, reform proposals also tend to highlight the importance of a more participatory and reactive decision-making mechanism. This is because findings such as those by Buthe emphasize that the incorporation of cost-benefit analyses of domestic interest groups into the regulatory power debate within the SPS measures should be imperative. Ensuring that all member states' voices, including the most disadvantaged ones, are heard could alleviate feelings of exclusion that have caused resentment within the organization. Incorporating the perspectives of various actors not only improves the legitimacy of the WTO but also results in a more equitable system of international trade. Inclusivity could allow decisions to be made through consensus, consequently resulting in greater cooperation among states and effectiveness of global trade negotiations. Apart from this, restructuring the WTO's approach to international standards and regulatory policies is crucial to achieving substantive reform. Buthes analysis suggests that the way in which delegation of regulatory authority can transform national policy-making autonomy is an issue that requires renewed attention from the WTO. This requires the WTO to revisit its structures governing practices, particularly considering local priorities. It requires balance between national and international cooperation to achieve maximum trade gains at the least political costs. It will help reform the delegated powers and align them with member states' domestic political circles so that the WTO can regain trust in being able to facilitate equitable trade. In the process, the organization would not only learn how to adapt to contemporary challenges but also reconfirm its position as an integral force in the future of world business.

10.6.1. Suggestions for Improving Dispute Resolution

Effective processes of dispute resolution are imperative in guaranteeing the integrity and efficacy of the World Trade Organization (WTO) in the face of contemporary challenges. Among the suggestions to strengthen such mechanisms is making the process of resolving disputes more transparent. Greater transparency would not only instill greater confidence in member states but also provide stakeholders, including non-state players, access to and an ability to understand proceedings. Such inclusion would give rise to a sense of accountability and adherence to decisions, thus strengthening the legitimacy of the WTOs decisions. Moreover, by providing more apparent channels of communication between disputants, the WTO will be in a position to neutralize adversarial aspects in disputes and promote cooperative resolutions. This postulate is aligned with demands for comprehensive reform evident in various academic formulations, whereby transparency is recognized as a key element for building cooperative international relations in multilateral environments. Further, incorporating alternate dispute resolution (ADR) means into the WTOs agenda can be a pivotal inclusion. ADR techniques, such as mediation and arbitration, would be more efficient and adaptable means of resolving conflicts among member states. By pushing parties toward such informal avenues, the WTO can take some load off its formal adjudicative process, which individuals tend to perceive as bureaucratic and slow. An emphasis on ADR in trade disputes would also be representative of a broader trend towards contested multilateralism, where states are expressly seeking new and diverse methods of dispute resolution and rule-making that align better with their interests (Morse et al., 2014). Furthermore, training in ADR as a profession among members can facilitate the capacity of the members to engage in effective settlement negotiations, encouraging a culture of negotiation over litigation. Finally, there should be a need to incorporate a broader understanding of global justice and equity into the resolution of conflicts. The WTO ought to be sensitive to the fact that trade disputes often have profound impacts on poor communities and low-income nations. By being actively involved in food sovereignty and other related issues of global justice (Edelman et al., 2014), the organization can begin making policies that take into consideration the broader socio-economic impacts of resolutions in trade. This focus on equity not only appeals to the legitimacy of the mechanism of dispute resolution but also encourages a more inclusive governance of world trade management. Adopting practices that prioritize listening to less privileged stakeholders will not only make the dispute rulings more equitable, but it will also enhance the overall credibility and relevance of the WTO in a changing global setting.

10.6.2. Enhancing Transparency and Inclusivity

In the World Trade Organization (WTO), inclusiveness and transparency remain still relevant issues that influence its performance and legitimacy. With the continued evolution of global trade, the same applies to the need for the WTOs activities to become more transparent. Member states tend to lament the opaque negotiation processes and decision-making channels that prevent wider participation by different stakeholders. Such transparency deficit could contribute to distrust, particularly from developing nations that believe they could be excluded from significant deliberations. The problem is also driven by claims of developing member status by powerful economies like China, which utilizes trade provisions intended to spur development among less developed nations to their advantage. By addressing these issues and facilitating inclusive discussion, the WTO can create a more balanced environment conducive to equitable trade activities and trust between its members (Hu et al., 2019). Increased inclusivity in the WTO system also calls for redefining membership entry and participation standards. At present, the categorization of nations into developing and developed does not reflect their trade potential or economic standing. As highlighted by ongoing controversies regarding reforms, certain nations exploiting their developing status have damaged the negotiation of future agreements by not adhering to transparency practices, such as timely notification and respect for commitments taken. Such inconsistency weakens the credibility of the multilateral trading system and poses barriers to achieving effective negotiations on priority issues such as fisheries subsidies and e-commerce. Therefore, revising existing frameworks to ensure fair participation and commitment fulfillment from all member countries will be the key to enhancing the WTOs openness and inclusiveness (Hu et al., 2019). Enhanced global governance through openness and inclusiveness can also learn from outside of mainstream economic platforms. Rockefeller Brothers Fund, for instance, is seeking to establish stronger democratic governance practices around the world based on transparency, accountability, and participation. The WTO, taking lessons from such models, may adopt similar types of strategies that are adapted to its own unique situation so that there can be access and participation for all members states irrespective of economic standing. Ensuring that everyone's heard can result in more comprehensive and fairer trade treaties that allow for the different needs and priorities of the world of trading. As the challenges facing the WTO become increasingly daunting, abiding by these values will not only secure its ongoing role in a rapidly evolving world but also enhance the legitimacy of its debates, enabling more balanced trade to flourish for all.

10.6.3. Adapting to Digital Trade and E-commerce

E-commerce and digital trade present challenges and opportunities for the World Trade Organization (WTO) as it adapts to the new global trade paradigm. Digital platforms have radically changed the way goods and services are traded across the globe, necessitating a rethinking of traditional trade regulations. The diffusion of online transactions raises enormous concerns in terms of intellectual property rights, consumer protection, and electronic payment systems. The capacity of the WTO to effectively mediate conflicts in this new era of internet is instrumental towards establishing a stable trade environment, as stakeholders must contend with diverse legal standards and technological platforms across borders. Also, understanding how the digital business impacts market accessibility and competition is vital in crafting policy that facilitates innovation as well as sound practice of trade, hence contributing to the sustainability of the global economy. Aside from regulation, e-commerce transition also necessitates greater focus on knowledge transfer in the digital economy, particularly concerning the services sector. Unlike traditional manufacturing, where knowledge transfer is usually heavily reliant on traditional channels such as patents and university partnerships, the services sector has particular dynamics. Here, two-way knowledge transfer, consumer engagement, and foreign direct investment play pivotal roles in facilitating competitiveness in a digitalized economy. As the world economy continues to evolve, it is necessary that the WTO acknowledges and reacts to these specific features that accompany services. This adjustment will allow greater inclusion of digital trade practices within its broader regulatory framework, ultimately empowering more efficient governance and facilitation of trade policy among member nations (Cowan et al., 2025). Furthermore, the WTO's ability to act upon digital trade is also linked with the complexities of intellectual property regulation as the culture and creative arts sectors increasingly become an information-oriented economy. The creative industry, as with all industries, must contend with the issues of digital distribution in terms of copyright, trademarks, and protection of art works. Ensuring that the intellectual property rights (IPR) system is sufficiently robust to overcome digital challenges is important to supporting creativity as well as ensuring market integrity. The WTO must communicate with stakeholders from various industries in order to establish standard and guidelines that lay out the nitty-gritty of digital trade, ensuring both the content producers and content consumers are adequately protected. Cross-stakeholder communication is vital to the WTO's continued relevance and utility as the world of global trade continues to change (N/A, 2002).

SUMMARY

The WTO stands at a crossroads, struggling with problems of the present that adversely impact its usefulness and validity. As globalization accelerates, it is faulted for its failure to address such problems as climate change, inequality, and trade distortions. These structural problems necessitate rethinking the WTOs structures and working methodologies. Stakeholders today advocate for more flexibility and inclusiveness, advocating for the need for flexibility in order to counter new trade dynamics and the complexities that stem from diverse regional arrangements and global alliances. Indeed, as the global economic system continues to evolve, the WTO must adapt to these complexities in order to ensure its legitimacy and working effectiveness, blending contrasting views and promoting problem-solving mechanisms through cooperation among member nations (Bigg et al., 2011). In addition, the future of the WTO hangs on its capacity to facilitate discussion of not only trade in goods but also new matters like digital trade and sustainable economic behaviors. The rise of bilateral and multilateral arrangements beyond normal trade patterns, due to regional blocs like ASEAN, indicates that the WTO must expand its focus. As seen in recent trade deals that involve far-reaching topics such as investment and competition policy, there is a strong momentum towards negotiating agreements that are more representative of the economic realities of today. The lack of explicit commitments in these negotiations serves to underscore the complexities of modern trade, demonstrating that while the WTO remains at the center, it must better tailor its strategies so as to incorporate these complex appeals for cooperation and broader modes of engagement between member states (Dayaratna et al., 2025). The WTO's future really lies in its ability to innovate and be proactive in addressing global trade governance. As member nations grapple with the ability to contend with new issues, the organization has a rare opportunity to redefine its mandate to not only deal with classical trade issues but also international problems such as climate change and economic inequality. Such a transformation is coupled with the assurance of embracing equity, sustainability, and inclusiveness in the conditions of trade. Through rethinking its role and promoting adaptive structures that facilitate collaboration and cooperation, the WTO can not only remain relevant but also become a key player in developing a global trading environment responsive to contemporary values and future demands (Bigg et al., 2011).

The WTO is facing several contemporary challenges that undermine its fundamental principles and operational efficacy. One of the key areas of disagreement revolves around increased nationalism and protectionism that is observable in most member states. This has generated tensions between pro-global liberalization trade forces and hard-line domestic pressures advocating for national interests. Policymakers are finding it hard to balance these competing demands, particularly with some nations pursuing bilateral trade agreements in a bid to circumvent the multilateral trade system. These trends can potentially fragment world trade standards, and chip away at the WTOs authority and ability to provide balanced terms of trade. While governments revisit their backing of world trade mechanisms, continued members' cooperation is essential for the survival of the WTO. Another subject of heated debate in the WTO context is the development of mega-regional trade deals. Such broad agreements will go beyond tariff reductions to even regulatory coordination and standards harmonization. The evolution of such trade agreements raises questions about the efficacy of the WTO's current framework in addressing the complexities of modern trade. With countries forming themselves in the process that might or might not have all members on board, the WTO risks being increasingly irrelevant in the case of preferential trade arrangements. The institution will need to navigate the consequences of these new arrangements so that they enhance and not weaken the multilateral trading system. Struggling with these forces is essential if the WTO is to continue to be relevant to the evolving realities of world trade. Lastly, the integration of sustainability and environmental considerations into trade policy challenges and provides an opportunity for the WTO. Greater understanding of climate change and its implications on the world economies has generated a pressing demand for environmental standards in trade policies. At the WTO, there have been debates regarding how to best strike a balance on these matters and promote trade. The member states more interested in expanding trade than the environment present obstacles to carrying out these debates. When stakeholders come to realize the interconnectedness of trade and environmental sustainability, the need for setting up frameworks that combine these two aspects becomes imperative. Joint efforts towards this would yield new approaches that maximize the WTOs mandate while addressing the world's pressing needs. Discussion on these issues becomes imperative in charting the future course of the WTO in a changing world (Havlik et al., 2025; Kerremans et al., 2013).

REFERENCES

1. Anderson, K. (2025). The new global economy: Opportunities and challenges for small open economies. https://core.ac.uk/download/pdf/6764307.pdf (accessed on 30th October 2025).
2. Bäumler, J. (2020). Between a rock and a hard place. https://core.ac.uk/download/322846649.pdf (accessed on 30th October 2025).
3. Bigg, T., DeSombre, E., Halle, M., et al. (2011). Beyond Rio+20: Governance for a green economy. https://open.bu.edu/bitstream/2144/22899/1/Rio20TFC-Mar2011.pdf (accessed on 30th October 2025).
4. Bochniarz, H. (2025). Is the WTO still relevant to the global economy? https://core.ac.uk/download/pdf/6457620.pdf (accessed on 30th October 2025).
5. Born, G. (2012). A new generation of international adjudication. https://core.ac.uk/download/62560047.pdf (accessed on 30th October 2025).
6. Boulin, J. Y., Lallement, M., Messenger, J. C., et al. (2025). Decent working time: New trends, new issues. https://core.ac.uk/download/pdf/6330846.pdf (accessed on 30th October 2025).
7. Bussmann, R. W., & Sharon, D. (2018). Medicinal plants of the Andes and the Amazon - The magic and medicinal flora of Northern Peru. *Ethnobotany Research and Applications, 15*. https://doi.org/10.32859/era.15.2.001-295 (accessed on 30th October 2025).
8. Büthe, T. (2008). The globalization of health and safety standards: Delegation of regulatory authority in the SPS Agreement of the 1994 Agreement Establishing the World Trade Organization. https://core.ac.uk/download/62553315.pdf (accessed on 30th October 2025).
9. Chadha, R., Davenport, S. V., & Gale, R. (2025). Competition policy reform in agriculture: A comparison of the BRICs countries. https://core.ac.uk/download/pdf/6418559.pdf (accessed on 30th October 2025).
10. Cowan, R., Soete, L., & Tchervonnava, O. (2025). Knowledge transfer and the services sector in the context of the new economy. https://core.ac.uk/download/pdf/6937059.pdf (accessed on 30th October 2025).
11. Dayaratna, B. O. G., & Whalley, J. (2025). Beyond goods and services: Competition policy, investment, mutual recognition, movement of persons, and broader cooperation provisions of recent FTAs involving ASEAN countries. https://core.ac.uk/download/pdf/6976728.pdf (accessed on 30th October 2025).
12. Edelman, M., Weis, T., Baviskar, A., Borras, S. M., Holt-Giménez, E., Kandiyoti, D., & Wolford, W. (2014). Introduction: Critical perspectives

on food sovereignty. *The Journal of Peasant Studies, 41*, 911–931. https://doi.org/10.1080/03066150.2014.963568 (accessed on 30th October 2025).

13. Fazial, F., Irshad, A. A., Abd Hamid, M. S., & Mohd Najib, N. W. (2025). Integrating zakat management into Ekonomi Madani: A literature review on contributions to Sustainable Development Goals (SDGs). *International Journal of Entrepreneurship and Management Practices*. https://www.semanticscholar.org/paper/99d55fac62312f444329755f6c4ebdebe7a67c42 (accessed on 30th October 2025).
14. Goldstein, J. L., & Steinberg, R. H. (2008). Negotiate or litigate? Effects of WTO judicial delegation on U.S. trade politics. https://core.ac.uk/download/62553324.pdf (accessed on 30th October 2025).
15. Gray, K., & Gills, B. K. (2016). South–South cooperation and the rise of the Global South. *Third World Quarterly, 37*, 557–574. https://doi.org/10.1080/01436597.2015.1128817 (accessed on 30th October 2025).
16. Gruin, J. (2011). "Freedom" through repression: Epistemic closure in agricultural trade negotiations. https://core.ac.uk/download/210634522.pdf (accessed on 30th October 2025).
17. Halliburton, M. (2017). India and the patent wars: Pharmaceuticals in the new intellectual property regime. https://core.ac.uk/download/219376560.pdf (accessed on 30th October 2025).
18. Hattunen, A. (2021). Maailman Kauppajärjestön tyhjät lupaukset sukupuolten tasa-arvosta: Buenos Aires -julistuksen jäljillä. https://core.ac.uk/download/491391255.pdf (accessed on 30th October 2025).
19. Havlik, P. (2025). Russian economic and integration prospects. https://core.ac.uk/download/pdf/6277456.pdf (accessed on 30th October 2025).
20. Helfer, L. R., Hathaway, O. A., Goldstein, J., Lutz, E., Chayes, A., Raustiala, K., et al. (2003). Constitutional analogies in the international legal system. https://core.ac.uk/download/62563345.pdf (accessed on 30th October 2025).
21. Higgott, R. A. (2009). Not just a "second order" problem in a wider economic crisis: Systemic challenges for the global trading system. https://core.ac.uk/download/47382.pdf (accessed on 30th October 2025).
22. Hite, K., & Shackleton Dann, M. (2016). The Rockefeller Brothers Fund's Democratic Practice Global Governance Portfolio: Impact assessment, 2010–2015. https://core.ac.uk/download/86445418.pdf (accessed on 30th October 2025).
23. Hu, W. (2019). China as a WTO developing member, is it a problem?

CEPS Policy Insights No. 2019/16, November 2019. https://core.ac.uk/download/286731365.pdf (accessed on 30th October 2025).

24. Ikenberry, G. J. (2018). The end of liberal international order? *International Affairs, 94*, 7–23. https://doi.org/10.1093/ia/iix241 (accessed on 30th October 2025).
25. Kerremans, B., & Orbie, J. (2013). Theorizing EU trade politics. https://core.ac.uk/download/55851683.pdf (accessed on 30th October 2025).
26. Kim, C. G., Koo, W. W., & Moon, W. (2025). World Agriculture Organization (WAO): New global governance for agricultural trade. https://core.ac.uk/download/pdf/6672600.pdf (accessed on 30th October 2025).
27. Kreuder-Sonnen, C., & Rittberger, B. (2020). The LIOn's share: How the liberal international order contributes to its own legitimacy crisis. *Harvard CES Open Forum Series 2019–2020*. https://core.ac.uk/download/323112021.pdf (accessed on 30th October 2025).
28. Lamy, P. (2025). The future of the multilateral trading system. https://core.ac.uk/download/pdf/30677758.pdf (accessed on 30th October 2025).
29. Mearsheimer, J. J. (2019). Bound to fail: The rise and fall of the liberal international order. *International Security, 43*, 7–50. https://doi.org/10.1162/isec_a_00342 (accessed on 30th October 2025).
30. Mehling, M., van Asselt, H., Das, K., Droege, S., & Verkuijl, C. (2019). Designing border carbon adjustments for enhanced climate action. *American Journal of International Law, 113*, 433–481. https://doi.org/10.1017/ajil.2019.22 (accessed on 30th October 2025).
31. Moon, W. (2025). Conceptualizing multifunctional agriculture from a global perspective. https://core.ac.uk/download/pdf/6273024.pdf (accessed on 30th October 2025).
32. Morse, J. C., & Keohane, R. O. (2014). Contested multilateralism. *The Review of International Organizations, 9*, 385–412. https://doi.org/10.1007/s11558-014-9188-2 (accessed on 30th October 2025).
33. N/A. (2002). The American Assembly: Art, technology, and intellectual property. https://core.ac.uk/download/71349265.pdf (accessed on 30th October 2025).
34. Newell, P. (2018). *Transformism* or transformation? The global political economy of energy transitions. *Review of International Political Economy, 26*, 25–48. https://doi.org/10.1080/09692290.2018.1511448 (accessed on 30th October 2025).
35. Rauh, C., & Zürn, M. (2019). Authority, politicization, and alternative

justifications: Endogenous legitimation dynamics in global economic governance. https://core.ac.uk/download/228065838.pdf (accessed on 30th October 2025).

36. Ruhullah, M. E., Ushama, T., Nurul Ain, B. N., & Moten, A. (2025). Al-'Ulama Warasatul Anbiya: Theological leadership, wasatiyyah (modernization) in advancing Sustainable Development Goals (SDGs). *Profetika: Jurnal Studi Islam*. https://www.semanticscholar.org/paper/ce88a8a4328fb21e9c4b9d941397ddc944873fc9 (accessed on 30th October 2025).
37. Singh, L. (2025). Globalization, national innovation systems and response of public policy. https://core.ac.uk/download/pdf/7302625.pdf (accessed on 30th October 2025).
38. Steinbock, D. (2011). The Eurozone debt crisis and the role of China. *EU Centre Policy Brief Number 3, November 2011*. https://core.ac.uk/download/5091271.pdf (accessed on 30th October 2025).
39. Wiegratz, J. (2008). Beyond harsh trade? The relevance of 'soft' competitiveness factors for Ugandan enterprises to endure in global value chains. https://core.ac.uk/download/51232.pdf (accessed on 30th October 2025).
40. Yu, P. K. (2014). TPP and Trans-Pacific perplexities. https://core.ac.uk/download/144230028.pdf (accessed on 30th October 2025).

Index

E

F

G

H

I

J

L

M

N

O

P

Q

R

S

V

W